PURCHASING

PRINCIPLES AND APPLICATIONS

Fourth Edition

PURCHASING

PRINCIPLES AND APPLICATIONS

Stuart F. Heinritz
Senior Editor, Purchasing Magazine

Paul V. Farrell
Editor, Purchasing Magazine

PRENTICE-HALL, INC., *Englewood Cliffs, N.J.*

Library of Congress Catalog Card No.: 65-16435

Printed in the United States of America C-74210

PRENTICE-HALL INTERNATIONAL, INC., *London*
PRENTICE-HALL OF AUSTRALIA, PTY, LTD., *Sydney*
PRENTICE-HALL OF CANADA, LTD., *Toronto*
PRENTICE-HALL OF INDIA (PRIVATE) LTD., *New Delhi*
PRENTICE-HALL OF JAPAN, INC., *Tokyo*

PREFACE

Each new advance in the art and science of purchasing has been built on a solid foundation established by purchasing people themselves.

When management, under the severe competitive pressure of the past few decades, demanded more from purchasing, it was forthcoming. Purchasing executives, responsible for spending at least half the money taken in from sales, recognized that the scope of their function was greater than that of a mere service activity handling the paperwork generated by decisions made elsewhere. Purchasing departments began to refine their negotiating and cost-reduction skills and make purchasing "a profit-making function."

That refinement of skills, that broadening of responsibility continues at a vigorous pace. Purchasing's potential for profit making and contribution to corporate long-range objectives, which Stuart Heinritz has analyzed in previous editions of this book, is materializing. Purchasing people have sought new management responsibility; they have geared their operations to their companies' long-range planning; they have streamlined their administrative work; they have actively recruited more highly educated personnel for their departments; they have worked closely with other departments in the best interests of their companies.

New material in this edition reflects these improvements in purchasing techniques and policies, and the increased importance of purchasing in the corporate structure. It covers such areas as personnel for purchasing, the techniques of negotiation, the role of purchasing research, and purchasing's responsibility in planning and forecasting. The emerging concept of materials management is analyzed. The section on purchasing procedures has been completely updated to include latest developments in contract buying, small orders, and electronic data processing. New case studies have been added to help the student test his own understanding of the changes that are taking place in modern purchasing.

The authors are grateful to many purchasing executives for their contributions and also to the following educators for their invaluable advice: Professor Richard A. Johnson, College of Business Administration, University of Washington; Professor John B. Klein, School of Business, University of Colorado; Professor John M. Purcell, State University of New York, Agricultural & Technical Institute; and Professor Joseph T. Rogers, Business Administration Division, Peirce Junior College.

STUART F. HEINRITZ
PAUL V. FARRELL

CONTENTS

PURCHASING

PRINCIPLES AND APPLICATIONS

1

THE PURCHASING FUNCTION

EVERY INDUSTRIAL ACTIVITY requires materials and supplies to work with. Before a wheel can start turning in the manufacturing process, the materials must be on hand, and there must be assurance of a continuing supply to meet production needs and schedules. The quality of materials must be adequate for the intended purpose and suitable to the process and equipment used. Failure on any of these points may entail costly delays (with cost frequently exceeding by a wide margin the value of the materials themselves), inefficient production, inferior products, broken delivery promises, and disgruntled customers.

To maintain a favorable competitive selling position and satisfactory profits, the materials must be procured at the lowest cost consistent with quality and service requirements. Cost of procurement, and cost of maintaining material inventories, must also be kept at an economic level.

These elementary considerations are the basis of the whole function and science of industrial purchasing.

Material cost as a factor of product cost

In the average of all manufacturing industry, more than half of the total dollar income from the sale of products is expended in the purchase of materials, supplies, and equipment needed to produce the goods. Figures of the Bureau of the Census, United States Department of Commerce, show that purchased materials and fuel represent 54.7 per cent of the aggregate value of national output, in terms of finished product cost.[1] Later reliable

---

[1] United States Department of Commerce, Bureau of the Census, *Sixteenth Census of the United States, 1940—Manufactures*. Washington: United States Government Printing Office, 1942. This is the last such census to give data on purchases.

studies substantiate this finding.[2] It can readily be confirmed by reference to published statements in the annual reports of manufacturing corporations. Such reports consistently show purchases as the largest single factor of industrial cost, and in many cases they are larger than all other factors combined. From this standpoint alone, the purchasing function calls for serious attention on the part of management.

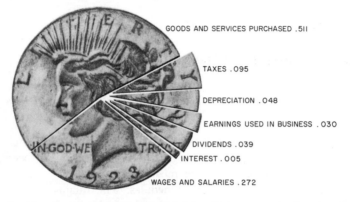

GOODS AND SERVICES PURCHASED .511

TAXES .095

DEPRECIATION .048

EARNINGS USED IN BUSINESS .030

DIVIDENDS .039

INTEREST .005

WAGES AND SALARIES .272

Fig. 1-1. How the Sales Dollar Is Distributed in 100 Representative Manufacturing Companies. Data for 1963 from the First National City Bank of New York.

In the majority of manufacturing companies, materials costs are found to be reasonably close to the average, from 40 per cent to 60 per cent of total product cost. But in special cases, purchases may range widely beyond these limits, according to the type of business and the kinds of materials used.

In the basic processing of a single raw material which, in the processed state, makes up the bulk of the finished product, the purchase cost of material is generally a high proportion of finished-product cost—up to 85 per cent or more. Examples of this are the manufacture of cotton cloth and food packing. A high degree of mechanization, by reducing labor cost per unit of

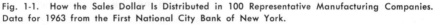

[2] For example, the First National City Bank of New York annually makes an analysis of the disposition of receipts by the 100 largest manufacturing companies in the United States. The figures for 1963, as reported in the August, 1964 issue of the bank's *Monthly Economic Letter,* are:

Total receipts from sales, revenues, etc.		100.0%
Total costs of operations		93.1
Costs of goods and services purchased from others	51.1%	
Wages, salaries and employee benefits	27.2	
Provision for depreciation and depletion	4.8	
Interest paid	0.5	
Federal income tax	5.4	
Other federal, state, local, and foreign taxes	4.1	
Net income		6.9
Dividends paid	3.9	
Retained in the business	3.0	

product, also tends to make material cost a higher percentage of the total, even though the materials themselves may be relatively low in unit cost. Most mass-production industries come within this category. The same is true of assembly operations, where product components are purchased in more highly fabricated form and have thus acquired additional costs in the earlier stages of fabrication, prior to purchase.

On the other hand, in extractive industries like mining or oil production, where the product is not manufactured from purchased materials but comes from natural deposits, the purchase ratio is relatively low. Manufacturing operations that involve highly skilled workmanship and a large labor factor applied to smaller quantities of material also show purchases as a smaller percentage of total cost, even though the materials used may be more expensive in themselves. In service industries where, after the original facilities have been installed, supplies are the somewhat incidental means of implementing the service, purchases are likely to be relatively low in proportion to the total cost of doing business. For example, a typical railroad operating statement shows expenditures for equipment, materials, and supplies, including fuel, as slightly less than 25 per cent of the total cost of providing and maintaining the railroad service. Even so, this item has represented an expenditure of nearly $35 million annually.

In some manufacturing industries, despite rising wages, the ratio of purchased material cost to total product cost is generally rising. This fact is due in part to increasing mechanization. It is also due, in great measure, to the growing trend toward specialization in manufacturing. The automobile industry, for example, buys batteries and tires, wheels and axles, carburetors, springs, bumpers, grilles, completely wired dashboard assemblies, and many other parts from specialized makers of such products, to be incorporated into the finished car. Thus, the prices paid for these items by the automobile manufacturer include the supplier's labor and indirect charges and his profits. Yet, for the automobile manufacturer, these prices represent true "purchased material costs." In 1940, when more of the actual parts manufacturing was still being done in the automobile plants, average material cost in this industry was about 52 per cent of total product cost. Twenty years later, when many components were procured in fabricated form, material cost had risen to 62 per cent of the total.

The dollar amounts involved in purchasing, even in companies of moderate size, are substantial. They demand prudent, skillful administration. Efficiency in purchasing affords opportunities for making important savings and avoiding serious waste and loss. The effect on product cost is such that it may easily spell the difference between leadership in an industry and an untenable competitive position. Management properly gives close and continuous attention to labor costs, production efficiency, and costs of distribution. The materials item is sometimes taken for granted, as if it were a fixed cost and nothing could be done about it. Yet in terms of the value received in return for purchase expenditures, this factor also reflects good or poor management and performance. It is, in fact, of equal importance with other functions of industrial activity and the other elements of product cost in attaining successful, profitable company operation.

The simple mathematics of the situation, using the figures from Footnote 2, are that a reduction of five per cent in the cost of purchased materials, which is a rather modest purchasing goal, is the profit equivalent of a 36 per cent increase in production and sales volume, which might be an ambitious quota, difficult to attain. Or, an increase of five per cent in material costs due to inept purchasing would wipe out two-thirds of the net income available for dividends.

Effect of purchasing on other costs

Direct expenditure for materials is by no means the only way in which purchasing affects end-product costs. The effect of delays due to lack of materials has already been noted. Shutdowns and waiting time at machines may be charged to production costs, but the end result is the same. More insidious is the situation where purchased materials are on hand as needed but are not uniform in quality or dimension, or are otherwise of inferior workability. Improper materials impair manufacturing efficiency and add to the "hidden" costs of production. In addition, they may entail extra costs of closer inspection and result in excessive waste and rejections which sacrifice not only the spoiled material itself but also the time and labor expended on it.

Such instances obviously show faulty or inadequate purchasing performance, which could be avoided by giving more and better attention to the buying function. But there are other cases in which purchasing may be done strictly in accordance with stated requirements, on time, and at a favorable price, yet the end cost may be unnecessarily high. This occurs, for example, when the specification does not give enough consideration to the availability of material, or to the possibilities of alternative materials, or to commercial standards of size and formulation. Factors such as these are inherent in the economics of purchasing decisions. The most advantageous end costs can be attained only when the purchasing factors are weighed and balanced against factors of utility and usage, when material cost is considered in its relation to other costs, as a part of the over-all operating plan.

Sound purchasing frequently discloses cases where it is more economical to buy more expensive materials, as either product components or operating supplies, when the additional cost will be offset by manufacturing economies. The reverse may also be true, in other cases. It may be economical to incur some additional manufacturing cost to take advantage of substantially cheaper materials that are adequate for the purpose. Or, it may be found economical to abandon certain manufacturing operations that are presently performed in the plant, when parts so produced could be bought at lower cost from an outside supplier.

A management function

Purchasing is not an end in itself. Materials and supplies are bought because they are needed to be used. Since the activities of purchasing have the primary purpose of implementing the work of other departments by pro- curing these goods, it is sometimes regarded as merely a service function. Purchasing can be carried on under this concept, with partial effectiveness. The implication, however, is that purchasing considerations are subordinated to the aims, desires, and policies—or even to the preferences and whims— of the departments served. This is to sacrifice, by default, the larger benefits and full potentialities of scientific purchasing and decisions.

The modern view is that purchasing's role is coordinate with those of other major phases of company activity. It is neither subordinate nor domi- nant, but works closely with other departments toward the common purpose of profitable operation. This viewpoint gives scope both for the service aspects of purchasing and for the special contributions of purchasing science and skill. Where the purchasing officer is thus "a member of the management team," the principles of economical, scientific purchasing can be applied without hindrance, on their own merits, and there is a constant incentive for improved purchasing methods and performance. Also, suggestions re- garding materials and policies can be initiated in purchasing, with the assur- ance that they will receive consideration, weighed against other facts or in arriving at a final decision.

In this sense, purchasing is a function of management. In yet another sense, purchasing is in itself a true management function. It involves the management of materials in flow, from the establishment of sources and "pipelines," through inventory stores, to the ultimate delivery at production stations as needed. At every stage there are decisions to be made as to quality, quantity, timing, source, and cost. And these decisions must be keyed to constantly changing business and economic conditions that alter the im- mediate objectives and policies of purchasing from month to month, even from day to day.

A review of the varied conditions that have prevailed at some time or other over a relatively short span of years shows how purchasing must be adjusted to current demands. Among these have been periods of extraordinary expansion and high activity; periods of recession and retrenchment; eras of "profitless prosperity"; prolonged "sellers' markets" and "buyers' markets"; material shortages during which manufacturing schedules were determined not by how much could be made and sold, but by how much raw material could be purchased; and great technological advances that introduced many new materials and processes, made others obsolete, and substantially changed the character of things to be purchased. In addition, there has been the enormous expansion in the production of defense goods to meet the demands of the cold war. Possible cancellation of contracts, close government supervision, and rapidly changing technological requirements are just a few of the factors that have to be considered in defense procurement.

With changing conditions such as these to contend with, today's good purchasing policy could be actually disastrous tomorrow. Constant close attention and a maximum of flexibility are essential. The changes must not only be recognized; they should be anticipated, and purchasing methods developed to cope with them successfully.

Responsibility for purchasing

Purchasing responsibility, like other major management and operating functions, is generally delegated to a specific person or a special department in the company organization. In few concerns of any substantial size today do individual departments do their own buying, of either production materials or operating supplies. In some cases, the specialized purchasing department comes under the jurisdiction of the production manager. This is a carry-over from earlier days, when purchasing was regarded primarily as a service to the manufacturing department. Most companies set up purchasing, or materials management, as a completely separate department, with the chief purchasing officer reporting directly to the executive who has the over-all responsibility for profitable operation, that is, the president, executive vice-president, general manager, or plant or divisional manager.

This system of allocating responsibility and concentrating authority for buying is known as *centralized purchasing*. Its advantages are those which are inherent in the economic principle of the division of labor and in all functional organization:

1. Better control is assured by isolating the materials factor, with one person or department directly responsible to management for handling this function, and one complete set of records pertaining to purchase transactions, commitments, and expenditures.

2. Concentration on purchasing develops specialized knowledge, skills, and procedures that result in more efficient and economical procurement.
3. Better performance may be expected in other departments when superintendents, office managers, and other department heads are relieved of the detailed buying responsibility and of the interruptions and interviews incidental to buying.
4. Divorcing the purchasing function from the influence or domination of other departments, whose primary interests lie in other directions, affords a greater likelihood that the economic and profit potentials of purchasing will receive more consideration on their own merits and thus may make a greater contribution to over-all profitable operation.

When is it economically feasible to maintain a separate purchasing department? Variations in individual conditions make it hard to set any arbitrary standard or limit. A rough rule of thumb is that annual purchases of a half-million dollars or more, corresponding to a million dollars or more in annual sales volume, constitute a full-time purchasing job. However, the principle of centralized purchasing can be applied effectively in smaller companies; there are many instances of this, where a purchasing agent has additional duties such as office manager, traffic manager, storekeeper, production control manager, or the like.

Objectives of purchasing

The purchasing responsibility is sometimes defined as *buying materials of the right quality, in the right quantity, at the right time, at the right price, from the right source.* This is a broad generalization, indicating the scope of the purchasing function, which involves policy decisions and analyses of various alternative possibilities, prior to the act of purchase. The significance of the definition depends, of course, on the interpretation of what is "right," and requires the consideration of many factors, which are discussed in detail in later chapters. At this point, we are more concerned with the objectives to be attained.

The fundamental objectives of purchasing for a manufacturing industry may be summarized as follows:

1. To maintain continuity of supply to support the manufacturing schedule;
2. To do so with the minimum investment in materials inventory consistent with safety and economic advantage;
3. To avoid duplication, waste, and obsolescence with respect to materials;
4. To maintain standards of quality in materials, based on suitability for use;
5. To procure materials at the lowest cost consistent with the quality and service required;
6. To maintain the company's competitive position in its industry and to conserve its profit position, insofar as material costs are concerned.

The same principles apply to purchasing in fields other than that of manufacturing industry. In a public utility company, for example, the first point would be to support the service, operating, and construction schedule, rather than the manufacturing schedule; in purchasing for a municipal government, it would be to support the various services, such as police and fire protection, maintenance of streets, parks, and public buildings, garbage collection and disposal, and all the other activities essential to a complete civic administration. In buying for a hospital, a university, or a governmental unit, where the profit motive and competitive factors are absent, the sixth point would be rephrased to express a similar thought directed toward getting the maximum value for the expenditure of a fixed budget appropriation for materials or, to take a word from the slogan of one eminently successful municipal purchasing department, toward increasing the "mileage" of the tax dollar.

Scope and limitations of purchasing authority

Purchasing is done not for its own sake, but to implement other phases of company operation. It starts, in every case, with a need that is established in the company's operating program.

Thus, a purchase requires authorization. This may be formal or informal. Sometimes it exists only in the form of a manufacturing quota for a given calendar period, the purchasing agent being apprised of this quota and all that it entails in the way of material and supply requirements. Sometimes it is embodied in the bill of materials, either for a standard line of products or for products built to special order. At other times it is expressed in the form of a purchase requisition for required material. For standard materials in common and repetitive use, the purchasing agent customarily has considerable latitude for the exercise of judgment in purchasing for stock in advance of specific requirements. His decisions are based upon experience, rate of use, sales estimates, and other indicators, and are usually in conformance with an established inventory policy.

In purchasing for a government unit or for institutions, purchases for a particular department or account are usually strictly limited by the annual budget or the unexpended portion thereof (which is another form of authorization).

In governmental purchasing, and in about 20 per cent of industrial operations, there is a monetary limit to the amount that may be spent for any single purchase without securing specific approval of the expenditure from general management. These monetary limitations vary from a hundred dollars in some cases to several thousand dollars. Frequently, in a single company, such limitations are scaled according to the type of purchase involved, being generally closer in respect to items of equipment and capital purchases and more liberal in respect to materials and supplies.

Purchases of capital equipment are usually controlled by special regulations, and purchasing department participation may be limited to procuring the basic data on what is available for the purpose and placing the order after a decision has been reached by committee or executive action. This is discussed in detail in Chapter 18. Some raw materials may also be excluded specifically from purchasing department jurisdiction under certain conditions, although this is less prevalent than formerly. The modern trend is to bring even the most specialized commodity buying within the general framework of the purchasing department, although with somewhat greater latitude and independence of action than for standard or routine requirements. Some examples of this are presented in Chapter 3.

The general statement of purchasing objectives limits the purchasing department to procurement for actual or anticipated use. This rules out purchases made primarily for the purpose or in the hope of inventory value appreciation or speculative profits on materials. Such buying—though it may be effected through the purchasing department—is a matter for general management to decide. The outlawing of speculative purchases, however, does not preclude the exercise of purchasing judgment in adjusting the buying and inventory program to economic and market conditions. The purchasing agent may extend coverage in anticipation of rising prices and work closer to actual current requirements when a price decline is in prospect.

Ultimate responsibility for the type and quality of materials to be bought must rest with those who use them and are responsible for results. In this sense, the using departments are in the relation of customers to the purchasing department, and they must be satisfied. But this does not place the responsibility or authority for selection in the using department. Rather, theirs is a responsibility of accurate definition or specification of the product, in terms of formula or analysis, accepted commercial standards, blueprints or dimensional tolerances, or the intended purpose of the material. Most industrial materials, supplies, and equipment are procurable in competitive markets, from a variety of sources, and it is the function of purchasing to select the particular material and source most advantageous to the company, patronizing two or more alternative sources if it is desirable to stimulate competition or assure continuity of supply, always bearing in mind that the essential requirement, as defined, must be met.

In addition to quality, the request for materials involves a statement of the quantity desired and the date or time when they will be needed. It is the responsibility of the purchasing agent to check these factors against the actual need, from his knowledge of the operating program or from his record of past purchases and use, and to question any apparent deviation from normal

Title: Director of Purchases

BASIC FUNCTION:

Responsible to the Vice President-General Manager for directing the purchasing activities of the Company in accordance with established broad policies.

BASIC OBJECTIVE:

To secure for the Company its requirements of raw materials, purchase parts, equipment, and operating supplies at the lowest possible cost consistent with accepted standards for quality and service.

MAJOR DUTIES AND RESPONSIBILITIES:

1. Policies and Programs
   a. To recommend to the Vice President-General Manager broad purchasing policies and programs in accordance with his forecast of economic and price trends in the domestic and foreign markets.
   b. To establish procedures for the control of purchases.
   c. To coordinate Company specifications with those of the trade.
   d. To search for new materials of present or future interest to the Company.
   e. To promote standardization of all purchases.
2. Organization
   a. To develop and maintain a purchasing organization that adequately meets the needs of the Company.
   b. To carry out Company's personal relations policies.
   c. To approve position description of all immediate subordinates.
   d. To approve employment, promotion, change in compensation, or other employee movement personnel in the organization.
3. Negotiations and Procurement
   a. To engage in negotiations for materials requiring commitments over extended periods.
4. Sources of Supply
   a. To engage in the development of additional or alternate sources of supply for important materials.
   b. To direct Purchasing Agent and Assistant Purchasing Agent in similar activity.
   c. To promote, in collaboration with the Chemical Research and Mechanical Engineering Divisions, sources of supply for new or improved materials.
   d. To direct the maintenance of a list of acceptable vendors, a record of purchases, and a record of prices and terms of purchase.
5. Relations with Vendors
   a. To promote and maintain good Company relations with principal vendors.
   b. To direct Purchasing Agent and Assistant Purchasing Agent in similar activity.
6. Contracts
   To execute contractual agreements for the purchase of raw materials, purchased parts, equipment, and operating supplies, after view by the Company's Legal Counsel.
7. Purchase Forecasts and Budgets
   a. To prepare, in collaboration with the Controller's Division, purchase forecasts and expense budgets for approval and decision by the Vice President-General Manager.
   b. To submit such reports on the activities and future plans of the Purchasing Division as may be requested by Vice President-General Manager.
   c. To collaborate with Controller's Division in establishing purchase price standards.
   d. To review with Purchasing Agent and Assistant Purchasing Agent monthly material price variance statements submitted by the Controller's Division, and to recommend appropriate action.

LIMITS OF AUTHORITY:

1. To operate within established budget limits.
2. To implement major purchasing policy changes only after the approval of Vice President-General Manager.
3. To execute contractual agreements for the purchase of raw materials, equipment and operating supplies.
4. To execute Company purchase orders for items of capital equipment in excess of $500 and upon receipt of proper authorizations.
5. To approve recommendations of Purchasing Agent concerning employment, promotion, or change in compensation of personnel in the Division.
6. To approve expenses of Purchasing Agent and Assistant Purchasing Agent.
7. To present papers and make speeches to outside groups regarding Company activities and purchasing procedures only after obtaining approval of Vice President-General Manager.
8. To limit his line authority to his immediate subordinates.

RELATIONS WITH OTHERS:

1. Directly responsible to the Vice President-General Manager for the performance of the above duties.
2. Responsible for cooperating with all executives of the Company coordinating the activities of the Purchasing Division with other units of the Company.

MEASUREMENT OF PERFORMANCE:

The performance of the Director of Purchases will be measured by the effective degree with which he secures for the Company its requirements of raw materials, purchase parts, equipment, and operating supplies at the lowest possible cost consistent with accepted standards for quality and service, and the degree to which he satisfies the Vice President-General Manager with the performance of his duties.

Title: Assistant Purchasing Agent

BASIC FUNCTION:

Responsible to the Director of Purchases for purchasing new materials and purchased parts used in the manufacture of the Company's supply products.

BASIC OBJECTIVE:

To secure for the Company its requirements of raw materials and parts used in the manufacture of supply products at the lowest possible cost consistent with accepted standards for quality and service, and in accordance with established policies and procedures.

MAJOR DUTIES AND RESPONSIBILITIES:

1. Purchasing
   a. To purchase those items and materials for which he is responsible.
   b. To negotiate claims resulting from damaged or defective merchandise received from vendors.
   c. To negotiate the sale of scrap and surplus equipment only after approval of the Director of Purchases.
2. Sources of Supply
   a. To assist in the development of additional or alternate sources of supply.
   b. To promote, in collaboration with the Chemical and Research Engineering Division, sources of supply for new or improved materials.
   c. To maintain a list of acceptable vendors, a record of purchases, and a record of prices and terms of purchases.
3. Relations with Vendors
   To promote and maintain good Company relations with vendors.

Fig. 1-2. Typical Job Descriptions for a Purchasing Department.

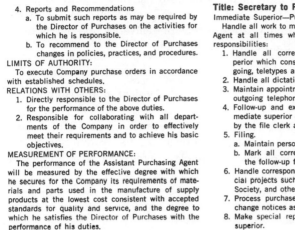

4. Reports and Recommendations
   a. To submit such reports as may be required by the Director of Purchases on the activities for which he is responsible.
   b. To recommend to the Director of Purchases changes in policies, practices, and procedures.

LIMITS OF AUTHORITY:
To execute Company purchase orders in accordance with established schedules.

RELATIONS WITH OTHERS:
1. Directly responsible to the Director of Purchases for the performance of the above duties.
2. Responsible for collaborating with all departments of the Company in order to effectively meet their requirements and to achieve his basic objectives.

MEASUREMENT OF PERFORMANCE:
The performance of the Assistant Purchasing Agent will be measured by the effective degree with which he secures for the Company its requirements of materials and parts used in the manufacture of supply products at the lowest cost consistent with accepted standards for quality and service, and the degree to which he satisfies the Director of Purchases with the performance of his duties.

Title: Secretary to Purchasing Agent
Immediate Superior—Purchasing Agent
Handle all work to maintain the office of Purchasing Agent at all times which consists of the following responsibilities:
1. Handle all correspondence for immediate superior which consists of pending, incoming, outgoing, teletypes and telegrams.
2. Handle all dictation for immediate superior.
3. Maintain appointments and handle incoming and outgoing telephone calls as required.
4. Follow-up and expedite correspondence for immediate superior each day. Follow-ups are pulled by the file clerk and put on secretary's desk.
5. Filing.
   a. Maintain personal files as directed.
   b. Mark all correspondence for filing either in the follow-up file, firm file or commodity file.
6. Handle correspondence and files required on special projects such as United Fund, NAPA, Cancer Society, and other civic and charitable activities.
7. Process purchase orders, shipping releases and change notices as required.
8. Make special reports as required by immediate superior.

Fig. 1-2. Continued

requirements, even though the authorization of the request may otherwise be in good order. This is a part of his duty to avoid duplication, excessive stocks, and unnecessary rush orders that would disrupt the procurement program and incur extra transportation costs.

When the quantity and delivery requirements have been established, it is the responsibility of purchasing to decide whether the goods shall be bought in a single lot, or in a series of smaller transactions over a period of time from one or more suppliers, or on a single long-term contract with delivery schedules to be specified according to the need. All of these considerations, weighed in conjunction with quantity discounts, carrying charges, market conditions, and the like, have a bearing on ultimate cost of the material, so that there is a considerable range of opportunity or advantage open to purchasing judgment, even within the strict specification of quantity and delivery requirements.

Commercial aspects of the transaction—negotiations as to price, delivery, guarantees, terms, and conditions of the contract and adjustments as to over- and undershipments or deficiencies in quality—are wholly purchasing responsibilities.

The extent to which the purchasing department is responsible beyond the point of issuing the order varies in different companies. Instances can be found where this act marks the end of purchasing jurisdiction, but they are not typical; the test of purchasing performance lies in satisfactory deliveries against the order. In the great majority of companies, the purchasing function is interpreted to include the follow-up for delivery, reconciling receipts and vendors' invoices with the purchase order, and passing invoices for payment.

In well over half the cases, it includes the responsibility of storeskeeping and complete accountability for materials until they are issued to the using departments. Inspection and quality-testing of deliveries for acceptance are sometimes included in the purchasing function.

Typical purchasing activities

Operating a purchasing department to meet these responsibilities involves a variety of detailed assignments, of both an administrative and a routine nature. Typical activities of even the simplest purchasing program include

Basic Information:
  Maintaining purchase records
  Maintaining price records
  Maintaining stock and consumption records
  Maintaining vendor records
  Maintaining specification files
  Maintaining catalog files
Research:
  Market studies
  Material studies
  Cost analysis
  Investigating supply sources
  Inspecting suppliers' plants
  Developing supply sources
  Developing alternate materials and sources
Procurement:
  Checking requisitions
  Securing quotations
  Analyzing quotations
  Choosing between contract or open-market purchase
  Scheduling purchases and deliveries
  Interviewing salesmen
  Negotiating contracts
  Issuing purchase orders
  Checking legal conditions of contracts
  Following up for delivery
  Checking receipt of materials
  Verifying invoices
  Corresponding with vendors
  Making adjustments with vendors
Materials Management:
  Maintaining minimum stocks
  Maintaining inventory balance
  Improving inventory turnover
  Transferring materials
  Consolidating requirements
  Avoiding excess stocks and obsolescence

   Standardizing packages and containers
   Accounting for returnable containers
   Making periodic reports of commitments
Miscellaneous:
   Making cost estimates
   Disposing of scrap and obsolete and surplus materials
   Handling reciprocal trade relations

Auxiliary functions

In addition to the activities which are distinctly within the province of purchasing, there are a number of responsibilities that are typically shared with other departments, by means of recommendations or by decisions reached through conference or committee action in which the purchasing agent or his representative has a voice. Among these responsibilities are

Office practice
Determination of whether to manufacture or buy
Standardization
Simplification
Specifications
Substitution of materials
Acceptance testing
Materials budget
Inventory control
Selection of capital equipment
Construction projects
Reciprocal trade policy
Production programs dependent on availability of materials

In some companies, certain relative activities are also assigned to the purchasing department. Among these are

Storeskeeping (in about 50 per cent)
Traffic management (Classification and routing of incoming traffic is quite
   generally regarded as part of the purchasing function. The complete respon-
   sibility for traffic management is on the purchasing department in about
   25 per cent of companies.)
Insurance
Real estate
Operation of garages and automotive equipment
Inspection
Salvage and reclamation
Materials accounting

The foregoing lists are not exhaustive. Activities vary somewhat among different companies according to the character of the enterprise, but the résumé indicates the scope and type of work that is generally included in a well-rounded purchasing program. One point that is made clear in this analysis is that the buying operation touches virtually every other department of the organization in some vital field beyond the actual procurement of materials and supplies for its needs. The closest sort of cooperation must be maintained, not only with production, but with finance, accounting, engineering, maintenance, sales, office management, and general management as well.

Purchasing as a concern of management

Top management has an obligation to see the total organization and profit picture, and to see each part in proper perspective. It has an obligation to demand not only that each part shall function adequately within its own area of responsibility, but that it shall make the greatest possible contribution toward the total operating and profit objectives. This entails defining the areas of functional responsibility and authority and correlating them in the larger scheme so that each will have scope to realize its full potential in the joint effort that constitutes successful company operation.

Purchasing is inescapably a part of that picture. Therefore, the manager must be at least "literate" in respect to the objectives, opportunities, and methods of modern purchasing.

Without this understanding of purchasing principles, management lacks the means of even a rudimentary appraisal of purchasing performance. It is not enough to delegate the act of buying and to charge the buyer to procure needed materials at lowest cost. The inadequacy of this approach is at once apparent in that most common of all admonitions to purchasing men, "The cheapest buy is not always the best buy." But the moment we go beyond this concept of price buying, as we must, the matter becomes more complex. The question for management becomes: "How much can I expect of the purchasing department? Where does it fit into our management and operating policy?"

There is no single, universal answer to these questions, as this study will abundantly show. But the answer in any given case may be surprising, for the developments in purchasing science and the experience of progressive purchasing departments reveal a potent profit tool that management can ill afford to ignore. The sharpness of that tool and the way it is used are matters that management, first, and then the purchasing agent, must determine. Viewed in this light, purchasing is more than just another job to be done; it is an integral part of successful management.

2

PURCHASING AND MANAGEMENT

IN MANAGEMENT SCIENCE, the three major responsibilities common to all manufacturing industry are generally listed as finance, production, and sales, and functional organization resolves itself first of all into these three broad divisions. The typical "success story" of American industry, starting from small beginnings and one-man management, finds the owner-manager in charge of all three. But with the growth of the business, it becomes necessary to enlist additional executive assistance and to delegate repsonsibility. The division of responsibilities is generally according to this three-part plan, with the original manager either retaining the active direction of the phase closest to his interest and genius, or supervising all three in the role of general management. In corporate organization, the latter situation is most typical, with a board of directors or executive committee supplanting the individual as the policy-making and directing head of the business. Up to this point the three functions have been subordinate factors, but now' they become separate executive responsibilities, coordinate in rank, reporting to and coordinated by a common general management body.

But this division is not final. With continued growth, as each of these three major functions increases in responsibility and complexity, the same process of division continues. First comes the development of specific subordinate functions within each division, then the setting up of these functions as separate departments in the charge of department managers. Many of the latter eventually report directly to the general management instead of through the division of which they were formerly a part. Thus they achieve independent status on a coordinate plane. Sales promotion and advertising may be divorced from sales management proper, with a sales promotion manager and an advertising manager, responsible not to the sales manager but to general management. All these functions were originally included in the sales division and must, of course, continue to work harmoniously in order to achieve the most effective results.) Similarly, the finance or treasurer's department may be subdivided to include a comptroller's office, cost accounting department, credit department, payroll department, transfer agent, and the like. Some may be of subordinate authority and some of independent and coordinate responsibility.

Historically, purchasing is allied to the production division. Some procurement of materials is also involved in implementing the work of finance, where accounting forms, office machinery, and supplies are required, and of sales, where catalogs, promotional material, salesmen's cars, and branch office equipment are used; but in the typical manufacturing operation, the bulk of purchased materials goes into the product and its fabrication, and its procurement is the first step of the production process. This is the nucleus of the purchasing program.

In the simple three-part division of responsibility, the production division embraces a wide variety of activities that are subject to specialized and independent administration in the more highly functionalized organization of large-scale industry. They include the design of the product to be manufactured (subsequently set apart as design and engineering departments); planning the schedule of operations (production control or planning department); procurement (purchasing) and stocking (stores) of materials and supplies required; and production itself. Other typical functions are plant engineering, power, maintenance, and the like.

The first step in specialization along functional lines is to assign the responsibility for each of these activities to a particular individual or group under the direction of the production manager. The second step is to set them up as separate departments, independent of direct supervision or of the jurisdiction of the production manager. This historical background is evidenced in the organization charts of typical industrial organizations. In about one-fourth of the companies maintaining purchasing departments, the purchasing agent reports to the production manager or some higher production executive, such as the vice-president in charge of operation; in about 5 per cent of the companies, he reports to the treasurer or other financial officer, reflecting the responsibility of committing the company to important expenditures of its working capital. But in the great majority of cases—approximately 80 per cent—the purchasing department has developed beyond this intermediate stage of subordinate responsibility; it is recognized as having a separate, specialized function equivalent to and independent of production and directly responsible to the general management or the board of directors.

The evolution of purchasing

Along with this evolution of broad managerial responsibilities, there has been a corresponding process of development in the actual conduct of purchasing activities.

In the first stage, when purchasing is indiscriminately done by foremen, master mechanics, department heads, superintendents, or whoever happens to need materials and supplies at the moment, there is typically a complete absence of planning and control. Each department makes provision for its materials needs independently of the others and according to its own policies, which are likely to be dictated chiefly by expediency. Buying is a secondary consideration; purchasing and material costs lose their identity in total departmental costs. There are few significant purchasing records and practically no standards of performance and value sufficiently concrete for intelligent appraisal at the management level. Duplication, inconsistency, and waste in materials are almost certain to follow.

Standards of quality under such conditions are matters of individual opinion or preference and vary widely within the same organization. The standard of price is merely "the market." The standard of quality is summed up in the principle of having "plenty" on hand and getting more when needed—a thoroughly unscientific and expensive policy. Without adequate records and planning, there are frequent emergency requirements which must be procured with even less than the usual attention to proper purchasing. In every department of the shop and office, time is wasted and primary activities are neglected or interrupted for interviews with salesmen and details of buying.

In the next stage, where routine purchasing duties are assigned to a purchasing clerk within the department, some of these shortcomings are remedied or at least improved. Records are kept and executive time is conserved. But so long as purchasing is regarded as simply a clerical function, issuing purchase orders as directed, without the incentive to acquire knowledge of materials and sources or the opportunity to exercise judgment, there is little improvement in basic purchasing performance. The purchasing clerk may handle interviews on repetitive requirements of standard materials, small miscellaneous items of minor value, or those that the production manager may relegate to him as unimportant. Under these circumstances, the only way that the "buyer" can show accomplishment is to secure a better price; the first emphasis is, therefore, upon shrewdness and the ability to drive a sharp bargain.

With slightly more independence and authority, when purchasing is set up as a separate department, though still under the direction of the production manager and subject to his final decisions, the buying procedure is systematized for greater efficiency. Records are developed from the purchase orders as a guide to buying practice. Some elementary market studies may be instituted to take advantage of seasonal trends and market fluctuations. Requirements are consolidated for quantity purchase, and standardization may be introduced on a limited scale. A start is made toward the conscious development of more satisfactory vendor relationships. Competition may be stimulated by inviting competitive bids, and alternative sources of supply are established. Emergency requirements are less frequent.

At this stage, the emphasis is primarily on procedure, which is very help-ful as a step toward better purchasing performance. But there is still no policy-making authority on the basis of purchase considerations. There is no consistent, long-range purchasing program. Although some of the larger op-portunities for service, efficiency, value, and economy in buying are doubtless apparent to the alert and imaginative purchasing man, under these conditions he can achieve or approach them only to the extent of making suggestions to his superior.

The development of truly centralized purchasing as a distinct functional responsibility, independent of production jurisdiction, came with mass-production operations, large-scale corporate organization, and the increasing complexities of modern distribution. With a separate purchasing department, under the direction of a responsible purchasing executive and having this function as its primary interest and responsibility, price consciousness and efficient procedures are still matters of concern, but they no longer receive first emphasis for their own sake. Price is balanced against the other factors of quality, quantity, and timing, to the end that the greatest ultimate value may be obtained for purchase expenditures. Procedure is considered as a means to an end, serving to implement an established purchasing policy. And techniques of research and analysis are added to help realize the full potential of purchasing toward making and conserving company profits.

What management expects of the purchasing department

Having established centralized purchasing, management expects, first of all, the competent performance of purchasing duties and the accomplishment of the basic purchasing objectives outlined in Chapter 1. It expects a depart-ment that understands and accepts the responsibilities of its function in the over-all organization. It expects a department that is efficiently administered, developing appropriate policies and procedures that will result in economical cost of procurement as well as economical cost of materials. It expects a well-informed department that can serve as an information center for the entire company on the commercial and market aspects of materials—availability, cost, trends, and so forth—and so can aid in the formulation of broad business policies.

Management expects its purchasing people to be "company men" as well, putting company interests and objectives ahead of departmental interests. It expects a department that can get along with other departments and work with them toward the attainment of company objectives without compromising sound purchasing principles.

Management expects the purchasing department, in its contacts and dealings with supplier companies and their representatives, to act with fairness, courtesy, and dignity, and to maintain high standards of business relationships. This public relations aspect of purchasing is now recognized as one of the most important opportunities and responsibilities of the purchasing department.

With the development of purchasing science and the broadening concept of the scope of purchasing activity, the plaint of progressive purchasing men is that management expects too little, rather than too much, of the purchasing department. It is well, therefore, at this point to note also what purchasing expects of management. It expects buying authority commensurate with its responsibilities. It expects a clear-cut definition of its activities and authority, particularly where they impinge upon the activities of other departments. It expects the backing of management in the enforcement of approved purchasing policies and procedures throughout the company. It expects management to provide the physical and technical facilities for efficient purchasing work.

Beyond this, purchasing expects management to have an understanding of the larger aims of progressive purchasing practice, so that the legitimate scope of its activities may not be unduly circumscribed; to grant purchasing a voice

HOWE
SOUND

HOWE SOUND PURCHASING POLICIES ARE DESIGNED TO:

1. Be ever mindful of our Company's general business objectives and develop to the maximum every sound opportunity towards the fulfillment of those objectives.

2. Purchase materials of a suitable quality in proper quantity at best over-all value to the corporation and to have materials delivered where and when required.

3. Keep suppliers currently informed as to our purchasing practices and procedures.

4. Have purchasing personnel available in all plants at reasonable times to interview salesmen.

5. Get prompt and effective evaluation of suppliers' proposals and to make certain that they receive the most complete possible consideration in relation to all areas of the Company's operation.

6. Treat confidentially all information, either written or oral, furnished us by suppliers in connection with their products.

7. Respect the proper channels of authority in the supplier's company and promote harmonious business relationships with supplying firms.

8. Keep all purchasing on an objective basis. For this reason our employees are not permitted to accept gifts or gratuities in any form from any supplier or prospective supplier, at any time.

FUNCTIONAL ORGANIZATION OF PURCHASING

Statement of Organizational Policy

Howe Sound's purchasing program has been established so that the New York Corporate Purchasing Office has the responsibilities for establishing and administrating our purchasing policies and co-ordinating purchasing activities of our Product Divisions.

What Activities are Centralized

Certain select commodities and services as they are used commonly throughout the Product Divisions are purchased or contracted for by the New York Office. Such practice facilitates communications between vendors and Howe Sound and provides mutual advantages through volume sales and purchasing by the New York Office. It further provides one point of contact where suppliers can discuss Howe Sound total requirements.

Fig. 2-1. Typical Company Statement on Purchasing Policies and Organization.

in policy-making councils and decisions; to listen with an open mind to purchasing proposals affecting materials usage in other departments and company investment in materials; and to permit the department to extend its activities and influence where benefit to the company can be demonstrated.

The purchasing department should regularly make available to management and to all interested departments its special knowledge and appraisal of economic and market conditions. Purchasing is in a unique position to acquire valuable information through its own continuing study of markets and through day-to-day contact with a variety of supplier industries, whose salesmen have personal and up-to-date knowledge of what the feeling is in their own companies and those of their customers. New products and processes, and new applications of old materials, typically come first to the attention of the purchasing department. Labor relations in supplier industries, and other factors affecting present and future supply, can be significant indicators in the formulation of sound business policies. Purchasing department reports can be a valuable service to management, supplementing other research.

Purchasing authority

Reference has been made in the preceding sections to the "authority" of the purchasing department and the purchasing officer, and more such references will be made in the balance of this chapter and in the discussion of organization for purchasing. It will be evident from the context that the authority mentioned is not standard or implicit in the function itself but is widely variable, in kind and degree, according to varying circumstances and individual cases. Before leaving the consideration of purchasing-management relationships, therefore, the concept of purchasing authority should be clarified.

Basically, authority is conferred by management along with the delegation of duties. The general management principle applied here is that authority should be commensurate with the responsibility and with the capacity to meet responsibility. Both of these criteria are for management to appraise and decide. The first is the more important, for the presumption is that if the person charged with responsibility does not have the required abilities, management will find or train one who has.

The scope of authority in any given case can therefore be interpreted, first, as corresponding to the functional responsibilities assigned by management in specific areas of decision and action. For example, when we say that it is outside the province of purchasing to decide *what* shall be bought for a particular purpose or need, but that purchasing does have the authority to select the *source* from which it is bought, the distinction is not one of privilege but of two different responsibilities—for suitability and for value.

The purchasing agent is given authority to buy, but the particular purchases must first be authorized by a specific evidence of need—a requisition originating in another department, a minimum stock quantity established by inventory policy, the bill of materials for a factory work order, or some other, similar means of authorization. And of course the purchasing agent, like everyone else in the organization, is answerable to his superiors in management for the manner in which he exercises his authority. Thus authority must be deserved and earned.

The scope of responsibility suggested in the preceding section is very broad. But even the simple delegated authority to buy may be circumscribed qualitatively, by stated exceptions to the general rule, or quantitatively, by placing a monetary limit on commitments made by the purchasing department. Limitations on authority may reflect basic management policy in the assignment of responsibilities, or they may be based on management's appraisal of the department's capacity to take responsibility. The factor of capacity works the other way, too. The purchasing agent with initiative and ability, seeing ways to improve purchasing service and performance by broadening the scope of his activity, may persuade management to rewrite its definition of his authority. Or, in the absence of formal authorization, he may assume added responsibility, acting originally beyond the scope of his stated function; if such activities do not infringe upon the authority of other departments.

Purchasing and production

The insistence on the separation of purchasing from direct control by the production department does not imply any basic divergence of interest. It is still a primary function of purchasing to serve the production program, and the latter must be satisfied. The relationship between the two departments should be considered rather from the viewpoint of their common objective, which is to contribute most effectively to the company's over-all advantage. From this viewpoint, there is excellent reason why neither should dominate the other. At the same time, there is compelling reason for the closest possible cooperation.

Final decision as to the type and quality of materials to be purchased rests with design or using departments, but this decision does not extend to the selection of source, which is a prerogative of purchasing. Preference as to source or brand may be indicated, and should be considered in purchasing so long as no sacrifice of other buying factors is involved. It should not be binding unless better reasons than personal preference or past usage can be presented. When required products are identified by a manufacturer's brand name or number, this description is usually qualified by the phrase "or equal," to give the buyer greater latitude of choice; the burden of proof is then on purchasing to show that alternative products are actually equal in suitability for the purpose. To increase the assurance of supply and to maintain competition, purchasing seeks to establish two or more sources for all items in regular use. Production and other using departments should therefore test alternative materials and supplies from various sources, at purchasing's request, and indicate those that are satisfactory for inclusion on an "approved list"; choice of product and supplier then is determined by purchasing, with the assurance that the selection will be acceptable to the user.

In making requests to purchase, using departments are responsible for providing complete and accurate information on what is required. The purchasing department has the duty of buying to fulfill any legitimate, properly authorized requisition; it has the privilege of questioning any requisition, as to either material or quantity specified for purchase, if in its judgment the request is out of line with current usage or best buying policy. This is in no sense a challenge to the authority of other departments. It is simply a prudent precaution, consistent with purchasing's position as a watchdog over purchase expenditures, against duplication, possible errors in description or estimating, or occasional misuses of requisitioning privileges. Usually, purchasing also has the privilege of revising quantities on a requisition for purposes of buying most advantageously, provided that the total requirement is procured in time to meet the need. Examples of this are the adjustment of quantities to conform with economical lot sizes, quantity discount brackets, or standard packaging and shipping units, and the deferring or anticipating of purchases to take advantage of expected market fluctuations.

So far as is practicable, specifications should be developed to define the need in such a manner that compliance with the specification insures acceptability of the product purchased. The purchasing department should have a voice in the preparation of such specifications to avoid special details that would restrict the sources from which materials might be procured or that would entail extra costs for unnecessary deviations from commercial standards and tolerances.

In ways like these, flexibility and competition are made possible in purchasing, for company benefit, without prejudice to the interest of the plant man who has to use the material.

Production or operating departments should advise purchasing promptly, and as far in advance as possible, concerning the program to be carried on, contemplated work schedules, special projects or contract jobs to be undertaken, new products to be produced, changes in design that will affect items to be purchased, and any significant changes in rate of production. In the absence of specific information, the routine guide of the buyer is the record of past consumption, and this would be a misleading criterion in the event of a change of schedule, leading to possible shortages if requirements are increased without notice, and to excessive inventories and losses through obsolescence if certain parts are discontinued or their use curtailed. The aim at all times should be to permit a planned program of procurement for systematic purchasing. "Lead time" in buying involves not only the supplier's manufacturing cycle and a normal period for delivery, but should also include a reasonable time for finding the best source and negotiating an advantageous purchase.

Data furnished to purchasing should also include a realistic statement as to when materials will actually be required to be on hand for use. The safety factors of timing, anticipation of requirements, forward coverage, and delivery schedules are matters of purchase policy and planning. A realistic statement of need fixes purchasing responsibility, whereas unwarranted requests for delivery in advance of the actual need tends to reduce the flexibility of the purchasing program, and generally to increase the risk of wasteful buying.

Purchasing, in turn, has the responsibility to keep using departments informed as to the status of their requests for material. A copy of the purchase order is usually routed to the requisitioner to show that the need has been provided for. If the vendor's delivery promise does not meet the time specified on the requisition, or if later delays make it necessary to revise delivery schedules, using departments should be advised of this so that schedules can be adjusted.

The purchasing department's file of vendors' catalogs should be available for reference by appropriate operating personnel at all times and duplicate copies obtained for plant use whenever this is indicated for greater convenience. Buyers should refer to plant departments any new products or equipment which come to their attention that seem to be applicable to plant needs. If a standard stock list is maintained, showing items regularly carried in inventory, copies should be provided for everyone having occasion to write or approve purchase requisitions.

A complete and up-to-date list of all surplus materials and equipment should be maintained, to facilitate the filling of requisitions by transfer instead of by purchase when such action is feasible, and to permit the prompt disposal of such surplus if no opportunity for use is reasonably expected to occur.

Contacts with suppliers are primarily in the domain of the purchasing department. Effectiveness of negotiation and buying can be seriously impaired by commitments implied or preferences expressed to suppliers' representatives by plant personnel. Even though such statements may have no real weight in the ultimate purchasing decision, they can easily lead to misunderstandings and friction in supplier relationships and also within the company. It should therefore be made clear, and enforced, that the salesman's proper channel of approach is through the purchasing department. This benefits the seller as well, since it entails one authoritative point of contact instead of many of doubtful value, and avoids the waste of time on both sides in seeking out potentially influential plant contacts by "back-door selling" methods. At the same time, it assures the salesman of receptive, informed purchasing consideration for his product when a source of supply is to be selected.

There are, of course, occasions when it is desirable to grant a seller's representative access to plant personnel for discussion or demonstration of technical details and methods of usage or application of a product. Purchasing can facilitate such contacts, when indicated, by directing the salesman to the proper person or persons in the plant and arranging the meetings for specific purposes, under proper controls. If the matter under consideration is still in the negotiating stage, it is frequently advisable to have a purchasing department representative present to acquire first-hand information for later purchasing dealings.

The same principle should be observed in all dealings with vendors, such as correspondence relating to orders, changes in specifications, quantities or delivery requirements, rejections, and adjustments. This is all a part of centralized purchasing responsibility.

Purchasing and engineering

Cooperation between purchasing and engineering departments is chiefly concerned with matters of product design and specification preliminary to the actual production requirements.

The purchasing agent and the engineer traditionally differ in their approach to the materials problem in that the engineer tends to specify wide margins of quality, safety, and performance, whereas the purchasing agent tends to narrow such margins and work to minimum requirements. The engineer, by temperament and training, seeks the ideal material or design or equipment, frequently with insufficient regard for cost, and the purchasing agent seeks adequate materials or equipment, with perhaps insufficient regard for desirable margins of quality. The two viewpoints have been brought much closer together in recent years as an increasing number of men with engineering training and experience have entered purchasing work. In a considerable number of companies, also, the appointment of a purchasing engineer, attached to the purchasing department staff for the express purpose of reconciling the two viewpoints with a full appreciation of both, has helped to arrive at an optimum solution of purchasing problems that involve technical considerations.

The purchase engineer is usually a staff adviser to the purchasing agent, directing research on qualities and costs, developing purchase specifications, and sometimes handling the purchase of such items as electric motors and controls to be incorporated in a manufactured product. Whether such a man is actually included in the purchasing department organization, and despite the fact that it is the purchasing agent's responsibility to become technically competent in respect to the materials and products regularly purchased, it behooves the buyer to take advantage of the knowledge and counsel of the engineering staff on any and all points where such counsel can aid toward more effective selection of materials.

Engineering specifications may call for excessively close dimensional tolerances. These may add to product quality and uniformity, but they often place the requirement outside the scope of commercial standards, restrict the number of potential suppliers, raise costs, and increase the percentage of rejections, without any significant increase in utility. Cooperation with the purchasing department will frequently result in arriving at a more practicable standard, affording substantial economies.

Standardization of materials and dimensions in product design is a field in which purchasing and engineering cooperation can yield very beneficial results. Such a program is logically initiated by the purchasing agent because of its possibilities in the direction of reducing the number of stock items, permitting the consolidation of requirements, increasing purchase quantities, and reducing inventory investment. The final decision is within the province of the engineer, whose judgment is invaluable in determining where, how, and to what extent the principle can be applied without jeopardizing product quality.

As in the case of the purchasing-production relationship, cooperation between purchasing and engineering is most effective if it starts at the planning stage, when designs and specifications are still formative and flexible.

Purchasing and accounting

Every purchase made represents an expenditure or commitment of company funds. It sets in motion a series of accounting operations, such as charging the expense to the proper contract or department account, the verification and approval of the invoice, payment of the charge, and final audit. In the case of extraordinarily large or unforeseen expenditures, it may require special financial arrangements or credit considerations. Under some forms of government contracts, there are further requirements that must be met in order to secure prompt reimbursement for the expenditure. The relationship between purchasing and accounting departments is therefore a vital one, and frequently starts before the purchase is actually made.

It is essential that purchasing forms and procedure be correlated with accounting requirements and methods, to avoid duplication of work on clerical entries and the necessity of checking back to secure essential information. It is customary to have a carbon copy of each purchase order routed to the accounting department at the time the order is issued, for determination of cost data and distribution of charges to the department or job concerned. The carbon copy also provides original data for final checking and audit when the transaction is completed. By means of this duplicate copy, the routine processing of the information can be done simultaneously in the two departments, each handling that portion of the work for which it is responsible, without waiting for the actual receipt of the materials and invoice from the vendor, and requiring only the reconciliation with the receiving report to complete the paper work incident to the transaction. Sometimes, as a matter of information, these order copies are supplemented by a daily or weekly summary report of commitments in dollar totals, to provide a quick view of the financial situation with respect to materials accounts.

Some of the accounting operations are customarily handled by invoice clerks in the purchasing department, particularly the verification of prices and terms, and in most cases the verification of extensions and totals as well. The receiving report is also routed through the purchasing department, to denote completion of deliveries, and this is also checked against the vendor's invoice. When the proper entries have been made to purchase and stock records, the receiving report is attached to the invoice, and the latter is stamped or certified for payment and forwarded to the accounting department. Prompt clearance is important in order that payment may be made within the discount period. Invoices upon which a cash discount privilege may be earned by prompt payment are sometimes flagged for immediate attention.

Purchasing and sales

Sales departments should keep purchasing informed of sales quotas and expectations as a guide to probable quantity requirements of materials. Purchasing should also be advised when special contracts or new products are contemplated, in order that the necessary preliminaries of the purchasing program may be undertaken well in advance of the actual need.

One of the functions of the purchasing department is to prepare estimates of the cost of materials for use in sales quotations and in the planning of product lines within a stated price range or cost limitation. The purchasing department can be of great assistance in determining how much quality or quantity can be built into a product or item within such limitations and in suggesting means of cost reduction or quality improvement to enhance the salability of the product, thus contributing to the competitive position of the company as compared with the rest of the industry.

Reciprocal trade relations constitute another subject upon which sales and purchasing departments must work closely together, in respect to both general policy and its specific application. Many purchasing departments have organized their records and procedure with a view to analyzing and using this factor most intelligently, just as records and policies have been organized to take account of seasonal and market fluctuations, rates of operation and consumption, and similar factors.

Purchasing department files and daily mail provide a wealth of first-hand information on the sales policies, promotional methods, and similar activities of other manufacturers and examples of how other companies handle special situations. This accumulation of material is of particular value in that it has been objectively received and appraised by the purchasing staff and that it makes available a practical basis for determining what policies, what sales approach, and what type of sales material are most effective. The sales executive has on hand, in his own purchasing department, an invaluable business laboratory. He should make use of its experience.

Purchasing and stores

The relationship between purchasing and stores departments is inherently so close and so basic that the two are combined in more than half of industrial organizations. Functionally, the effect is to extend the responsibility for materials from the point of acquisition to the point of issue and use. The activities between these two end-points are chiefly of a custodial nature, including the receipt and care of purchased items and accountability for material stocks, both physically and in accurate record form. This is the continuation of a single process. Except for the verification of quantities actually received against purchase orders, there is no purpose of "checks and balances" to be served by separating the two functions. The administration of stores may be a job of considerable magnitude in itself, but widespread experience shows that it can be handled effectively within the general framework of the purchasing department.

There are cogent reasons for combining the purchasing and stores functions. Inventory stores are implemented wholly by purchasing action. A large part of the purchasing program is usually initiated by requisitions from stores departments, to replenish stocks. Duplication of records can be minimized. Stores records are essential to the buyer, not only as to receipts and quantities on hand, but as to disbursements and rates of use. This information is vital to the formulation of a sound purchasing policy and program, for inventories and stock turnover are among the measures of purchasing performance and efficiency. The determination of maximum and minimum stock quantities is not primarily a control over purchasing, but a guide; it is purchasing's means of controlling inventory investment, of maintaining balance, and of assuring the adequacy of supplies in relation to the need. As a mere quantitative measurement, such figures have little meaning. As a matter of fact, they are effective only to the extent that they are adjustable—and adjusted—to the use requirements and purchasing policy which they implement.

To fulfill purchasing objectives, it is necessary also to know that materials are definitely correlated to the purchase order when received, and that they are issued and applied to the purposes for which they are procured. Special attention should be given to inactive and slow-moving items, to avoid losses from depreciation and obsolescence and the accumulation of excessive carrying costs over a long period of time. All are properly chargeable to the materials account and add to the cost of materials up to the time of use or disposal, and thereby come within the scope of purchasing responsibility. The accountability for materials cannot be divided without sacrificing efficiency and control.

In any event, there must be a daily, detailed flow of information between the buying and the stores divisions. Purchasing must advise stores regarding orders placed and deliveries expected in sufficient detail so that they may be readily identified, promptly placed at the service of using departments, and accurately accounted for. Stores, in turn, must keep purchasing advised regarding the fulfillment of orders and the status of inventories, as noted above.

The most common point of issue in this general area is the responsibility for inventory control—the determination of quantities, coverage, and balance among items carried in stock. This is sometimes set apart from purchasing as a special, independent function. Inventory control is undeniably a major consideration in management policy, with significant effect upon the costs of operation. However, even more than the physical control of stores, it is inherently linked with purchasing. Determination of optimum ordering and inventory quantities is a part of modern purchasing science. (See Chapter 8.) In a purchasing department that understands the full import of its responsibilities and is conscientious and competent in meeting them, inventory control factors are weighed against commercial aspects of the transaction as a standard procedure in making buying decisions. To segregate this phase from the act of procurement is, then, a duplication of function. If it is imposed as the dominating policy, dictating or limiting decisions on quantity and timing, it can actually negate many of the opportunities and economic advantages of sound and comprehensive centralized purchasing.

Purchasing and traffic

Purchased materials have to be brought from the supplier's plant or warehouse to the point of use, and transportation charges make up a distinct and sometimes substantial part of ultimate delivered cost. The purchasing department is therefore concerned with incoming traffic costs. Purchasing usually takes cognizance of this by giving preference to nearby sources, or to those that are strategically located in relation to good transportation facilities, as one means of minimizing this cost factor. But the problem is not altogether so simple. The availability of a variety of alternative transport methods, proper freight classification, consolidated shipments, and the like, offer additional means of savings. Further, the development of newer services, such as fast freight, truck-rail combinations, and air express, have materially extended the economical purchasing radius and are to be considered in buying policies and decisions. The purchasing department can therefore make good use of expert traffic knowledge.

Most purchase orders include shipping instructions for the vendor. The easy notation "Ship best way" is a default of this responsibility of buying. A well-informed traffic department determines what is the "best way" for various types of shipments from various source locations, and this information is incorporated in the purchasing department's vendor file for quick reference and application when orders are issued. Other traffic services to purchasing include the tracing of shipments, expediting in transit, and the handling of claims on shipments damaged in transit.

Where no separate traffic department is maintained, purchasing usually has this responsibility in respect to incoming traffic. In smaller organizations, where a complete division of functional responsibilities is not practicable, the combination of purchasing and traffic is frequently found.

Purchasing and quality control

Purchasing's first responsibility in respect to quality control is to procure materials and products that conform to the specification. The quality control department usually handles acceptance testing of purchased materials. In that case, it should be made clear to purchasing, and through purchasing to the vendor, what test methods are to be applied and what are the criteria of acceptability. Such advance information minimizes the chances of misunderstanding and controversy and, in the long view, aids substantially in the procurement of consistently acceptable materials.

In the case of rejections, it is important to observe the principle previously stated: that complaints and adjustments be handled through the purchasing department and not directly between quality control and the vendor. Only in this way can satisfactory vendor relationships be maintained. It is also important from the standpoint of keeping purchase records accurate, for a rejected shipment means that the need has not been satisfied and the purchasing responsibility has not been ended.

Acceptance testing should be done promptly upon the receipt of a shipment, and the results reported to purchasing, rather than waiting until goods are issued from stores to production departments. Vendors' warranties are generally limited in time. Each day of delay makes adjustment more difficult, or even impossible if the warranty period has expired. Meanwhile, shortcomings in quality may multiply owing to the vendor's assumption, in the absence of prompt corrective action, that previous shipments have been satisfactory to the buyer.

Purchasing has a further interest in the general field of quality control as practiced by vendor companies. (See Chapter 7.) It helps in the selection of vendors and can substantially reduce the necessity and expense of acceptance testing at the buyer's plant. To get maximum benefit from this buying technique, it should be correlated with the quality control practices and standards in the buyer's own company.

Purchasing prerogatives

Four prerogatives of the centralized purchasing department should be emphasized.

First, selection of the supply source is wholly a matter of purchasing authority. The need to buy originates in other departments, and required quality is defined. So long as these measures of *what* to buy are satisfied, the decision on *where* or *from whom* to buy is the responsibility of the purchasing agent. The exception (which is actually outside the realm of scientific purchasing) is in the case of a management policy of reciprocity. (See Chapter 20.)

Second, all contacts with vendors and their representatives should be made through the purchasing department, from the first sales interview, through the process of negotiation and ordering, follow-up for delivery, and correspondence relating to materials and purchases, to approval of the vendor's invoice or any adjustments that may be necessary. Legitimate contacts with technical and plant personnel should be arranged only with the knowledge of the purchasing department and are not to be conducted or construed as in any way prejudicing the purchasing department's freedom of negotiation or its latitude of choice in selecting the supplier. Some exceptions may arise in centralized purchasing for branch plant requirements. (See Chapter 3.)

Third, it is the duty of the purchasing agent to check purchase requests against the need. It is his privilege to suggest modifications of the requested quality for purposes of more economical or more expeditious procurement, and to revise quantities on a particular order so long as the total quantity is procured in time to meet the need.

Fourth, the commercial aspects of the purchase are wholly within the jurisdiction of the purchasing department. These include the manner of purchase, the price, the terms and conditions of the order or contract, packing and shipping instructions, and the like.

It will be recalled that the purchasing responsibility is defined as buying materials of the right quality, in the right quantity, at the right time, at the right price, from the right source. Quality is definable in the specifications; the other factors are matters of judgment and decision. In the buyer's constant search for the most advantageous purchase, these prerogatives must be reserved to him as the means of making his judgment and decisions effective.

WHO PURCHASES WHAT

To help you find the person who is looking for your type of product, refer to the following:

COMMODITY (PRODUCTION)	LAUNDRY GROUP BUYER	DIVISION MATERIAL COORDINATOR		
		CLYDE	MARION	ST. JOSEPH
BALLASTS (Fluorescent)	R. N. PHILLIPS	R. J. CELEK	D. E. SHOUP	D. A. KIBLER
BEARINGS	M. A. HYDE	L. H. KRAMER	A. J. NICOLOSI	R. W. BAKER
CASTERS	J. C. WARREN	L. H. KRAMER	–––	D. A. KIBLER
COIN MECHANISMS	J. C. WARREN	–––	A. J. NICOLOSI	F. M. ROWE
CONTAINERS & WOOD	R. J. ZIMMERMAN	L. H. KRAMER	A. J. NICOLOSI	D. A. KIBLER
DECORATIVE METAL	R. E. SCHULTZ	R. J. CELEK	A. J. NICOLOSI	R. W. BAKER
DIE CASTINGS	R. E. SCHULTZ	R. J. CELEK	E. L. WILLIAMS	R. W. BAKER
ELECTRICAL CONTROLS	R. N. FRUEH	R. J. CELEK	D. E. SHOUP	F. M. ROWE
FASTENERS	J. C. WARREN	L. H. KRAMER	J. E. ROBBINS	F. M. ROWE
FELT, FIBER and CORK	R. D. HUMBERG	L. H. KRAMER	E. L. WILLIAMS	R. W. BAKER
FLUORESCENT HARNESSES	R. N. FRUEH	R. J. CELEK	D. E. SHOUP	R. W. BAKER
GAS CONTROLS	R. N. PHILLIPS	–––	L. N. HEISER	R. W. BAKER
GLASS	J. C. WARREN	L. H. KRAMER	L. N. HEISER	R. W. BAKER
HEAT ELEMENTS	R. N. PHILLIPS	–––	D. E. SHOUP	F. M. ROWE
IRON CASTINGS	M. A. HYDE	R. J. CELEK	A. J. NICOLOSI	R. W. BAKER
JUNCTION BLOCKS	R. N. FRUEH	–––	D. E. SHOUP	D. A. KIBLER
LAMPS	R. N. PHILLIPS	R. J. CELEK	J. E. ROBBINS	R. W. BAKER
LOCKS	J. C. WARREN	–––	L. N. HEISER	F. M. ROWE
MOTORS and PROTECTORS	R. D. HUMBERG	R. J. CELEK	E. L. WILLIAMS	L. J. POWERS
PAINT	R. J. ZIMMERMAN	R. J. CELEK	D. A. MEDDLES	L. J. POWERS

Fig. 2-2. Typical List of Buyers and Commodities They Purchase at Whirlpool Corporation.

3

ORGANIZATION FOR PURCHASING

EFFICIENT CONDUCT OF PURCHASING presupposes a department specifically assigned to this duty, headed by a responsible purchasing officer who is accountable to management for the performance of the function, and a department adequately staffed to carry on the procurement activities.

In a small company, with a relatively limited volume and variety of purchases, the department may consist of only the purchasing agent and a clerical assistant. Purchasing may even be a part-time assignment, where the purchasing agent serves in a dual capacity, being, for example, also office manager or manager of building and office services, or has other assigned duties in addition to his buying responsibilities. So long as the purchasing authority is centered at one point, this is not inconsistent with the principles and definition of centralized purchasing.

Purchasing under such circumstances requires close personal cooperation with plant superintendents and operating personnel. With a wide variety of products to be purchased, the one-man purchasing staff must rely largely on the judgment of his associates for the proper selection of many of the items required. Efficient operation depends on his ability to organize his own time and to develop the simplest procedures and records for doing the job.

In the larger company, the various functions and activities are divided and assigned to various individuals, and the duties of each become more specialized. The buying itself will be done by several people, each specializing in particular types of commodities. Organization becomes more important, both in respect to the internal structure of the department and in its relation to the over-all company plan. The duties of the chief purchasing officer, as head of the department, tend to become more of a policy-making and administrative nature rather than actual buying.

In very large companies, purchasing departments number up to several hundred employees. There is no clear correlation between the dollar volume of purchases and the size of the purchasing staff. This varies widely according to the character of the enterprise and its purchasing problem, the scope of the purchasing responsibility, and the extent to which related activities, such as expediting, storeskeeping, traffic management, and materials control, are included.

Purchasing in the general organization plan

As was noted in Chapter 1, the majority of centralized purchasing departments (more than 80 per cent) report directly to the top executive officer who is responsible for profitable operation—president, executive vice-president, general manager, or works manager, as the case may be. This includes branch plant and divisional purchasing departments in multi-plant organizations, where the plant purchasing agent is apart from the general purchasing department at company headquarters, with considerable independence of authority, and reporting to the branch or divisional manager responsible for that operating unit. This situation is discussed in greater detail in a succeeding section of this chapter.

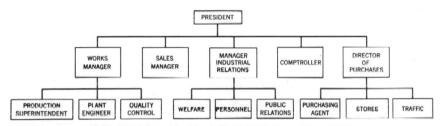

Fig. 3-1. Place of the Purchasing Department in the Company Organization.

Wherever the purchasing agent reports directly to top management, he is in the first tier of executives, on the same organization plane with the production manager, sales manager, comptroller, manager of industrial relations, and the heads of other function divisions.

In a smaller number of manufacturing companies (about 20 per cent), the purchasing department is under the jurisdiction of the production or manufacturing division, and the purchasing agent reports to the production manager, who is in turn responsible to top management. Here the purchasing agent is in a secondary tier of executives, and his function is regarded as a subordinate one. Purchasing is still centralized, and many of the advantages of centralization still accrue, but the emphasis and evaluation of purchasing performance are primarily on the service aspect of buying rather than on the management aspects of materials procurement as an independent factor of cost control.

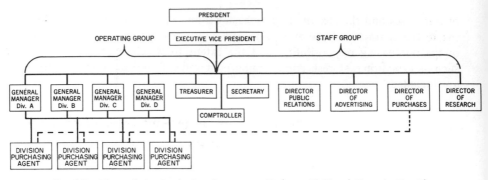

Fig. 3-2. Place of the Purchasing Department Under a Divisional Organization Plan.

A third type of organization, chiefly characteristic of very large companies and of diversified industries operating under a single management, separates the operational and managerial phases of the purchasing function. Separate buying departments are set up at the divisional level as respective parts of the division organization plan. A general purchasing department at company headquarters serves the entire organization as a staff facility. It counsels top management on broad purchasing and materiel policies, conducts general and specific purchasing research programs that are made available to all buyers, sets policies for the guidance of divisional purchasing departments, coordinates purchasing policies and activities throughout the company, and gives assistance on specific purchasing problems where needed. It does little or no actual buying and has no responsibility for the details of procurement beyond evaluating purchasing performance at the various divisions and pointing out means for improvement. In most cases, it has no jurisdiction over the hiring or firing of divisional purchasing personnel, although it usually sets up the buyer-training programs and has decisive influence in the transfer of persons with superior buying talent to positions of greater responsibility and opportunity among the divisions, thus enhancing the caliber of the over-all purchasing activities and keeping open the way for advancement on the purchasing ladder.

There are many variations of this system, corresponding to particular company organization and operating conditions. A few representative examples will illustrate how it is adapted to individual situations.

A. A large chemical manufacturing company has five operating divisions, each headed by a general manager who reports to the president of the corporation as the chief executive officer. In the central organization there are ten "general staff departments" which report to the executive committee of the board of directors. Purchasing and traffic together constitute one of these staff divisions, being jointly under the supervision of the Director of

Purchases and Traffic. The other staff divisions are: treasury, patent, legal, foreign operations, engineering, development, central research, advertising, and accounting.

B. In a textile manufacturing company operating five plants, widely separated geographically, there are four executives reporting directly to the president and treasurer: the comptroller, the vice-president in charge of sales, the vice-president in charge of advertising, and the vice-president in charge of manufacturing. The general purchasing agent and the production manager serve in a staff capacity to the vice-president in charge of manufacturing. The same official heads the line organization of operations at all five plants, through the respective works managers.

C. A large corporation manufacturing both industrial and consumer goods has three organization groups reporting directly to the president. One of these groups consists of ten operating divisions, set up according to product classifications, each headed by a general manager and including a divisional purchasing department. A second group includes all foreign and export activities. The third group is composed of ten "auxiliary departments": purchasing, industrial and public relations, traffic, business research, general development, engineering, advertising, legal, distributing branches, and Pacific Coast division. The head of the purchasing department in this instance is also a vice-president of the corporation. There is also a fourth, separate division of finance and accounts, which reports to the company's finance committee, which in turn is responsible to the president and the board of directors.

Departmental organization

The internal organization of the purchasing department is concerned with the performance of the function itself rather than with its relationship to other functions. Here the organization pattern is much more consistent.

As was previously noted, the one-man department presents no problems of organization, since all activities are embodied in the one person. In the two-man department, the situation is not much more complex. The assistant is exactly what that term implies, taking on such responsibilities as may be delegated to him by the purchasing agent. There is likely to be no more formal division of buying duties than the retention of major materials and contract items for the purchasing agent's attention while the assistant handles the procurement of supplies and routine requirements. Each would normally do his own follow-up on orders and clear the invoices for the goods he purchases. In any such limited department, there is an advantage in having both buyers familiar with the entire purchasing program, to gain greater flexibility of operation and to maintain continuity of work during the temporary absence of either man.

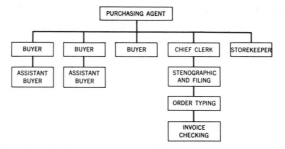

Fig. 3-3. Organization Plan of a Medium-sized Purchasing Department.

Where the volume of purchasing has grown beyond the capacity of any such simple arrangement, organization becomes essential to efficient operation. The buying staff itself is necessarily larger, and the incidental services and paper work of procurement increase proportionately. This requires coordination and direction. It is no longer efficient nor feasible to have each buyer personally responsible for the detailed procedures that make up the complete transaction. He is relieved of clerical and routine tasks so that he may become a specialist in buying—in the evaluation of quality, selection of sources, and negotiation—and usually a specialist in one or a few particular commodity groups. The other departmental activities are similarly divided and specialized, so that they may effectively support the buying operation, and usually with a less expensive type of personnel.

In the fully organized purchasing department, the chief purchasing officer (usually having the title of "Director" or "Manager of Purchases") is chiefly concerned with administrative and executive duties. He establishes and directs over-all purchasing policies, handles major aspects of trade relations with supplier companies, coordinates the purchasing program and procedures with the operating requirements of other departments, represents purchasing in plant management and policy meetings, assigns purchasing representation on interdepartmental committees and projects such as standardization and methods, and is directly responsible to top management for efficient departmental administration, morale, training, and performance.

The director of purchases may or may not take part in actual negotiation and buying. If he does so at all, his participation is usually limited to major contracts and items which involve substantial volume and dollar value and represent matters of policy as well as of procurement. He may also take part in the initial consideration of new supply sources or of new materials that affect product design and manufacturing methods. For the most part, he is concerned with summary reports of purchasing activities, order status, and cost trends rather than with the individual purchase transactions.

He may have one or more staff assistants, for business and economic research, cost and value analysis, engineering counsel and coordination, the handling of reciprocal trade relations, or other specialized services.

The assistant director of purchases, or purchasing agent, is directly in charge of the buying staff and of general office operations. He assigns the buying responsibilities and directs the work of the buyers or buying groups. He is concerned with the actual, day-by-day purchases, and in many companies all purchase orders pass over his desk for noting and review before they are released to the vendor. Through a chief clerk or clerical supervisor, he supervises the necessary office services of record keeping,

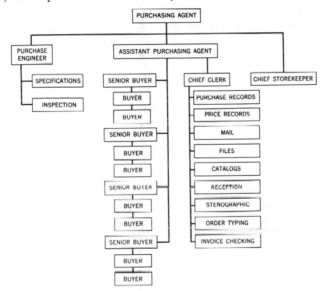

Fig. 3-4. Organization Plan of a Large Purchasing Department.

filing, order typing, invoice checking, mail distribution, catalog library, and the like. He may also have under his supervision separate sections for follow-up and expediting, traffic, and the disposal of surplus and waste materials.

If storeskeeping comes within the jurisdiction of the purchasing department, there will also be a chief storeskeeper, usually reporting to the director of purchases, on the same organizational level as the assistant director.

The buying staff

Buying assignments are usually specific, item by item, with a definite responsibility for each item or commodity classification that is regularly purchased. So far as is practicable, items that are related by nature or by source (rather than by end product or using department) are grouped for buying purposes. In a department of moderate size, where such assignments are made to individual buyers rather than to a buying group or section, this principle may have to be modified somewhat so as to distribute the work load evenly, but the major classifications at least will be identified with particular buyers—steel buyer, electrical goods buyer, and so forth—who have direct and sole responsibility for procurement of the stated products. For each such buying assignment, it is customary to name an alternate from among the other buyers, who can assist with or take over the buying in a classification other than his own as may be required from time to time.

In larger departments, assignments are made to commodity buying sections, each headed by a senior buyer or assistant purchasing agent, with one or more buyers and assistant buyers under his direction. Where this type of organization is in effect, the commodity groupings and assignments can be completely consistent. Equal distribution of work load among the several buying sections is not essential, because the size of staff in each group can be adjusted to the load and understudies or alternates are available within the section.

The advantages of organization according to specific, related commodity assignments are:

1. Buyers become specialists in a particular field. Concerned with a limited range of items, they can acquire a better knowledge of the materials and products, their characteristics, and their applications, and greater familiarity with marketing practices, economic influences, and sources of supply in that field. All of this makes for superior purchasing skill.
2. Duplication and overlapping are eliminated, and situations are avoided where buyers in the same organization may in effect be competing with each other for supplies.
3. There is greater opportunity to review requirements of related items, sometimes resulting in beneficial standardization, and making it possible to combine requirements, gaining maximum quantity buying advantage, with fewer interviews and purchase orders.
4. Vendor contacts are concentrated, conserving time and effort for both the salesman and the buyer. The salesman of a given material or of a related product line usually needs to make only one contact in the purchasing department, and that contact is with a buyer having specific authority.

There can be no standard purchasing classification of commodities that will be applicable to all companies. Requirements vary widely among different industries. The item that is of primary importance and volume in one plant may be used in insignificant quantities, or not at all, in the plant next door. The division and assignment of buying responsibility must be tailored to the individual case.

In a representative large automobile manufacturing company, the buying sections in the purchasing department are:

(a) *Bodies and Frames.* (Subsections: Tooling; Passenger and Commercial Car Bodies and Frames; Wood and Fabricated Trim; Stampings and Hardware.)
(b) *Machined Parts and Stampings.* (Subsections: Chassis Stampings; Standard Parts; Machined Accessories; Machined Assemblies.)
(c) *Rough Castings, Forgings, and Die Castings.* (Subsections for each of these classifications.)
(d) *Rubber, Plastic, Electrical, Gaskets and Accessories.* (Subsections for each of these classifications.)
(e) *Raw Materials.* (Subsections: Nonferrous Metals; Sheet and Strip Steel; Bar, Wire, and Miscellaneous Steel; Coal and Iron Ore.)
(f) *Maintenance, Repair, and Operating Supplies.* (Subsections: Printing and Office Equipment; Building and Plumbing Supplies; Hardware and Laboratory Supplies; Electrical, Hospital, and Photographic Supplies; Chemicals and Operating Materials.)

In this company, machine tools and major plant equipment are bought by a separate purchasing unit under the direction of the manufacturing manager.

A representative metal fabricating company classifies its purchases in the following groups:

(a) *Metals.*
(b) *Electrical Parts.*
(c) *Machine Tools and Mechanical Parts.*
(d) *Chemicals, Stores Supplies, Automotive Equipment.*
(e) *Office and Drafting Supplies.*
(f) *Printing, Office Machines, and Furniture.*

A public utility company uses the following basis of organizing its purchases:

(a) *Building Materials.*
(b) *Mechanical Equipment.*
(c) *Castings, Tools, and Hardware.*
(d) *Electrical Equipment.*
(e) *Fuel.*
(f) *Office Equipment and Supplies.*
(g) *Restaurant Supplies.*

These are specific cases, listing only the general group classifications according to which buying duties are assigned in the respective companies. Sometimes this is enough to set the pattern of responsibility. Usually, however, there would be a more detailed tabulation of the items coming under each group heading. And within each buying section, there would be definite buying assignments among the several buyers, for orderly administration if for no other reason.

A more comprehensive listing of representative commodity classifications and buyers' assignments is given below. Some of these may not be applicable at all in some companies. Some would be major classifications in one company and subordinate items in another.

Abrasives
Accessories
Automotive Equipment and Supplies
Building Materials
Castings
Chemicals
Drafting Supplies
Electrical Materials and Parts
Electronic Parts
Fabricated Parts and Assemblies
Fasteners
Forgings
Fuel
Glass and Glass Products
Hand Tools
Hardware
Instruments
Insulating Materials
Iron and Steel
Laboratory Equipment
Lubricants, Petroleum Products (except Fuel)
Lumber
Machined Parts
Machinery and Plant Equipment
Maintenance, Repair, and Operating Supplies
Nonferrous Metals
Office Machines and Furniture
Office Supplies
Packaging Materials
Paint, Varnish, Lacquer, Finishing Materials
Paper and Paper Products
Plastic Parts
Printing
Refractories
Rubber Products (except Tires)
Safety Equipment
Screw Machine Products
Services
Shipping Room Supplies
Stampings
Subcontracting
Textiles
Welding Equipment and Supplies
Wood products

The diversity of products in this tabulation re-emphasizes the importance of specialization in purchasing, through organization.

Special commodities. In a number of industries where the end product is made up largely of a single raw material, as in the case of cotton textiles, the procurement of that material constitutes a distinct activity quite apart from the general purchasing program and department. This is particularly true in the case of products of nature, where the evaluation of quality and the actual purchasing often must be done at markets or auctions at the point of production. For example, in cigarette manufacturing, the purchase and seasoning of leaf tobacco may be vested not merely in a separate department, but in a separate, affiliated corporation. Large users of wood customarily have a timber agent entirely independent of the purchasing department; he buys standing timber or leases timber rights, and schedules cutting operations to provide the lumber for manufacturing needs. In the woolen textile industry, the wool buyer may spend the greater portion of his time in the distant wool markets of Australia, South America, and the Near East purchasing the particular types of staple desired.

Project purchasing. Purchasing for special projects, such as new plant construction, or highly complex made-to-order equipment, is frequently set up as a separate division within the purchasing department. This makes it easier to handle special requirements of the project, avoid delays, and obtain cost information in the early planning stages. Project purchasing calls for the use of buyers with a high degree of technical knowledge and training who can work closely with design and engineering departments.

Field operations, such as drilling and laying of pipelines in the petroleum industry, are customarily handled on a project basis. Purchasing for product development and research laboratories, where requirements are highly specialized and there can be no consistent, continuing materials program, often come within this category also.

Project purchasing has received its biggest impetus in recent years, however, from military and related procurement. Defense contractors who must bid on such things as complex electronic systems have representatives of the purchasing department participate in the preparation of such bids. Perkin-Elmer Corporation, for example, which makes among other things, highly complex cameras and reconnaissance systems for the military, uses the project buying approach. [1] Procurement and purchasing engineers assist engineering, sales, and management personnel in the preparation of bids in several ways. They provide cost estimates on new materials and parts, analyze specifications that may cause suppliers trouble, and indicate probable

---

[1] Somerby Dowst, "Purchasing by Project," *Purchasing Magazine,* April 8, 1963, p. 88.

lead times on delivery of materials. Without such specific procurement data, the planning group might make an unrealistic bid, and the company might end up losing money on the job or failing to deliver it on time.

Planning for actual purchasing goes on during the proposal stage in the Perkin-Elmer system. Procurement engineers start searching for sources of new and unusual components and collect data for decisions on whether to make or buy certain items. If the company is successful in its bid, the purchasing program is then actually under way. The procurement engineers leave the actual negotiation and buying of parts to the purchasing engineers assigned to that project and move on to new projects.

Generally speaking, project buyers purchase only special items or materials used in the end product. Common items or standard components (fasteners, for example) used in both the company's regular and custom-made lines are purchased by the purchasing department's commodity buyers.

Materials management

The evolution of purchasing discussed previously is by no means ended. Purchasing has been given specialized department status, along with clearly defined responsibilities and authority. But its role in an increasingly complex mass-production industry is not fixed, particularly in respect to its relations to other functions.

Purchasing will continue to coordinate its efforts with those of other specialized departments—traffic, inspection, engineering, production, and so forth. And in the very process of integrating its operations with those of other groups involved in the materials cycle, purchasing may move in new directions. Interdependence of functions may lead to a crossing of lines of authority in some companies and under some circumstances. This in turn would require new definitions of responsibilities and possibly new patterns of organization to administer them properly.

Does purchasing's responsibility in a highly integrated plant end, for example, with the issuance of the order? If purchasing's negotiations with the supplier involve transportation costs, packaging methods, and delivery dates, how far does purchasing's obligation extend in these matters? Should purchasing not have some interest in or even control of traffic and receiving to see that the supplier meets all requirements that were part of the negotiated price? Similar questions can be asked at the other end of the materials cycle—whether, for example, purchasing's concern with ordering quantities and inventory levels should directly involve it in material control and even in production scheduling.

Questions like these have led a number of companies to experiment with a broad concept of materials procurement that goes beyond basic purchasing. Known generally as *materials management,* it has been used in a number of industrial firms in recent years. The scope of the materials management organization varies considerably from company to company, depending on the size of the enterprise, the nature of its products, and, in many cases, even on the availability of personnel to handle the position of materials manager.

A broad definition by an early proponent of materials management shows the extent to which the concept may be carried:

> Materials management is the planning, directing, controlling, and co-ordinating of all those activities concerned with material and inventory requirements, from the point of their inception to their introduction into the manufacturing processes. It begins with the determination of material quality and quantity, and ends with its issuance to production in time to meet customer demands on schedule and at the lowest cost.[2]

Under this definition, materials management could include, in addition to purchasing any or all of the following functions: inbound and outbound traffic; receiving and receiving inspection; determination and control of inventories, including raw material, in-process, and finished goods inventories; warehousing and shipping; material handling; and production planning and scheduling.

In practice, the concept has been modified in a number of ways to meet special conditions, and there is no widespread agreement on what materials management really embraces. The definition above would seem to set the limits on what it could be; but numerous companies are using the term much more loosely.

Even purchasing executives, who are in the most logical position to assume the position of materials manager in the average industrial organization, are not completely in accord as to what materials management covers. Of 50 purchasing executives surveyed by the University of Wisconsin Management Institute, a high percentage (95 per cent) said that materials management should include inbound traffic and receiving in addition to buying. But only 60 per cent favored bringing outbound traffic, materials handling, and receiving inspection within the scope of the organization. And only 40 per cent advocated making production planning and scheduling part of materials management.

Some of the more successful materials organizations in industry reflect these differences of opinion. The General Electric Company, for example, has pioneered in the use of materials management in the broadest sense of the term. Its Metallurgical Products Division has even extended the

---

[2] L. J. De Rose, "The Role of Purchasing in Material Management," *Purchasing Magazine,* March, 1956, p. 115.

materials group's scope to include an order service department that handles and monitors customer orders. The inclusion of this function is not typical of the G.E. materials approach, however.

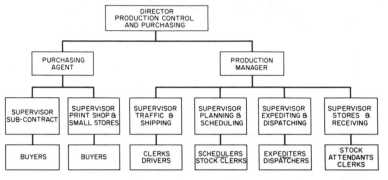

Fig. 3-5. Organization Plan of a Materials Management Group That Includes Production Control.

In addition to purchasing and customer service, the Metallurgical Division organization, which is headed by a materials manager, includes production and inventory control, receiving and warehousing. As described by Materials Manager T. S. Teague, it gives practical meaning to the theoretical definition of materials management previously quoted:

> Materials management establishes the requirements, provides the availability, determines the value and price levels, and controls the flow of materials from the initial development of the production requirement (coming from the receipt of the customer's order or from marketing's schedule of anticipated sales) until the final delivery of the product to the customer.[3]

A modification of the G. E. system is that used by Lenkurt Electric Company, San Carlos, California. It takes in buying, inbound traffic, inventory control, and receiving and stores. It has no control over shipment of finished goods, nor over production planning and scheduling. Purchasing personnel are divided into four groups, each headed by a senior buyer and each with its own responsibilities for planning, buying, routing, receiving, storing, and disbursing specific commodities. The head of the materials organization has the title of "Manager of Purchases and Materials."

Apparatus Division of Texas Instruments, Inc., also has a modified materials management organization, although it is not designated as such. It is headed by a purchasing agent and includes groups of buyers (assigned to specific division products, primarily defense items) and a material control group. The latter has responsibility for stores, collating and packaging

---

[3] "Four Approaches to Materials Management," *Purchasing Magazine,* June 17, 1963, p. 55.

spare parts and systems for the divisions customers, and shipping and receiving.

The great advantage of the materials management type of organization reported by those companies that have adopted it is the improved communication and coordination between departments that it permits. Materials management provides a central administration where conflicting function or departmental interests can be balanced out in the over-all interest of the company. Centralized responsibility and control also make for smoother, faster flow of materials from the time they are requisitioned by using departments to the time they are shipped out to customers as finished products.

Among the more specific ways in which a centrally controlled materials organization has helped a number of companies to improve efficiency and to reduce costs are these:

1. Control of inventories is made easier and simpler. The traditional conflict caused by the efforts of manufacturing, on the one hand, to build up stocks of raw material and parts, and of purchasing, on the other, to keep them to a minimum, have been resolved. Production planning and control and purchasing have found it easier to come to agreement on minimum and maximum stocks when they are working more as a team than as separate groups with separate interests. Losses caused by obsolescence or deterioration of surplus materials are eliminated, as are the dangers of shutdowns necessitated by material shortages.

2. Clerical work is sharply reduced. As responsibility for materials moves from department to department, records are almost inevitably duplicated. Many production control departments, for example, retain file copies of the requisitions they issue to purchasing, and in turn demand copies of the purchase order. With production control and purchasing in one office under one individual, a single file copy of either form serves both. Similar reductions in the generation and filing of paper work can be made in every department involved in the materials cycle, leading, in turn, to substantial cuts in the clerical force required. (Before the adoption of materials management in an eastern electronics firm, various functions involved in handling materials accounted for 10.5 per cent of the total plant work force. A year after the new organization was formed, the percentage had dropped to 7.1. During this time the total work force had increased by 74 per cent, but the number of material personnel had gone up only 18 per cent.)

3. Assorted problems of delivery scheduling, emergency orders, and storage are minimized. Purchasing can arrange delivery schedules on the basis of its knowledge of inventory levels and production requirements. Emergency or rush orders are less frequent because of understanding between production control and purchasing. Better regulation of the flow

of materials into the plant permits better use of storage facilities and coordinated movement of materials into the production line.

Materials management is particularly suited to—and has been most widely adopted by—those companies which manufacture to customers' orders. Such operations often involve fluctuating inventory levels, engineering changes by the customer, and irregular production scheduling. Placing the responsibility for materials in one department enables management to keep informed on the status of every order by checking with one source. In a less coordinated system, basic information about a particular job—what materials had been requisitioned for it, the status of purchase orders placed against the requisitions, the condition of inventories, and manufacturing progress on the job—would have to be gathered from four different departments.

In those companies producing highly standardized items for stock, on the other hand, good communication and coordination between departments handling material generally have been developed by experience. Inventory levels and production schedules are usually established on the basis of sales forecasts and historical usage, and the manufacturing operation is generally more stable and predictable than is the case in the manufacture-to-order companies. In such cases, good control has already been built into the materials system and the plant manager, or vice-president of operations or whatever top executive the departments concerned report to, is, in fact, a materials manager already.

Branch plant purchasing

In multi-plant operations, which are frequently found in enterprises of moderate size and are almost universal among the larger companies, the question arises of whether to do all purchasing for the entire organization at one central point, or to set up a separate purchasing department for each operating division or plant location, each with a considerable degree of autonomy in buying. Both methods are in use, but, as was suggested in an earlier section of this chapter, the trend in organization practice is toward the latter plan.

This is popularly referred to as *decentralization* of purchasing. However, the term should be applied with some reservations, because it refers to over-all management policy rather than to the purchasing function itself. Centralization or decentralization of purchasing under these circumstances is usually a matter of degree. The branch plant or divisional purchasing department is organized on the same pattern as already outlined, and every principle of centralized purchasing is observed in its operation. Furthermore, the system is in no way inconsistent with effective central management control.

The reasons for establishing separate plant or divisional purchasing departments may be summarized as follows:

1. The plant or division manager is responsible for the efficient and profitable operation of that company unit. On the principle that responsibility and authority should go hand in hand, he should have jurisdiction over purchases as well as production, because a large percentage of his costs and a major factor in the efficiency and continuity of production are represented in the procurement function.

2. If the branch or division is large enough to be considered an economical operating unit, it is usually large enough to realize the advantages of volume purchasing on the basis of its own requirements. It is, in most instances, as large or larger than many complete independent companies in the same field, where centralized purchasing is profitably used, and the corporate relationship to other divisions is merely incidental in this comparison. The law of diminishing returns applies to centralization in the organization and procedure for purchasing as well as in the mechanical phases of industrial operation. Good management seeks to find the method of maximum efficiency, rather than to apply even a proven principle like centralized purchasing arbitrarily.

3. Where the geographical distance between plants is significant, purchasing by remote control from a central office entails a time lag that may result in serious delays in procurement. It involves duplication of paper work and records. It sacrifices the direct, daily contact with departments where needs arise and materials are used. It is poorly adapted to cope with emergency requirements promptly. These shortcomings and added complexities of procedure tend to offset the benefits that might be expected from complete centralization of purchasing operations where branch plants are concerned. In even the most competent departments set up under such a plan, it is usually found necessary to have a purchasing department representative stationed at the plant, and the most effective utilization of such representatives would seem to be in the direction of more, rather than less, delegation of independent responsibility.

4. Each plant or division usually has some unique requirements and differences in operating conditions that affect material needs and procurement. Transportation, climatic conditions, storage facilities, plant equipment and usage, local trade customs and ordinances, and suppliers' distribution policies all have a bearing on purchasing programs. The plant purchasing department is in the better position to understand and adapt to these factors. Where two or more branch plants have some common requirements, suggesting an advantage in joint procurement, it is entirely feasible to regard

this as the exception to the general rule and to handle it accordingly, rather than the other way around.

5. The public relations aspect of purchasing must be considered, as well as the more objective factor of over-all purchase volume. It is now generally conceded that a company has an economic responsibility to the communities in which its plants are located. Good will can be fostered by purchasing from nearby sources, or through local distributors and sales representatives, so far as is practicable. Although such policies can be carried out even though purchasing is done from a distant, central point, they are likely to be more effective, consistent, and personalized when locally administered. Certainly they are more closely identified with the local community, in the public mind.

Complete centralization

The arguments for complete centralization of purchasing for a multi-plant manufacturing company stress the cumulative requirements of the entire company and the consequent opportunities to combine these requirements for greater quantity-purchasing advantages and tactical purchasing power; the desirability of having a single buying policy and procedure for the whole organization; the need for central controls as a means of evaluating purchasing activities and maintaining high standards of performance. It is pointed out that the staff responsibilities of the chief purchasing officer can be most surely effectuated through his direct administration of all buying.

In this view, plant location in itself is a relatively unimportant detail. The purchasing department is not necessarily located at the plant in any case. It is regarded more as a part of the general executive organization than as a part of the manufacturing operation. Particularly in metropolitan areas, it is not unusual to find a company's executive and purchasing offices in the business center of the city, whereas the manufacturing plants are located in outlying factory sections, sometimes several miles distant. With modern telephone, telegraph, and teletype facilities, the greater distance to plants in other cities need be no great obstacle to efficient buying service.

There are advantages other than mere volume in a single purchasing program for the entire company. For example:

1. Quality of purchased materials and parts is more readily controlled when they are bought on one contract from one source than when the orders are placed with several unrelated sources by as many different buyers.

2. There is added flexibility in that shipments on existing orders or contracts can be allocated and directed to various plants as needed instead of

initiating a new purchase. The transfer of materials from one plant to another may be the quickest and most economical way of meeting an emergency.

3. One plant's surplus may be used to fill another's needs without making an additional expenditure or commitment, at the same time getting a better return on the value of such surplus.

4. Losses from obsolescence of parts due to changes in model or design can be minimized by concentrating the "balancing out" process of manufacture on the existing model in a single designated plant.

5. A higher degree of specialization and consequent purchasing skill can logically be expected in respect to special types of commodities, as compared with a situation in which the same responsibility is delegated to several buyers at the various plants.

Centralized control

Judging from actual business practice, there is no one best answer to this question of centralization versus decentralization of purchasing for branch plants. In about 25 per cent of multi-plant companies, purchasing is strongly centralized; the great bulk of all buying is done at a central office, with a minimum of buying authority (usually restricted to emergency requirements and supply items of small value) granted to the branches. The trend has been away from this system as multi-plant operation has become more prevalent and as branch plants and divisions have become larger and more important on their own account. In about 15 per cent, buying for each plant is largely delegated to local plant management, with almost complete autonomy of authority and action. In the majority of cases, a compromise has been adopted, seeking to achieve the advantages of both methods. This usually takes the form of a decentralized system with centralized coordination and controls. Some of the specific means of accomplishing this include:

1. Uniform policies, forms, and procedures at all plants, established through a company-wide purchasing manual; uniform quality standards established by company-wide specifications.

2. Continuing review of all purchasing activities by having copies of purchase orders routed to the central office. Systematic monthly reports from all branch purchasing departments, correlated at the central office and redistributed to the branches in a summary report form, with buying recommendations.

3. Dollar-value limitation on branch plant purchases. Orders or contracts in excess of the stated limit are subject to approval by the central department.

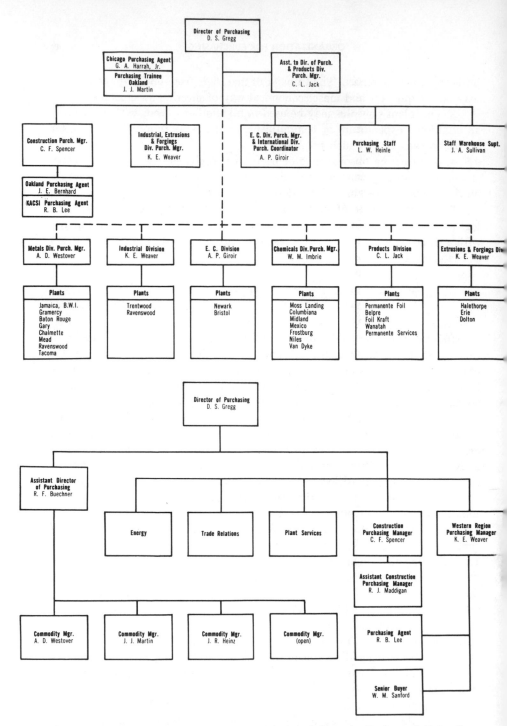

Fig. 3-6. Multi-plant Purchasing Organization Before and After the Purchase of Major Commodities Was Centralized.

This corresponds to the regulation in many purchasing departments that orders amounting to more than a stated dollar value must be approved by the head of the department or by some higher executive.

4. Certain items, usually major materials in common use at two or more plants, are designated as contract items and are purchased by the central department for all plants. In some cases, the initial requirement of a new item is purchased by the plant purchasing department, with subsequent review to determine whether it shall be classified as a contract item. A variation of this is to delegate the purchase of specified items to a designated plant purchasing department where the item is used in greatest volume.

5. Contracts for items in common use are made by the central department, with provision for shipment to all company locations. Branch plant buyers are expected to issue release orders against these existing contracts, but have the option of buying independently if they can improve on the terms of the contract for their individual plant requirements through special local circumstances or for any other reason. This assures buying on the most favorable terms in all cases and may lead to revision of the central contracts to extend the benefit to all branches.

In some companies, centralized control of commodities used in a number of plants has led to more highly centralized headquarters purchasing organizations. Kaiser Aluminum Corporation, for example, has moved approximately 40 per cent of all its purchases into central purchasing in Oakland (see Fig. 3-6). Commodity specialists at headquarters handle all corporate requirements for commonly used items like pitch binder, petroleum coke, and corrugated boxes. Any item not specifically assigned to the central office is the direct responsibility of plant purchasing offices. Headquarters continues, however, to provide local purchasing agents with policy guidance and administrative assistance.

Departmental budgets

Departmental operating budgets are primarily a means of accounting and administrative control, and they are customarily calculated for the calendar or fiscal year. In the majority of cases, each department head makes out his own estimate of the cost of running his department, preparing his budget from previous experience and from his knowledge of the work to be done and the personnel required, prevailing salary scales and increments, and the like.

The simplest forms of departmental operating budgets cover the essentials of salaries, expenses, and supplies. Where detailed cost accounting systems are maintained, there may be an allocation of such expenses as rent, light, heat, postage, telephone, and telegraph. Some budgets are broken down into detailed classifications including the above, plus printing and stationery, travel, entertainment, furniture and equipment, insurance, and the like. In some cases, a distinction is made between the fixed charges over which the department has no control (tax items, insurance, depreciation on equipment, and others) and controllable expenses on which administrative care and skill can be exerted. In the latter group, definite limits may be placed on certain items, such as entertainment, subscriptions, and membership dues, whereas such items as travel, postage, telephone, stationery, and the like, are more flexible because the job to be done will eventually determine the amount necessary, just as the manufacturing program ultimately determines the materials to be purchased.

Departmental operating budgets are in more common use than purchase budgets for materials and supplies, and close adherence to budgeted amounts is more generally required.

4

PERSONNEL FOR PURCHASING

THE CALIBER and effectiveness of a purchasing department depend not only upon its organization and procedure, but even more upon the personnel through which its policies and systems are carried out. To maintain a high standard of personnel, there should be a consistent plan of selection and training for key positions and for progress upward through the department to the positions of responsibility. It is true that a departmental staff reflects the leadership of the department head, but the department that is bound up in the person of the one "indispensable" man is a weak department. There must be delegation of responsibility and the capacity to accept responsibility. Consequently, one of the important characteristics of leadership is attention to sound training.

Qualifications for buying

The scope of the purchasing activity and responsibility and the qualifications needed in a buyer have been indicated throughout this study. They have been codified for many individual companies through the process of job analysis, and on a more general and inclusive basis in the *Handbook of Descriptions of Specialized Fields in Management and Administration,* compiled by the National Roster of Scientific and Specialized Personnel and undertaken as a part of the work of the War Manpower Commission, Bureau of Placement. A section of the study is devoted to purchasing, as one of these specialized fields, and was made available in 1945.

In discussing purchasing personnel, the *Handbook* states: "Professional skill in purchasing is acquired by academic training and practical experience, and is applicable and interchangeable in any field to the solution and administration of management problems."

Qualifications as to both academic and experience training, most likely to lead to success as a purchasing execuive, are listed as follows:

(a) College education; preferably a graduate engineer, with additional training in economics and business administration.
(b) Practical training in the production, stores, accounting, and engineering departments.
(c) Practical training in all sections of the purchasing department; experience in, or familiarity with, clerical positions, and service as buyer and assistant purchasing agent.

This statement is amplified, and somewhat modified, by the following commentary:

> Such training should qualify a person to handle a managerial purchasing position in any organization. Having acquired these basic qualifications in one company, a purchasing executive can be expected to meet the needs of another company by becoming familiar with its material requirements and organization policies.
>
> As in other specialized fields of management, comparable education, secured through study of commodities and markets, and practical experience in the company organization, may be substituted for and may compensate for basic academic training as a prerequisite for administrative positions in purchasing.

Despite the value of practical experience, a college degree has become increasingly important as a prerequisite for obtaining an industrial buyer's position. E. F. Andrews, Vice-President—Purchases of Allegheny Ludlum Steel Corporation, describing a trend, points out that five years before a little over 30 per cent of the buyers in his department were college graduates; today, 90 per cent hold degrees. [1]

A study by the Milwaukee Association of Purchasing Agents show the following degree of specialization of the college-trained purchasing man:

Field of Specialization	Per Cent
Business Administration	44.7
Engineering	22.0
Liberal Arts	12.9
Law	1.5
All other fields	18.9

Commenting on the results of the survey, the Project Development Committee on Purchasing As A Career of the National Association of Purchasing Agents said: [2]

---

[1] Speech delivered at the International Management Congress, New York, Sept. 18, 1963.

[2] Reprinted from the booklet, *Purchasing As a Career* (1962), distributed by the National Association of Purchasing Agents, New York.

Probably the ideal college training would consist of an undergraduate degree in engineering (at least for metalworking firms) and a master's degree in business administration. For the student who seeks a career in purchasing and cannot devote more than four years to college training, it is generally believed that business administration training would be best, provided it was supplemented by elective work in technical subjects to the greatest extent possible.

The existing programs of study available at most collegiate schools of business provide the college student with the basic tools needed for a career in purchasing, according to the Committee. It suggests that 50 per cent of the student's work be in liberal arts and the remainder in economics and business. Courses recommended for inclusion in such a program would be:

General Economics
Accounting Principles
Business Communications
Commercial Law
Statistics
Business Organization and Management
Marketing Principles
Corporation Finance
Industrial Purchasing
Sales Forecasting
Price Policies
Traffic Management
Production Planning and Control
Cost Accounting

In addition to the above, the Committee says, the student could consider as free electives any general industrial engineering courses offered by his university.

Personal qualifications

Personnel selection starts with the character and capacity of the individual. For the routine clerical operations in the purchasing office, the basic qualifications would include intelligence, ability to learn, accuracy, speed, and the ability to get along with fellow workers. The opportunities for advancement in this area generally consist of supervisory positions. For these the desirable characteristics are a sense of responsibility and loyalty and the capacity for leadership.

For positions in the line of buying, leading eventually to top responsibility for purchasing management, the requirements are of a higher order. They include integrity, analytical skill and objectivity, resourcefulness, initiative, practical imagination, and the ability to meet and deal with people. The personal qualifications also include a good educational background, preferably a college degree. In lieu of formal academic training, however, the man seeking a career in purchasing should have the ambition and perseverance to acquire the equivalent educational qualifications through evening and extension courses. In either case, he should not consider the completion of any formal course as the end of learning, but should be alert to the opportunities for further study in pertinent fields and conscientious in keeping up to date on continuing developments in purchasing and in industry.

Seeking human material

Having set up a specification for purchasing personnel, in the form of a list of the qualifications desired, the next step is to seek a source of supply. First on the list of prerequisites cited above is a college education. A logical first source, then, is among college graduates having the necessary academic background. This is a source regularly cultivated in the standard personnel recruiting programs of many large companies. Where this method is a part of company policy, the recruiting for purchasing is usually handled as a part of the general program, with the specific assignment to purchasing following a screening and training program during which special aptitudes are disclosed.

The indicated preference for graduate engineers is consistent with a trend that has been in evidence for a number of years, but it is by no means an absolute requirement. Recent studies indicate that over 20 per cent of industrial purchasing executives have a background of engineering training, as compared with less than 10 per cent in 1940. This trend reflects the increasing complexity and importance of technical knowledge of materials and products purchased, but generalization is likely to be misleading. There are many positions in purchasing where engineering training is but a marginal requirement and certainly not essential; there are other assignments where very specialized technical qualifications are important—a textile engineer, electronics engineer, or metallurgical engineer, for example. "Engineering" is a broad term, covering not only the inclusive branches of chemical, electrical, and mechanical engineering with their several specialized subdivisions, but also the science of management and methods engineering, in which the technology of materials plays a minor role. The engineering requirement or preference, therefore, is a selective rather than a general rule, depending on the company's type of business and on the type of materials purchased.

The case for the graduate engineer is well stated by the purchasing executive of a large company manufacturing technical products, who has made technical education a requisite in the personnel policy of his department. He stresses the point that it is more practicable to take a technical specialist and train him in the application of that knowledge to problems of procurement than to take a nontechnical person whose qualifications may otherwise be excellent and try to supply him with the required technical knowledge and training of the specialist. This argument has additional force in the particular case, because his large organization, like many other large organizations, has provision for an executive training program extending from 12 to 18 months before the specific assignment to purchasing or other duties is made. Other companies, especially smaller ones, may require more immediate results. It should also be pointed out that highly specialized technical knowledge, although extremely valuable in a particular application, may also be a limiting factor. The broader the base of academic training, the greater is the opportunity for advancement to more general responsibilities.

The second academic qualification cited—training in economics and business administration—points to another preferred source for purchasing personnel, namely, the colleges of business administration. This is direct training for managerial positions. The majority of such schools now offer basic courses in the principles of procurement as a standard or elective part of the curriculum, and a few offer such courses as a major field of specialization.

The second general qualification, practical training in plant and purchasing departments, is obviously one that must be acquired on the job. It is well established that this process can be greatly accelerated in the case of the person having an adequate academic training. But the requirement in itself suggests another fruitful source of purchasing personnel—extension or evening colleges, whose students usually are engaged in acquiring practical business experience while studying, and business or engineering schools operating on the so-called "cooperative" plan, under which academic and practical training are carried on in alternating terms throughout the course, grounding the student in both phases.

Personnel recruiting for purchasing is by no means limited to the college field. It has been pointed out that practical experience in the company organization may compensate for the academic requirement. Thus, the selection may be made from among persons of aptitude and promise currently employed in various departments of the company, with or without the formal educational credits.

General training program

The first objective of a general training program for any new employee is orientation—an understanding of the job in terms of its own activities, objectives, and responsibilities, and in relation to over-all company objectives and operations.

If the new employee in purchasing comes to his work without previous experience in the company, or without previous business experience, so that all of his practical training must be acquired on the job, one part of that training should be the opportunity to see the workings of other departments and their relationship to purchasing. Such assignments as internal tracing and expediting of materials, the investigation of complaints regarding materials and deliveries, and even messenger service that takes him out into the plant, the storeroom, the laboratory, and the drafting and accounting departments on missions concerning materials, purchasing service, and records—all contribute effectively to this end.

The objectives of this general training, which may be carried on coincidentally with specific job training, include:

> Knowledge of the company's processes, equipment, and product.
> Knowledge of production and maintenance materials and how they are used.
> Knowledge of the flow of materials and of form and record controls.
> Knowledge of other departments and their work, and of the purchasing department's relationship to them.
> Knowledge of company policies.
> Knowledge of purchasing policies.

The general course of training outlined above is predicated on the supposition that the new employee in the department is without specific experience in purchasing work. The case of the employee who comes with a background of purchasing experience in some other organization presents a special case. The functional job analysis quoted above stresses the fact that basic qualifications and training are applicable to purchasing in any field. Many examples of successful transfer from purchasing in one industry to purchasing in another very different type of industry could be cited to support this statement; such cases present the most convincing evidence of the essentially professional nature of a purchasing career. The trained and experienced purchasing man is presumably capable of stepping into any purchasing assignment. But although this may seem to obviate the necessity of further apprenticeship in preparation for the job, it does not eliminate the need for general orientation. Products, processes, and equipment vary rather widely even among individual companies within the same industry; material requirements or standards vary; systems and controls, although following a generally standard pattern, have individual peculiarities developed to adapt the plan to particular conditions and types of organization; and, finally, company policies are likely to be highly individualized. The new man, however competent and experienced in procurement, must adjust himself to all of these factors in order to achieve maximum effectiveness in his new responsibility.

It should be noted here that wide observation of purchasing practice indicates that, in the majority of cases, where a man goes from a purchasing position in one company to the purchasing department of another company, his services are generally sought in the capacity of department head. Typically, within the department, purchasing work is among the more stable occupations, and orderly advancement is the general rule. Among the conclusions to be drawn from this observation is the somewhat unfortunate indication that training programs are frequently deficient, to the extent that men who are deemed competent to fill every other purchasing responsibility are not always ready to step into the positions of top responsibility. This is a point worthy of serious consideration by every purchasing executive and by company managements. There should be no ceiling to advancement in purchasing for the man who is really qualified in buying. Sound selection and comprehensive training of purchasing personnel are two of the more obvious means of correcting the situation.

Training on the job

Although the popular conception of a purchasing job is that of buying, this is a culmination rather than a starting point. It is generally accepted in the field that a minimum of two years' experience is required to fit a person for a position at a buyer's desk. This would include both the general phases of orientation and training plus work at other duties within the department. Extensive experience in other departments, of a nature pertinent to the knowledge and consideration of materials and their procurement, would naturally accelerate progress in the purchasing department itself, but it does not take the place of familiarity and experience with the actual mechanics of processing a requisition or carrying out a purchasing transaction. There is a practical advantage for every buyer in knowing not only how, but why, procedures are handled as they are. This knowledge gives significance to details that might otherwise be slighted, perspective to the process as a whole, and smoothness and coordination to the whole procurement operation.

In the earlier chapters on departmental organization, it was pointed out that, although the purchasing function is in the position of a staff assignment with respect to the company organization as a whole, within the department it is adapted to the "line" type of organization, with definite lines of authority and responsibility integrating the entire operation. In most purchasing departments, whether large or small, there is a well-defined sequence or relative rank of the various assignments, affording a logical course of progress without necessarily cleaving to a rigid pattern of seniority in promotion. Typical stages of such progress would include the following:

1. Routine clerical, file, and mail distribution duties; report to the chief clerk; provides general familiarity with departmental procedures and records, how and why used.

2. Invoice checking; report to chief clerk; provides familiarity with purchased materials list and with receiving procedure, contact with receiving and accounting departments; stresses importance of accuracy and demonstrates purchasing responsibility in committing the company to expenditures. Detecting and correcting a single, simple error at this stage is practical and valuable experience in showing what can happen to an order after it has been placed and the transaction is apparently closed.

3. Requisition checking, stock records, internal expediting; report to buyer; provides familiarity with purchasing program and flow of materials, contact with stores and using departments; demonstrates purchasing responsibility and policy in respect to stated requirements and how these needs are filled.

4. Follow-up and expediting; report to buyer or head of buying group; provides familiarity with specific materials from the procurement angle, first direct contact with vendors, evaluation of vendors' service and reliability, first independent responsibility.

5. Assistant buyer; report to buyer; first direct dealing with vendors' sales representatives, first decisions on supply sources, first responsibility for negotiation and terms committing the company to a purchase agreement. This work generally starts with standard catalog items, bought on established maximum-minimum stock basis, or issuance of release orders and shipping instructions against contracts in force, all under direct supervision of the buyer who is responsible for the items. Scope of items bought and independent authority are broadened as capacity is demonstrated, up to the point where the employee is ready to serve as a buyer with certain commodities or items definitely assigned to him for procurement.

This regular progression of duties, with actual experience in the major phases of purchasing department operation, provides a comprehensive course of training on the job that should equip the buyer with the necessary knowledge of policy and procedure to think and act in accordance with that policy and to coordinate smoothly with the over-all buying program. It should provide a foundation of general preparation in and for purchasing that can later be applied, at the "buyer" stage, to almost any group of items in the company's list of requirements as the need for such an assignment may arise. For, as was pointed out in the summary of qualifications, familiarity with particular commodities and products is something that can be acquired and superimposed on the basic purchasing knowledge. If there is a specific opening or buying assignment in view as the objective of the training, it would, of course, be logical to take it into consideration at the "assistant buyer" stage, so as to have a definite apprenticeship in the handling of these particular items. Typically, however, the objective of training up to this point is more general in nature, and versatility or flexibility is an important factor. Although specialization is a characteristic of purchasing department organization and operation, there is likewise a need for interchangeability of personnel in respect to commodity responsibilities, and there may also be an element of progression from one product group to another group of greater importance. Thus, the basic training is the essential feature of the training program.

Training away from the office desk is highly important. The trainee should be encouraged—and opportunities made, if necessary—to visit suppliers' plants, to develop a diversity of personal contacts in the trade, in supplier industries, and in purchasing associations, and to acquire a first-hand knowledge of how materials are made, marketed, and used. The value of these outside experiences can be greatly enhanced by following up each one with a personal conference or a written report to his immediate superior.

A continuing program

A proper conception of training recognizes the fact that it is never a completed job. The experience of many successful departments, even when the staff is stable and well-established and its personnel reasonably experienced and competent in their respective positions, shows that there is much benefit to be derived from a continuing program of training, whether or not it is referred to as such. The emphasis placed upon education and discussion forums in the program of the National Association of Purchasing Agents and the policy of that organization in making advanced study courses available to its membership are testimony to the fact that even those who have arrived at positions of leadership in their company organizations and in their profession can profit by such projects. It is even more true in respect to a departmental group that operates as a coordinated working unit with one common purpose.

There are several ways in which a continuing training program can be handled. Among those that have proved most effective are the following:

Refresher courses. These may be conducted annually, or biennially, for a three-month period. Meetings are held weekly on company time, from 4 to 5 o'clock on Monday afternoons, for example. Attendance is usually compulsory for specified grades of personnel throughout the entire department. A formal course of study is followed, based on the department manual or selected from some standard text on purchasing. The class is generally led by some senior officer of the department, but not necessarily by the department head himself. Free discussion is encouraged but is held to prescribed subjects for each session so as to cover the topics in an orderly and comprehensive manner. Written examinations are not recommended, but it may be desirable to summarize the points of emphasis on a mimeographed sheet for each session, apart from the printed manual or text, as the equivalent of a student's notebook. The fundamental principles of purchasing are stressed, interpreted in the light of specific company policy and procedure.

Such a course can be made progressively more advanced from year to year, according to the capacity and need of the staff, and for variety. Topics eliciting the greatest interest and points on which more emphasis is desired can be developed in course outline for studies in intermediate years.

Periodical staff meetings. These are less formal than the organized refresher course and do not have the "schoolroom" atmosphere that is sometimes resented by older and more experienced members of the department, but
they can be made equally effective from the training standpoint with careful
planning and good leadership. Meetings are held regularly, monthly or twice
a month, on company time; for example, from 11 o'clock till noon on the
specified dates. Attendance is limited, but it is compulsory for those eligible to
take part, all other appointments being subordinated to this conference.
Eligibility is defined in some cases as including all buyers and all those who
have other workers coming directly under their supervision. Such a plan brings
in the heads of the various sections such as filing, invoice checking, and
expediting, whose attendance is usually of value in a discussion; at the same
time, it keeps the group and its programs and deliberations distinctly above
the elementary and theoretical plane, being of a nature and caliber to represent
the transaction of real company business. The training is probably regarded as
incidental by those who are receiving it, if indeed they recognize it as training
at all.

A group of this kind provides an excellent opportunity for indoctrination
in policy matters and for setting up uniformity of practices. It is a logical
and effective place to have representatives of the company management and
of other departments explain the work of the organization as a whole, what is
expected of purchasing in relation to these other operations, and how it can
be coordinated to best advantage. Occasional speakers or discussion leaders
from the outside, qualified to present some topic or viewpoint pertinent to
purchasing work, may be introduced from time to time. Informal round-the-
table discussion of specific local or departmental or purchasing problems can
be developed to good advantage and usually with good response, general participation in such discussions being encouraged.

Outside training. Earlier in this chapter it was pointed out that the
chronology of training is variable—that academic or formal studies can be
superimposed on departmental experience, if such happens to be the need in
an individual case, with the same effectiveness as if the normal sequence were
followed, taking basic academic qualifications and supplementing these with
training on the job. This principle is well worth consideration in its application to the continuing training program. Facilities for the study of purchasing,
and of related business and economic subjects, are available in many cities,
scheduled for evening classes to meet exactly this need. One of the objectives
of the educational program of the National Association of Purchasing Agents
has been to foster the establishment of such courses.

The facilities can be effectively used in the company training program,
especially for the smaller departments where specific company training for a
limited personnel would be impracticable. It is generally taken for granted

that this type of education is a responsibility of the individual, and not of the employer, but there is much to be said in favor of encouraging such studies and of providing an incentive in the form of partial or complete payment of tuition charges. Unlike the company programs cited in the preceding paragraphs, these courses are not on company time. Therefore, although it is not proposed that trainees be compensated for time spent in such studies, it is logical to regard the actual costs—for designated trainees and for approved courses—as a legitimate training expense.

Somewhat similar training facilities are available in junior purchasing associations, or junior memberships in some of the active senior chapters. It is significant that some of the most successful of these junior organizations have had their origin in study groups where a strong desire has been felt to continue the training program on a self-administered basis—convincing testimony to the serious objectives of the organization and the values that its members find in the study program. Membership and active participation in such groups are also to be encouraged as a continuing process of training.

Careers in purchasing

Up to this point we have considered the matter of purchasing personnel only from the viewpoint of management—the company with a purchasing job to be done and the executive responsible for administering the department. The discussion is not complete without a consideration of the subject of all this concern, the person entering upon purchasing work. What does purchasing promise him that will lead him to accept the job offer or the assignment to purchasing duties? For what sort of business life does this training equip him? What opportunities and rewards are his if he chooses a career in purchasing?

Purchasing is an occupation of wide variety and interests. The buyer deals with a wide range of materials and products, and these are constantly changing, in themselves and in their economic relationships, through technological developments and progress. The products are procured from many different sources, affording the buyer direct and stimulating contacts and familiarity with a range of supplier industries far broader than the experience of workers concerned only with the internal company operation. In the regular course of his activities, he deals with many people—those for whom and from whom he buys—in a variety of business and personal relationships. And the economic conditions under which he does his buying are constantly changing, so that one day's problems are never quite the same as those of the day before.

Purchasing is a challenging and competitive occupation, with large responsibilities in both the quality of supply service provided and the magnitude of expenditures. It calls not only for knowledge and routine efficiency, but for resourcefulness, for skill in negotiation and good judgment in decisions, and for imagination and initiative in the continuing search for greater value.

Purchasing is a useful, essential part of the company activity. It offers the satisfactions of pride in the end product that embodies purchased materials and in the profit results made possible through wise and effective procurement.

Purchasing is a growing field, soundly established but still in the developmental stage, with many horizons yet to be explored and many opportunities yet to be fully realized and exploited as the function moves toward the broader concept of materials management. The man in purchasing has the opportunity for constructive service to industry and management by contributing to the knowledge and techniques of procurement science, to the broader scope of purchasing service, to higher professional standards and management status, and to a share in the rewards of such advances.

Purchasing is steadily winning increased recognition in every progressive company as an integral and important part of industrial management. It has prestige within the company organization. It participates in management councils and policy decisions and has the authority to administer and carry out the programs to fulfill its functional responsibilities.

The upgrading of purchasing in the management organization is reflected in the levels of compensation. Salary scales that once lagged behind those of technical and sales divisions are now commensurate with the basic responsibility of purchasing and fully on a par with those of comparable positions in other departments. And there is increased participation in executive profit-sharing plans as the profit potentials of purchasing are better known and as better means of evaluating purchasing performance are used. The salaries of top executives in purchasing, which represent the ultimate measure of opportunity, are equivalent to those of the top executives in sales, production, engineering, and finance.

Purchasing is among the more stable of industrial occupations. Numerically, the field is smaller than the employment opportunities in technical, plant, and sales activities. On the other hand, it is less subject to sudden and wide fluctuations that characterize employment levels in these other areas along with fluctuations in business volume. The major exceptions to this generalization occur in periods of intense plant expansion or emergencies like war production, involving temporary peak loads of purchasing expenditure; but these are generally undertaken on a project basis rather than as a part of normal business operation.

Partly as a corollary to this stability, advancement in purchasing is typically steady rather than rapid; but, with the growth of industry and the increasing demands made on purchasing, the opportunities for rapid advancement in the larger departments are greatly enhanced for the qualified younger buyer with an alert, constructive approach to the procurement function and

DATE PREPARED	**PURCHASING MANPOWER INVENTORY**	LAST NAME	FIRST	MIDDLE
MARITAL STATUS		PRESENT JOB TITLE		GRADE
DATE OF BIRTH		DIVISION & LOCATION		

BUSINESS EXPERIENCE

(SHOW RCA & PREVIOUS EXPERIENCE)	FROM	TO	POSITION (DUTIES & RESPONSIBILITIES)

EDUCATION

INSTITUTION & LOCATION	FROM	TO	MAJOR & MINOR FIELDS
HIGH SCHOOL OR COLLEGE			

YEAR	OTHER COURSES & TRAINING		

BUSINESS MEMBERSHIPS, ASSOCIATIONS, SPECIAL SKILLS

CSP 100   (OVER)

PERFORMANCE APPRAISAL

REVIEW DATES	PROMOTABILITY	PROMOTABLE TO
	PURCHASING AGENT'S APPRAISAL	
	IMMEDIATE / 1 YEAR / 2 YEARS OR MORE / NOT APPARENT / NEWLY HIRED ☐ ☐ ☐ ☐ ☐	BUYER Y / BUYER A / BUYER MGR. / PURCHASING AGENT ☐ ☐ ☐ ☐
	OTHER APPRAISAL	
	IMMEDIATE / 1 YEAR / 2 YEARS OR MORE / NOT APPARENT / NEWLY HIRED ☐ ☐ ☐ ☐ ☐	☐ _____ SPECIFY

RELOCATION	INDIVIDUAL'S PREFERENCE	CURRENT SALARY	DATE OF LAST INCREASE	
☐ WILL RELOCATE				☐ SEMI-MTHLY
☐ WILL NOT RELOCATE				☐ MONTHLY
				☐ YEARLY

Fig. 4-1. Records Used By Headquarters Purchasing to Analyze Qualifications of Buyers, Purchasing Agents, and Administrators in a Multi-plant Company.

good leadership characteristics. In the modern concept of scientific materials control, the upper echelons cannot be filled adequately on the basis of seniority alone.

The top of the ladder in purchasing, which every purchasing man can logically set as his goal, and which he may attain, is not only a position as department head, but a vice-presidency in the company organization.

It is no mere happenstance that the newer ranks of purchasing are made up largely of those who have definitely elected purchasing as a career field. Some significant testimony on this point comes from the training director of a large manufacturing company in which the purchasing department plays an important role and has earned high regard within the company.[1] This company annually recruits some 200 talented graduates of business and engineering colleges for its executive training course. They spend the first year working for several weeks in each of the major departments in turn; at the end of this time, having had the chance to sample all types of activities and to evaluate and compare the opportunities offered, each trainee is asked to state his preference for a permanent assignment. Up to 1955, about one trainee in 20 chose purchasing. In 1957, the figure was one trainee out of every 13, which is about par in relation to staff personnel requirements. In 1958, one out of every 9 trainees requested assignment to the purchasing department.

Instances such as this reflect not only the appeal of purchasing work, but the opportunities for business advancement which it affords as well. Our concern here is primarily with the career aspects of purchasing itself. It should not be inferred from this, however, that opportunity is circumscribed in any way or limited to that function. The purchasing department is an excellent training ground for advancement to positions at the general management level. The inclusion of purchasing indoctrination in executive training courses is evidence that this is regarded as essential knowledge and experience in any well-rounded training for management responsibility. The work of procurement brings the buyer intimately into touch with the requirements and operations of virtually every other phase of the business. The qualities required and developed in purchasing work—analytical skill, foresight, organization and punctuality in meeting responsibility, ability to deal with people, imagination, resourcefulness, and respect for ultimate values—are precisely those which make for success in the broader fields of management. And with increasing reliance being placed upon purchasing as a vital part of profit potentialities, there is little chance that the really competent purchasing man will be unnoticed or overlooked in general management plans.

---

[1] "Career Men for Purchasing," *Purchasing Magazine,* June 9, 1958, page 67.

5

BUYING THE RIGHT QUALITY

WHAT, WHEN, HOW, how much, from whom, and at what price to buy are decisions that must be made in the purchasing department, and the rightness of these decisions determines how well the responsibility is fulfilled.

This and the following chapters deal with the principles underlying these decisions, which, together, make up the process of purchasing. Strictly speaking, they are not "steps" in purchasing, for the factors are so completely interdependent that in most cases they must be considered simultaneously. To take a very simple example, the buying decision may involve a choice between one quality of material at one quoted price and another quality at a different price, from another source. Obviously, in this case, it is impossible to consider either quality, price, or source without considering the other factors at the same time. There is no fixed chronology or sequence. Nevertheless, each factor has its own characteristics and values which must be separately understood and weighed in arriving at a right decision before we can balance them in seeking the inclusive objective—value.

The three major factors entering into every purchasing decision are: quality (of the item purchased), service (provided by the supplier), and price (paid by the purchaser). Buyers generally state that they consider quality first, or of first importance, service second, and price last, in making a purchase. This is another way of saying that, unless the quality of the purchased item is adequate to satisfy the requirement, superlative service on the part of the supplier and all-but-irresistible price appeal are both in vain. Quality, then, is a logical starting point in consideration of the purchasing process.

Quality must be defined

In the vocabulary of purchasing, *quality* has a special meaning. It is not a generalization or an attribute to be characterized simply as "high" or "poor."

It is specifically the sum or composite of the properties inherent in a material or product. These properties can be measured and defined. The significant ones must be defined in order that the buyer may know what he should ask his supplier to furnish and may know what he is getting. This definition of quality, in greater or less detail, becomes the ordering description for every item—the essence of the purchase order.

Significant elements of quality for materials and components that go into a manufactured product include: analysis and dimension; physical, chemical, and dielectric properties; workability; uniformity of analysis and dimension, to insure uniform results in standard processing and to permit the use of mass-production methods with a minimum of spoilage or readjustments of machinery; and special characteristics tending to increase the salability of the purchaser's product, such as appearance, finish, finishing properties, desirable bulk or weight, and the acquired quality of popular acceptance.

When dealing with maintenance and operating supplies, significant properties would include utility, ease of application or use, efficiency, economy of use, and durability.

When dealing with machinery and equipment, the properties to be considered include productivity, versatility, dependability, durability, economy of operation and maintenance, and time- and labor-saving features.

For purchasing purposes, quality can be defined in a number of different ways, appropriate in varying degrees to various types of purchases. Among these ways are: complete and detailed specification; reference to established market grades or particular brand-named products which sum up certain combinations of qualities; actual sample, in which case the product itself is its own definition of the quality desired. Purchasing by each of these methods is discussed in following sections of this chapter. Of course, for many common items, such as hardware, for example, a simple statement of type and size is usually sufficient.

Every definition of quality is predicated on some standard of measurement, understood by both the buyer and the supplier. Here, again, there are various methods that are applicable, depending on the type of item under consideration and the purpose for which it is to be used.

Chemical analysis is one method of measurement. The composition of an alloy determines its physical properties and its adaptability for a specific use. The formula of an ink is important in relation to the surface upon which it is to be used, the conditions to which it will be exposed, and the necessary permanence. The formula of a cleaning compound measures its usefulness and safety on various types of material and its efficiency in removing various types of dirt or foreign matter. The strength and purity of chemical substances have a direct bearing on their action and methods of use. The sulphur, ash, and B.T.U. content of coal tell whether the fuel is suitable for use in a particular power-equipment installation and measure the heat efficiency which may be expected from its combustion. These and scores of similar examples can be cited as elements of quality which can be accurately determined in the laboratory and which have a direct relationship to the utility and value of the product.

Physical tests provide a measurement of quality in respect to such properties as the tensile strength and shearing strength of metals and fibers, the bursting, folding, and tearing strength of paper, dielectric properties, elasticity, ductility, opacity, resistance to abrasion or shock, resistance to sunlight or moisture, and many others. Ingenious testing machines have been devised for accurate measurement of these properties in terms of standard and comparable units, and accelerated tests under controlled conditions can be used to simulate the effects of use over long periods of time. Frequently the results of such tests are more important and revealing to the buyer than the basic chemical composition determined by analysis. For example, a special alloy, defined by analysis, may be desired and specified for the particular characteristics of ductility or hardness which go with that composition; to the buyer, the effect rather than the means is the essential consideration, and a physical measurement of the desired properties may afford a more direct and positive assurance of satisfaction.

Dimensional measurements indicate such quality factors as precision finishing and conformance to stated tolerances. The thread count of a woven textile and the thickness of a leather belt are quantitative measures that are significant in respect to utility and quality.

The most direct and obvious measurement of quality in the purchasing sense is the measure of performance. In each of the foregoing illustrations of methods available, it has been pointed out that the units of measurement of these various properties are primarily useful as a guide or indicator of suitability or performance. They provide a means of comparing various degrees of quality. Sometimes it is desirable to use all quality measurements available in evaluating a product. In some cases it may be possible and more practicable to measure performance directly rather than to go through the intermediate step of measuring specific properties or quality factors that may be expected to give the desired results.

Machinery is a common example of this situation. It is possible to describe and define a piece of complicated equipment in terms of dimension and design, giving the component elements of each part. As a matter of fact, this is a necessary step for the designer and builder of the machine. But dimensions, design, and structural materials are means to an end, which is performance or productive ability; and it is this latter characteristic that interests the buyer and is the measure of quality for him, because he is essentially purchasing what the machine will do. All the other factors are meaningless if the equipment turns out to be inefficient or unsuited to his purpose. Consequently, performance or guaranteed output is the basic measure of quality, and a proper specification or description of quality would make this the responsibility of the machine builder, rather than mere conformance with the physical factors involved.

To cite another example, the quality of paint can be described in terms of its composition, the amount of white lead, zinc oxide, or pure linseed oil per gallon and the methods of grinding and compounding. Certain quality results would be expected if these directions were observed. But looking once more past the means to the desired end—the finished painted surface—other considerations arise. Among these are the covering properties, ease of application and cleaning, and wearing qualities under given conditions of use and exposure. These factors are more important measures of quality to the buyer than the composition itself, and they could well be made the basis of his quality description and tests.

There are sound and practical reasons why the "use specification" is becoming increasingly popular as a method of defining and measuring quality. As a general rule, it is good purchasing policy to inform the supplier or bidder as fully as possible regarding the specific use for which his product is intended, how it is to be applied, and the performance it is expected to give. There is no compulsion on the buyer to do this, and there are some cases where it might not be desirable to do so, as in the case of special applications developed in the user's company or other confidential or competitive situations. However, these are the exceptional cases, not the general rule. Ordinarily, by enlisting the cooperation of the seller and inviting his suggestions and advice, a more satisfactory purchase can be made. Another point to be considered is that the law places the basic responsibility on the seller that goods must be reasonably adapted to the purpose for which they are sold; if the seller is not advised of this purpose. and if the goods conform to other stated quality requirements, the buyer has no recourse in the event that they do not live up to his expectations in use.

Two warnings should be expressed in this connection. Inviting one or more potential suppliers to prescribe a product or material for a particular purpose does not relieve the purchasing agent of his responsibility of selection and purchase; the judgment and decision are still a part of his function and cannot be delegated to the seller. Nor does this policy condone the purchasing policy often urged by sellers, to select a responsible supplier and leave the problem in his hands. Up to a certain point, the principle expressed in this suggestion has merit, but its acceptance as a complete buying policy is a direct negation of purchasing responsibility.

One further point, of a negative nature, must also be stressed. Quality is *not* measured by price. The assumption that higher price in itself denotes higher quality has been disproved so often and so thoroughly that no thoughtful buyer can proceed on this basis. Examples are legion, in every selling field, that identical material is available at varying prices from different sources, and that if a thorough search is made, higher quality can be procured from some sources at a lower price than is asked for the lower quality offered by others. The old saying that "you get just what you pay for" is a half-truth whose shortcomings have often been demonstrated and learned by the hard and costly method of experience. It can be accepted only with the modifying influence of careful and objective judgment. Under competitive conditions, variations in quality tend to be reflected in varying prices, but this is the broadest sort of generalization.

Suitability, the basic consideration

One of the objectives of purchasing has been defined as buying the right quality. "Right quality" does not necessarily mean the best quality available, however desirable that might be. Purchases are made to meet specific requirements. Quality must therefore be related to the need. In the purchasing vocabulary, "right quality" means the best quality *for a purpose*. That involves both economic and physical considerations.

The measurements of quality previously cited presuppose that, for most materials, a considerable range of quality is available to the buyer, from superior quality at one end of the scale to inferior quality at the other end of the scale, with numerous gradations in between. Which grade is "right"? For intelligent and effective purchasing, it is assumed that the buyer knows, or will learn, the quality required and the qualities available. His task will then be to correlate his information, to compare and select.

It has already been stressed that suitability and adequacy of material for the intended purpose are the basic requisites of quality in a purchasing decision. This is absolute, and substantially reduces the area of choice by eliminating everything that does not measure up to this standard. Thus, the buyer's definition of right quality starts with establishing the *minimum acceptable quality*. He may not actually purchase this minimum-quality material, though in many instances this would be the proper course. Before making that decision, he makes a further study of values. Superior quality may be desirable, although not actually essential. Sometimes he can find such superior quality at no additional cost, or at merely a nominal increase that represents better value received for his expenditure. But real value, too, is value for a purpose. If the buyer pays premium prices for quality in excess of the need, the extra dollars spent are sheer waste. The purchasing responsibility is to procure adequate quality at the lowest cost. The purchasing agent who searches for the less expensive quality of material that will yet be suitable and acceptable for the purpose is still making quality the first consideration. There are some uses for which the lowest and least expensive grades of material will be entirely suitable. In that case, the lowest quality is the right quality, for the concept of value is rooted in utility rather than in intrinsic worth.

On the other hand, there are instances in which the best quality available is none too good. The purchasing agent may seek the most highly refined material or the product manufactured to the most exacting precision stand-ards, if that is what the company needs, and no price may be too high. In-deed, the buyer may be justified in making every effort to induce suppliers to extend the upper quality range and to encourage improvements that would enhance the highest qualities presently available. Many technological ad-vances, such as the science of alloying metals, for example, to increase their resistance to heat, fatigue, and strain, have their impetus from this constant search for superior and special-purpose materials.

Producers and buyers look at the quality scale from different viewpoints. The producer designates some median point as "good," grading other qualities upward through "better" to "best," and downward from his central point through "fair" to "poor." The buyer selects some median point as "satisfac-tory"; anything below that quality level would be "not good enough," and anything above it would be in a "better" classification, grading into "too good" as additional costs outweigh utility for the purpose in hand. To pur-chase materials that are either not good enough or better than necessary represents potential waste.

The decision as to what constitutes the right quality is not altogether a purchasing prerogative. But as a practical matter, on the bulk of requirements for which there are generally accepted commercial standards, it is left for the purchasing agent to decide. He will certainly have a voice in the decision in any case, and his suggestions, if well founded, will carry considerable weight. But functionally, it is a responsibility of the operating branch where materials and supplies are to be used to define, or at least to approve, the minimum acceptable quality standards. From that point on, the selection of products meeting these established standards, from whatever source, is the responsibility of purchasing, and it is important that the quality standards adopted permit the purchasing agent the greatest possible flexibility of selection and procure-ment.

Availability, the practical requirement

If it is true that the purchase of unsuitable materials is useless, it is equally true that the specification of theoretically right qualities is futile unless the specified items are available. No purpose at all is served unless and until the goods are bought and delivered. This is a practical consideration that may modify the decision as to the right quality to be purchased.

Availability does not mean merely that a desired material can somewhere, somehow, be found and purchased, or that a desired product is capable of being manufactured. The practical definition of availability requires that an item be readily and economically procurable, in sufficient quantity to serve continuing needs, within a reasonable purchasing lead time, and preferably from alternative sources. Where such conditions are not present, the "rightness" of quality specification or selection is open to serious question. In such a case, good purchasing practice dictates that an effort should be made, with the approval of specifying and manufacturing departments, to bring the requirement into line with the facts of availability.

Sometimes this can be accomplished very simply by finding a standard product that is suitable and adequate for the purpose, in place of one that is specially designed or is procurable from only one source or may require special facilities for its manufacture. In purchasing, commercial standards are practically synonymous with product availability. Obviously, this easy answer does not apply to all items; but, in any case, the specification should be reviewed to see that a product is made of standard materials and that it can be produced or fabricated with ordinary facilities.

Availability can be improved by developing new and more convenient sources. There are many instances where large companies have encouraged potential vendors to enter new fields, install new equipment, or expand existing facilities, so as to become suppliers of needed items. This is done by giving the vendor the assurance of reasonably long-term contracts, by financing the purchase of new equipment or otherwise subsidizing production costs in the early stages, and by providing technical assistance if needed.

Availability is both a current and a long-range factor. Purchasing departments of large equipment manufacturers, for example, regularly carry on research as to the future availability of copper, aluminum, steel, and other materials that are vital to their own production plans, just as producers try to foresee future markets. Buyers project their estimated needs for these essential materials ten years or more in advance, and correlate these figures with forecasts of primary producing capacity over the same period and the percentage of such output that they may reasonably expect to be able to procure. By this means they can anticipate future difficulties in availability before the situation becomes critical and can adjust their own planning accordingly. (See Chapter 13.)

Cost, the economic aspect

Beyond the considerations of suitability and availability, without which no satisfactory purchase can be made, there is a third important factor in determining right quality—the factor of value. Cost of materials is a basic element of product cost and, because of this, it helps determine the competitive position of the company as a seller and the net profits that accrue after the product is sold. To keep this cost at a minimum is the direct responsibility of purchasing.

The right quality to buy, then, is the quality that satisfies the requirements already mentioned, and that does so at the lowest cost consistent with these requirements of suitability and service. The definition of desired quality largely determines the purchase cost, both because of the intrinsic costs of materials and manufacture involved, and because competition among suppliers tends to set a fairly uniform market price level. The buyer's first duty, then, is to explore the market to find the most favorable price at which the desired item is offered. He will seek suppliers who are efficient producers, whose costs are correspondingly favorable. And he will invite competition among suppliers so as to reap the advantage of this factor also.

A thorough job of quality selection and purchasing, however, is not quite so simple as that. Cost is not measured by price alone, even after the cost of purchasing, transportation, and receiving have been added. Ultimate cost, the significant factor, includes the cost of operations involved in utilizing or converting the purchased product and must be measured in terms of end results. The cost of paint, for example, is not merely the price per gallon; ultimate cost depends also upon the labor required to apply it and the square feet of surface coverage it provides. An expensive paint that is easily applied and gives good coverage is more economical than a cheaper paint that takes longer to apply and may require an extra coat to give the desired result. Similarly, a material having qualities of workability that save man-hours and machine-hours in fabricating operations, or having superior surface qualities that eliminate a finishing operation, may cost more per pound but actually represents lower cost, greater value, than a cheaper material that may otherwise be adequate but does not have these special properties. The balancing of all these costs is a necessary step in determining the right quality to buy.

Responsibility for defining quality

Quality must be defined for every commodity or product to be purchased, and it is expressed in such a way that:

(a) The purchasing department knows just what is required.

(b) The purchase order or contract is made out with a proper description of what is wanted.

(c) The supplier is fully informed of the buyer's quality requirements.

(d) Suitable means of inspecting and testing can be applied to see that delivered goods meet the stated standards of quality.

(e) Goods delivered in conformance with the quality definition will be acceptable to the buyer's company.

The quality definition may be very simple or very complex, according to the item concerned, and, as previously noted, it may be expressed in a number of different ways. It must be sufficiently specific to provide an accurate and adequate ordering description, which becomes a matter of record in the purchasing department, usually on the purchase record card for each item regularly purchased, as a direct reference in the issuing of purchase orders. In some systems, commodities and parts are identified by a numerical code, but this is basically a reference to the quality definition itself.

Responsibility for the factor of suitability in the quality definition rests ultimately with the departments responsible for product quality and performance and for using the purchased items. This part of the definition should be restricted to minimum essential quality requirements, leaving the greatest possible latitude for considerations of availability and value in purchasing without sacrificing the necessary suitability. If, for any purchasing reasons, it seems desirable to modify the basic definition of quality, this is done only with the approval of design and using departments. In the preparation of formal specifications, even though they are primarily of a technical nature, the best practice is to approach the matter as a joint project of technical, manufacturing, and purchasing personnel, so that all phases of quality, use, and procurement may be considered from the start and full agreement reached.

Purchasing by brand name

The simplest method of defining quality, although not always the most satisfactory, is to identify a material or product by the manufacturer's own brand name. This identification is an inclusive designation of quality, including the supplier's implied warranty that certain standards of quality and product performance will be maintained, and a reasonable assurance of uniformity in composition and workmanship. From the purchasing viewpoint, this method has the advantages of simplicity in ordering, normally well-organized distribution and, consequently, ready availability, and the fact that elaborate inspection and tests can often be eliminated, because the delivery of the specified brand fulfills the obligation of the contract and it may be assumed that the quality implications that are inherent in the brand name have been observed. It has the serious disadvantage of limiting procurement to a single supplier and thus eliminating the competitive element except insofar as competition may exist in the distribution of the product.

The effectiveness of this method, of course, depends entirely on the integrity of the supplier and what his brand name stands for. In this connection it should be noted that a manufacturer's brand name, where the details of production control are directly under his own supervision, is a more reliable standard than a distributor's or "label" brand, for which the actual production may be in any one of several supplier plants and production control one step removed. The distributor's intentions may be the best, but he is not always in a position to make them effective. This and similar considerations should be given the closest attention in determining the extent to which reliance can be placed on a trade-name designation.

Incidentally, the acceptance of trade names by executives and operatives in the using departments, whether on the basis of hearsay, prejudice, or favorable experience, is a potent force for satisfactory interdepartmental relations and better utilization of materials. Operators, whether by accident or design, seem to do better work and get better results when working with materials in which they have confidence, and consumer acceptance of a finished product may be enhanced by the use of known components. This, of course, is a situation subject to many abuses, and to accept it unquestioningly as a determining reason for the selection of particular products and materials is a negation of good procurement and the purchasing function.

The greatest shortcoming of purchase by brand name is its restriction on the buyer's selection of supply sources and the elimination of competition. This is sometimes unavoidable, as in the case of patent and license monopolies, or in the purchase of repair and replacement parts or accessories for equipment, which it is generally advisable to purchase from the original manufacturer. But most items, and most types of materials and equipment, are available in comparable quality from competitive sources or are in competition with adequate alternative items. This is, in fact, one of the principal reasons for having a special purchasing department: to discover or develop such alternate sources of supply.

One further point for the purchasing agent to bear in mind is that, because brand or trade names do represent specific compositions or qualities, competition can be enhanced and substantial savings frequently effected through a knowledge of what the trade name stands for. Cleaning compounds of comparatively simple chemical formula with no increased utility value command premium prices by virtue of their packaging and sale under brand designations, and purchasing can be far more efficient if chemical terms are used.

When it is desirable, for convenience or any other reason, to use a brand or trade name as the descriptive term or definition for a company requirement, prudent purchasing practice overcomes this restrictive factor by adding the phrase "or equal." On the initial requisition for a material or product that has not previously been used or purchased by the company, design or production men may be aware of a particular branded product known to be suitable for the purpose, and they naturally specify that brand as the product wanted.

Lacking time for market search, analysis of products, and the development of a more definitive product description, it is incumbent on the purchasing agent—and is good purchasing practice as well—to order the stipulated brand. But there is no assurance that this is the only suitable material, or even the most suitable. It immediately becomes the purchasing agent's responsibility to seek possible alternatives. "Or equal" is his authorization to undertake this responsibility.

Purchasing by sample

The actual description or definition of quality is sometimes avoided by inviting prospective suppliers to match a sample submitted by the buyer. This may be the simplest method of indicating what is wanted, and sometimes, as a result, it is the lazy buyer's method. Unfortunately, the apparent saving of effort in the first instance may be more than offset by the necessity of detailed inspection and test to determine that the delivery actually does match the sample. Furthermore, no definite standards are set for the record or for future purchasers.

The practice is justified under certain conditions: in the case of special, nonrepetitive items; or when absolute quality requirements are not a significant factor; or when the size and importance of the purchase do not warrant the effort and expense of formulating a more definitive buying description. It is likewise justified when used in respect to particular aspects of quality, such as color, which is best defined by comparison with a standard sample. It should be noted that grading standards for some commodities, such as cotton, are based on standard samples accurately selected and maintained under government auspices.

It should likewise be noted that a good deal of selling and bidding is done on the basis of samples submitted with the bid. Some purchasing departments, particularly in the governmental buying field, require the submission of samples with bids. However, this is supplementary to, and not in place of, other forms of product description. Having on hand samples of what the bidder proposes to furnish on a contract permits a comparison of qualities and values to be made before placing the order, and later permits a comparison of actual deliveries against the samples submitted.

Formal specifications

There are some items, usually of a technical nature, whose quality cannot be sufficiently defined by any of the preceding methods, so that a more formal and detailed specification is necessary. Most technical standards (as, for example, the standards for composition and properties of the various alloy steels) are compiled in specification form and can be adopted and used in procurement. The same is true in respect to many manufactured items. Standard specifications of this sort are as easy to use as brand names and are more accurately descriptive and subject to analysis and test. Because they are widely accepted as industry standards, they have the same commercial advantages as market grades in that they are a part of the language of their respective industries or trades and represent materials or products that are directly comparable on the basis of equal quality.

However, because standardization has not yet reached universal or national status, and because there are different sets of standards applicable to various items, some cautions should be observed. One point that buyers must watch in purchasing on standard specifications is that some producers will quote on "our equivalent" for the industry standard. This is not necessarily to be interpreted as an indication of inferior quality; it does indicate that there is some deviation from the standard, although there is an implication that the quality is generally comparable and adapted to the same applications. These claims may be entirely justified. The notation corresponds, from the seller's side, to the buyer's own "or equal" qualification. But because the value of buying on specification depends on strict adherence to quality requirements as stated in the terms of the specification, it becomes the buyer's responsibility to determine whether the alternative or variant product offered is in fact acceptable for the intended purpose.

Standard specifications do not cover all materials, nor all requirements. A material of standard composition and properties may have to be bought to special tolerances of dimension or surface finish, and manufactured parts frequently have special features that must be specified in detail, beyond the information that can normally be indicated on a blueprint. For the procurement of such items, a formal specification is prepared in the buyer's own company, for its own individual use.

As previously noted, the writing of a specification is best undertaken as a group project, with representatives of technical, manufacturing, and purchasing departments participating, so that the finished specification will be satisfactory to and in the best interests of all concerned, and in the best interests of the company as a whole. Although these viewpoints may sometimes be in conflict as to the details of a particular specification, they all have the common objective of arriving at the best decision for the company. The work should be done in the spirit of cooperation toward that end, rather than in a spirit of conflicting aims and unwilling compromise. A standing committee on specifications is the approved agency for this purpose. This provides the orderly channel for initiating a specification whenever the need or desirability for such action arises, and also a means of review and revision as needs or circumstances arise. A provision for periodic review of all specifications is wise policy. For, although the specification itself is a very precise document, to be observed strictly in all its details, it should not be permitted to "freeze" quality standards to the detriment of product improvement or to rule out the consideration of new materials or methods. Working together on such a standing committee fosters an understanding and appreciation of all three viewpoints and makes for smoother, more consistent action.

From the purchasing agent's standpoint, a satisfactory specification must:

1. State exactly what is wanted, clearly, definitely, and completely. This is necessary for his own information and guidance in buying, and also for passing along the information to the supplier;

2. Provide the means or basis for testing deliveries for conformance with the specification. Without this check on actual deliveries, the specification loses much of its force as a purchasing tool;

3. Avoid nonessential quality restrictions that add to cost and to the difficulty of procurement without adding to utility and value;

4. Avoid definitions that unnecessarily restrict competition;

5. Conform, so far as possible, to established commercial and industrial standards, and to company standards for other materials in regular use.

As in all purchasing, the consideration of the material or part to be specified should begin with an analysis of the function it is to perform, rather than writing the specification around a particular design or merely describing some predetermined quality. When the quality factors necessary to fulfill the functional need have been determined, they must be stated in such a way as to assure the procurement of the proper quality, yet with sufficient flexibility to permit the application of good purchasing practice in that procurement. The purchasing agent has a major responsibility at this stage in making the specification a practical and effective tool for achieving ultimate value as well as precise suitability.

For example, one of the important purposes for using specifications in buying, beyond defining the material, is to provide a uniform quality standard as a basis for comparing competitive bids. Many specifications, however, are so closely written around a particular product that all competition is effectively excluded. Such specifications, of course, should be avoided if that is in any way possible. Generally it is possible, because for the great majority of industrial requirements there are a variety of products or sources wholly adequate for the purpose, and the restrictive features are frequently nonessential to the intended application even though they may be entirely consonant with it. They have frequently been included, either by accident or by design, because the definition has been approached from the standpoint of describing a product known to be suitable for the purpose rather than describing the basic requirements of the purpose itself. Thus, an engine may be specified with a prescribed number of cubic inches' piston displacement, which might limit the buyer's choice to a single make, whereas a definition in terms of the power to be developed would be inclusive enough to admit this model, as well as several acceptable alternates, without sacrificing any significant measure of desired quality. The definition should, therefore, be rewritten from the viewpoint of the requirement, and all nonessential limiting references should be eliminated. This is also a strong argument for the adoption of existing standard specifications and established commercial grades if these are available and suitable, in preference to setting up a new and special definition, even at the expense of some slight compromise in design.

Specification outline and use

The drafting of the specification should follow a definite pattern or outline. This has a dual advantage. It is a guide for the specification writer or committee, indicating the full range of details that should be included, thus preventing oversights, loopholes, or omissions. It facilitates reference by users of the specification, because certain types of information are consistently found in a particular section or sequence. Such a pattern in common use is as follows:

In the body of the specification, there are separate sections devoted to special areas of information:

A. Reference to applicable standard specifications, if any, which are thus incorporated into the specification and made a part of it without transcribing the actual text. Printed copies of the standard specification may be attached for the sake of completeness and for convenience in reference. The use of standard specifications is recommended, where appropriate to the purpose. They take advantage of the wealth of technical skill embodied in existing standards, save research time and effort required in the formulation of an independent, individual specification, and help keep purchase requirements in line with standard industrial practice.

B. Statement of the various types, grades, classes, and sizes of material covered by the specification. Where a material is used in a variety of forms or dimensional ranges, the repetition of identical quality standards is mere duplication, serving no useful purpose. It is therefore customary to have one specification covering an entire group of items where the same quality standards apply.

C. Statement of the use for which the specified material or equipment is intended. This is not merely a verification of the suitability of the purchased item. It is a guide to usage and a precaution against misapplication of materials.

D. Statement of the kind of materials and workmanship required in a fabricated item covered by the specification, and of any special methods of production or manufacture that are required. Control of quality in a purchased item may involve control of the fabrication or processing as well as of the component raw material.

E. General requirements common to all of the types, grades, and classes of the material covered.

F. Detail requirements peculiar to each type, grade, and class included in the specification.

G. Inspection and test procedure to be used in determining conformance with the specification, including location at which inspection will be made.

H. Instructions as to packaging, labeling, marking of shipments, and so forth.

I. Notes and special instructions to bidders, rules regarding submission of samples with bids, where and how additional copies of the specification may be obtained, and similar information.

Complete files of existing specifications are maintained in the technical, purchasing, and inspection departments; and, in addition, there will probably be copies of some purchase specifications in the hands of suppliers. With this wide dispersion of basic quality information, it is essential that all copies be kept strictly up to date to prevent confusion and errors in ordering and deliveries. Whenever a specification is revised or discontinued, or superseded by a new specification, this should be made clear to everyone concerned. The new specification is identified by number and effective date, with the notation that it supersedes a particular previous one. As an additional precaution, all outstanding copies of the outdated specification should be recalled and destroyed. Therefore, the central specification file, in the purchasing department, should list all persons or departments to whom copies have been issued, and whenever copies are sent out to vendors for bidding or ordering purposes, this fact should be posted to the record.

In addition to these uses, specifications may be distributed to design and requisitioning personnel within the company so as to avoid requests for special, nonspecification items when there are materials covered by specification that are suitable to the purpose.

Alternatives and substitutions

Whenever quality is defined, whether by formal specification or by any of the other methods mentioned, it follows that no deviation from the stated quality definition is permissible on the basis of purchasing judgment alone without approval of the other departments concerned. The practical means of providing the necessary flexibility in procurement have already been noted: defining quality in terms of minimum requirements, so that anything above these minimum properties will satisfy the definition; the inclusion of approved alternative products in the basic identification of quality; the "or equal" provision; and the avoidance of unduly restrictive factors in a formal specification. Despite these precautions, circumstances sometimes arise that make some deviation necessary.

The obvious and extreme case of this is a condition of material shortages that make the specified material or quality unavailable for purchase, or an urgent delivery-time requirement which is less than the necessary lead time or procurement cycle. In such a case, the purchasing agent must find the most feasible alternate or substitute that is available and secure approval as to its suitability for the purpose. Such approval may be limited to the immediate quantity required, and does not necessarily establish a continuing approval for the substitution, although it may be so extended.

A second case is that where a delivered material or product does not conform to specified quality but is close enough to be usable, perhaps with some reworking or other adjustment in the manufacturing process. The inspection department notes the deviation, which would normally make the shipment unacceptable. But if the deviation is not too serious, if rejection would entail any considerable delay in securing a replacement, and it is in the interest of maintaining the good will of the supplier, the purchasing agent will take steps to determine whether the delivered item is usable and suitable and what additional costs or inconvenience will be involved in using it. If this is a practicable solution, he will then negotiate an equitable price adjustment with the supplier to compensate for the inferior quality and value, accepting the goods on this basis. Such action definitely does not set a precedent for compromising or modifying the quality definition on future purchases or shipments.

A third case arises when specifications are sent to potential suppliers with an invitation to bid, and a bidder submits an alternative proposal, offering a product that differs from the one specified but is intended for the same purpose. It is entirely possible that products so offered are suitable and that they may have superior advantages of economy, convenience, or end-product improvement. If they are acceptable to the other departments concerned, the logical step is to establish the non-conforming product as an approved alternate or to revise the original specification. Some companies, indeed, include on their inquiries a statement that they are receptive to alternative suggestions, for this is one of the potent means of improving specifications and buying practice in the light of suppliers' specialized knowledge.

When alternative proposals of this nature are accepted, on items for which bids have been solicited, some questions of purchasing ethics may be involved. First, there is a responsibility to vendors who have conscientiously bid on the exact specification, only to find that the order or contract is to be placed on a different basis. Should the bid invitation be reopened so that all may have an opportunity to bid competitively? At the same time, the originator of the improved suggestion is entitled to practical recognition for his imagination and initiative in the buyer's interest as well as his own, even though the buyer is not bound to commit himself permanently to a single source of supply for the item and good purchasing practice demands that competition be invited. The matter is usually resolved by giving the initial order to the supplier who has earned it by his superior initiative and by giving him preferential consideration, at least, on succeeding orders. His margin of advantage may be narrowed as other suppliers bid on the revised specification, but such initiative should be encouraged. It represents an element of value that is extremely important and is not measurable by the ordinary standards of quality definition and competitive prices.

The search for such opportunities, the scientific determination of right quality in terms of cost reduction through reduction of producers' costs, has given rise to an important purchasing activity known as Value Analysis. Although it questions—and sometimes challenges—existing definitions of required quality, it is not an encroachment upon the authority of the specifying departments, because the recommendations prompted by such analysis are still subject to approval and acceptance by those who are ultimately responsible for setting the standards of quality and suitability. Value analysis simply adds another dimension to the definition of quality.

Formal value analysis is not carried on in all purchasing departments (although the practice is increasing), nor is it equally adaptable to all types of purchases. In departments where it is practiced, it is typically set up as a special activity, with special personnel, directed to special projects, and in many cases it is undertaken as a joint activity with technical and manufacturing departments. In other words, it is an adjunct to, rather than a part of, the regular purchasing process. It is mentioned here briefly because of its concern with and effect on the quality factor. A more detailed description of the principles and methods of value analysis appears in Chapter 15.

6

STANDARDIZATION

MASS-PRODUCTION TECHNIQUES are predicated on the principle of uniformity and interchangeability of materials and parts. To this extent, the vast majority of manufacturing companies are committed to the policy of standardization in their product lines, and this is reflected to some degree in the standardization of their purchase requirements. When this principle is carried one step further, to coordinate these "standard" requirements with the standard product lines and quality grades of supplier industries, additional advantages accrue in the form of quicker availability, alternative sources, and, again, in the economies of mass production by the supplier as compared with the cost of a custom-made item.

These advantages are obviously of primary importance in purchasing. Theoretically, it is possible to determine and define the ideal quality—in terms of composition, dimension, physical and electrical properties, and other attributes of a material or product—for each individual purpose, and this ideal quality could be procured, at substantial cost of money and time. In some special instances, this may be necessary, but in most cases it is both impractical and unnecessary. Industry has found the answer in standardization of materials and products, so that the selection may be made not from an infinite number of possible qualities and sizes, but from a more practicable range, broad enough to meet the majority of requirements satisfactorily, yet sufficiently limited and well established as to acceptance and use to permit mass production and ready availability. Even so, there is a great deal of designing, manufacturing, and purchasing done on the basis of special specification, where reasonable standards could be adopted with no sacrifice of utility or satisfaction and with substantial advantages of economy and convenience.

Good purchasing practice extends the concept of standardization by promoting the consolidation of similar requirements into a single specification, wherever possible. For example, fewer types of cleaning compounds or fewer grades of lubricants than are ordinarily requested for specific applications might adequately serve the plant's maintenance needs. If so, there would be fewer items to buy and carry in stock, and those that are required could be purchased in larger quantities to better advantage. The same principle can be applied to production materials, as, for example, fewer sizes of fasteners, tubing, bar stock, and an endless list of other items.

Before dealing with these matters in detail, it will be well to review the broader aspects of industrial standardization.

Engineering standards

We take it for granted that an electric lamp bulb, regardless of the particular manufacturer, will fit the sockets of our lighting fixtures; that the plug on the appliance cord will fit the standard outlets of our house or factory wiring system; that the freight cars and coaches of any railroad will fit the rails in any part of the country; that fire hose and couplings, called into emergency service in a neighboring community, will be adaptable to the equipment there. Because we have come to accept these things as a matter of course, it is easy to overlook the long and complicated process through which such a situation has been achieved. Standardization is a relatively modern development, and the process is not yet finished.

The public, or buyers', interest in standardization is of direct importance as it affects the further stages of product fabrication. Standardization of screw threads makes possible the use of stock machine screws and bolts in standard tapped holes. Standardization of pipe fittings makes it possible to install plumbing and heating fixtures in existing piping systems, and to alter or expand these as required. The list could be extended to great length, affecting many materials and products in common use in our daily living. It will be noted that in the latter examples cited, the principle of standardization has been extended to design as well as to simple dimension.

Standardization has also been applied to the composition of materials. A typical example of this is the SAE steels, a series of alloys of specified composition and known properties, defined, identified by numbers, and recognized by all buyers and producers of steel. The number of possible varieties of such steels, the nature and proportion of component elements, and the particular properties attained, are almost infinite. Thus, these standards provide a variety competent to serve the great majority of industrial needs within a limited number of items suitable for economical mass production and maximum availability from many sources.

Typically, such standards are developed through the cooperation of producers and users, taking advantage of the experience and technical skill of both groups and coordinating these efforts through various national technical societies or governmental agencies.

Among the agencies that have actively sponsored the development of industrial standards are the American Standards Association, American Society for Testing Materials, Society of Automotive Engineers, American Society of Mechanical Engineers, National Electrical Manufacturers Association, and others. The federal government has also taken an active and effective interest in such projects through the National Bureau of Standards and various procurement agencies. [1]

These organizations have helped to provide, in their respective fields, a large body of technically sound standards covering a wide range of basic requirements and extending into the field of manufactured products, and have incorporated features of safety and adequate performance as well as convenience. With the participation of representative users and the disinterested service of the sponsoring agency, they are of more general applicability and acceptability than standards that are written from the producers' viewpoint alone. They are available for use by all industry, a matter of official record, readily identified by numerical or code systems that are understood by all concerned and are capable of being substantiated by standard test methods.

Government standards

The federal government has contributed to industrial standardization in four ways. As mentioned above, it has placed the services and facilities of the National Bureau of Standards at the disposal of industry, on request, as a coordinating and sponsoring organization for the development of standards. This service is reinforced by the promulgation of such standards and by the sponsorship of a certification plan indicating adherence to standards by manufacturers, which substantially lessens the burden of individual tests.

Second, as a large consumer and buyer of a great variety of products, it has developed standards for its own purchases. These standards originate with the various procurement agencies, principally the Army, the Navy (and a joint board of these two agencies), and the Federal Bureau of Supply.

The formulation and promulgation of government standards is a

---

[1] As an indication of the buyer's concern with standards and standardization, it may be noted that the National Association of Purchasing Agents is one of the member organizations of the American Standards Association, took a leading part in the standardization of oil-field tubular goods, and maintains an active standardization group as a part of its own organization,

responsibility of the Federal Bureau of Supply. The work begins with a technical committee, 72 such committees being maintained to deal with various types of products. Collaborating in the work are all departments and agencies of government which may be interested as users of the item under consideration, as well as representatives of the trades and industries involved, including both engineering and management personnel, in order that the standard may be expected to bring into conformity the use requirements and the productive capabilities of the industry which is to produce the item, in terms of the most practicable and acceptable commercial practice.

An Industry Advisory Council has been established, collaborating with the Standards Division of the Federal Bureau of Supply to bring government standards and procurement practices more closely into line with industrial purchase requirements and prevailing manufacturing practices. The membership of the Council includes representatives of the American Standards Association, the American Society for Testing Materials, the Society of Automotive Engineers, the Manufacturing Chemists Association, the American Society of Mechanical Engineers, and the National Electrical Manufacturers Association, technical experts from a number of leading industrial companies, and, significantly, the General Purchasing Agent of a large manufacturing corporation to represent the industrial purchasing viewpoint.

Intended as an instrument of purchase, governmental standards are expressed in terms of a buying description or specification, known as a Federal Specification, which becomes mandatory for use by all departments and agencies of the government. There are approximately 1,700 of these Federal Specifications in current use.

Although primarily conceived as purchase standards for the use of governmental procurement agencies, the influence of federal standards has been much wider than this original function would indicate. They have been a powerful force in advancing the general principle of standardization in manufacture and availability, as well as in procurement. The government is at all times a considerable factor as a buyer in many market fields, and in wartime a dominant factor. As such, its standards of quality must be observed by manufacturers, and in procurement by government contractors and suppliers, through every stage of fabrication from raw materials to the finished product.

A third major contribution of government to standardization has been the compilation of a directory of all standard specifications, including non-governmental standards, those of the technical societies and of individual large manufacturers, for the benefit of producing industry and purchasing executives. The advantage of knowing what work has been done and what results are available is that duplication of effort is avoided and a multiplicity of similar but not identical standards eliminated. The cause of over-all standardization is thus advanced.

Simplification

A fourth contribution of government is the project of simplification, closely allied to standardization and sponsored by the National Bureau of Standards. Simplification is a commercial and selective process rather than a technical one. Its objective is to reduce the excessive variety of types and sizes of manufactured products by determining which of these are the most important, and by restricting and concentrating production to these items. Over a long period of years, there is a natural tendency toward wide variety in any line: types and sizes that are standard for one or a few users but in little demand outside this restricted outlet; obsolescent or unnecessary items still maintained in producers' catalogs and stock through inertia and to meet occasional demand; and those whose chief reason for existence is to maintain a "complete" line. In the typical industry it will be found that by far the greatest part of the business is done in a relatively small number of these varied types and sizes, and that a considerable part of the rest of the demand could be converted to the more popular numbers with no real sacrifice of utility.

The process of simplification analyzes sales and uses from this standpoint, with a view toward the elimination of unnecessary variety by common consent of the producing industry. Usually it is undertaken through the medium of trade associations representing the bulk of producing capacity and output. When a group of manufacturers, distributors, and users agree to cooperate and concentrate their operations on a definite and relatively small list of variations, simplification becomes simplified practice.

Under the sponsorship of the National Bureau of Standards, nearly 200 specific schedules of simplified practice have been accepted and made effective. The reduction in the number of commercial varieties of the products involved has run from 10 per cent in some cases to as high as 98 per cent in others, without any loss of utility in serving the purposes for which the products were intended. [2] A few typical examples affecting industrial items in wide use may be cited:

---

[2] The reduction of commercial varieties and sizes by 90% or more is startling but by no means exceptional. For example, Simplified Practice Recommendation 81-28, Binders' board, 718 to 10 (98.6%); S.P.R. 157-37, Steel horizontal firebox heating boilers, 2,328 to 38 (98.4%); S.P.R. 64-30, One-pound folding boxes for coffee, 100 to 2 (98%); S.P.R. 7, Rough and smooth-faced brick, 75 to 2 (97%); S.P.R. 120-40, Ice cream brick molds and boxes, 30 to 1 (97%); S.P.R. 15-35, Blackboard slate, 120 to 6 (95%); S.P.R. 74-30, Hospital and institutional cotton textiles, 454 to 26 (94%); S.P.R. 126-41, Set-up paper boxes, 1,084 to 75 (93%); and others.

Coated abrasive products, reduced from 8,000 varieties to 1,755
Box board, reduced from 244 different thicknesses to 96
Welded chain, reduced from 1,831 varieties to 1,214
Steel drums and barrels, reduced from 66 sizes to 26
Files and rasps, reduced from 661 varieties to 377

Some of the more obvious advantages accruing from these programs have been summarized by E. W. Ely, Chief of the Division of Simplified Practice, as follows:

For the manufacturer: Less capital tied up in slow-moving stocks; simplified inspection requirements; longer factory runs with fewer machine changes; less idle equipment; less stock to handle; larger production units; less special machinery; more prompt deliveries; less chance of error in shipment; less obsolescence in material, equipment, and stock.

For the distributor: Increased turnover; eliminating of slow-moving stock; staple lines, easy to buy and quick to sell; greater concentration of sales efforts on fewer items; less capital invested in new stocks and repair parts; less storage space required; decreased overhead and handling charges.

For the consumer: Better values than otherwise possible; better service in delivery and repairs; fewer items to be carried in inventory.

Standardization cuts product costs

Standardization, then, can be a potent tool of purchasing. An adopted standard is essentially a definition of quality which becomes the purchasing agent's ordering description for the item. A standardization project or program must be effected through those in the company organization who design the product, thereby creating the need for specific materials and parts, and those who requisition and specify materials and supplies for plant use. The initiative and pressure for standardization, however, may logically come from the purchasing department, which has the responsibility for economical procurement and is in the strategic position of being a clearinghouse for the requirements of all departments, so that variations in usage and specification among various departments can be most readily detected here.

The most convincing argument for specifying and purchasing standard products, rather than those which are items of special manufacture, is the factor of cost. A survey of representative manufacturers of industrial products reveals the following significant cost comparisons: 23 per cent of the manufacturers estimate that special items cost from 10 to 15 per cent more to produce than comparable standard items; 47 per cent estimate the additional cost at from 25 to 50 per cent; 17 per cent estimate that the extra cost runs even higher than 50 per cent. Only 12 per cent report that no substantial extra cost is involved.[3] The type of product and the supplier's facilities and organization for handling special work naturally influence these calculations, but the general conclusion is clear that deviations from standards mean higher costs and less value received for the purchaser's dollar. This is confirmed by value-analysis studies that show many instances where simply switching from a specially fabricated part to a standard part of equal utility results in cost savings of as much as 75 per cent.[4]

Along with this cost advantage is the factor of greater availability and more prompt delivery. Standard items are normally "shelf items" which can be promptly furnished from manufacturers' or distributors' stocks, or which have a regular place in the supplier's production schedule so that delays are minimized. Special items, on the other hand, must be fitted into the production schedule, often involving a delay of weeks or months. Thus, the normal procurement cycle or lead time is lengthened by the addition of scheduling procedure and the actual production cycle. Procurement of emergency fill-in quantities becomes excessively difficult, if not impossible.

In the survey previously referred to, 300 purchasing departments reported their experience with respect to their requirements of ten common items. They showed practically unanimous agreement (93 per cent) that deliveries of standard items were appreciably faster than deliveries of special items. In six of the ten product groups, more than 90 per cent of the special orders presented serious difficulties in securing delivery as needed; at the same time, among companies using only standard items, similar difficulty in securing delivery was relatively negligible.

Standardization cuts inventory costs

One of the chief benefits of standardization is the possibility of reduced material and supply inventories. With fewer types and sizes and qualities of items to be carried in stock, a smaller total inventory can support the manufacturing program. The prudent quantitative safety margin on a single item protects requirements for all of its various uses or applications. There is greater flexibility in meeting the demands of changing rates in the usage of any given item, and the danger of incurring losses through obsolescence is minimized. Reduced total inventories release working capital for other, more productive purposes. This is a constant objective of management.

At the same time, stock turnover is faster, so that there is less accrued carrying cost to add to the real cost of material up to the time of use.

---

[3] "Specify Standard Types and Sizes," *Purchasing Magazine,* May, 1942, p. 62.

[4] "How to Get the Most from Value Analysis," *Purchasing Magazine,* May 6, 1963, p. 41.

Along with these considerations, there is the obvious corollary that smaller physical inventories require less space and storage facilities, and fewer storeroom personnel, and that fewer items in stock means fewer stores records to maintain.

Organizing a standardization program

An effective company standardization program depends upon definite assignment of responsibility and continuing attention to the subject. In some companies it is set up as a function in itself, under the supervision of a standards engineer or of a director of standards. More common practice is to undertake standardization as a committee activity. This is perhaps the more logical procedure, because standardization is essentially a process of securing agreement among those responsible for specification and use of materials, those responsible for product design, and those charged with the procurement of the needed items. All of these factors should be represented in any form of permanent committee organization, with provision for participation on particular projects by individuals or department heads directly affected.

Purchasing department representation on a company standardization committee is essential, not only because purchasing is deeply concerned with promoting materials standards for company use and procurement, but because of the specific contributions that purchasing can make to the over-all project. As already noted, the purchasing department is in the unique position of dealing with the material needs and requests from all departments and is thus more likely to be aware of variations in usage and opportunities to reconcile such variations in an acceptable standard. Also, its familiarity with commercial standards, gained from day-to-day dealings with vendors, and its knowledge of the additional costs entailed by the use of nonstandard items, are prime data in any consideration of this sort. As a matter of fact, where no standardization committee has previously existed, the purchasing department frequently is the one to initiate such an activity; often as not, the purchasing representative serves as its chairman. The representative is usually an assistant purchasing agent or senior buyer, selected for his qualifications as a coordinator and given time to devote to standardization work.

One of the first objectives of the program is to establish standard nomenclature for all materials used. Analysis of stockroom inventories often reveals instances of duplication where identical items may be carried under two or more identifying descriptions. This can easily happen when an item is requisitioned by and purchased for different departments, each of which uses its own term to describe the item; or if a part is identified by the manufacturer's part or catalog number, or by the company's own part number for a particular end use in product assembly, it is often the case that two or more such parts are actually identical and interchangeable, although they may be independently requisitioned, purchased, and recorded. Effective standardization of materials cannot be achieved without standard means of identification.

Analysis of stockroom records reveals other pertinent information: excessively slow-moving items and materials carried in a multiplicity of sizes and grades. Data of this sort can be the starting point for study regarding the feasibility of standardization in particular areas. Another starting point may be found in purchase records. All materials do not pass through a central stockroom and do not appear on stores records. But in the usual organization of a purchasing staff by commodity groupings, related items are generally handled by one buyer, and it is usually a simple matter to detect similar products used by several departments, excessive varieties of a single basic product purchased, and deviations from normal usage.

Aims of a standardization program are: (1) adoption of company-wide standards for materials used for like or similar purposes; (2) correlation of these company standards with established industry standards to the greatest possible degree; (3) reduction in the number of varieties and sizes to be purchased.

Using a standard stock catalog

The work of a standardization committee generally results in decisions as to what materials and supplies are to be carried in stores as standard stock items. This information is frequently incorporated in a standard stock list or catalog, usually a mimeographed list showing all stock items, identified by standard nomenclature with whatever cross-reference may be required, and detailing all sizes of each item regularly carried in stores. Requisitions are expected to conform to this list, and users can expect immediate supply of listed items. The list is revised as new items are added by action of the committee, or as standards are changed in view of changing requirements and usage. On common supply items, requests for nonlisted varieties are automatically questioned and are procurable only under exceptional circumstances, for good reason.

The standard stock catalog is also used by designing and drafting personnel as the means of conforming so far as possible with sizes and varieties already stocked, rather than specifying new requirements. In this case, the standard stock catalog is not necessarily restrictive, tending to hamper the creative skill and technical judgment of the designing engineer, but is intended rather as a guide, setting up a warning signal against unnecessary diversification of requirements. The burden of proof as to the essentiality of a new specification is upon the one who deviates from the established standard.

It should be emphasized that standards should never be static, freezing existing practice and placing a bar in the way of progress. They should always be subject to revision and improvement, in tune with changing conditions and technological advancement. One of the principal functions of a standardization committee is the continuous review of company standards to the end that they may at all times be a sound tool for best operating practice and most economical procurement.

7

QUALITY CONTROL—INSPECTION

INSPECTION OF DELIVERIES, including the application of appropriate tests in some cases, is essential to insure that the quality of the delivery is in conformance with the order and as represented by the supplier. This does not imply any lack of confidence in the supplier, but is a prudent routine precaution on the buyer's part. One of the basic reasons is to assure that no improper materials go into the production process. It is likewise a check on purchasing, for the responsibility for procuring material of proper quality cannot be lightly delegated or taken for granted. The most accurate and painstaking attention to the specification of quality factors in purchasing is wasted unless there is a positive check on the quality that is actually received. Consequently, a provision for inspection and testing is included in standards and specifications, and provision for inspection and tests is also made in the routine of receiving deliveries. The very fact that inspection is indicated tends to make the vendor more careful to see that goods of proper quality are delivered.

Inspection—where and when

The manner of inspection—when and where it is to be done, and how simply or elaborately—depends largely on the type of product or material under consideration and on its importance to the buyer. Inspection is an expense to the account of the buyer, and it is obviously unsound to incur an expense of this sort out of proportion to the value and significance of the purchased material. But when the quality and salability of the end product are involved, when manufacturing efficiency is likely to be affected, or when large amounts of labor are to be expended on the material in the process of fabrication; when other component materials are to be used in connection with it so that material expense is multiplied; when personal safety of workers is at stake; or when purchase value is dependent on certain analyses, it is equally obvious that careless or inadequate inspection is just as inexcusable. Some purchases will warrant complete tests of the entire delivery; in other cases, representative sampling will be sufficient. As a general rule, any purchase important enough to warrant the preparation of a formal specification will call for inspection and test, to an extent and in a manner defined in the specification itself.

Sometimes inspection is made at the manufacturer's plant, before shipment. This has the advantage of eliminating freight charges for return and reshipment in the event of rejection, and is consequently adapted to purchases in which transportation costs are a considerable factor, such as heavy products and those procured from distant plants. The procedure is likewise indicated when shipments are to be made direct to a distant location, as for export, where the return of rejected merchandise for adjustment is impracticable, or where inspection at destination is too late to do any good as far as receipt of satisfactory and usable deliveries is concerned. To generalize, this policy is the logical one whenever the possibility of commercial adjustments is not adequate and where initial shipments of assured quality are essential. The military services consistently inspect products at manufacturers' plants prior to shipment.

Inspection at the source involves the cost of training and maintaining a staff of capable field inspectors. It also entails the delegation of authority to such inspectors for decisions as to the acceptability of product, because the system becomes excessively slow and cumbersome if reference must be made to the home office whenever a question or doubt arises.

Typically, quality inspections are made at the buyer's plant on receipt of materials, on the basis of representative samples from each shipment. Standard methods are prescribed for securing a representative sample of such nonhomogeneous materials as coal for fair analysis. On unit items, this of course presents no serious problem. Bulk materials, such as those received in tank car deliveries, are generally tested before unloading. Other materials are received, and if sampling and tests are required before acceptance, they are segregated pending the completion of these tests to avoid the possibility of their going into general stock or even into use before the proper inspection has been made.

On some items the entire lot is tested, but these are in the nature of special cases. Large castings would generally be included in such a category, and parts where extreme precision is essential. Safety rubber gloves for use in connection with high voltages would be subjected to individual dielectric tests before acceptance—and where such equipment is in common use, the same procedure would probably be followed after each use, before the equipment is reissued.

Considerable use is made of independent commercial testing laboratories and services, usually by agreement between the buyer and the supplier. Such establishments have the advantage of excellent facilities for a wide variety of tests—physical, mechanical, chemical, X-ray, electrical, optical, photometric, and the like, adapted to all sorts of materials and products—and their impartial findings are accepted as final.

It should also be noted at this point that there is increasing use of a manufacturer's certification of quality to obviate the duplication involved in acceptance testing after careful tests have been made in the production process itself. Where such certification can be relied on, this phase of procurement is greatly simplified. A specific guarantee of this sort technically places the responsibility on the seller. It has been developed to the point where some steel producers, for example, furnish an individual analysis and heat-treating specification with each shipment made from a given heat of steel. Certification also has some more general aspects, such as the certificate of the Underwriters' Laboratories as to the safety and electrical properties of certain products and equipment. The function of acceptance testing should not be confused, however, with the subject of manufacturers' guarantees, which form the basis for arbitration or legal action in the case of product failure.

Latent defects, which are not detectable by ordinary testing methods, are also a special subject.

Responsibility for inspection

In larger organizations, where the volume of such work is greater and where a higher degree of functional organization usually obtains, the tendency is to regard inspection as a wholly separate function, independent of purchasing, receiving, stores, production, and other technical departments.

For routine inspections of quality, where a simple visual inspection or reliance on package labels is sufficient, the responsibility is generally in the receiving or stores department, which may or may not be under purchasing supervision. It is coupled with the routine receiving responsibility of inspection for quantity delivered.

Where actual tests are to be made, a more technical type of personnel is required than would ordinarily be found in receiving or stores work. If technical or laboratory departments are maintained in the company, both personnel and equipment for inspection and test are likely to be found there, and it is logical to assign the actual testing operation to such a department. In the absence of specialized facilities of this nature, technical personnel of the using department—usually those who have set the standards and agreed to the purchase specification—can logically be called upon to make the inspection to determine whether deliveries are in conformance with those standards. Or, as noted above, the responsibility may be placed in the purchasing department. In considering any of these arrangements, it should be remembered that inspection is merely the measurement of quality; it does not involve the decision as to acceptance, rejection, or adjustment, but provides the basis on which that decision will be made. The manner and flow of reports leading to that decision are discussed in a later section.

When inspectors are assigned to a supplier's plant, with responsibility and authority for making such decisions, a closely coordinated organization is required. The function is distinctly a part of the procurement process, and the inspector is generally a part of the purchasing department. But because he must be intimately familiar with technical and use requirements, it frequently happens that he is assigned to the purchasing department from a technical, engineering, or manufacturing department for this special purpose.

When outside laboratory service is employed for acceptance testing, it is the usual practice for such arrangements to be made by and for the account of the purchasing department. Inspection is a purchasing expense, and reports are made to the purchasing officer, on the basis of the purchase specification.

Inspection procedure

To correlate the inspection procedure with normal receiving routine, the first step is to determine what deliveries will be subject to test beyond the mere identification of merchandise. This is done at the time the order is placed, and generally follows an established policy in respect to certain materials, including those covered by formal specification.

However this responsibility may be assigned, the testing department receives a notification of expected shipments by means of a carbon copy of the purchase order.

When the shipment arrives, the testing department is promptly notified by the receiving department. Ordinarily the goods are received, identified by purchase order number, and checked for quantity, then segregated pending inspection before being placed into general stores available for issue and use. In many cases, the actual taking of a sample for test purposes is also done by the receiving department in accordance with established regulations, and the properly identified sample is delivered to the testing department. In the case of tank cars and other shipments of bulk material which is to be tested before unloading into the company's tanks or bins, the official receipt of the shipment may be delayed until the sample has been taken and the test made.

Mr. _____

Copy to _____   **Notice of Arrangement for Trial**   No. _____

Copy to _____   **of Material or Equipment**   Date _____

Copy to Stores Dept.   Subject _____

Copy to Purchasing Dept.   _____

We have authorized _____

to send us for purpose of   Laboratory Test   the following material _____
                            Factory Test

_____

_____

Proposed Use _____

_____

    (is   )
This (is not) covered by an order.   Order No. _____ Date _____
You will be notified when material is received.
Please arrange to test this material as indicated above and furnish report of results.

                        Signed _____

RECORD OF RESULTS

Please answer the following for complete history of test for future reference:

I. Where was material tried _____

_____

                                    (Better _____

II. How does material compare with material now standard (As good as _____

                                    (Not acceptable _____

III. If in your opinion product is better, give reason _____

_____

_____

IV. Would you like more of this product for further trial? _____ How much _____

V. If product is as good as, but no better than product we are now using, would you object to a change,
    if there is a price advantage ? Yes_____
                                    :No _____

If answer is Yes, state reason _____

_____

_____

VI. If product is not acceptable, state reason _____

_____

VII. Remarks _____

_____

_____

                        Signed _____

    Analysis slips, sieve test reports or any memoranda that has bearing on results of test, should be
attached to Purchasing Dept. copy.

    Keep duplicate for your file, send original to Purchasing Dept.

Fig. 7-1. Report on a Test of New Material.

It is of the utmost importance that tests be made as promptly and as expeditiously as possible, consistent with the character of the particular test procedure. A maximum time limit of 48 hours after receipt of the goods may be set for the completion of this work, and it is not unusual to set a 24-hour schedule as preferred practice. There are sound practical reasons for this: avoiding demurrage charges, conserving storage space, making materials available for use, and permitting prompt entry to stock or inventory records so as to keep material records up to date. From the purchasing standpoint, it is necessary to clear the record promptly in order to maintain the purchasing schedule, for, if the delivery is not acceptable, it will be necessary to replace the purchase on a shorter procurement cycle than normal, and early information affords a correspondingly longer time for the placement of the second order with the expectation of receiving the goods in time to meet the scheduled requirement. It is also desirable as helping to facilitate the passing of the invoice for payment and the taking advantage of cash discounts.

There is also a legal consideration in that rejection for deficient quality must be made within a "reasonable" time, and the interpretation of the courts has been that the responsibility for inspection devolves upon the purchaser as soon as the goods come into his possession. Consequently, any considerable delay in making the necessary tests may result in forfeiting the privilege of rejection or adjustment. (This does not apply to latent defects that are not discoverable until a certain amount of work, in fabrication or use, has been expended on a product. Where such conditions are likely to be encountered, special provision may be made in the contract to permit an equitable adjustment, or trade customs covering the situation may prevail. Many technical developments have been made in recent years, such as X-ray inspection of large castings, to keep such problems at a minimum.)

When the test has been completed, a test report is prepared showing the results and containing any comment or recommendations that may be indicated, with the reasons therefor. Sometimes this report is made in a space provided for the purpose on the testing department's copy of the purchase order. More typically, it is made on a special report form. The original copy of the report, attached to the purchase order copy, is forwarded to the purchasing department, a duplicate being retained in the testing department's files.

If the test report is favorable, and delivered goods are found to be satisfactory, no difficulty is raised, of course. The goods are immediately released to stores or to the using department. The purchasing department signifies acceptance by attaching the inspection report to the invoice along with the receiving report which vouches for the quantity delivered, and the vendor's invoice is approved for payment.

On the other hand, if goods delivered on an order fail to meet the specifications set forth in the order, the vendor has not fulfilled his part of the agreement and there is cause for rejection. The engineering, production, or testing department of the buyer's company is wholly within its province in refusing to certify the use of such goods, and outright rejection of the shipment may be clearly indicated. This is the simplest case, and the ordinary terms of sales transactions make provision for handling the situation. There are many instances, however, where the situation is not so clean-cut—cases of borderline quality where the goods are usable although substandard, differences of interpretation and of test conditions, errors or omissions in the original statement of requirements, and the like. Under these circumstances, the problem is a matter of vendor relationships as well as of technical compliance.

For these reasons, and in accordance with the principle that vendor contacts are a function of the purchasing department, the test report is not made directly or arbitrarily to the vendor as a rejection, but is essentially a report to the purchasing department, whose performance on a particular procurement has failed to satisfy its responsibility to the specifying or using department. It then becomes a matter for commercial adjustment between the purchasing department, which placed the order, and the vendor. The test report is the evidence upon which the purchasing department undertakes the adjustment.

Science of quality control

The term "quality control," which has been used in this discussion in a broad descriptive sense, has acquired new and special significance with the development in recent years of scientific sampling and inspection methods and their application not only to the measurement of product quality and precision, but also to the control of quality in manufacturing operations. This function is now widely recognized in management organization for production, much valuable technical literature on the subject has been developed, and there is an active professional association in the field— The Society for Quality Control.

Among the accomplishments of this new science are: the determination of sample lot sizes for accurate measurement of conformance to quality standards to specified degrees, thus reducing the amount of unit inspection required and in many cases eliminating the need for 100 per cent inspection; measurement of the range and distribution frequency of deviation from standards, within and beyond acceptable tolerances; analysis of this information for correction and control of manufacturing processes; and development of graphic methods for presenting the information.

The charts shown in Figure 7-2, with accompanying interpretations, illustrate a few of the infinite number of variations in quality distribution frequency that may be disclosed by such inspection. It is obvious that such information regarding product quality is valuable to the purchaser or user as well as to the manufacturer. The following are specific advantages of

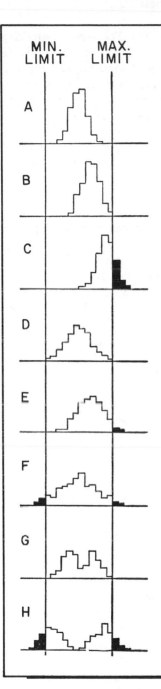

MIN. LIMIT   MAX. LIMIT

A — Product range substantially less than specified and distribution is well centered. Consider using smaller sample on subsequent lots.

B — Product range substantially less than specified but distribution is off-center. Production of defects imminent.

C — Product range substantially less than specified but distribution is badly off-center, producing defects above max. limit. Vendor can meet tolerance and eliminate defects by centering the distribution.

D — Product range approximately same as specified and distribution is well centered. Slight shift off-center will produce defects at one limit. Vendor may require increased tolerance.

E — Product range approximately same as specified but distribution if off-center producing defects above max. limit. Vendor must reduce product range through change in process or by better control and distribution must also be centered. May require increased tolerance.

F — Distribution is well centered but exceeds specified range and defects are occurring at both limits. Change in process or better control required to reduce range. Vendor may require increased tolerance.

G — Double distribution suggests possibility of two sets of tools, change in process or material during running of this lot. Vendor can easily hold tolerance since range of either distribution is smaller than specified.

H — Same as G except that the two centers are far enough apart to cause defects outside both limits. No increase in tolerance needed. Condition should be easily corrected.

Fig. 7-2. Graphic Presentation of a Quality Distribution Frequency.

quality control methods in relation to purchasing. (1) The vendor practicing scientific quality control may generally be accepted as the more reliable and desirable bidder. (2) Quality control methods of sampling and test can be (and frequently are) effectively applied to incoming inspection of deliveries. (3) The practice of some vendors of sending a copy of the quality test report with each shipment gives an accurate picture of the quality of the parts delivered and largely eliminates the need for elaborate inspection by the purchaser; it is similar to, and much more precise than, the form of certification issued by vendors asserting that products conform to established standards.

Acceptance or rejection

It is probably academic to argue the point of where the technical responsibility for acceptance or rejection of a delivery lies. But it is important to bear in mind these two distinct stages of responsibility—the obligation of the purchasing department to procure materials of the right quality, and the obligation of the vendor to deliver in accordance with the order. It is a basic purpose of inspection and testing to confirm or certify the action of the purchasing department, and to guide the buyer in his decision as to whether the contract requirements have been satisfactorily met in the delivery. The buyer will naturally rely on these findings as an integral part of the procurement process. Certainly any prudent purchasing officer will always consult with technical and using departments in the event of any substantial deviation from specified quality before making a decision as to the disposition of the goods.

Several alternative methods of procedure are open to the buyer in respect to substandard deliveries. These include:

1. *Outright rejection.* The goods are returned to the supplier, at the latter's expense, on a shipping order and invoice issued at the direction of the purchasing department. The supplier is notified of this action and of the reasons therefor. It should also be made clear at this point whether the original purchase order is considered as still in force and unfulfilled, or whether the transaction is terminated through default of the supplier. When dealing with well-established sources of supply, the first of these alternatives is generally used, but the invoice for returned merchandise should nevertheless be issued as a means of keeping the accounts in order, especially because vendors' invoices refer to specific shipments, identified by case numbers, packing slips, and other shipping documents.

2. *Return for replacement.* This procedure applies particularly to fabricated parts, but it can be used for materials as well. Accounting procedure

is customarily handled through a memorandum invoice or credit memo pending receipt of the corrected or satisfactory delivery.

3. *Technical or engineering adjustment.* It is frequently practicable for a qualified representative of the vendor to come to the buyer's plant to make necessary adjustments on faulty equipment or to assist in working out a satisfactory application of materials that do not perform in accordance with the buyer's expectations and understanding. Because the objective of the purchase is to achieve certain desired results, and the objective of the seller is to deliver materials and equipment adapted to the buyer's need, this may be the most forthright and satisfactory solution for both parties. It may be the means of saving additional transportation costs and of avoiding the loss of time involved in a new procurement. If the supplier is promptly notified of the need for such additional service before goods can be finally accepted, it does not prejudice the buyer's privilege of rejecting the delivery for cause, and it serves to cement rather than to strain the relationship between buyer and supplier.

4. *Price adjustment.* If goods are usable, although not strictly in accordance with the purchase specification, a price renegotiation in line with the value actually delivered may be the simplest and most satisfactory means of adjustment, although it does not actually correct the condition of a faulty delivery. It should be noted that repeated instances of this nature, regardless of the vendor's willingness to make the adjustment, are indicators of an unsatisfactory and incompetent source of supply.

Whatever method of adjustment is decided on, two principles should be consistently observed. The vendor must be promptly notified that a delivery is unsatisfactory, and for what reason; and the negotiation or adjustment should be carried on by or through the purchasing department. This latter point is not merely a matter of prerogative, although it is in accord with the principle previously stated that all dealings with vendors are within the province of this department. It is primarily a functional responsibility, because the procurement is not complete until a satisfactory delivery has been made and accepted. The contractual relationship has been effected through purchasing, and the personal contacts, both with the vendor and within the buyer's own organization, to aid in effecting a proper adjustment or settlement are generally centered in the buyer who placed the original order. Furthermore, it is essential to the accuracy of purchasing department records in respect to the individual requirement and order, and in respect to experience with individual vendors, that this department retain its responsibility until the purchasing assignment in any particular transaction is completed. This is the only way in which a purchasing program can be consummated and proper controls be established.

8

BUYING THE RIGHT QUANTITY

THE SECOND DECISION a buyer must make, after determining the right quality to buy, is how much to buy. The need for materials has a quantitative, as well as a qualitative, factor. When a requisition or request to purchase comes to the purchasing department, it generally specifies not only the item that is needed, but the quantity needed as well. However, except in the case of custom types of manufacture, or materials to be purchased for a particular project, or special, nonrepetitive requirements, this statement of quantitative need is by no means a complete answer to the buyer's problem. Purchasing can be done on the basis of immediate need or on individual requisitions, but for the great bulk of industrial purchases this is a cumbersome and uneconomical policy.

Most material and supply requirements for a manufacturing operation are continuing requirements, and the cumulative or total need is a far better guide to effective purchasing than the day-to-day needs. Most requirements can be forecast well in advance with a high degree of accuracy on the basis of sales quotas, bills of material for the end product, projected plant operating schedules, and records of past experience in respect to rates of use. But even if a whole year's needs could be anticipated by such means, it would obviously be impracticable, as well as unnecessary, to purchase the total quantity at one time (although it is sometimes advisable to cover the total need by contract). It is the purchasing agent's responsibility to have sufficient quantities on hand as needed. Purchase quantities therefore must maintain a balance with operating needs and with the advantages of volume buying, aided by the cushioning effect of an inventory reservoir of materials, to which current purchases are added and from which currently needed quantities are withdrawn.

Thus, in purchasing, just as the term "right quality" has the special meaning of suitability or quality *for a purpose,* so "right quantity" has the special meaning of quantity to be purchased *at a time*. And just as there is a most suitable and economical quality of material, there is a most economical ordering quantity.

Optimum ordering quantity

Because quantity is a mathematical figure, there have been many attempts to develop a formula for determining the most economical ordering quantity. Besides the basic need, there are many factors to be taken into consideration—unit cost of the item in various lot sizes, the average inventory resulting from purchases in different quantities, the number of orders issued, cost of negotiating and issuing a purchasing order, and cost of carrying materials in inventory. Calculation of the last item alone involves a number of additional factors, such as interest on the inventory investment, overhead charges on storage space, stores department personnel, insurance, depreciation, and the like. Some of the earlier formulas contain no less than 15 variables. Consequently, although they were mathematically correct, they were too complicated and cumbersome for practical use in connection with any extensive and diversified commodity list.

This difficulty has been largely overcome with the development of computers which are able to relate variables far beyond the capacity of individuals to do so, and to give direct readings of the answers to complicated calculations in a matter of seconds whereas manual calculation would involve excessive time and effort. Computers are now widely used in a variety of purchasing operations; in some cases, indeed, they implement an entire purchasing system so far as standard stock items are concerned. The key to their value and effectiveness is their ability to determine optimum ordering and stock quantities from the data furnished and to control reorder points and quantities once proper inventory standards and policies have been established. The use of computers in purchasing is essentially a method, and is described in detail in a later section (Chapter 19) in connection with purchasing procedures. We are here concerned with the principles of quantity determination, which must be understood in order to feed the required information into a calculating device and to set up a program for processing the data. This is important, too, because many purchasing departments do not have access to computers, and the results must be obtained by simpler means.

Meanwhile, a number of practical working formulas have been developed, based on the known factors. The problem can be worked out to determine economical ordering quantity in terms of the number of units per order, the dollar value which this represents, or the number of weeks of coverage at a given rate of use. All of these methods are equally serviceable, because they are merely different ways of expressing the same quantity, and the answers can readily be translated into either of the other two units of measurement, as desired. One such formula that has gained wide acceptance and has proved its effectiveness as a purchasing guide is:

$$Q = \sqrt{\frac{2\ AB}{I}}$$

where: Q = Economic order quantity (in dollars)
A = Annual usage (in dollars)
B = Cost of issuing a purchase order (in dollars)
I = Cost of carrying inventory (as a decimal percentage of inventory value)

The mathematics of arriving at this simplified calculation are beyond the scope of this discussion. The important point is that, once the factors of order cost and inventory cost have been determined for any given company operation, the determination of optimum ordering quantity is directly related to a single variable, the total annual usage of the item under consideration.

To give meaning to the formula it is essential, of course, to have reasonably accurate values for the two cost factors. Relatively few companies have detailed information on purchase-order cost. In lieu of an elaborate cost analysis, a satisfactory working value can be found by taking the total cost of operating the purchasing department, including all salaries, expenses, and overhead charges, on an annual basis, and dividing this by the number of purchase orders issued during the year. (Rather surprisingly, perhaps, this will show an average cost in the neighborhood of $10 to $15 per order.)

The information on average inventory carrying cost is more generally available in most accounting systems. Here, however, the average cost is likely to be misleading, because the order quantity formula is to be applied to individual commodities, and there will be a wide range of actual carrying costs due to differences in the physical bulk of various items, the type of storage facilities and protection needed, rates of depreciation, and so forth. It would be excessively difficult, and would serve no useful purpose, to calculate a specific carrying cost for each individual item. But, instead of taking one average cost figure of, say, 25 per cent on total inventory, it is quite feasible to classify the commodities into three or four groups having similar storage characteristics, and to assign an average carrying cost to each group. This might range from as little as 10 per cent up to 50 per cent or more. Applying the appropriate group figure in the formula obviously gives added accuracy and value to the calculation of ordering quantity. An example of this method, and of the difference it makes in the resulting order-quantity determination, is shown in the parallel columns of Figure 8-2.

The limitations of a formula such as this are readily apparent. Most important of these is that it does not give effect to changes in the unit price of the material or product concerned. A change in unit price changes the value of *(A)* annual usage, in dollars, and consequently changes the economical ordering quantity. This can be adjusted by inserting the revised value in the formula and making a new calculation. But this adjustment does not take care of the more significant fact that the direction of current price trends and the anticipation of price changes may actually be determining influences in purchasing policy regarding the quantity to be bought at any given time. Certainly they would tend to modify any decisions predicated on a stable price situation. Similarly, the formula does not (except through a recalculation, as in the case of a price change) reflect the price advantages of volume buying and quantity discount schedules.

Even supposing that the price factor is stable and that the formula produces a precise theoretical determination of the most economical ordering quantity, it is quite likely that the resulting figure will have to be adjusted somewhat arbitrarily to bring it into conformity with commercial practice in respect to unit packages, established quantity-discount brackets, economical manufacturing quantities, full-carload or truckload quantities, and so on. This is somewhat analogous to the classic jibe at engineering practice which calculates a structural strain to three or four decimal places and then adds a 50 per cent safety factor.

There are other limitations where specific materials are concerned. Any formula must be interpreted and applied with common sense, and the ordering-quantity formula is no exception. For example, no matter what the formula says, bulky materials, such as excelsior, cartons, and filler materials used in the paper and leather industries, must be ordered with available storage space in mind, because space may effectively limit the quantity that can be handled. Nor is it sensible to order materials that are subject to deterioration in such quantities that the supply will exceed the shelf life of the material. Portland cement, batteries, photographic paper and film, cellulose tape, and enameled wire are examples of items on which such caution must be exercised.

Benefits of using the formula

Despite these limitations, the mathematical approach to determination of best order sizes is steadily gaining in acceptance and usage, for sound reasons of policy and because of the very substantial demonstrable savings and benefits that have resulted where this method has been consistently used as a guide within the proper scope of its application.

It has already been noted that the decision on best quantity is quite a complicated one if all the pertinent factors are considered, and the list of purchased commodities typically runs up to thousands of items. Without some sort of approved mathematical procedure to simplify the calculations, an excessive amount of time and effort may be expended on this one aspect of the purchase, for the larger and more significant items, while scant attention may be given to any accurate determination of best quantity for the great majority of items on the list. There will be a tendency to rely on other, less scientific standards of quantity, such as mere precedent. Experienced buyers may make a quick, intuitive appraisal of the factors and come fairly close to the right answer most of the time. The popular presumption has been that this intuitive judgment is reasonably satisfactory, but there is no assurance that this is so, and the improved performance where mathematical methods have been put to work suggests that intuition is far from reliable where ordering quantities are concerned.

The ordering-quantity formula substitutes facts for judgment.

It establishes a definite relationship between the significant variables in the situation and eliminates the variable of personal judgment, so that quantity decisions are consistent and are in accord with policy.

It can be used on machine calculators or converted into tabular form for direct reference, so that the scientific method can be applied to every item on the list with a minimum of effort.

For the great majority of stores and supply items, the mathematical method can be relied on completely, relieving the buyer of all responsibility on this score, with the assurance of having correct decisions which are reflected in superior performance. For example, the purchasing department of the Bell Telephone Laboratories, as early as 1940, devised a series of conversion factors based on the formula which made it possible to reduce inventories automatically by $28\frac{1}{2}$ to 42 per cent of dollar value while supporting the same volume of requisitions and maintaining a superior standard of service, as compared with the situation when stock control, ordering point, and order quantity were based on the judgment and decisions of experienced stockkeepers and buyers.[1] Thus, the often neglected area of operating supplies and standard parts, representing a great number of different items which must be purchased and stocked, sometimes in relatively small amounts but in substantial total volume, is readily brought under scientific purchasing control.

---

[1] R. H. Wilson, "Inventory Cut 42 Percent," *Purchasing Magazine,* August, 1940, page 49; "Stockroom Purchasing," *Purchasing Magazine,* February, 1941, page 47; "A Universal System of Stock Control," *Purchasing Magazine,* September, 1941, page 80.

For production materials, and other items where the final determination of ordering quantity involves a consideration of price trends, seasonal factors, advance coverage, or other elements not provided for in the mathematical calculation, the formula nevertheless furnishes a useful starting point. Under stable conditions, it may be directly applied. In any case, the necessary modifications may be made more intelligently, and with a clearer understanding of costs entailed, than if there were no basic standard of optimum quantity.

In addition to these uses in quantity decisions, the formulas have established some important and hitherto unrecognized principles of costs and cost relationships in respect to inventory control, which is inseparable from the problem of how much to buy. Among these are:

Total cost is at a minimum at the point where restocking cost is equal to carrying cost for a given quantity.

Within reasonable variation of order size (plus or minus 20 per cent), the total cost varies very little; beyond these limits, total cost goes up rapidly either way.

Ordering too little usually costs much more than ordering too much.

A change in the cost of carrying stock has a much greater effect on the most economical order size than does a change in the cost of restocking. (Mathematically speaking, optimum size of order varies in inverse proportion to the carrying cost and in direct proportion to the square root of the reorder cost.)

Using the formula

It is only in unusual cases that the order-quantity formula is calculated for each individual order. Once the optimum quantity is established for an item, it is valid until there is some change in one of the variable values—annual usage, carrying cost, or cost of ordering. The appropriate quantity is therefore noted on the purchase order record card for each item, along with maximum and minimum stock quantities and ordering point, so that the information is immediately available by direct reference when the item is to be reordered.

Also, there are some practical short cuts for making the actual calculation. One of these is the nomograph chart, a graphic device having parallel logarithmic scales so placed in relation to a reference line that the calculation can be made simply by laying a straightedge across the chart connecting the appropriate values in any given problem and finding the answer by direct reading at the point of intersection on the scale. This is essentially the same principle as in the operation of a slide rule, but is even simpler

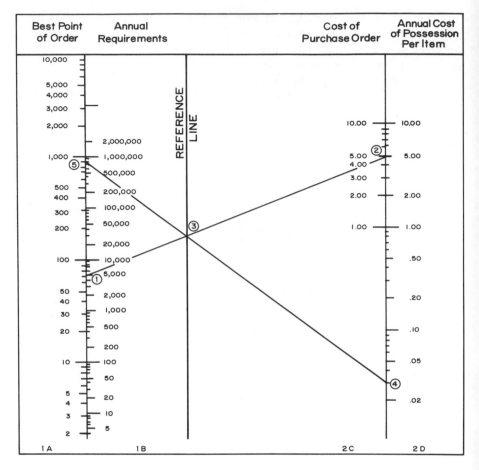

Best Point of Order	Annual Requirements		Cost of Purchase Order	Annual Cost of Possession Per Item

Fig. 8-1. Nomograph for Determining the Most Economical Ordering Quantity. Example: annual usage of item is 5,000 units; cost of issuing purchase order is $5.00; cost of possession in $.03 per year. Enter chart at 5,000 on scale 1B (1) and draw a straight line to 5.00 on scale 2C (2). This line intersects the reference line, establishing point (3). Draw another straight line from .03 on scale 2D (4) through point (3) on the reference line, continuing it to intersect left hand scale at point (5). A direct reading on scale 1A at point (5) shows the most economical ordering quantity to be 900 units.

for a specific type of problem. An example is shown in Figure 8-1. In some purchasing departments, such a monograph is printed on the reverse side of the requisition form. Then, in the case of a new or nonstocked item, the buyer can use the requisition as a work sheet and determine the economical ordering quantity in a few seconds without going through the arithmetical process.

The most widely used method is to make up a table based on constant values for ordering cost and carrying cost, calculating the economical order quantity for each of a wide range of annual-usage values. This is permanent and universally applicable. All the buyer needs to know is the annual dollar usage of an item, and he can find the economical order quantity by direct reference in the table. In cases where there are several different carrying costs for different types of material, a separate table is made up for each of the several values for this factor, and commodities are classified and coded to indicate which table applies.

Order-quantity table

An order-quantity table developed by the purchasing department of the Meter Division of Westinghouse Electric Corporation is shown in Figure 8-2. This was originally undertaken as a means of eliminating material shortages that had occurred under the previous normal purchasing policy of buying repetitive stores items in lots representing a three months' supply. The accomplishment of this objective has been one of the great advantages resulting from its use, but it has also revealed previously unsuspected opportunities for economies in purchasing and inventory cost.

This table is calculated on the basis of four different rates of stock-carrying cost: (A) 11 per cent per year, (B) 25 per cent, (C) 50 per cent, and (D) 100 per cent. Annual usage, in dollars, is shown in a range from $1 to $10,000. The economical order quantity is expressed as a multiplier representing, decimally, the number of years' (or fraction of a year's) supply to order. To use the table:

1. Find, by reference to the stock record card, in which of the four stock-carrying rate groups the item is classified (for example, Code B, 25 per cent per year).

2. Note annual usage of the item, in dollars (for example, $750 per year).

3. Find the figure in column B, opposite $750 in Annual Use column (.194).

4. Multiply: $750 × .194 = $145.50.

5. Result: Best ordering quantity is the commercial quantity closest to $145.50 in cost, or about ten weeks' supply. To avoid repeated calculations, order quantity is entered on the purchase record card. It is subject to revision if the rate of use changes or if the item is reclassified.

Examination of this table clearly shows the error of applying one time-coverage standard (for example, three months' supply) to all items, regardless of the rate of use. It indicates that, for an item in the 11 per cent carrying-cost classification, used at a rate of about $1,000 per year, the three months' supply is the economical quantity to buy. But for items in greater use, or with higher carrying costs for the same dollar usage, smaller orders and shorter coverage are indicated. For less used items, it calls for orders greatly in excess of common practice.

BEST ORDER QUANTITY MULTIPLIER

Annual Use $	Year's Supply to Order				Stock Carrying Rate Code	Annual Use $	Year's Supply to Order			
	.11	.25	.50	1.00			.11	.25	.50	1.00
	A	B	C	D			A	B	C	D
1	8	5.3	3.75	2.65		260	.495	.328	.232	.164
2	5.6	3.70	2.62	1.85		280	.477	.316	.224	.158
3	4.6	3.08	2.19	1.54		300	.460	.308	.219	.154
4	4.0	2.65	1.87	1.32		325	.444	.294	.208	.147
5	3.6	2.38	1.69	1.20		350	.427	.284	.199	.142
6	3.26	2.16	1.56	1.08		375	.412	.273	.193	.137
7	3.03	2.00	1.42	1.00		400	.400	.265	.187	.132
8	2.84	1.88	1.33	.935		425	.388	.257	.182	.128
9	2.68	1.77	1.25	.885		450	.377	.250	.177	.125
10	2.52	1.67	1.18	.836		475	.368	.244	.173	.122
12	2.30	1.53	1.08	.765		500	.360	.238	.169	.120
14	2.14	1.42	1.00	.710		550	.341	.226	.160	.113
16	2.00	1.32	.936	.663		600	.326	.216	.156	.108
18	1.90	1.25	.885	.626		650	.314	.208	.147	.104
20	1.79	1.19	.840	.593		700	.303	.200	.142	.100
25	1.60	1.06	.750	.530		750	.292	.194	.137	.097
30	1.45	.968	.682	.482		800	.284	.188	.133	.0935
35	1.35	.900	.635	.448		850	.275	.182	.129	.0910
40	1.25	.838	.592	.419		900	.266	.177	.125	.0885
45	1.2	.790	.559	.395		950	.260	.172	.121	.086
50	1.13	.747	.530	.374		1000	.252	.167	.118	.0836
60	1.07	.682	.485	.342		1100	.242	.160	.114	.080
70	.960	.636	.450	.318		1200	.230	.153	.108	.0765
80	.896	.594	.420	.297		1400	.214	.142	.100	.0710
90	.840	.556	.394	.278		1600	.200	.132	.0936	.066
100	.800	.530	.375	.265		1800	.190	.125	.088	.063
110	.767	.508	.359	.254		2000	.179	.119	.084	.059
120	.730	.484	.342	.242		2500	.160	.106	.075	.053
130	.704	.468	.328	.232		3000	.145	.096	.068	
140	.675	.447	.317	.224		3500	.135	.090	.064	
150	.653	.433	.306	.216		4000	.125	.084	.059	
160	.632	.420	.296	.210		4500	.120	.079	.056	
170	.614	.407	.287	.203		5000	.113	.075		
180	.595	.395	.279	.198		6000	.107	.068		
190	.580	.384	.272	.192		7000	.096	.064		
200	.560	.370	.262	.185		8000	.089	.059		
220	.540	.357	.253	.178		9000	.084	.056		
240	.515	.342	.242	.171		10000	.080			

Application of the Table
(Using Stock Carrying Rate Code A)

If you use $10,000 per year, order 1 month's supply per order

1,000	3 months'
250	6 months'
65	1 year's
15	2 years'
5	4 years'
1	8 years'

Fig. 8-2. Best Order Quantity Table.

CHART FOR DETERMING STORES ORDERING QUANTITIES

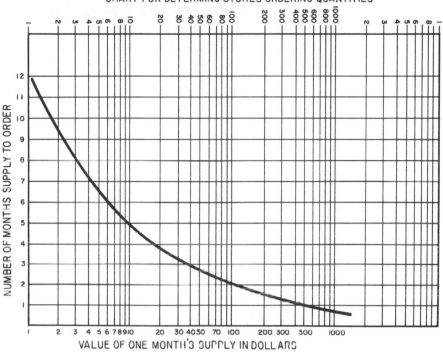

Fig. 8-3. Curve Showing Economical Stores Ordering Quantities.

The mathematical, or theoretical, calculation of most economical purchase quantity on these items of limited use, where purchase of from one to several years' supply is indicated, runs counter to all the traditional concepts of prudent coverage and active stock turnover; yet the table has amply justified itself in actual use. It is easy to visualize mountains of inventory piling up under these schedules, but this did not occur. The reason for this is that the "long" orders are more than compensated for by closer scheduling on the major items that make up the great bulk of purchases. In this division, for example, there are about 8,000 different items purchased for stores, but 250 of these account for more than two-thirds of the dollar volume; half of the total dollar volume is represented by only 40 items. The indicated purchase quantity for any item used at a rate of $10,000 per year is one month's supply per order, so that current investment is consistently low and turnover is high

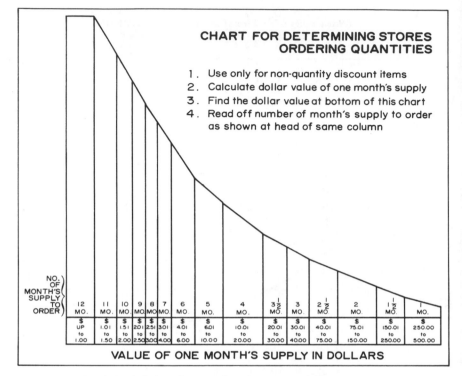

Fig. 8-4.   Ordering Chart Based on the Economical Quantity Curve.

on this predominant portion of the inventory. Meanwhile, the elimination of frequent repeat orders on the minor items, purchased according to the table, reduced the number of purchase orders issued from 15,000 to 5,400 per year, with consequent substantial savings in the cost of purchasing, magnified by a corresponding reduction in the expenses of receiving and accounting.

Additional benefits resulting from this method of quantity determination are reported by the purchasing agent as follows:[2]

1.   During a period when the company was spending more dollars than ever before, fewer purchase orders were being placed per month than at the bottom of the depression.

2.   Despite an all-time high of production volume, the buying staff was reduced by two-thirds and total purchasing department personnel from 37 to 21.

3.   Buyers were enabled to expend nearly their entire time on constructive negotiation, whereas formerly a significant portion of their time was devoted to expediting.

---

[2] B. D. Henderson, "Purchasing Profits through Inventory Control," *Purchasing Magazine,* November, 1947, page 106.

4. Follow-up action has been eliminated on 80 per cent of the orders placed.
5. The record shows only one stock-out[3] per account in seven and one-half years. On the average, there are only 15 to 20 items reported as delaying production out of more than 2,000 open purchase orders, as compared with a high of 325 items out of 3,000 open orders prior to the adoption of this system.

A variation of this method that puts the precalculated information into simple graphic form is shown in Figures 8-3 and 8-4. The first step is to plot the most economical order quantities as a curve on a chart having as its horizontal scale the value of one month's supply in dollars (corresponding to the Annual Use column of the table) and a vertical scale showing the number of months' supply to order (corresponding to the Multiplier column of the table). The shape of the curve is such as to make a logarithmic scale most feasible on the horizontal axis. As a matter of policy, the scope of the chart is limited to purchase quantities of not less than one month's supply nor more than a year's supply.

The second step is to note where the curve intersects the lines indicating best order quantity as equivalent to 12 months' supply, 11 months' supply, 10 months' supply, and so forth, and draw vertical lines from these points down to the base line of the chart, showing the corresponding readings in terms of the dollar value of one month's supply. The result is shown in Figure 8-4, a simple and practical guide to determining economical order quantities according to the rate of use of the various items. As in the case of the quantity tables, this calculation is accurate for only the one value of inventory-carrying cost used in the original formula; for different rates of carrying cost, additional charts must be drawn and commodities classified and coded to indicate which chart applies. In a moderately simple operation, two such values may be sufficient to cover all cases with reasonable accuracy. In large, complex operations, with a wide variety of items carried in inventory, the items can usually be grouped within not more than four classifications. Four charts, corresponding to the four columns of the Multiplier table, will serve for the entire purchasing program.

Effect of quantity discounts

The best-order-quantity formula is predicated on a constant price factor. Fluctuations in price are taken care of by the fact that these are reflected in

---

[3] A "stock-out" is the inability to fill a requisition for a stores item from stock on hand, that is, the failure of the inventory policy or formula (or of purchasing performance) to anticipate fully the requirement for that item. In setting ordering points and quantities, this is a calculated risk.

the figure of annual usage or value of a month's supply. But there is another important price variable that is closely related to order quantity—the quantity discount offered by many suppliers, by which the unit price of a product or material is reduced in successive stages as larger quantities are purchased. "Cheaper by the dozen" pricing is a common practice in industrial distribution as well as in retailing, and the price differentials may be very substantial and alluring. If the optimum quantity indicated by formula comes close to the point of such a price "break" or bracket, common sense would dictate adjusting the quantity purchased so as to take advantage of this extra saving. But if the formula does not actually give the answer to this problem, it does suggest that the lower unit cost must be balanced against the extra investment and the extra cost of carrying inventory over a longer period, to determine whether the lower unit cost thus earned represents a real saving to the purchaser.

This factor does not lend itself to generalization or precalculation. Each case must be individually considered. However, there is a simple mathematical approach based on determining the return, or "profit," on the extra investment if the larger quantity is purchased. Figure 8-5 shows a work sheet for this purpose, by which a useful calculation can be made in a few minutes.

For example, consider an item of stainless steel tubing priced at $42.20 per hundred feet in small lots, and at $33.60 in lots of 1,000 feet or more. It is used at a rate of about 150 feet per month, and is generally requisitioned in lots of 500 feet, or about three months' supply. Problem: to determine whether it would be more economical to buy nearly seven months' supply at the lower price. The applicable inventory-carrying rate is 12 per cent per year, or 1 per cent per month. Freight charges amount to $4.00 on a shipment of 500 feet, and $7.50 on a shipment of 1,000 feet.

Following the calculations on the work sheet, we find:

1. Total cost of an order for 500 feet is $215.00.

2. Total cost of an order for 1,000 feet is $343.50.

3. Additional investment entailed by ordering 1,000 feet at one time is $128.50.

4. Total cost of 1,000 feet, ordered in two lots of 500 feet, is $430.00.

5. Cost saving on 1,000 feet, ordered at one time, is $86.50.

6. Additional period for which the additional investment must be carried is (approximately) 4 months.

7. Additional inventory-carrying cost is $5.30, making the total cost of additional investment $137.80.

8. Cost saving (5) divided by total cost of additional investment (7) represents a return of nearly 65 per cent on the additional investment, over a seven-month period.

Because this is many times greater than the normal return on investment,

QUANTITY DISCOUNT ADVANTAGE WORKSHEET
TPFC-1135   DIVISION   DATE
MATERIAL

VENDOR   ADDRESS

1. COST TO BUY REQUISITIONED (SMALLER) QUANTITY NOW:	2. COST TO BUY RECOMMENDED (LARGER) QUANTITY NOW:
SMALLER QUANTITY	LARGER QUANTITY
TIMES: UNIT PRICE ....PER	TIMES: UNIT PRICE ....PER
EQUALS· COST OF GOODS	EQUALS: COST OF GOODS
PLUS· FREIGHT	PLUS: FREIGHT
EQUALS: TOTAL COST	EQUALS: TOTAL COST

3 ADDITIONAL INVESTMENT REQUIRED TO PURCHASE LARGER QUANTITY NOW:	4. ULTIMATE COST TO BUY LARGER QUANTITY, BY MEANS OF SMALLER QUANTITY RE-ORDERS:
TOTAL COST FROM 2 ABOVE	QUANTITY (FROM 2 ABOVE)
MINUS: TOTAL COST FROM 1 ABOVE	TIMES: UNIT PRICE (FROM 1 ABOVE) ....PER
EQUALS· ADDITIONAL INVESTMENT	EQUALS: ULTIMATE COST
	PLUS: FREIGHT (EST. FROM 1 ABOVE)
	EQUALS: TOTAL ULTIMATE COST

5. SAVINGS WHICH WOULD RESULT FROM BUYING LARGER QUANTITY NOW·	6. PERIOD OF ADDITIONAL INVESTMENT:
ULTIMATE COST TO BUY LARGER QUANTITY (FROM 4 ABOVE)	LARGER (RECOMMENDED) QTY. = ... MOS. SUPPLY
MINUS: COST TO BUY SAME QUANTITY NOW (FROM 2 ABOVE)	LESS: SMALLER (REQ'ND.) QTY. = ... MOS. SUPPLY EQUALS: MONTHS ADDITIONAL INVESTMENT MUST BE CARRIED MONTHS

7. COST OF CARRYING INVENTORY IF LARGER QUANTITY IS PURCHASED NOW.	8. RATE OF RETURN ON INVESTMENT:
ADDITIONAL INVESTMENT (FROM 3 ABOVE) X.01 (CARRYING COST PER MO. 1% OF INV.) TIMES: MOS. ADDITIONAL INVESTMENT MUST BE CARRIED (FROM 6 ABOVE)	DIVIDE TOTAL SAVINGS (FROM 5 ABOVE) $ BY TOTAL COST OF ADDITIONAL INVESTMENT (FROM 7, AT LEFT)
EQUALS: CARRYING COST OF INV.	EQUALS: 0._____, EQUALS_____% RATE OF RETURN ON INVESTMENT
PLUS: ADD. INVESTMENT (FROM 3 ABOVE)	
TOTAL COST OF ADDITIONAL INVESTMENT	

THE PERCENTAGE FIGURE DEVELOPED IN BLOCK 8 IS THE RATE OF RETURN ON THE EXTRA INVESTMENT REQUIRED TO PURCHASE THE RECOMMENDED LARGER QUANTITY NOW. IT SHOULD BE COMPARED WITH THE PREVAILING RATE OF RETURN ON INVESTMENT IN THE DIVISION CONCERNED, TO DETERMINE THE ADVISABILITY OF PURCHASING THE LARGER (RECOMMENDED) QUANTITY.

PREPARED BY _____

Fig. 8-5. Work Sheet for Calculating Quantity Discount Advantage.

it would probably be advisable in this case to buy the larger quantity and take advantage of the price discount. This is not always the case, nor is the decision always in the hands of the purchasing department. In many companies the procedure is to submit such cost comparisons, with buying recommendations, to the inventory control department. There may be other considerations, such as maintaining inventory balance, or greater fluidity of assets, or conserving working capital for other essential purposes in the businessness. It is part of the purchasing responsibility, however, to determine the most economical buying policies and to follow them so far as is consistent with purchasing authority and within materials budgets.

Quantity determination by policy

Mathematical determination of most economical order quantities is a useful device, particularly in respect to inventory items in regular use, and is a guide in all quantity decisions, but it does not automatically provide the answer to the problem of deciding the right quantity to buy. It is not equally applicable to all classifications of purchased items, nor to all types of require-ments. The decision on quantity may be a matter of policy, in which the economical lot size is only one of several factors to be considered. And there are a number of different buying methods, other than purchasing for the replenishment of inventory, especially adaptable to various types of require-ments and having a definite bearing on the decision of how much to buy at a time. A complete purchasing program will probably make use of all these methods, according to circumstances and need. The more important of these are:

1. *Definite quantity contracts* with predetermined deliveries scheduled over a period of time. This method is particularly adapted to raw materials and components for scheduled operations and assembly, where quantity re-quirements and rate of use are reasonably well known in advance. The con-tract quantity in this case is the total estimated need for the contract period, usually three months or a year, or a base supply to cover the bulk of estimated needs, to be supplemented by open-market purchases as required.

For the buyer, this method has the advantages of utilizing total purchas-ing power represented by the entire quantity requirement over the contract period, without incurring a heavy inventory investment at any one time; assuring continuity of supply and prudent coverage of requirements at known cost; placing procurement on the basis of materials flow corresponding to rate of use; and accomplishing in a single negotiation and transaction what would otherwise entail repetition and duplication of purchasing effort and detail. For the seller, it affords an assured outlet for his production and greater opportunities for mass production, advance planning, and stable operations. The latter consideration is frequently a means of securing favorable price terms beyond the normal quantity differentials, for the seller may utilize the backlog of contract orders to maintain his organization and production during slack periods, figuring it largely as the means of meeting his basic overhead costs.

2. *Continuing contracts,* similar to the above but without the specific

THE A. B. C. SUPPLY CORP.
2001 NORTH END DRIVE
RIVERTOWN, PA.

ORDER NO. 120-555555-10

INQUIRY NO. S-079-6

VENDOR CODE 89898

TERMS 2% Std. Terms FOB Delivered

ITEM	STOCK NO.	COMM. CODE	IDENTIFICATION & SIZE	UNIT	PREPRICE
	INVESTMENT				
1	95903-00202	203	1/8" Std. Galv. Pipe 20	Ft.	8.20 C
2	00204	203	1/4" Std. Galv. Pipe 21 Ft. Random Lengths	Ft.	9.98 C
	EXPENSE				
5	94903-09108	961	2" Jenkins Fig. 49 Gate Valve	Pc.	13.25 ea
			Swing Check	Pc.	4.95 ea

GENERAL ⊗ ELECTRIC

PURCHASE ORDER

Address All MAIL TO— 2901 E. LAKE RD. ERIE 1, PA. To Location Checked

☐ EQPT. PURCH. 3-42
☐ LOCO. PURCH. 3-14
☒ R & U PURCH. 1-20F

SHIP TO ▼

GENERAL ELECTRIC COMPANY
LOCO. & CAR EQUIPMENT DEPT., ERIE PLANT

A.B.C. COMPANY
DEF STREET
CHICAGO, ILLINOIS

3501 EAST LAKE RD., ERIE 1. PA.

MAIN AVE., ERIE 1. PA.

DATE ISSUED
MO. DAY
12 5 1

FOR DH ROBINS 20E

MARK PACKAGES AND DOCUMENTS

SHIP PER STANDARD INSTRUCTIONS OR AS SHOWN BELOW

VENDOR	COMM.	ACCOUNT NO.	P	ORDER NO.	SHIP ON
89898		SEE ATTACHED SHEETS		120-555555-10	STANDING ORDER

ITEM	QUANTITY	DESCRIPTION

THIS PURCHASE ORDER IS TO COVER THE CONTINUING PROCURE-
MENT OF STANDARD GENERAL STORES ITEMS.

RELEASES WILL BE AUTHORIZED BY GENERAL STORES ON A POST
CARD FORM. REFERENCE WILL BE MADE TO STANDING PURCHASE
ORDER NUMBER AND ITEM NUMBER.

IF MATERIAL CAN BE FURNISHED BY DATE REQUESTED, SUPPLIER
NEED NOT CONFIRM RECEIPT OF REQUEST TO RELEASE. INFORMA-
TION SHOULD BE SUPPLIED TO BUYER ON ANTICIPATED LATE
DELIVERIES.

SUPPLIER SHOULD FURNISH TWO COPIES OF PACKING LIST FOR
RECEIVING PURPOSES.

PRICES ON ATTACHED LIST ARE NEGOTIATED PRICES AND ARE
NOT SUBJECT TO CHANGE EXCEPT AS RENEGOTIATED THROUGH
R&U PURCHASING.

PACKAGES SHOULD BE MARKED WITH PURCHASE ORDER AND
ITEM NUMBERS.

INVOICES MAY BE PROVIDED ON A MONTHLY BASIS, IN
DUPLICATE. INVOICE SHOULD LIST SHIPMENTS BY DATE
AND ITEM NUMBER.

"This order is placed subject only to the terms and conditions on the face and reverse side hereof and does not constitute the acceptance of any terms and conditions contained on any previous quotations whether or not referred to herein. The purchaser hereby objects to any terms and conditions contained in an acknowledgement form or otherwise, different from or in addition to the terms and conditions on the face and reverse side hereof."

GENERAL ELECTRIC COMPANY LOCO & CAR EQPT. DEPT., ERIE PLANT

INSTRUCTIONS:
• IMPORTANT-RETURN ACKNOWLEDGMENT WITH PROMISE.
• INVOICE EACH ORDER SEPARATELY IN TRIPLICATE.
• PACKING SLIPS MUST ACCOMPANY EACH SHIPMENT: ATTACH TO OUTSIDE OF CASE.

LC-431 REV. (12-60)

OP SMITH   BUYER

Fig. 8-6. Continuing Order Lists Major Material and Prices and Explains Release Procedure to vendor.

limitations of quantity and duration, so that it has greater flexibility. In a typical arrangement of this sort, requirements are projected three months in advance; firm delivery instructions are issued for the first month, and the supplier is authorized to proceed with the manufacture of the second month's quantity at his convenience and to procure raw materials for the third month's estimated requirement. The quantity need is reviewed every 30 days and projected as before so that, in effect, there is a firm three months' contract in force at all times. (See Figure 8-6.)

3. *Term or requirements contracts,* for a specified duration of time but not for a fixed quantity, this being subject to the buyer's needs as they develop.The quantity is usually estimated within stated maximum and minimum limits, with deliveries to be ordered and released as required. The method is used where requirements of a material or product are expected to be substantial, but total quantity and the scheduling of use cannot be accurately known in advance. It is particularly useful in connection with materials that are fabricated in two or more stages, with the possibility of variation in specific requirements of the later stage, as when varied dyeing or finishing operations are to be specified in the delivery instructions but basic production up to the semifinished stage can be carried out in advance. It is also frequently employed in connection with materials that are used in common by two or more plants of the purchasing company, one central contract being issued for the over-all quantity requirement, with delivery instructions to come from the various plants as required.

The advantages to the buyer are as noted above, plus the effect of putting major requirements in the position of "shelf goods" for prompt shipment, with the supplier accepting the responsibility for maintaining adequate stocks to make this possible. The advantages to the seller are similar to those noted in the previous case, although without the same degree of assurance as to regularity of shipment. Two of the chief benefits to him are that a single sales operation suffices for the complete transaction, and that for the duration of the contract he is not under the necessity of making a competitive selling effort to secure the orders for whatever quantity of the contract item may be required.

4. *Open-market purchases.* This method is indicated when quantity requirements of an item are either small or variable; when market and competitive conditions suggest the advisability of a flexible purchasing condition; when goods are readily available on short notice, when they conform to industry standards, or when special requirements are known sufficiently in advance to permit ordering and delivery time without endangering the continuity of operations.

5. *Group purchase of related items,* usually those that are used in small quantities as individual items but which make up a substantial order and

commitment when combined in a single or "blanket" order to one supplier. It can be done either as an open-market purchase or on short- or long-term contracts. It calls for periodic review of stock by related classifications of items, or the review of related items whenever a requisition is received for an individual item. A variation of this scheme is a monthly or quarterly contract on the "requirements" basis as outlined in the third case above. This might cover a list of mill supplies or small tools, for example. Bids would be invited, either on an item-by-item basis or in the form of a generally applicable discount from list prices. After selecting the most favorable over-all proposal, all requirements for these items are passed along to the successful bidder in the form of memorandum orders to be delivered as needed and billed on a single invoice at the end of the month or contract period. The advantages are that small and relatively unattractive "retail" quantities are consolidated into substantial business; that great savings in clerical and accounting procedure accrue to both buyer and seller because single small transactions are not made the subject of a formal purchase order and are not carried individually through accounting records. It is the logical answer to the otherwise justifiable complaint that the cost of formal purchasing and the cost of filling small orders may sometimes be greater than the value of the material concerned. Contract buying is discussed at greater length in Chapter 19.

6. *Special purchases,* applicable to nonrepetitive items —equipment purchases, special parts, items that are not regularly carried in stores, materials and supplies for a particular project. The quantity in such cases is, of course, determined by and equal to the specific need. The method of purchase depends on the nature and size of the project. No generalizations can be made for this broad and miscellaneous category; some of the more important aspects, such as the purchase of capital equipment, are separately discussed.

7. *Purchase strictly for requirements,* as indicated by requisitions received. Quantity is dictated by the individual request. This is the least flexible and least desirable of all purchase policies, affording a minimum opportunity for the application of sound purchasing principles and the development of a planned purchasing program. Except insofar as it includes the classification of special purchases outlined in the preceding paragraph, it is held to a minimum wherever centralized purchasing organization prevails.

Basic quantity requirements

The basic information regarding total quantity requirements and rates of use in a continuing operation comes from two sources: the record of past experience, which is available in purchasing department records and reflected in maximum and minimum stock quantities; and projected sales quotas and manufacturing schedules, which establish purchasing policies in the first place and are the basis of subsequent modifications. With modern scientific management, these projections of material requirements can be made with a high degree of accuracy. Sometimes manufacturing programs are set for an entire season or year in advance; more typically, they may be set for a quarterly period, with provision for review and revision monthly, so that there is at all times a reasonably accurate knowledge of what requirements will be for some time in advance. Manufacturing schedules can be broken down into detailed bills of materials, normal rates of waste and spoilage are known from past experience, and the normal ratio of nonproduct or operating supplies can be calculated to the operating rate. On the basis of this information, total requirements for the period can be forecast to take advantage of quantity buying, deliveries can be scheduled to meet the need, and purchasing policies can be established so as to make possible the most economical and efficient procurement.

It is essential that the purchasing officer be completely and promptly informed of manufacturing or operating plans and schedules. The most desirable means of accomplishing this is to have the purchasing executive represented in, and participating in, the management councils where such decisions are made. His whole responsibility depends on such plans, and the successful execution of the plans depends on his knowledge and performance, to the same extent as design, manufacturing, sales, and finance. In many cases his special knowledge of materials and their availability, of new developments and trends in use, and of commercial standards can contribute much to the wisdom and practicability of the projected program.

In operations where products are made to special design and special order, forecasting of material requirements cannot be done with such detailed accuracy. In such cases the record of average requirements as reflected in purchasing experience, where materials data is compiled and recorded, may be of even greater relative importance in planning. Under these circumstances it is even more essential that the purchasing department be apprised of needs and of projected activity than under a continuing schedule, and at as early a stage as possible. To cite a typical example, orders may be received for three large installations to be built to special order, each one involving, as a matter of special purchase, a quantity of condenser tubing. Before a detailed bill of materials can be drawn off, these separate projects must go through the engineering or drawing board stage. One of these may take considerably longer to detail than the others, or the three may be engineered consecutively, coming to the purchasing department as three separate requirements, in limited quantity, within a relatively short space of time but each demanding separate and urgent procurement. If these three projects were known to the purchasing agent at the time the sale was made, with even approximate quantities, much time could have been saved; one order and one receiving operation, with all their attendant record and accounting detail, would have done the work of three; and a substantial saving in cost could have been effected by reason of the quantity involved.

Factors influencing quantity

Having the basic information regarding scheduled quantity requirements, or any request to purchase, the buyer has several factors to consider in arriving at a decision as to the right quantity to purchase at a time—a quantity that will maintain continuity of operation according to schedule, that will represent the most economical unit cost, cost of procurement, and cost of handling, and that will take best advantage of commercial usage and market trends.

The first factor is the time required for delivery, from the time the order is issued until goods are received. If the item is one that must be fabricated before shipment, this would include not only the time in transit, but the time required for manufacture and a prudent allowance for the supplier's own scheduling of production, because it is not safe to assume that production will start immediately upon receipt of the order. The sum of these three constitutes the procurement cycle, or lead time required in placing the order to insure delivery when needed. The scheduling of purchase starts with the required delivery date and is calculated in reverse chronological order. In any time of scarcity and great demand, when production facilities are overcrowded and orders must wait their turn, the procurement cycle lengthens. Conversely, when markets are easier, the cycle shortens to actual production and transit time, and on many standard items of the "shelf goods" variety that are normally carried in stock by suppliers, it may amount to the delivery time only.

For items that are in continuing use, where long lead times are involved, the quantity and timing of orders are calculated on the basis of the length of the procurement cycle and normal rate of use so that, ideally, stock will be replenished just as the last material from the previous order is being used. However, to minimize the risk of running out of stock, two prudent precautions should be taken. One is to supplement the lead-time calculation with a specific promise of delivery on the part of the supplier. The other is to maintain a reasonable reserve or "insurance" stock as a cushion for unexpected demands and delayed deliveries. (See Chapter 9.)

The second factor, or set of factors, affecting purchase quantity has to do with commercial usage in respect to manufacture, packaging, and shipment. There is a minimum economical manufacturing quantity, directly reflected in unit costs. The quantity will vary in respect to different types of products and the facilities of various suppliers, some being organized and equipped for long runs and mass production, whereas others can operate efficiently on a comparatively short-run or custom basis. There are basic costs of machine setting, tool and die changes, and the like, incurred in every order, to be spread over the unit cost whether the quantity be large or small. It does not follow that costs and prices will be automatically or proportionally reduced as ordering quantities are increased beyond the minimum point. The cost of batch processing, for example, may be constant for any quantity more than the minimum. The process may be such that it is feasible only in exact multiples of the minimum quantity, or new costs of reconditioning tools and dies may be incurred after a given volume of production has been accomplished. The supplier's schedule of quantity discounts is a fairly reliable indicator of the quantity economies that can be achieved.

Similarly, there are quantity economies in the cost of transportation, which is a definite part of the buyer's unit cost. Freight rates are quoted on the basis of carload and less-than-carload lots, and this differential must be taken into consideration in the quantity determination. As in the case of manufacturing costs, this factor tends only to set a minimum quantity advantage. If purchases are made in carload lots, there is rarely any saving in unit transportation cost to be gained by ordering two or more carloads. There are various ways of meeting the less-than-carload quantity problem. One possibility is an arrangement for mixed carloads or combination shipments of related products from the same supplier. Other methods of transportation should also be considered. Truckloads of various sizes, all less than the freight carload, are frequently feasible and economical.

The standard commercial unit of packaging also has a bearing on the purchase quantity. Although many items are procurable on a bulk basis or are specially cased or crated according to the quantity ordered, most products are packaged in standard unit quantities—wrapped reams of paper, bolts or rolls of specific or approximate yardage, barrels or drums of standard capacity, cartons of a hundred, or a gross, or a thousand, or multiples thereof. Insofar as purchase quantities can be made to conform with these standard units, it is advisable and economical to do so. Vendors customarily, and properly, make an additional charge for fractional or "broken" package units, and apparent savings from calculating requirements down to the last decimal place may be more than outweighed by increased unit costs.

There are other trade customs which must be considered in respect to quantity. In the production of special castings and some other fabricated parts, the manufacturing process is such that it is not always possible to come out even in the end, with precisely the number of units ordered. The producer's allowance for defective parts may not have been enough, or it may have been too liberal. Trade custom in these industries has established a reasonable leeway, plus or minus, for the producer in meeting this problem, that is, a stated percentage short of the quantity ordered is considered as satisfying the order, and a stated percentage of overage must be accepted by the purchaser. These conditions are generally written into the contracts in the industries where they apply. This, of course, can result in either a shortage or a surplus for the buyer, and this possible variation in delivered quantity must be considered in addition to the buyer's own allowance for spoilage in his own company's operation, in determining the right quantity to buy. On parts that are regularly reordered, shortage or surplus on any particular lot can be compensated for by adjusting the quantity on succeeding orders. On parts that are procured for a specific purpose, a shortage can present a more serious problem. Experience may be the only guide as to which suppliers are most likely to come closest to the quantity actually needed and ordered.

The third factor affecting purchase quantity includes the storage facilities available and the cost of carrying inventory, both of which tend to set a maximum on the quantity to be purchased at one time. The importance and the effect of this factor have already been considered in discussion of the economical order-quantity formula.

The fourth factor in determining how much to buy is the condition and trend of the market for the commodity. This is a major consideration in setting both purchasing and inventory policies. In periods of advancing prices, the indicated policy is to extend the period of coverage (that is, to increase purchase quantity), whereas in periods of declining prices the reverse is true. This is discussed in greater detail in Chapter 9. The effect of price trends and changes is also reflected in the order-quantity formula, because, for an identical physical quantity the value of the Annual Use factor, expressed in dollars, goes up or down according to the unit costs prevailing.

9

STORES CONTROL

NO STUDY OF purchasing is complete without a consideration of the inventory phase through which most purchased materials pass between the time of acquisition and the time of use. In the present study, for example, this close relationship and correlation has already been noted in several instances. The purchasing responsibility to have materials on hand when needed (Chapter 1) implies the existence of an inventory reservoir as part of the procurement process. One of the principal reasons for standardization of quality (Chapter 5) is its effect in reducing the variety and volume of inventories. The whole science of economical order quantities (Chapter 7) and forward buying (Chapter 8) depend upon a knowledge of inventory costs, which constitute an important factor in the purchasing determinations. Finally, repeated surveys of actual practice show that, in a preponderant number of companies, the responsibility for inventory control is vested in the purchasing department, entirely or in part, and in well over half the cases, administration and operation of the physical stores department are under purchasing jurisdiction.

Responsibility for inventory control

There has for some time been a growing awareness of the importance of inventory control as a planning and policy function in over-all company management. This is reflected in organization trends, which follow one of two general principles: (a) making inventory policy a joint responsibility enlisting the judgment of several phases of management, for example, purchasing, production, stores, finance, and executive, or (b) establishing a separate department with the specific function of materials planning and control.

As long ago as 1939, the National Association of Purchasing Agents noted that "The definite majority trend is away from control of inventory as a responsibility of the purchasing department alone."[1] At that time it was reported that the purchasing department was solely responsible for inventory in 41 per cent of the companies represented in the survey, and that it shared the responsibility with other departments in another 39 per cent. There was no information on separate departments for materials control.

Nine years later, the National Industrial Conference Board reported that the purchasing department was primarily responsible for inventory control in 43 per cent of the companies surveyed and shared the responsibility in another 53 per cent, being thus involved in all but 4 per cent of the cases. The role of the specialized materials control department is indicated by the finding that, where primary responsibility did not rest in the purchasing department, it was usually in the hands of some form of planning or control department.[2]

By 1951, a survey of 484 manufacturing companies showed that 11.4 per cent had separate materials control or inventory control departments, with complete responsibility in respect to raw materials and production items (fabricated parts and components), but concerned with maintenance and operating supplies in only 2.9 per cent of the cases. Joint responsibility existed in about 20 per cent of the companies. The purchasing department had complete or partial responsibility in a substantial majority of cases, in all three categories: raw materials, 69.2 per cent; fabricated parts and components, 54.1 per cent; and supplies, 64.5 per cent. The second most prevalent influence in inventory control varied according to the type of item. For raw materials, it was executive management (17.8 per cent). For production items, it was the production department (35.5 per cent). For supplies, it was the stores department (28.3 per cent).[3]

Objectives of inventory control

Inventory stocks are the means of implementing many of the functions and goals of purchasing. They provide the assurance of having the items on hand when needed and afford the added protection of reserve stocks, theoretically untouchable but practically serving to fill needs when extraordinary demand develops or when current procurement fails, for example, when deliveries are delayed or rejected. They provide the flexibility that enables the purchasing department to apply economical buying policies which would not be

---

[1] *Handbook of Purchasing Policies and Procedures,* National Association of Purchasing Agents, New York, 1939.

[2] F. R. Lusardi, *Purchasing for Industry* (Studies in Business Policy, No. 33), National Industrial Conference Board, New York, 1948.

[3] B. Melnitsky, *Management of Industrial Inventory,* Chilton Publications, Book Division, New York, 1951.

possible in purchasing strictly according to current needs, for example, to take advantage of quantity discounts for lower unit prices, to make forward purchases in anticipation of price advances, and to adjust ordering quantities to conform to commercial packaging standards, economical manufacturing lots, and full-carload or truckload shipments for minimum transportation costs. All of these uses of inventory are taken for granted. They suggest the conclusion that proper inventory quantities are merely the result of scientifically determined purchase quantities.

In fact, however, inventory management has standards and objectives of its own, which importantly influence purchasing policy and quantity decisions. The relationship is a mutual one, working both ways.

The mathematical determination of economical ordering quantities (Chapter 8), by whatever formula or method, always involves an inclusive factor representing the cost of carrying inventory, and the variable rates for this factor found in some of the ordering tables show that this is not simply a matter of the interest on the inventory investment. There is, of course, the basic consideration of efficient stores administration and operation, and this depends in part on inventory policies. Handling and record-keeping costs vary, as do purchasing costs, with the size and frequency of orders and deliveries, and there are optimum quantities from the viewpoint of inventory management which do not necessarily coincide with the optimum quantities for purchasing. The limitations of actual storage facilities have already been noted as a modifying factor in purchasing policy. The whole area of the cost of providing and maintaining storage and handling facilities is a problem of inventory management. And whereas the buyer may concern himself with the summary figure of annual or monthly usage, the person responsible for inventory control analyzes the more detailed record of the number of demands per month or per day as a necessary item in setting order-review points and minimum stock quantities. Thus stock-outs are avoided when using departments call upon the stores department to furnish their operating needs.

Further, the investment in materials is a factor of financial policy that may outweigh the considerations that pertain strictly to purchase quantities and costs. There may be excellent reasons of circumstance or policy that suggest a materials investment policy in which potential purchase savings are sacrificed for the sake of fluidity or conservation of capital resources or their application to other business purposes. Management decisions of this sort are often implemented through inventory policies and control.

Thus, it is true that purchasing and inventory policies usually go hand in hand, but they are not one and the same. They have the common objective of seeking the lowest practicable ultimate cost of purchased materials. But there are occasions when a company's inventory policy determines or modifies purchasing policy, rather than the other way around. This is one of the reasons for setting up inventory control as a joint responsibility, where such an or-

ganization plan is in effect. The purchasing department that has the responsibility for materials control in addition to procurement must have this
broader viewpoint of the total function of material control and be able to
adjust both purchasing and inventory policies to attain the over-all management objective.

Statistical inventory control

Like economical order quantities, appropriate and economical inventory
quantities can be scientifically and mathematically determined. Also, as in the
former case, the formulas must be applied with judgment and must be in a
practical, workable form so that they can be readily used and so that the labor
of calculation does not offset their value as a business tool.

At the outset, some facts should be noted about the nature of inventories.
The typical industrial inventory comprises several thousand items. Every one
of these is, in its own way, essential to the company operation, but dollarwise
and in volume of usage, their significance varies widely. In a representative
case, 25 per cent of the items may account for 75 per cent of total volume or
the dollar value passing through inventory over any given period; the other
75 per cent of items then represent a relatively small percentage (25 per cent)
of total dollar value. This is a conservative ratio. Instances are fairly common
where as few as 10 per cent of the items account for as much as 80 per cent
of dollar value.

It follows that the same policies cannot be economically applied to both
classes of items. If an inclusive policy of maintaining 30 days' supply of all
items were adopted, it would entail the issuance of an unreasonable number
of purchase orders every month. The vast majority of these would be for
excessively small amounts where the cost of purchasing is disproportionate to
or actually greater than the value of the purchased merchandise. On the items
of larger usage, the inventory investment would be burdensome or even pro-
hibitive, and quantities on hand would tax normal storage facilities. A purchasing staff undertaking such a program, with the entire range of thousands of
items coming up for procurement each month, could not possibly give adequate
attention to all, or perhaps to any.

The economics of this situation, from the purchasing standpoint, is reflected in the ordering-quantity tables (Chapter 8), which indicate that the
items of smaller usage and annual dollar volume should be ordered less frequently, for longer forward coverage, up to a full year's supply, whereas the
items of larger usage and value should be ordered more frequently, in quantities for much shorter-term coverage.

From the inventory standpoint, a similar conclusion is reached, expressed
initially in a more general statement of principle in setting inventory policies.

For the 25 per cent or 10 per cent of large-volume and -value items, the indicated policy of inventory control calls for careful analysis and planning, close individual attention item by item, and maximum flexibility to adjust stocks to current conditions. For the 75 per cent or 90 per cent of small-value items, where individual analysis is neither practicable nor warranted, the indicated control policy is based on probability factors, which can be mathematically calculated and applied.

Size of safety stock

Probability, by definition, is not an exact science. A policy based on the laws of probability implies the calculated risk of deviations from the normal pattern—in this case, the risk of stock-outs, which inventory control specifically seeks to avoid. This risk is minimized by providing safety or reserve stocks. The lack of even a small item like a label or the tiny liner for a bottle closure can halt production just as effectively as lack of some major ingredient of the product to be packaged. Thus, it becomes even more important to make provision for a safety stock for the small items that are controlled by formula than for the larger items that are under continuous individual attention. It costs money to maintain safety stocks beyond the normal, expected usage. The effect, in total cost, is to trade this "insurance" expense for manpower by releasing the time of buyers and inventory analysts for closer control of the larger items.

Determining the proper size of the reserve stock is a basic problem in inventory control. Too large safety stocks represent a wasteful expense and can be a very serious item. A fact about inventories that is not always recognized is that, although safety stocks may represent a relatively small percentage of the total value that passes through inventory over the course of a year, they can amount to 60 per cent or more of inventory content at any given time, which is the basis of inventory-carrying cost. On the other hand, too small safety stocks defeat the purpose. A study made in one large manufacturing company showed that its plants could operate successfully, without serious effect on production, if $1\frac{1}{2}$ per cent of stores items were out of stock at any one time. If 3 per cent of the items were out of stock, production losses were serious. At 5 per cent, schedules were completely disrupted and the purchasing department had a difficult time in providing the needed items.[4]

The first step, then, is to determine the degree of protection desired, that is, not to exceed one stock-out in two years, five years, and so forth. From this starting point, the calculation of necessary reserve stocks is a rather com-

---

[4] B. D. Henderson, *Proved Policies of Inventory Control,* Address before the Public Utilities Buyers Group, National Association of Purchasing Agents, February, 1951.

plicated statistical process. The number of demands per month, over a period of a year, is plotted on a Poisson distribution curve to establish a frequency-of-occurrence ratio, and from this an inverse accumulation ratio is calculated. (See Figure 9-1). In this example, with an average or expectation of three demands per month, the inverse accumulation-ratio table shows that .034 of the area of the curve (shaded area) lies to the right, or above six demands per month. This means that 96.6 per cent of the time, the number of demands will be six or less, and 3.4 per cent of the time there will be six demands or more. Assuming a restocking period of one month, then, to limit the chances of a stock-out occurring more than 3.4 times in 100, the time to place a restocking order is when the stock balance reaches the equivalent of six demands, and the safety stock would also have to be six demands' worth, or three in addition to the expected three demands during the restocking period.

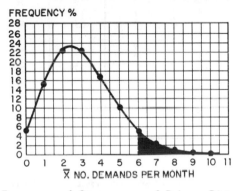

Frequency of Occurrences of Poisson Dist.
X=3

No.	Frequency of Occurrence Ratio	Ratio (Inverse Accumulation)
0	.049	.951
1	.149	.801
2	.224	.577
3	.224	.353
4	.168	.185
5	.101	.084
6	.050	.034
7	.022	.012
8	.008	.004
9	.003	.002
10	.001	.001
∞	∞	∞

Fig. 9-1. Poisson Distribution Curve for Determining Safety Stock Requirements.

ORDER REVIEW POINTS
TABLE OF PROTECTIVE STOCK FACTORS

Protection
1 Stock Out in 2 Years

RESTOCKING FACTOR		DEMAND FACTOR			
No. of Restk. Orders Per Year (N$_r$)	Factor (R)	No. of Demands During Delivery Time (N$_d$)	Factor (D)	No. of Demands During Delivery Time (N$_d$)	Factor (D)
1	.00	1	.85	13	3.00
1.2	.35	2	1.20	14	3.10
1.5	.75	3	1.45	15	3.20
1.7	.95	4	1.65	16	3.30
2.0	1.15				
2.5	1.45	5	1.85	17	3.40
3.0	1.65	6	2.00	18	3.50
3.5	1.85	7	2.20	19	3.60
4.0	1.95	8	2.35	20	3.70
4.5	2.10				
5.0	2.20	9	2.50	22	3.95
6.0	2.35	10	2.60	24	4.10
7.0	2.50	11	2.75	26	4.20
8.0	2.65	12	2.85	28	4.35
9.0	2.75				
10.0	2.85			30	4.50
11.0	2.90			40	5.20
12.0	2.95			50	5.85

Instructions:

A. RESTOCKING FACTOR
1. Obtain (N$_r$) number of restocking orders per year from order quantity table and read Factor R.

B. DEMAND FACTOR
1. Obtain number of demands during past three months from ledger and divide by 90 days to get demands per day.
2. Obtain delivery time in days and multiply by number of demands per day to get number of demands during delivery time (N$_d$) and read Factor D.

C. PROTECTIVE STOCK
1. Calculate protective stock; multiply the Restocking Factor R, times the Demand Factor D.

D. ORDER REVIEW POINT
1. Add protective stock to the number of demands during delivery time (N$_d$) to get order review point in demands.
2. Obtain past 90 days' issues or sales from ledger; divide by the number of demands in the past 90 days to get the average size of demand.
3. Calculate order review point in units by multiplying the ORP in demands times the average size of demands.

Fig. 9-2. Table for Calculating Order Review Point.

Going on from this relatively simple example, conversion factors can be calculated for various desired degrees of protection and varying numbers of demands per delivery period. These, in conjunction with the frequency of restocking orders, make it possible to determine accurately the required safety stocks and ordering points to provide the desired protection. A representative table of this sort is shown as Figure 9-2.

The determination of safety stocks by such a method is more than a means of scientifically implementing inventory policies. It is a guide to policy decisions, for it establishes a relationship between inventory investment and the quality of supply service at various inventory levels. For example, if management should wish to improve the service from 6 per cent stock-out to 4 per cent stock-out, it knows that this can be done only with an increase in inventory equivalent to a 10-day supply. Knowing the value of a 10-day supply of inventory (for example, $100,000) and the carrying cost (for example, 9 per cent), it is clear that such a decision would cost $9,000, and this would be balanced against the cost savings resulting from fewer interruptions to production or the additional profits or sales advantages resulting from better service to customers. The decision would be based on actual cost data rather than on unsupported judgment, and it could be carried out easily by inventory clerks if they were issued instructions to use the appropriate inventory and ordering tables.[5]

Control of working inventory

In the control of working inventory, exclusive of the safety stock, the basic formula is the one cited in Chapter 8 for the determination of most economical ordering quantities, which establishes certain relationships between annual usage, ordering quantity, cost of ordering, and cost of carrying inventory. The formula stands for a specific use and it is not, therefore, an all-purpose answer to every inventory problem. But all of the factors are present, or can be derived from the values expressed in that relationship. For example, number of orders is derived by dividing annual usage by order quantity; average inventory quantity is half of the ordering quantity, assuming a constant rate of use and replenishment of stock at the time that previous inventory supply is exhausted; total inventory and total number of orders are the sums of these factors as applied to individual items. Any of these values can therefore be expressed mathematically in terms of the original factors, and the factors can be mathematically transposed in the equation without affecting its validity.

---

[5] W. F. Hoehing, "A Statistical Method of Inventory Control," *Purchasing Magazine,* February, 1955, page 92.

In establishing the economical ordering quantity, the problem was to arrive at lowest ultimate cost of maintaining the inventory supply, item by item. The formula showed that this could not be accomplished by applying the same ordering frequency to all items regardless of the total quantity (annual usage) involved. It was accomplished by increasing the frequency (decreasing the amount) of orders on items of large annual usage, and by decreasing the frequency (increasing the amount) of orders of small annual usage, to the point where the cost of acquisition and the cost of possession were equal.

If lowest inventory cost were the only objective, if unit costs were stable regardless of quantity, and if usage were at a constant rate, this would be the whole story of statistical inventory control. But none of these conditions consistently prevail.

There are two variables in the formula—size (or number, or frequency) of orders, and annual usage of items. The formula shows the relationship to be between the numerical value of the former and the square root of the latter. Mathematically, this is expressed by saying that order quantity is a function of the square root of annual usage. This can also be written as the formula:

$$Q = K\sqrt{A}$$

Standing by itself, this has little practical meaning. It is the problem of the inventory analyst and controller to find or assign appropriate values of the constant K to make that relationship meaningful in the attainment of specific inventory objectives and in the carrying out of current inventory policies. By standard statistical methods that are too involved for this discussion, and by taking cognizance of the additional factors pertinent to a particular problem, the skilled analyst can compute K values to adjust ordering frequency and quantity to desired inventory levels (at a sacrifice of purchase economy but to the advantage of total net cost of materials), or to reduce the number of orders issued, or to take best advantage of quantity discounts, or to cope with conditions of variable usage or variable lead times.[6]

Inventory-control policies thus arrived at are translated into buying terms in the form of reorder points and quantities—maximum and minimum stock limits—for the various inventory items or classifications. It is a responsibility of the inventory-control phase of management or procurement to keep these instructions up to date, consistent with current conditions and policies.

As in the case of optimum purchase-order quantity (Chapter 8), the calculations involved and the implementation of the entire program can be greatly expedited by the use of automatic computers and application of the principles of integrated data processing.

---

[6] For a detailed exposition of these methods, see W. E. Welch, "Tested Scientific Inventory Control," Greenwich, Conn., Management Publishing Corp., 1956.

Inventory classification

Successful inventory management is greatly aided by a logical system of classification covering all inventory items for purposes of control, cost accounting, storeskeeping, and issue. There is no necessary correlation between such a classification and the grouping of commodities for purposes of procurement; in fact, the two types of classification frequently differ within the same company. For purchasing, the classification is logically based on the related nature and source of the various items. For inventory purposes, it is more logically based on the end use or function of the item, the purpose for which it is purchased. In both cases, the starting point is a system of standard nomenclature and identification, to avoid duplication in purchasing or stocking identical items under two or more different designations. The identification code or system, obviously, should be the same in both the purchasing and stores classifications.

There is no standard system of inventory classification appropriate for all companies, because of variations in material requirements. However, there are some general principles that apply.

For purchased inventory items, major divisions are usually set up for production materials (which are incorporated in the end product and are a direct material cost of that product) and nonproduction items (supplies, which are an operating expense). In some companies, depending on organization and policy, there is a third major division of capital expense items. Inventories of materials in process and of finished goods are outside the scope of this discussion, since purchasing responsibility usually terminates when goods go from stores into production.

The production material classification is generally subdivided into raw materials, semifinished materials, and fabricated parts and components, sometimes a fourth division is provided for items purchased for a special project or end use, as, for example, items bought to fulfill a government contract under which materials must be separately accounted for. If some parts are fabricated for stock in the company's own plant instead of being procured by purchase, they are classified in the same way as if they were bought from an outside source. The only difference in procedure is that, when the time comes for stock replenishment, a work order is issued instead of a purchase order.

Nonproduction materials are similarly subdivided. Major headings under this category would include: fuels, operating supplies, maintenance and repair items, and stationery.

The process of subdivision is continued until there is an appropriate classification for every item. If an item is used for both production and nonproduction purposes, like a common bolt that is a component of the end product and is also used in plant maintenance, it is listed only once, under the major-use category. If an item is stocked in several different sizes, each size is treated as a separate item under the appropriate subhead.

One important purpose of inventory classification has been suggested—in accounting and distribution of costs for the various types of material. Another is in connection with the operation of physical stores, which are usually arranged in much the same way—raw materials, production parts, and supply stores, with related items in adjacent locations so far as is possible. Classification is especially helpful where mechanized accounting systems are in use and where identification is according to a numerical code, so that entries automatically fall into the proper group or account.

For control purposes, the summary figures, by groups, are useful in analyzing usage and in maintaining a properly balanced stock. Top management is more interested in such summary information than in individual data, except for a few critical key commodities. It is obvious that inventory policies can be set collectively for many categories, from the standpoint of both investment and supply service. Thus, classification simplifies the mechanics of control.

The most comprehensive published inventory classification is that covering the wide range of materials used by the United States Government in its various departments, bureaus, and establishments. This "Commodity Classification for Storage and Issue" was compiled under the direction of the Standards Division of the Federal Bureau of Supply, and appears as Section II of the Federal Standard Stock Catalog. For comparison, see also III, "Commodity Classification for Purposes of Procurement," which is on a different basis altogether.

Inventory records

The basic inventory record is the perpetual inventory. This is a continuing, current record of receipts, disbursements or allocation of material, and balance on hand and on order, of every item in stock, showing the complete inventory position.

This information originates in the stores department, and the record is typically kept in that department, with some provision for making the data readily available to other departments as needed. In the small purchasing department which also has the responsibility for stores and for stock control, it is a common practice to incorporate the inventory record directly on the purchase record card, showing also the maximum and minimum stock quantities, ordering quantity, and any other purchasing information required to implement the established, prevailing inventory policy for the item. Where this type of record is used, the record of disbursements is usually in the form of a summary figure obtained from the stores department, showing total monthly usage in a single entry instead of listing the individual issue transactions.

In the more specialized and completely organized systems of inventory control, whether under purchasing jurisdiction or in a separate department, mechanized records and posting have almost universally supplanted manual methods of record keeping. This has not only eliminated many hours of tedious clerical effort and minimized errors of transcription and calculation; it provides a far more useful management tool by making it possible to present more complete information in analytical form, more quickly and at more frequent intervals. One particular system, for example, makes it possible to furnish the purchasing department with a weekly inventory recap which is automatically subtotaled by commodity groups (for example, plumbing supplies, machine parts, work clothing, and so forth), together with current, cumulative, and past average usage data, information on open orders and split shipments, and indicated reorder and follow-up action. This is only a part of the information developed in this particular record. It establishes average prices which are used in pricing withdrawals, calculates inventory valuation, accumulates material costs on specific job orders, and signals job closings for the invoice department. In providing more and better information of this sort, it has eliminated several individual records and forms previously required and has reduced travel and processing time on others.

All perpetual inventory records are periodically checked against actual stock for accuracy, and any discrepancies are adjusted in the record. In the system just described, the current inventory figure is verified by spot checks of selected items in each classification. In all cases, good management requires a complete physical inventory at least annually. The current record is accepted as adequate for control and operating purposes, but it does not constitute a real audit.

Inventory valuation

The simpler forms of inventory records are concerned only with quantity. Even so, the annual inventory must be priced to provide an accurate valuation for this asset, and current financial information is also desirable for several reasons. Where such information is incorporated directly in the current stores record, the term "stores ledger" is commonly used instead of "perpetual inventory." Such a record is properly, and almost necessarily, maintained outside the stores department, in purchasing or materials control. Indeed, it is the policy in some companies to withhold all price information from the stores department by blocking out the "price" column on stores department copies of purchase orders, and making this department responsible only for prompt and accurate reporting of quantitative receipts and disbursements. Where a stores ledger is maintained, material requisitions and bills of material can be priced directly from the ledger cards instead of from supplementary records, and the totals and trends of inventory investment can be readily summarized for a single item or for a commodity group.

From an accounting standpoint, the stores ledger is usually set up as a subsidiary ledger, controlled by and balanced with one or more controlling accounts in the general ledger.

In standard accounting practice, there are several alternative methods of pricing inventory. Each of these gives a somewhat different interpretation of inventory values, and the choice of a particular method will depend on (1) general accounting policy and (2) tax advantages. The five methods most generally used are outlined in the succeeding paragraphs. They are all acceptable for tax purposes, with the proviso that once a particular method has been selected as the basis for tax returns, it cannot be changed at will to gain a temporary tax advantage but must be consistently observed in subsequent returns unless a written application to change is filed with and approved by the Tax Commissioner.

1. *Cost or market, whichever is lower.* This method considers replacement cost as the true measure of value. If the market price declines, the loss or depreciation in value is taken at once, rather than maintaining a fictitious book value in excess of current worth. If the market price advances, the "paper profits" of inventory appreciation are disregarded until they become real profits when the material is used. As a pricing or marketing policy for the end product, the higher replacement cost of materials is then properly considered.

2. *Average cost.* This accounting method prices all withdrawals from inventory at the average unit cost of the total supply of the item in stock at the time. It has a stabilizing effect by evening out price fluctuations, yet in the long run it reflects the actual purchase cost of materials.

3. *First in, first out.* This pricing method, which is also referred to as "oldest lot first," is based on the theory that materials will be used in the same order as received, and that actual cost should be applied. However, the physical observance of this policy is not essential to the application of the accounting method. It is a satisfactory method where stock turnover is reasonably rapid, or where normal fluctuations in material costs can be absorbed in the product price. It serves to "clean house" by disposing of those lots (values) that have been held longest in stock. Consequently, inventories are carried in asset accounts at values that approximate current market prices most closely.

4. *Last in, first out.* This pricing method reverses the procedure described immediately above. Current issues of material are priced at the unit value of the lot most recently received. The theory is predicated on the premise that the reserve stock is economically the equivalent of a fixed asset. In this method, the aggregate book value of an inventory tends to remain stable over

a period of time, while current usage is priced to reflect current market values and costs.

This method is a relatively recent development in accounting practice. It was adopted by the American Petroleum Institute in 1934 as the uniform method of inventory evaluation, and has come into more general use since 1939, when income tax regulations regarding its use were liberalized. It is appropriate under certain conditions: when the ratio of inventory to other assets is large; when inventory consists principally of basic raw materials accounting for a large part of end-product costs; when inventory turnover is slow because of long processing cycles; and when the cost of raw materials is such an important factor that fluctuations in such costs cannot readily be absorbed in the ordinary cost of business. Because it has the effect of reducing profit margins when material prices are rising, and increasing profit margins when material prices decline, it is advantageous from a tax standpoint in industries where the long-range trend of material prices is upward. It is not suited to operations where the manufacturing cycle is short, where inventory turnover is rapid, or where specific purchases must be correlated to current sales, as in the manufacture of most consumer goods, especially style merchandise.

5. *Standard cost.* This pricing method irons out minor fluctuations in cost by setting a standard unit cost for each item, thus providing a stable basis for cost calculations as materials are withdrawn from stock and used. The standard cost should approximate actual cost as closely as possible. It may include a small margin of safety, but it defeats its own purpose if it is calculated with a profit factor. Provision must be made to account for deviations from actual cost,[7] and for revision to a realistic basis in the event of any major change. This method is particularly appropriate in connection with the mass production of standard products. It is sometimes cited as an advantage of standard costs that they provide an incentive for the purchasing department to keep actual prices paid at or below the given standard, but this argument is really irrelevant. Standard costs are essentially an accounting device.

Inventory turnover

One result of effective stores control is a healthy rate of inventory turnover. This does not necessarily mean the highest possible rate. For, although

---

[7] A supplementary account is kept in the cost department, detailing such variations, which are totaled on a summary sheet at the end of each accounting period. The net adjustment to the inventory account is made by journal entry, with an offsetting debit or credit in the inventory variations account. At the end of the fiscal year, the latter account is entered into profit and loss.

rapid turnover does reduce inventory investment, it must be balanced against the need for adequate reserve stocks, the quality of supply service, the desirability of prudent forward coverage, and the economies of quantity buying, which are equally important objectives.

The fallacy of regarding turnover rate as the measure of stores efficiency can be readily seen by remembering that the rate can be doubled very simply by halving the purchase-order quantity and issuing twice as many orders at more frequent intervals. This may be a very expensive way of buying, and at the same time it jeopardizes the reliability and continuity of supply. Extremely high turnover rates are practicable and advantageous only insofar as they can be achieved within the scope of these other factors.

Inventory turnover is a selective matter. No over-all rate is applicable to all items in the stock list. At one end of the scale may be a replacement part for a power-generating unit, representing a substantial investment; it is absolutely essential to have this part on hand, even though it is expected that it will not be needed more than once in five years or longer. At the other end of the scale are standard shelf items of hardware, procurable at short notice from a local dealer. In between are scores of classifications differing in significance, availability, rates of usage, and length of procurement cycle. In setting a standard for inventory turnover, therefore, certain broad groupings should be separately considered. Within each group, a reasonable goal or policy can be set, to be effectuated through stores control. Then comparisons between successive periods, for each group, will have significance that is completely lost in an over-all figure. Regarded in this way, turnover rate can be a useful indicator of stores operating efficiency and a guide to inventory and purchasing policy.

Surplus materials

A final objective of stores control is the detection of inactive stock items which increase the inventory investment without contributing any corresponding service or utility. Such a condition may arise from any one of many reasons: overrequisitioning, overbuying, or overdeliveries; abandonment of projects or cancellation of sales orders; changes in design or specifications; undetected errors in materials accounting; materials stored in the wrong location and consequently "lost." These conditions rarely come to light of themselves. An alert storekeeper familiar with his stock may notice particular items or lots that are not being called for, and may question their place in the inventory. But in dealing with a stock of several thousand separate items, complete reliance cannot be placed upon this chance. A comprehensive system of stores control therefore initiates direct action, which can be taken in three ways:

SHIPPING AUTHORIZATION

THE MARTIN COMPANY
BALTIMORE 3, MARYLAND

MARTIN ORDER NO.	SUPPLEMENT NO.
DATE	CUST. ORDER NO.

SOLD TO	SHIP TO	INSPECTION REQ'D
		☐ Supply Affidavits ☐ See Notation Below
		REQUESTED BY

SHIP VIA	☐ PREPAID ☐ COLLECT	F.O.B.	AUTHORITY

ITEM NO.	QUANTITY		Packed By	Checked By	DESCRIPTION	UNIT PRICE	AMOUNT
	ORDERED	THIS SHIPMENT					

SHIPPED VIA	SHIPMENT NO. ☐ 1 ☐ 2	NO & KIND CONTAINERS	Gr. Wt. (Lbs.)	B/L NO.

SHIPMENT SUMMARY

Item	1 Shipment	Date	Bal. Due	2 Shipment	Date	Bal. Due	Item	1 Shipment	Date	Bal. Due	2 Shipment	Bal. Due	Date

INSIDE – PLANT TRANSPORTATION RECORD

FROM	SHIPPING CLERK	DATE	DRIVER	DATE	RECEIVER	DATE

TRUCK PASS

DATE _____

TIME IN _____ A.M. _____ P.M.   TIME OUT _____ A.M. _____ P.M.

TRUCK _____
MAKE   LICENSE NO.

COMPANY _____

DRIVER _____
SIGNATURE   LICENSE NO.

FROM _____

DESTINATION _____

SIGNED _____
DEPT. HEAD OR ESCORT

Fig. 9-3. Forms Used in Scrap
Disposal Control Program.

SCRAP TALLY
MARTIN

065384 (11-56)

SOLD TO _____

ADDRESS _____

DESCRIPTION OF SCRAP

SHIPPING AUTHORIZATION	LOCATION	DATE
GROSS WEIGHT	TARE WEIGHT	NET WEIGHT

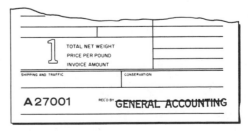

1	TOTAL NET WEIGHT	
	PRICE PER POUND	
	INVOICE AMOUNT	

SHIPPING AND TRAFFIC	CONSERVATION

A27001   REC'D BY   GENERAL ACCOUNTING

1. *Periodic review of stock records* on a systematic basis, taking a specified section each week or month so that the entire list is covered once or twice a year. Items which have not been called for during the past six months or for which the rate of use has fallen off so that stock quantities represent excessive coverage are noted and brought up for analysis and action.

2. *Analysis of physical inventory* at the time the annual inventory is taken. Any material that has actually been in stock a year or more is noted and comes up for review.

3. *Periodic "clean-up" campaigns,* extending beyond the storeroom itself into all departments. This provides for review of materials that have been issued from stores but have not been used for the anticipated purpose, those held in subsidiary stockrooms and tool cribs and thus outside normal stores supervision, and capital items such as furniture and equipment that have fallen into disuse or have been replaced by more modern equipment.

Standards can be set to indicate the basis upon which an item should be declared surplus, for example, materials for which there have been no disbursements during the past quarter, quantities in excess of the past six months' requirements, equipment and tools that have not been used during the past year, and materials and supplies in manufacturing departments for which there is no open order.

If there is no reason for holding such items against some future contingency, a decision is made as to the manner of disposition. There are several alternative possibilities:

> Utilization, as is, as a substitute for currently standard material or in some other product or model.
> Utilization by transfer to another department.
> Utilization by charge-out at a percentage discount from standard costs. (An oil company found this method effective in securing acceptance of outmoded models of pumps and other service station equipment by station managers whose compensation was calculated on the ratio of sales to investment and costs.)
> Utilization by remanufacture.
> Return to original manufacturer.
> Sale as surplus material.
> Sale as scrap.

The three last-named methods of disposal generally come under the jurisdiction of the purchasing department. Whatever disposition is made, it serves to convert a continuing liability into an asset, reduce the investment in stores, maintain a clean inventory, and increase stock turnover by eliminating inactive items.

10

BUYING AT THE RIGHT PRICE

PRICE IS WITHOUT QUESTION a consideration of major importance in any purchase transaction, but to the uninitiated in purchasing science it is a highly overrated factor. There is a curiously contradictory attitude toward this aspect of the buying responsibility. Management properly expects its purchasing agents to negotiate and buy at the most favorable price levels obtainable and is likely to judge the efficiency of its purchasing department on the basis of prices paid; yet the characterization of a purchasing agent as a "price buyer" is used as a derogatory term. No honest purchasing man will deny a keen interest in the prices of the materials he buys, but he will be just as honest in declaring that price is generally the last factor to be considered, for price is meaningless unless it is predicated on adequate quality, assured delivery, reliability and continuity of supply, and satisfactory commercial relations. Price is just one of the terms and conditions of a purchase order, no more nor less important than any of the other terms or details set forth in such an agreement. Certainly the sales function is fully as price-conscious as is purchasing, perhaps in part from an exaggerated notion of its importance in purchasing psychology and in part because of a sound recognition of price as an economic and competitive factor in distribution and in profitable company operation.

Price objectives

Basically, price is rarely if ever considered alone or for its own sake but in connection with other factors as a means to certain objectives of economical and efficient company operation. A few simple concepts fundamental to all good purchasing should be noted at this point. Some of them have been suggested in previous chapters, but they should be specifically considered in relation to the price factor.

Low ultimate cost is the objective and responsibility of purchasing. Invoice price is one element of cost, but not necessarily the determining factor. This is readily apparent if a transaction is traced through its successive stages. The first checking point occurs at the time material is received, when delivered cost can be ascertained. A low price paid to a distant supplier may be outweighed by packing and transportation charges, so that delivered cost of the low-price item is actually higher. The second checking point comes when materials are issued to the using department. The buyer may have paid a lower price by reason of taking larger quantities at a greater discount, but the expense of handling and storage may have outweighed this price differential by the time the materials are actually required, issued, and put to use. The third checking point occurs after the materials have been used or fabricated and incorporated in the end product. Manufacturing costs have now been added, and the extent to which such costs have been increased by reason of inferior workability or difficulties in application must be weighed against a price which would have procured superior materials. At all three stages there is a balance that must be observed, and in considering the original or invoice price the purchasing agent must aim at ultimate cost rather than immediate unit price.

A common equation used in discussions of purchasing is that *value* equals *quality* divided by *price*. This is not a mathematical formula, but a means of expressing the general truth that value varies directly in proportion to the quality received and inversely in proportion to the price paid. It stresses the fact that the amount of investment in materials is less significant than what is obtained in return for the investment. If quality increases more rapidly than price in a series of offerings, the value is greater at the higher price—up to the point where the buyer would be paying for quality in excess of the need. Where quality has been defined in a specification, so that it can be considered as a constant in this equation, the comparison of values can be made in terms of price alone, and the lower price would represent the greater value. It should be noted, however, that this attention to price comes *after* quality has been fully considered and decided upon.

The purchasing responsibility is frequently defined as keeping the company in a favorable competitive position in its field, so far as costs of materials are concerned. Because this involves a consideration of what others are paying for similar materials, it carries the implication that there is a prevailing market price and that the purchasing agent must be familiar with market conditions in order to buy at or below their levels. The Robinson-Patman Act, for example, is aimed at eliminating price discrimination between buyers on the part of sellers, but the purchasing agent cannot rely on such regulations to assure him of equal price advantage. He will find differences of price between various potential suppliers in the same field, and differences according to customer classification, quantity discounts, and the like. He must therefore exert himself to be sure that his company is in the most favorable customer classification earned by the nature and size of the business, and he must adjust his policies and buying methods to take advantage of all available price economies. Otherwise, his company will have to overcome a competitive handicap as compared with another concern in the same field where a more astute procurement program is followed.

The purchasing agent's concern for price properly extends to every item procured through his department, however trifling in unit value or however small the unit saving may be. This is a part of his function, to avoid any needlessly high cost and to keep expenditures at the lowest level consistent with attaining the desired results. The scorn which is sometimes expressed concerning penny-consciousness in purchasing would be more appropriately directed at careless disregard of minor savings possibilities. For in large-scale operations, the field of industrial purchasing, the cumulative effect of small savings amounts to substantial totals. This is particularly true in mass-production industries, where even the smallest and least costly parts are magnified to significant proportions through repetitive use and large volume.

Who makes the price?

In the philosophy of business, it is the seller's privilege to name the price at which he is willing to sell his product. In the economics of business, that decision depends on how many buyers can be found who are willing to pay the price; otherwise, there is no market. From this angle it could be argued that the buyer makes the price. As a practical matter, neither of these positions can be categorically supported. Although in theory the seller is under no compulsion to sell, nor the buyer to buy, at any given price level, actually that compulsion does exist if business is to be done. Business cannot be conducted on the basis of the irresistible force and the immovable object. It is a process of arriving at a mutual agreement resulting in sales and purchases. The seller must find an outlet for his product and the buyer must find the materials needed by his company. Markets and prices are not made by quotations or offers, but by actual transactions.

It is true, of course, that there are periods in which sellers can exert the dominant influence, and other periods in which buyers are in the more favorable position. But these "sellers' markets" and "buyers' markets" are basically economic in origin and nature, and the resulting price advantages are temporary in that they shift from one side of the transaction to the other as the imbalance is corrected. Realistically, pricing policies follow these changing economic fortunes, but businesses that are built on long-range, continuing supplier-customer relationships do not press the advantage beyond maintaining a normally competitive position. The supplier who consistently sets his price at "all the traffic will bear" forfeits customer loyalty and can expect to fare worse than others when the economic tide turns. The buyer who is primarily an opportunist, looking for the hungriest supplier and capitalizing on that condition, can scarcely ask for consideration in price and service when problems of supply become more difficult.

For most standard materials and products, production costs and competition tend to establish a going market price that is approximately equal among all suppliers at any given time. This is presumably equitable and mutually satisfactory, representing a fair return to the seller and fair value to the purchaser under prevailing conditions. Buyers frequently test such markets, but rarely try to break them. The buyer is not a price censor. A generally established market price level is accepted as one of the economic facts of business life. The rightness of that price, from the buying standpoint, is largely a matter of being sure that regular supply sources are reasonably in line with the going market price, and that the purchaser is getting the most favorable terms and discounts warranted by the size of his requirements and orders.

Obtaining bids

For nonstandard materials, more complex fabricated products where design and manufacturing methods vary, and items made to the buyer's specification, no such ready-made market level exists. Asking for competitive bids is the buyer's simplest way of exploring price under these circumstances and evaluating the rightness of the quoted prices. To establish a right and realistic price, buyers properly insist upon firm bids, that is, the offer upon which a prospective seller will unequivocally stand in his bid for the order. If a bid is offered with the suggestion that the seller might revise it subsequently, offering a better price if necessary, the buyer can have no confidence that he will in fact receive the best, or right, price offer from that source.

If there is a wide range in quotations, the excessively high bid is clearly out of line, but the excessively low bid is just as much open to question on the grounds of its economic soundness and reliability. However, a reasonable variation is expected, for no two suppliers are exactly equal in manufacturing efficiency and competitive eagerness. If several or all quotations are identical, there is usually a suspicion of collusion to maintain an unjustifiably high price.

Having received competitive bids from a representative number of possible suppliers, the buyer can, of course, easily select the lowest price offer. Whether this is actually a "right" price he must judge by comparison with the other offers, with past experience, with the prices of similar products, and with his own knowledge of prices and markets.

A great deal of purchasing of both standard and special items is done on the basis of competitive bids. In governmental purchasing, which is very sensitive to charges of favoritism and patronage, which is specifically dedicated to the conservation of taxpayers' money, and where the buyer as a public servant must operate "in a goldfish bowl" for all to see, the bid system is usually mandatory. When a purchase is contemplated, it is advertised so that anyone interested may have the opportunity to bid. Sealed bids are received and held, to be opened and made public at a stated time, in the presence of all bidders who may wish to come. The order must be awarded to the lowest responsible bidder. If no bids are deemed acceptable, the purchasing agent has no alternative but to reject them all and start all over again, calling for new bids. If two or more low bids are identical, he may divide the business or toss a coin to determine the successful vendor—scarcely a scientific method of making a purchasing decision. The entire transaction becomes a matter of public record.

The chief shortcoming of such a policy is that it makes price the sole criterion of value. This can be justified on the principle that "all other things being equal" price is the determining factor, and by making the requirements

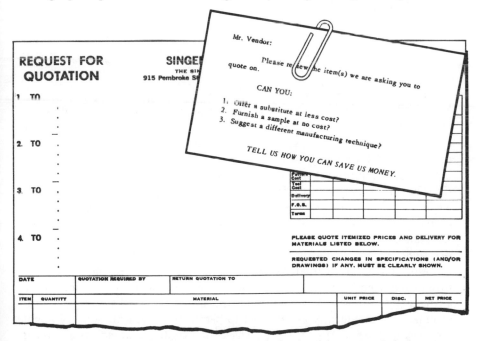

Fig. 10-1. Request for Quotation with Special Plea for Help on Cost Reduction.

of quality and service so definitive and clear that there can be no conflict or choice between suppliers on that score. Care must also be taken that the specification is not written so as to be preclusive, admitting only the product of one supplier. On important purchases, a performance bond furnished by the vendor with his bid is the buyer's assurance that quality and service will be as represented.

Industrial buyers are generally committed to the principle that bid price information is confidential, and they demand greater latitude in deciding where to place orders, so that due consideration can be given to factors other than price. They use the bid system primarily as a means of exploring or fixing the price factor. Frequently it follows, particularly in cases where competitive products and alternative vendors are adjudged to be equally acceptable, or on standard commercial items on which "all other things" are equal, that business is awarded on the bid basis. But this is not necessarily so. Bids are a useful tool, but not the only tool at the buyer's disposal in determining the right price at which to buy.

Buyers and sellers alike are critical of strict adherence to the bidding system for another reason. It gives no weight to past performance and service. Continuity of supply and healthy buyer-seller relationships are important and valuable considerations to both sides. Yet both are disregarded when successive transactions are considered only on the basis of current bids.

Negotiated prices

The alternative method of arriving at a price is through negotiation. Negotiation should not be interpreted as "trading" or compromise. It is the process of working out a procurement and sales problem together, to the point of reaching a mutually satisfactory agreement. Negotiation is not at all incompatible with competition. In almost all cases it starts with a competitive bid, a firm bid in respect to the conditions and requirements as known at the time. But it recognizes that this is by no means the last word, and that many modifications may be made in all factors to arrive at the most favorable balance between quality, service, and cost. Negotiation can be carried on simultaneously with several suppliers on a given project, maintaining competition right up to the point of decision.

Most buyers agree that negotiated bids come closer to the right price than merely competitive quotations, because all pertinent factors come under analysis and discussion in the course of the negotiation, and details of the requirement can frequently be adjusted to permit price advantages that would otherwise be missed. Most major purchases and contracts in industrial buying are negotiated. It is almost essential in the case of new products for which there is no prior manufacturing experience; otherwise, it is likely that a bidder will be impelled to include in his quotation a safety margin for contingencies and unknown manufacturing costs. These extra margins may or may not be warranted in the hindsight of actual experience, but the industrial buyer, unlike the federal government, has no legal recourse through renegotiation after a contract has been completed. Many of these problems can be resolved in the negotiating process.

In its military buying, the federal government has turned largely to negotiation rather than bid-and-award methods. The practice has been sharply criticized as extravagant, wasteful, and discriminatory, but such charges are certainly open to debate. The fact remains that the massive, complicated, and urgent requirements in this field could never have been fulfilled by any other method.

Skill in negotiation is an important asset to the buyer. It includes a knowledge of costs and values, the ability to marshal facts logically and convincingly, to deal with people, to set realistic price goals, and to pursue these goals firmly and persuasively. It is the buyer's responsibility in negotiation to make sure that his company receives every price advantage to which it is legitimately entitled. At the same time, he must understand and appreciate the seller's position. Although he has no ethical responsibility to safeguard the seller's profits, he is aware that the final price must be economically sound to make the price right for both parties. No purchasing program is stronger than its sources of supply, and to drive too sharp a bargain is to weaken the supplier or to eliminate him as a potential, continuing source of supply for future requirements.

A more detailed discussion of the philosophy and techniques of negotiation appears in Chapter 16.

Price related to cost

There are three general criteria of what a fair price should be. They assume (1) that price should bear a reasonable relation to cost (material *plus* manufacturing cost *plus* overhead and profit); (2) that price is the result of economic conditions (supply and demand); (3) that price is determined by competition. The purchasing agent must take all three of these influences into account in his analysis of price and in deciding what is the right price for a given product at a given time.

Cost sets a lower limit on the price at which a supplier can afford to make and sell his product. Prices based on cost plus a reasonable profit are fair to the supplier as well as to the buyer, but "cost plus" is a dangerous way to express price in a contract, because it tends to make the supplier careless of costs in the assurance that he will recover them, plus a profit, in any case.

The cost basis of pricing should operate as an incentive for the supplier to reduce costs. Where price directly reflects cost, the buyer can select the supplier having the most efficient management and the most economical production, and can share in those lower costs. The buyer can reduce costs by adapting the design and specifications of his own requirements to lower-cost materials and more economical production methods. It is not uncommon for large industrial companies to aid their suppliers in reducing costs by providing technical and management counsel, in the expectation of lower prices resulting from the cost savings.

The soundness of the principle of a price related to cost has long been recognized in certain types of contracts calling for price adjustments, up or down, in the event of changes in major raw material costs or prevailing wage rates. The standard coal contract endorsed by the National Association of Purchasing Agents and the National Coal Association contained such a provision, tied in with mine wage agreements, years before the idea was popularized under the descriptive term, "escalator clause." Contracts of this sort have their place in industrial buying and selling. However, because one of the primary purposes of a contract is to fix risk and commitments, escalator clauses should be limited to long-term agreements or contracts involving a long production cycle, as in the case of power-generating equipment or special machinery, where a period of years rather than weeks or months may be involved in filling the order. The cost basis of price escalation should be clearly defined in any case and, because the risk is transferred to the buyer's account, provision should be made for downward adjustment on the same basis in the event that costs decline.

Price analysis takes into account both materials and manufacturing costs. The first part is relatively simple, for even a complicated product like an electric motor can be quite accurately broken down into quantitative terms of its major material components—copper, cast iron, and insulation. The spread between material cost and quoted price represents manufacturing cost and profit. To appraise this part of the price, the buyer should have a knowledge of manufacturing processes and costs, and the various operations and handling involved. The cost experience of his own company on comparable operations frequently provides a rough but useful comparison.

One of the things that consistent price analysis shows is that the manufacturing differential is by no means a constant factor, but fluctuates in much the same manner as material costs. Sometimes that fluctuation may be justified by circumstances, and sometimes it is open to question. For example, if it is found that the differential is consistently on a percentage basis derived from material cost, similar to the percentage markup common to retail merchandising, rather than representing a true unit manufacturing cost, the buyer may be justified in challenging the computation, for the percentage markup is not a sound method of estimating or accounting for the cost and value of manufacturing operations. If the buyer's challenge is supported by facts based on analysis, he may not only secure a price adjustment without penalizing the producer's legitimate costs and margin but may also be doing a public service by checking at the source that process of pyramiding costs that leads to inflation at the ultimate consumer level.

Probably the most difficult problems in cost analysis for the purpose of price appraisal and negotiation are those concerning new and nonstandard products for which there is no prior manufacturing experience. This is difficult for the supplier as well as for the buyer, but production management science has developed some useful techniques for coping with such problems, and the buyer should be familiar with these methods, too. The first units of any new product are relatively costly to produce, but experience improves the efficiency of manufacturing methods and the productivity of workers, so that costs come down on succeeding products. The "learning curves" plotting this condition generally show rapid cost reduction on the first few units, then tend to flatten out as methods are standardized but continue downward at a lesser rate as workers steadily gain proficiency. When the curve is plotted on a log-log scale, it approximates a straight line. (See Figure 10-2.) This is projected to permit establishing a target level of production costs upon which a suitably profitable ultimate price can be predicated. The cumulative average line in this graph is higher than the unit cost line, because it includes the initial high costs, but eventually all of these costs are recovered in mass production at the improved rates. The buyer who understands the statistical basis of this phenomenon is likewise able to project a target buying price. He will reject the factual but unrealistically high costs of initial quantities, and will base his negotiations on total quantities, where long-run productivity has been established, or insist on a sliding scale in which the price of successive lots will fairly reflect the lower costs that result from "learning."

Supply and demand

The second, or economic, concept of right price is based largely on the law of supply and demand. As already noted, the operation of this economic law depends on freedom of market action, which has been so modified by modern political and business practices that the action of supply and demand is no longer the decisive factor affecting price, as assumed in classic economic and purchasing theory. Nevertheless, they are influences that cannot be ignored. Prices tend upward when demand exceeds supply, and tend downward when supply exceeds demand.

In this equation, the purchasing agent represents demand. Individually, his influence on the situation may be very small. Cumulatively it may be considerable, but buying policies and action are not a concerted effort except insofar as they represent a common reaction to prevailing conditions. When demand is high, the purchaser must bid up in order to get the goods he wants and needs. The indicated buying policies—to extend forward coverage in times of rising prices, and to buy only for immediate needs in times of declining prices—actually tend to exaggerate these price fluctuations rather than to modify or correct them.

In this concept, the rightness of prices at any given time is accepted as

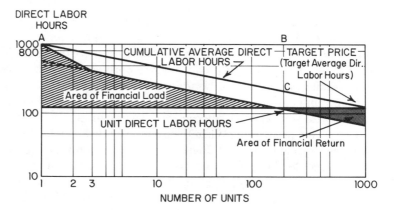

Fig. 10-2. Effect of the Learning Curve on Production Costs. The 80 per cent statistical curve shown here is fairly representative of average conditions in industrial production and is sufficiently accurate to be used as a starting point in most purchasing calculations. In general, the percentage to be used varies inversely as the amount of manual labor involved in the operation. The practical range for most production processes lies between 70 per cent (assembly operations, showing steeper initial decline) to 90 per cent (machine work with long runs and few setups). The 100 per cent curve (no decline) implies complete automation.

being determined by basic economic conditions outside of any effective individual control. The buyer's role, then, is to collect and interpret as accurately as possible the facts of supply and demand, the outlook for economic and political conditions, and the psychological temper of the business community, in order to gauge the probability and reasonableness of prices, current and future.

Competitive prices

The third theory is that price is determined by competition. In a sense, this is predicated on the two price theories already discussed, for it assumes that supply and demand conditions are such as to create a market and to establish a general price level reasonably above the cost of production. Given these fundamental conditions, it is common knowledge that there will be some variations in price—sometimes substantial variations—as between various suppliers. The purchasing agent must discover and understand these variations so that he can place his company's business at the most favorable price that will not jeopardize the equally important considerations of quality and continuity of supply, and that will not entail additional costs due to manufacturing or commercial difficulties, excessive spoilage, interrupted production, and so on.

Some of these variations are readily understandable. There may be lower manufacturing costs due to cheaper labor, cheaper power, strategic location in respect to raw materials or markets, better processes or better equipment, more complete mechanization, larger volume of operations, or highly specialized skills. All of these are legitimate competitive advantages, in which the buyer can logically share.

Some low prices are of less desirable origin. The willingness to work on lower profit margins, for example, may be an indication of some essential weakness in the supplier's organization, and entails the possible hazard of less adequate inspection or quality control, less attention to progressive research, and less reliable production and service. Low prices attributable to the exploitation of labor are now quite generally outlawed, but it must be kept in mind that any unsatisfactory labor conditions in a supplier's plant are likely to lead at any time to an interruption of supply through strikes and walkouts.

Low prices may be quoted on job lots and off-standard merchandise. This does not condemn the merchandise, which may be entirely usable. There is a legitimate outlet for such goods, but the offerings are generally avoided by purchasing agents who value uniformity of product, the assurance of continuing supply from regular vendors, and loyalty in business relationships.

Competition may also be used as a selling weapon, as in the case of a special introductory price to capture a new market or a new customer. This obviously offers no permanent advantage to the buyer, and the temporary advantage may be more than offset by long-range considerations. There is also the vicious and destructive "price war" to discipline a competitor or to drive him from the field by forcing him to sell below cost to meet price competition, a thoroughly uneconomic procedure and likewise, necessarily, a temporary measure. It can be argued that such situations do establish a market price, though it is temporary and usually limited to a local area, and that the buyer should accept it as such in order to maintain his own company's competitive cost position. In any event, his choice of policy lies between opportunism and stable relationships, and his buying decisions are made accordingly.

Purchasing policy, therefore, does not always seek the lowest price obtainable through competition. Yet it does seek competition as one means of evaluating the rightness of quoted prices and of keeping prices right. Competition is maintained by establishing acceptable alternate sources for purchased materials and products, by periodical checking of prices on even common, standard items, by the judicious division of business when quantities warrant, and by inviting competitive bids for comparison and analysis.

Discounts

There are three types of discounts which concern the buyer in his consideration of price.

Trade discounts. Many companies' pricing systems are set up with a series of discounts, on a graduated scale, that are applicable according to the company's classification of customers, without reference to the size of the particular order. Usually such a system is linked with the policy of distribution through franchised representatives, wholesalers, and local dealers; it makes possible an orderly chain of distribution by protecting the territorial rights, profit margins and incentives, and competitive equality of accredited middlemen. There are also other bases of customer classification, for example, according to the purpose for which goods are purchased, whether for export, for domestic resale, for fabrication, or for end-use. The price, then, depends to a considerable extent upon the classification in which a company is placed, and this involves an element of "rightness" from the purchasing standpoint.

Pricing on the basis of customer classification is not regarded as a discriminatory practice, so long as it is part of a logical and established marketing policy and is consistently observed. It sometimes comes in conflict with the logic of purchasing, however. This is the case when a buyer's purchases of an item are substantially greater than all of the distributor's other sales of that item, when orders are filled by mill shipments so that the distributor's role is only nominal, when the distributor does not actually perform the services associated with his function, such as maintaining stocks, extending credit, expediting deliveries, and the like, or when such extra services and conveniences are not needed or desired as a part of procurement. The force of these arguments (and of competition) is sometimes recognized by establishing special classifications for large users, by handling them as "house accounts" or "national accounts," or otherwise modifying the discount system in order to bring prices in line with quantity and service factors.

In any event, it is a part of the buyer's price responsibility to see that his company is in the most favorable customer classification warranted by the circumstances. And this is a proper subject of negotiation with the prime supplier, the distributor, or both.

Quantity discounts. The practice of offering lower unit prices on larger quantity orders has already been discussed in connection with the determination of ordering quantities and forward-buying policies. It has its basis in the economies of volume production and the reduction of selling, shipping, and accounting detail, in the added business assured by the larger orders, and the large user's importance as a customer.

The buyer's responsibility in this case is largely an internal one, to adjust his ordering practices to the most advantageous quantity price breaks. It is also a matter for negotiation in getting prices on products made to the buyer's specification, where quotations are asked on various lot sizes, and where cumulative quantity discounts based on total annual purchases instead of individual purchases may be obtained.

Cash discounts. The cash discount is quite a different matter. It is not a price concession or variation; it is an inducement for prompt payment of invoice charges, and it is earned only when payment is made in accordance with the stipulated terms. Nevertheless, because it affects the net disbursement, the discount is reflected in the total cost of materials, and purchasing must see to it that this potential saving is not jeopardized by carelessness in the terms of the contract or delay in the processing of invoices. The saving, though usually expressed in small percentages of invoice amount, is really a very substantial one. A commonly quoted discount, "2 per cent, 10 days— 30 days net," means that the seller is offering 2 per cent for 20 days' use of the capital amount involved, which is at the rate of 36.5 per cent a year.

Cash discounts are generally uniform throughout an industry, and this practice is consistent with their real function. Discounts for prompt payment are not properly a competitive pricing device. There are cases where such uniformity does not exist, and the varying differentials, if consistently offered by the respective sellers, constitute a cost factor that must be considered in the analysis of comparative costs. There are other cases in which cash discount terms are not stipulated on a vendor's invoice, but in which the standard discount may be allowed provided that the purchasing agent takes care to make this agreement a part of the contract.

Cash discount terms seem very simple, but they must be clearly defined by mutual agreement. For instance, in the absence of any other understanding, most vendors take the stand that the discount period starts with the date of the invoice. The purchasing agent can safeguard the position of his company by making it a condition of the order that the discount period shall be calculated from the date that an acceptable invoice is received by the buyer, thus anticipating and avoiding the loss of the discount when invoices are delayed or the lapse of the discount privilege pending necessary adjustments in the invoice charge.

For convenience in the handling of accounts payable, many companies have adopted the policy of making payments twice a month. But with the daily receipt of invoices, some cash discount periods normally expire on every business day. It is usually possible to make an agreement with vendors that the cash discount will be considered earned if invoices received during the first half of the month are paid on the 20th and invoices received during the second half of the month are paid on the 5th of the succeeding month. This sets up an average discount period of twelve and a half days. It is technically in violation of some standard invoice terms, but calls for prepayment in other cases. Such an arrangement is usually acceptable to vendors, because the basic objective of cash discounts is to encourage promptness and regularity of payment. However, a definite mutual understanding is essential; it is not a matter that can be arbitrarily decided by the purchaser's company.

The purchasing department's responsibility for this potential saving includes (1) seeing that proper cash discount terms are incorporated in the order, (2) securing invoices promptly from vendors, (3) processing invoices promptly and getting them to the accounting or disbursing office within the discount period, and (4), when unavoidable delays are encountered for adjustments in respect to deliveries or invoices because of some fault of the seller, making sure that the discount privilege is not waived pending such adjustment and notifying the vendor to this effect. These are all functions directly connected with the purchasing department procedure, and loss of a cash discount because of failure in respect to any of these steps is properly attributed to purchasing.

The concern for taking advantage of cash discounts involves more than the dollars and cents involved. A company's financial reliability and credit rating are judged by its consistency in discounting its bills, and this is an attribute that should be zealously cultivated. Conversely, the most common abuse of the cash discount privilege is by those companies that deduct the discount after the stated period has elapsed, apparently regarding this percentage as a part of price, rather than a privilege that must be earned by prompt payment in accordance with the terms of the order. Vendors are justified in taking a firm attitude and not permitting such abuse. The purchasing agent has no legitimate grounds for negotiation on this point.

11

SELECTING THE RIGHT SOURCE

TO MAKE A SATISFACTORY purchase, it is necessary to find a capable and willing vendor and to reach an agreement with him on the pertinent factors of quality, service, and price. It is sometimes stated that selection of the right source automatically takes care of every purchasing consideration; quality will be right, deliveries on time, and prices fair. It is not quite so simple, for, as set forth in previous chapters, there are specific purchasing standards for all of these factors. And, in any case, there is the problem of finding this ideal vendor. Traditionally, it is the seller who seeks out the potential customer. That is one important means of making the contact that may lead to the business relationship. But scientific purchasing does not leave the matter to this chance. The buyer seeks to find the best possible sources of supply for his needs. In some cases this will be a matter of making a choice from among many possible and approximately equally promising sources. In other cases it may be a problem involving extensive search to find one satisfactory supplier, or even to develop a source where none had previously been available.

Four stages of selection

In the actual process of source selection, there are four stages: (1) the survey stage, in which all possible sources for a product are explored; (2) the inquiry stage, in which the relative qualifications and advantages of potential sources are analyzed; (3) the stage of negotiation and selection, leading to the issue of an initial order; and (4) the experience stage, in which a continuing vendor-supplier relationship is established or the earlier steps are reviewed in the search for a more satisfactory source.

As in all purchasing problems, the starting point is the need for a material or product. The exact specifications may or may not be fixed, but its general nature and purpose are known. What is available on the market? Who makes such a product, or can make it? Who can supply it most satisfactorily and most economically?

The original survey of potential sources should overlook no possibilities. Trade directories provide comprehensive and well-organized listings of the whole range of manufactured products and manufacturers on a nation-wide basis, usually with at least a general indication of size and commercial rating. Supplementing these are regional directories such as those issued by state Chambers of Commerce and, on a still more local scale, the classified section of telephone directories. Specialized trade directories are available listing concerns which do not have product lines of their own but provide industrial services, such as foundries, screw machine shops, heat treaters, custom fabricators of plastic parts, and the like.

The buyer's library of manufacturers' and distributors' catalogs is another reference source of prime importance, provided there is an adequate indexing system. Many purchasing agents also have a commodity information file in which they have collected vendors' mailing pieces and data sheets, advertisements and new-product announcements from business magazines, and material that was not immediately pertinent when received but touched upon possible or anticipated needs. Some of this information is so new that it has not yet found its way into the standard catalogs, but the alert buyer has it on hand when needed.

In respect to items that must be made to order, the vendor's facilities and processes may be more important than his listed products. The buyer learns to identify the makers of similar products, involving the same manufacturing techniques and equipment, as potential suppliers of the custom-made item he needs.

Salesmen are an important source of information that is not always used to the utmost. There is a tendency in sales effort to promote a particular product or group of products that are known to be used by the buyer's company, which is therefore a logical prospect for such items, whereas other products for which a more immediate demand may exist (unknown to the salesman) are not even mentioned. Instances are commonplace where such sales opportunities—and buying opportunities—have been overlooked throughout a long period of business contacts and eventually disclosed through sheer accident, because the buyer did not know the complete range of the vendor's line and the salesman did not know the full extent of the buyer's requirements. Salesmen should therefore be encouraged to present the entire line of their company's products so that the buyer may recognize and note these potential sources for products or materials that might not otherwise come to his attention.

From the information gleaned from these various sources, the buyer can

WORCESTER PRESSED STEEL COMPANY
FOUNDED 1883

LIGHT AND HEAVY METAL STAMPINGS
HI-PAC PRESSURE CYLINDERS AND VALVES

100 BARBER AVENUE
WORCESTER 6, MASSACHUSETTS 01606

8 January 1964

Reference company
Att: Reference name
Address

Gentlemen:

(Company   ) (Address   )
is being considered as a supplier of   to
Worcester Pressed Steel Company. We understand you have worked
with them, and would be most grateful if you would check applicable statements, and return this letter to us.

I. Their quality rating with us is: Excellent___, very good___,
satisfactory___, fair___, poor___,

        A) On regular jobs_____
        B) On very difficult jobs____

II. In meeting deliveries their record is: Excellent___,
long, but meet promises___, meet most promises___, are frequently
late___, occasionally late, but not their fault___, often very
late___,

        A) We expedite as a matter of course____
        B) Requires little follow-up____
        C) Requires a lot of follow-up____

III. In connection with giving engineering assistance, they have
been: Most cooperative___, helpful and accurate___, helped us
save costs___, somewhat limited___, hard to reach___, neither
prompt nor very helpful___, don't know___.

IV. Handling complaints or rejects, they are: Cooperative
and responsible___, a bit tardy but fair___, settle eventually___,
hard to deal with___, don't know___.

V. Their quotes and costs are: Very low___, competitive___,
sometimes low___, sometimes high___, higher than competition,
but worth it___, generally high-priced___.

VI. Our experience is based on: One order___, fairly new to
us___, recent years___, or long-time association___.

VII. Any comments?

Thank you very much for your confidential opinion.

Sincerely yours,

WORCESTER PRESSED STEEL COMPANY

C. C. Fletcher

C. C. Fletcher, Purchasing Agent

Enc. (Addressed and stamped envelope)

Fig. 11-1. Pre-purchase Survey of Vendor Capabilities and Performance.

build a workable list of the most likely sources. He will select those who seem to combine the attributes of reliability and stability, appropriate manufacturing ability and experience, and reasonably convenient location to avoid excessive transportation costs. Some of them he may know by reputation or through their advertising. He will exclude those having very low capitalization or credit ratings, those whose products are not in the general quality range he requires, those outside his normal trading area, and any with whom he may have had previous unsatisfactory experience. If the product required is of a routine nature, he may send out a request for bids from such a selected list. If the product is more significant, and one for which there is likely to be a continuing need, there will be an intermediate stage of inquiry and research.

Study of supply sources

The second stage of supplier selection narrows the field from possible sources to acceptable sources. Inquiry at this stage is directed toward developing more specific information on vendors' production facilities and capacity, financial stability, product quality, technical competence, manufacturing efficiency, general business policies, position in the industry, progressiveness, interest in the buyer's order, and cooperative attitude. The aim at this point is to find those suppliers who are capable of producing the item in the required quality and quantity, who can be relied on as a continuous source of supply under all conditions, who will keep their delivery promises and other service obligations, and who are competitive as to costs.

It is probable that the buyer's inquiry will elicit a call by the vendor's sales representative. This provides an opportunity to appraise the caliber of the vendor's personnel and representation, his ability to understand the buyer's problem, and his initiative in helping to find the best solution. If the nature and importance of the requirement warrant, it may lead to interviews with technical personnel, the examination and trial of samples, and a visit to the vendor's plant for personal inspection.

Particular features to be noted at the plant of a supplier or prospective supplier are modernity and efficiency of equipment, facilities for technical controls and the importance attached to such controls, caliber of supervision and inspection, evidences of good management and good housekeeping in plant operations, practice as to the maintenance of raw material stocks, and the character of the operation, especially as it relates to purchasing requirements and practices. With such information, purchasing and production specifications may be correlated for maximum economy to both parties. Personal contacts should also be established with key men in management and production as a very helpful asset in the event that emergency or special requirements need to be discussed later at long distance.

The result of the study at this point should be a list of several acceptable supply sources, not only capable of furnishing the requirements, but with any of whom the buyer would be willing to place his order, confident of its satisfactory fulfillment. The list is not necessarily in order of preference, clearly indicating the one best source. It may come very close to that point of decision, but in the orderly process of vendor appraisal and narrowing of choice, there still remains the stage of negotiation where details and terms are considered, to determine where the best ultimate value lies. Basically this will be in terms of quality, service, and price. Beyond that, it will be influenced by the intangibles of interest, cooperation, and good will which enhance the value of all these factors. Beyond that, the decision may hinge on special circumstances—the smaller company where the order will have an importance that is lost in the larger operation, the company that has an engineer or superintendent particularly skilled in that type of production, or the company that has an open spot in its manufacturing schedule to accommodate the order.

As a matter of fact, there may be no *one* best source, for the buyer usually wishes to establish alternative sources for the products he buys, both as an added assurance of supply and to maintain competition. Then the decision as to where the bulk of the business will be placed will be made on the basis of a fourth and convincing criterion—experience.

The approved list

Before taking up the evaluation and rating of vendor performance, the practice of buying from alternative sources should be examined further. For reasons already cited, purchasing policy in most companies requires at least two supply sources for each item, and management generally supports this policy as being in the best interest of the company. Whether there should be more than two, and how many, is a matter of purchasing judgment and the way the list is used. It depends partly on the importance of the item, on competitive conditions in the supplier industry, and on the quantities involved, which might make it practicable to divide the business among several suppliers.

In the preceding sections we have traced the finding and selection of suppliers, assuming a new requirement with no procurement precedent. Acceptability of the source has been considered strictly from the purchasing viewpoint. It is assumed that the requirement has been defined or specified so that the delivered product, in accordance with the specification, will also be acceptable to all concerned. Deciding on the source, then, is entirely a responsibility of purchasing.

Now take another example. The company engineers have designed a product incorporating a common electrical part. For their development work they have selected such a part from a manufacturer's catalog or from an electrical supply house. Their main interest has been merely to find something that will serve the desired purpose. The selected part proves satisfactory and is incorporated in the product design. In drawing up a bill of materials for the first production order, the part is naturally specified by the manufacturer's name and catalog number.

When the purchasing agent receives the requisition to purchase, he is bound to conform to this request, and does so. However, he properly challenges the specification that ties the requirement to a single source, and succeeds in having it modified by the addition of the words "or equal." Now he has leeway for choice on succeeding orders, but because the original part was specified for its known successful performance, the buyer is not to be the sole judge of equality. He is not authorized to make a substitution arbitrarily, without the consent of the specifying engineers. Neither is it practicable for him to go to them for approval every time the item comes up for purchase and he wishes to consider an alternate.

So he promptly starts a search for acceptable alternative products and sources. When he locates a promising new source, he procures samples for inspection and test. Let us say that three such samples are approved as acceptable alternatives for the item first specified. Now, instead of a single source, the buyer has an "approved list" of four suppliers. He enters their names, along with that of the original supplier, on the purchase record card for the item. It is now his privilege to patronize any one of the four at his own discretion. Or, he has a mailing list ready-made for issuing invitations to bid, with the assurance that any one of the offerings will be acceptable as to quality and suitability. A typical purchase record card will provide space for recording up to eight alternative suppliers. The practice of using such "approved lists" is so universal that practically all the stock form designs issued by manufacturers or office systems equipment include this feature.

It is quite likely that the buyer will continue to purchase the bulk of his requirement from the source originally named, provided there is a real preference for the product and that the supplier's price and service are satisfactory. But he will also make some purchases from the others, or give them a chance to quote regularly in order to maintain their interest. An alternative source that is merely another name on a list represents no advantage either to the buyer or the seller. The approved list of supply sources must be used in order to be useful.

Two major criticisms are made of the approved list as a purchasing method. One of these is that it is discriminatory and serves to blacklist any potential supplier who is not included, whereas every seller should at least be accorded the privilege of quoting for business if he so desires. The other is that it imposes a limitation on the buyer himself and restricts the scope of his choice.

If either of these criticisms is justified, and it is quite possible in any individual case, it is an indication that the method is not being properly used. Flexibility and periodical review will overcome both objections. As to the first criticism, it is assumed that all qualified sources of supply have been investigated and have been given an opportunity to present their story when the list was being built, and that if conditions have changed in any essential particular or if new sources enter the field, that opportunity will be given. If they can at any time establish any good reason why they should be added to the list, or replace one of the suppliers already included, that claim should be given full consideration, because the purchasing agent is naturally interested in maintaining his list at the highest possible standard. Failing to establish this position, the opportunity to quote is an empty privilege, because other sources have already been adjudged more desirable. The purchasing agent has the responsibility to keep an open mind, but this does not lay on him any obligation to extend his list of preferred suppliers beyond practicable bounds.

As to the second criticism, the limitation on the buyer, if any, is a self-imposed one. In principle, that limitation is set by either of two conditions: the absence of additional competent sources, from technical or commercial angles, or the practical limits of a working list beyond the basic assurance of supply and reasonable competition. The purchasing agent's judgment may be questioned on either point, but the underlying principle of selection and approval is sound.

The purchasing department of one large railroad has established a policy or formula in respect to the approved list that has given generally satisfactory results even though the method is a somewhat arbitrary one. It is the practice in this company to list seven sources of supply for each item, business being allocated to the several sources according to the best judgment of the buyers. At the end of the year, the list comes up for review and revision. The amount of business given to each of the sources is totaled, and the two suppliers who have received the least business are automatically removed; if three or more have received no business whatever during this period, all of those in this category are removed. Then to bring the list up to seven for the succeeding year, at least two and possibly more than two new suppliers are selected and added, based upon sales presentations and purchase investigations made during that period. The reasoning behind this procedure is that the supply source receiving the least volume of business is of least value to the buyer's company, and the potential supplier who has not earned any awards over a year is simply "dead wood" on the buyer's list; therefore they should give way to some more promising source. Although an occasional injustice may be done by strict adherence to this system, it does provide a desirable measure of flexibility and "new blood" in the supplier list and constantly works toward the ideal of a completely active corps of vendors who are suppliers in fact as well as in name.

Evaluating suppliers' service

The real test of vendor selection is, of course, the test of experience, or satisfactory performance by the vendor once the order has been placed with him. It is listed here as the fourth step in selection because it does more than confirm or refute the buyer's judgment and decision. It is the deciding factor in whether the selected vendor will continue to receive the buyer's business or be replaced by another source.

The objective evaluation and rating of vendor performance has lagged behind the measurement of other factors in purchasing. The buyer is aware, in a general way, that some vendors require an excessive amount of expediting effort and are consistently late in their deliveries, and that rejections for inadequate quality are more numerous with some suppliers than with others. But his measurement of these shortcomings is likely to be chiefly in terms of his own annoyance. In comparatively few departments is it made a matter of record; in fewer still is there any attempt made to establish any sort of a performance rating; and in fewer still is it used for the objective comparison of vendors, as a scientific means of source selection.

A start in this direction is the "Vendor Rating" sheet maintained in one relatively small purchasing department. In this instance, a rating sheet is attached to each folder in the commodity information file, where vendors' product literature, catalog and price sheets, and the like, are kept. Vendors represented by information in the folder are listed in a column at the left side of the sheet, followed by six narrow columns in which entries are made by letter symbols. The first column states whether the vendor is an approved source. The second indicates whether he is a manufacturer, a manfacturer's agent, or a jobber. The third shows a rating of his financial stability. The fourth and fifth columns rate his manufacturing facilities and service facilities, respectively, as Excellent, Good, Fair, or Poor. The sixth column carries an experience rating, simply as Excellent, Satisfactory, or Unsatisfactory. A wide column at the right provides space for comment on "Other considerations." There is no set standard for these ratings; they represent the buyer's appraisal, which is presumably consistent. They do provide some element of comparison, because all suppliers of a given commodity are listed together on one sheet. They do not take vendors' price performance into consideration, but are used in conjunction with a "Summary of Bids" form when quotations are received.

A more comprehensive mathematical vendor-rating formula has recently been developed in the purchasing department of a large manufacturing company. It is known as the "Incoming Material Rating," rather than as a vendor rating, because the calculation is based upon experience with a single item or product; this is its logical application as a buying tool when procurement of that product is under consideration. It is designed to provide a comparative

VENDOR RATING REPORT

J. M. HUBER CORPORATION

COMPANY — Company: _____ DATE _____

TOTAL RATING

	Excellent (4)	GOOD (3)	FAIR (2)	POOR (1)
Size and/or Capacity	4			
Financial Strength		3		
Operational Profit		3		
Manufacturing Range	4			
Research Facilities			2	
Technical Service		3		
Geographical Locations	4			
Total 32	12	18	2	
.63 x Total = 20.16				

Management

	Excellent (4)	GOOD (3)	FAIR (2)	POOR (1)
Labor Relations		3		
Trade Relations		3		

Service

	Excellent (4)	GOOD (3)	FAIR (2)	POOR (1)
Deliveries on Time	4			
Condition on Arrival		3		
Follow Instructions		3		
Number of Rejections	4			
Handling of Complaints		3		
Technical Assistance			2	
Emergency Aid		3		
Supply Up to Date Catalogues, Etc.				1
Supply Price Changes Promptly	4			
Total 27	12	12	2	1
.69 x Total = 18.63				

Products:

	Excellent (4)	GOOD (3)	FAIR (2)	POOR (1)
Quality	4			
Price		3		
Packaging	4			
Uniformity		3		
Warranty	4			
Total 18	12	6		
1.25 x Total = 22.50				

Sales Personnel

1. Knowledge

	Excellent (4)	GOOD (3)	FAIR (2)	POOR (1)
His Company		3		
His Products	4			
Our Industry		3		
Our Company		3		

2. Sales Calls

	Excellent (4)	GOOD (3)	FAIR (2)	POOR (1)
Properly Spaced	4			
By Appointment		3		
Planned and Prepared		3		
Mutually Productive	4			

3. Sales-Service

	Excellent (4)	GOOD (3)	FAIR (2)	POOR (1)
Obtain Information		3		
Furnish Quotations Promptly	4			
Follow Orders		3		
Expedite Delivery		3		
Handle Complaints		3		
Total 43	16	27		
.48 x Total = 20.64				

Fig. 11-2. Vendor Rating Form. Total of points in each category is weighted so that maximum score in any one is 25.

evaluation of vendor performance in any case where an item is procured from two or more sources.

This formula is based upon the principles that (1) the evaluation of a vendor's performance must embrace all three of the major purchasing factors—quality, price, and service—and that (2) the relative importance of these factors varies in respect to various items. The first step, therefore, is to assign appropriate weights to each, adding up to a total weighting factor of 100 points. For example, in a given case, quality performance might be rated at 40 points, price 35, and service 25, and these percentages are subsequently used as multipliers for individual ratings on each of the three purchasing factors. The assignment of these weights is a matter of judgment. In the company where this system originated, the importance of quality ranges from 35 to 45 per cent, price from 30 to 40 per cent, and service from 20 to 30 per cent.

The quality rating is a direct percentage of the number of acceptable lots received, in relation to total lots received.

In rating price, the lowest net price (gross price minus discounts plus unit transportation cost) obtained from any vendor is taken as 100 points, and net prices from other vendors are rated in inverse ratio to this figure.

The service rating is a direct percentage of the lots received as promised, in relation to total lots received.

These three ratings are multiplied by their respective weighting factors and the results are added to give a numerical "Incoming Material Rating" for each vendor, for a given item. Perfect deliveries, on scheduled time, at the lowest net price, earn a rating of 100 points. Any rejections, lapses in delivery, or prices higher than the lowest quotation, reduce the rating. At the same time, there is an objective basis for determining the extent to which superior quality and service offset higher prices in over-all value and satisfaction, or vice versa.

> *Example:*
> Vendor A has delivered 58 lots during the past year, of which two were rejected. His percentage of good lots is 96.5. Multiplied by the weight factor of 40, this gives him a quality rating of 38.6.
> The lowest net price from any vendor is $0.93 per unit. A's price is $1.07. By inverse ratio, his price performance is 86.9 per cent. Multiplied by the weight factor of 35, this gives him a price rating of 30.4.
> Of the 58 lots delivered, 55 were received as promised. This is 94.8 per cent performance. Multiplied by the weight factor of 25, it gives him a service rating of 23.7.
> The sum of these figures gives him a total performance rating of 92.7.
> Vendor B, who furnished 34 lots during the same period, was the lowest-price supplier at $0.93 per unit, so has a price rating of the full 35 points. However, four of the lots were defective, giving him a quality rating of 35.3. Also, he was late with five deliveries, so his service rating is 21.3, for a total performance rating of 91.6.

In this instance, therefore, Vendor A is judged to be the more satisfactory source and the buyer is warranted in placing the bulk of the business with him in spite of his substantially higher price. If Vendor B could be induced to cut his delinquencies in either quality or service by one-half, or if the price factor were deemed relatively more important in respect to this item, B would have the better rating.

To facilitate the use of this rating method, the company has devised a calculator consisting of two plastic discs with logarithmic scales around the circumference of each, on the order of a slide rule, and with supplementary scales providing a direct reading for each of the three rating factors within the weighting ranges previously cited. With the aid of this device, the entire calculation can be completed in a few moments.

Establishing the supplier relationship

No purchasing department wishes—or could afford the time and effort— to go through the complete process of research and analysis of sources for each individual order. The aim of careful vendor selection is to find the one most satisfactory source, or a group of alternative sources with adequate and reasonably comparable qualifications so that succeeding orders for the same item can be placed with these same suppliers with confidence in the original selection. In other words, the decision as to a source of supply contemplates a continuing relationship over a period of time.

It is to be expected that this relationship, which has its origin in objective, impersonal analysis and decision, will become more intimate and personal in the course of doing business together. It starts with the expectation of satisfactory supply service. That expectation should not only be realized; it should improve with cumulative experience and understanding. The purchasing agent, on his part, should make every effort to foster that improvement and to make the relationship a mutually satisfactory one.

The means toward that improvement include:

Completeness and clarity of communication concerning the need, the application and usage of the purchased material or product, the scope and limitations of the product itself, the outlook for continued usage and probable quantities required, and any special requirements of either a technical or commercial nature.

Mutual understanding of the conditions and problems of both usage and production, resulting from that communication.

Mutual confidence in the statements and intent of both parties.

Mutual consideration—no unreasonable demands, as much notice as possible in the event of changes in schedules or instructions, a fair and open mind in the discussion of differences, and willingness to waive or modify non-essential details of the agreement if the modification does not impair quality of service and is substantially to the advantage of either party.

A genuine interest in the mutual problem of procurement and supply, rather than mere contract fulfillment. This includes suggestions for cost reduction in the product itself and in methods of packing, shipping, usage, and accounting.

Cooperation—an active effort to fulfill contract obligations, prompt shipment by the supplier to minimize the need for inquiries and expediting action, and prompt processing and payment of invoices by the buyer.

Continuous improvement of ordering methods and supplier service as the opportunities arise.

Cultivation of personal contacts in the buying and selling organizations, making for better liaison and good will.

The emphasis throughout is on mutuality of interest and action, for the procurement and sale are in fact a single transaction. Where such a relationship is developed, as it is in many cases, the sales representative becomes in effect a "member of the buyer's team," a sympathetic interpreter of the buyer's viewpoint within his own organization, and the buyer becomes a valued member of the vendor's "family" of customers. This does not imply any softness or weakening of either position in the discharge of the functional duties of buying and selling, nor in the responsibilities to the two companies involved.

Many companies have found it helpful to hold annual, or more frequent, suppliers' conferences, when vendors are invited to gather at the buyer's plant, to see at first hand how their materials or parts are used, to share in the pride of product, and to be briefed on the reasons for certain buying policies and for the insistence on certain quality specifications. Conversely, buyers find it advantageous to make periodic visits to the plants of their suppliers to see at first hand how the things they buy are produced and to keep in touch with the problems and progress of supplier industries.

Loyalty to vendors

A continuing buyer-seller relationship, based on mutual confidence and satisfaction, implies a policy (and, indeed, a responsibility) of loyalty to suppliers. This is the antithesis of opportunism and constant "shopping around" in purchasing. It is true that some cost savings can be made by such methods, but it is usually at the sacrifice of uniformity and continuity of supply, and of most of the factors that have been cited as making up good supply service. Especially, it sacrifices the assurance of supply that is the first responsibility in purchasing. Without established and loyal sources of supply, every recurring requirement presents a procurement problem of the first order and the work of the purchasing department is magnified beyond all reason and proportion.

Experienced purchasing agents are in practical agreement that the long-range considerations of reasonable cost and of satisfaction and value in respect to purchases are best attained through a consistent policy toward supply sources. And a sound purchasing program, like any sound business program, is based on long-range considerations. The buyer who relies on opportunism to gain an immediate advantage makes himself and his company the vulnerable prey of opportunism in selling.

A high rate of turnover among suppliers suggests either that the purchaser's company is basically an undesirable customer or that wrong decisions as to supply sources have been made in the first place.

Loyalty to a supply source does not mean that competition is eliminated or that the search for better value and more advantageous sources has been abandoned. It does mean that the established supplier is given an opportunity to work out the best terms and arrangements consistent with his ability to produce efficiently, and without prejudice to the buyer's interests. Thus, the established source of supply does have a legitimate competitive advantage, but he is still in competition. The advantage must be earned and maintained by service. One of the seller's chief incentives in this connection is the assurance of an outlet for his production among established customers, corresponding to the assurance of supply that the buyer expects. It is when good service and good relationships deteriorate, or when the seller is unable to match the superior service of a more efficient competitor, that the buyer changes his patronage.

It has already been noted that service and satisfaction tend to improve as a supplier gains experience and familiarity with the requirements, methods, and business practices of the customer. Purchasing agents frequently refer to the process of "educating" their suppliers along these lines. It may be a long process and not an inexpensive one in terms of energy, patience, and cost until a completely satisfactory relationship is attained. It is not to be lightly or indiscriminately undertaken unless there is a reasonable expectation that the result attained will pay dividends in satisfaction and value over a considerable period of business dealings. But as this goal is approached, the supplier's value as an asset to the purchasing program increases beyond any impersonal rating of potential service factors or competitive advantages. The purchasing agent therefore has a selfish interest in maintaining a consistent and loyal policy toward well-selected suppliers, and be logically regards the fostering of such relationships as one of the more important and constructive phases of his responsibility.

Loyalty begets loyalty. In a buyers' market, sellers depend heavily on the

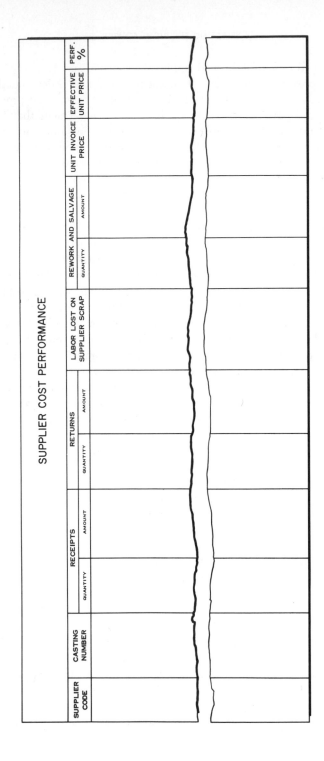

Fig. 11-3. Total Cost of Item Is Compared to Actual Invoice Price on This Computer-produced Record of Supplier Performance.

continued patronage of their established customers. In a sellers' market, buyers must rely on their established vendors for continuity of supply and fair dealing. Recognition of this mutual responsibility has been the means of carrying many companies through difficult periods. When such relationships are sacrificed to opportunism and immediate temporary advantage, the results of years of sales and purchasing effort are destroyed, giving place to resentment and blacklists. Every businessman of experience and foresight is aware that his company must play the role of both buyer and seller, and that the cycle of buyers' and sellers' markets will be repeated over the years, so that today's advantage will become tomorrow's need. The effects of such extreme changes in the business and economic situation are unfortunate at best. They are infinitely worse when they are expressed in a cycle of exploitation and retaliation in business dealings. Purchasing and sales departments have it in their power to mitigate this condition and to introduce a highly desirable element of stability if they will work together toward that end.

Developing sources of supply

The process outlined in this chapter has been based on the supposition that adequate sources exist to supply every need, and that the purchasing agent's problem is merely one of selection from among the available suppliers. In the majority of cases, and under normal business conditions, this assumption holds true; but the exceptions to the rule are equally important in the complete supply program and are likely to present difficulties that will put the procurement officer's resourcefulness to a severe test. His survey and search for the most satisfactory source may result in the discovery that no satisfactory or willing source can be found; yet the requirement exists and it is his responsibility to meet it.

Products or parts that have not previously been made, intricacies of special design, unusual requirements in the specification or difficult conditions of application and use, and the utilization of new or unfamiliar materials for which there is little precedent in treatment and fabrication are some of the factors that may lead to a situation for which no established supply source stands ready at hand. Or, from the standpoint of practical procurement, the only available sources may be too distant, prices may be exorbitant or out of line with budgeted costs for the product, production capacity may already be fully occupied so that no new customers may be accommodated, or the potential suppliers may simply be unwilling or uninterested in additional business.

Under any of these circumstances, the buyer's responsibility is not to select, but to create a satisfactory source. This is not a theoretical or fantastic situation. On the contrary, it was very common in the early days of the war production program when many types of production capacity were substantially short of demand and demand was rapidly increasing. For the many new plants that came into existence during this period, organized specifically for war production, and for those that engaged in new lines of manufacture so that they had no precedent or established supplier relationships for the new requirements, it was a basic and major problem. To a lesser extent it exists in every sellers' market, in the development of every new industrial area, and whenever a buyer seeks to improve on currently available supply conditions that fall somewhat short of being completely satisfactory.

The process in its earlier stages is not unlike that already described, except that the emphasis of the search is placed on qualifications, equipment, and experience in a similar type of operation that might logically be applied to production of the material or part in question. Then, in place of a process of elimination or narrowing of the field, the buyer must concentrate on the most likely sources, persuading them to undertake the desired production, and, if necessary, helping to implement their plant and personnel for such expansion or conversion of facilities as may be needed. In such cases, procurement is partly a matter of salesmanship, seeking to establish the buyer's company as a desirable customer in the same way that the salesman normally seeks to establish his company as a desirable supplier. Among the incentives offered are the steady flow of guaranteed orders over a period of time at a satisfactory price level, technical assistance in setting up the process on an efficient basis which will result in a satisfactory product, assistance in the procurement of raw materials even to the point of furnishing such materials for fabrication only by the supplier, so that risks of waste and spoilage in the initial stages are for the account of the buyer, and, sometimes, subsidizing the costs of new equipment and tooling until they may be absorbed by the volume of business that develops.

Subcontracting

Defense purchasing practice has brought into general business usage a term that had previously been largely confined to the vocabulary of the construction industries but is now a permanent part of the vocabulary and policy of procurement. A distinction is made between "prime contractors," whose contract is directly with some governmental procurement agency as buyer, and "subcontractors," who contribute to the fulfillment of that contract but have no direct contractual relationship with the government. Their own specific contracts are with the prime contractors or with "subcontractors of the first tier," as the process of subcontracting is repeated in successive stages down the line. The emphasis in this terminology is on the end product called for in the prime contract.

Essentially, subcontracting is purchasing, and the subcontractor is a supplier. In the defense usage of the term, there are certain special characteristics of the relationship that differentiate it from ordinary procurement and call for special handling. The purchased product is specifically identified with the project and end product of the purchaser; priority ratings on the material used follow through procurement and operations in both plants; and in wartime utilization of the purchased parts or products was definitely allocated. This presents a condition distinctly different from procurement of parts for stock or for application, at the buying company's option, to any need that might arise. Many of the terms of the prime contract are required to be passed along to the subcontract, by reference to the original document, even though there is no direct contractual responsibility between the subcontractor and the government, the ultimate recipient of the product. From the standpoint of the prime contractor's purchasing department unusually close contacts have to be maintained to see that schedules are properly and positively coordinated with the buyer's assembly program. Altogether, a much larger share of responsibility for the subcontractor's performance rests upon the purchasing agent than under normal conditions of procurement. Some variations from normal types of contracts have also been developed. For example, instead of contracting for delivery of a particular part or product, some companies contract for certain machine capacity and machine time in a subcontractor's plant, to be used as the buyer might direct. Under such an arrangement, the buyer furnishes raw materials, schedules production, and provides supervision.

As a result of these special conditions, the typical organization for subcontracting is a special division within the purchasing department for this purpose. In some companies, the procedure is considered as a separate managerial and administrative function, apart from the purchase of materials for use in plant production operations, and special subcontracting departments are set up outside the jurisdiction of the purchasing department. The reasoning behind such an arrangement is indicated by the fact that such departments are sometimes known as "outside production" departments.

In common industrial usage, the term "subcontracting" has reference to such parts or products as could be produced with the buyer's own facilities and would normally be manufactured within his own organization. Successful subcontracting, as suggested above, regards the operations of the supplier as part of a continuous process, leading up to and including the operations in the buyer's own plant. In this concept, the supplier's material control, production efficiency, scheduling, and service are definitely the concern of the buyer and his company, to be handled with the maximum of cooperation and mutual assistance. So far as the subcontracts are concerned, the supplier's operations are a part of his customer's operation, even though they are carried on under a different roof and a different management. This point of view is the practical embodiment of the essentials of a satisfactory relationship between purchaser and supplier.

Improper influence

This discussion would be incomplete without reference to some of the improper influences that may be brought to bear in buyer-seller relationships. Those that are obviously dishonest—bribery, misrepresentation, and the like—need no argument here; they have no place in legitimate buying or selling. The difficulty arises in connection with the subtler manifestations of those practices, where the difference between right and wrong, courtesy and abuse, is a matter of degree and intent. The purchasing agent cannot afford to place himself under any obligation that may conceivably affect his freedom of choice, and his only safe course is to hold himself above suspicion even on those minor counts that may seem to be too trivial to be dignified by making an issue of them. Purchasing agents must remember that they are quickly classified by salesmen according to the amount of entertainment they expect or will accept, and that they are equally at a disadvantage in the salesman's estimation whether a high price or a low price is set upon such favors.

It is natural and desirable that personal friendships develop in the course of business dealings, and the value of a business relationship is enhanced when this is the case. But personal friendship is not a proper basis for a purchasing decision. The absurdity of such a course of action is evident when, as frequently happens, the salesman changes his position and represents one of his former competitors. Such changes are often made on the supposition that a successful salesman "controls" certain accounts. Yet for a purchasing agent to change sources of supply forthwith is *prima facie* evidence that his earlier decision was unsound or unrelated to real considerations of value. Logic and good business both demand that the buyer's loyalty should be to the supplier company that has earned his patronage, rather than to any individual.

Pressure brought to bear through the influence of an important customer brings up the whole question of reciprocal trade relationships, which is discussed in detail in a later chapter. At this point it need only be noted that whenever such a consideration involves the compromise of purchasing principles and the sacrifice of purchasing efficiency, the problem is a matter of balancing the advantages to be gained by following either course. This is for management, rather than for the purchasing agent, to decide. It is quite possible that the decision may be in favor of reciprocal dealing and patronage; in that case it becomes a part of general company policy, a framework, outranking the policy of any one department, within which the purchasing department, like all others, must carry on its work.

Pressure brought upon the purchasing department through personal influence with a superior officer of the company has less justification. Where the purchasing department has proper status in the organization, with both the responsibility and the authority to perform its function to the best of its ability, such an approach may result in a special introduction assuring full and fair consideration, but should not affect the decision beyond this point. Management acts against its own interest and fails to get full value from its own purchasing department when it permits such influences to become dominant factors of purchasing action. Under such circumstances it cannot expect the highest standards of efficient purchasing performance, nor can it hold the purchasing officer accountable for failure to achieve those standards.

12

PURCHASING RESEARCH

RESEARCH, IN THE broad sense, is an intimate and continuing part of purchasing. Investigation and searching for new facts are definitely involved in the basic activities described in preceding chapters: finding the right quality and alternate materials, determining the right price, locating a source of supply, and selecting the right supplier. The careful preparation for a negotiating session is often a good-sized research project in itself. The accumulation and sifting of data that purchasing departments do in using more specialized techniques like capital-equipment buying, make-or-buy studies, the establishment of standards, and value analysis—all of which will be discussed in later chapters—are examples of research.

Until relatively recently, however, this type of research was considered almost incidental to purchasing. Indeed, few purchasing agents would have used the term to describe a process they felt was inherent in good buying. Fewer thought of establishing a specific, organized research activity in the purchasing department as a function separate from the buying group.

But purchasing, as much of an art as it is, could not long rely on intuitive judgment and a vaguely defined commercial sense to meet its obligations as a profit-making function. The surge of industrial and technological progress that followed World War II made research and the scientific approach in every important phase of company operation a competitive necessity. Purchasing was a logical place for a research activity to develop for several reasons.

In a highly complex, growing economy, buying becomes more than a series of individual, unrelated transactions carried out to meet particular requirements. Any buyer must have knowledge of the products he buys, supply sources, and current market conditions in the field. Beyond this, however, he must begin to concern himself with a much broader range of factors. Some of them immediately concern a particular buy; others have only long-range implications. But all of them ultimately affect purchasing performance and, therefore, company profitability.

A competent buyer must have some understanding of his company's long-range needs and the ability of supplier industries to meet them at reasonable prices. He must make some attempt to forecast long-range supply trends for various commodities, the outlook for substitute materials, and the speed of technological change in specific product fields.

A purchasing executive for a growth company in the electronics field, for example, may buy millions of dollars' worth of capacitors and resistors. Negotiating for this volume alone calls for a good deal of short-term purchasing research, however informal. But what of the long range? Will the requirements grow? What are the likely supply and price trends? Will, in fact, these items be in general use five or ten years from now, or will they be replaced by new developments in molecular electronics, for example? What suppliers appear to

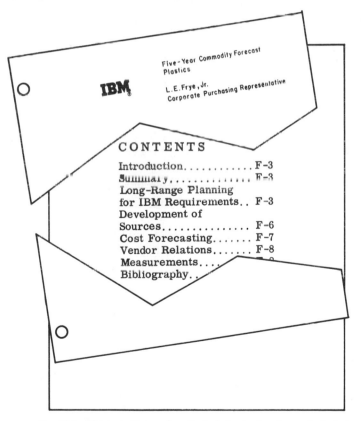

Fig. 12-1. Contents Page of a Typical Purchasing Research Project.

be the most progressive and farsighted? What are the prospects for imports?

The need for purchasing research is not limited to the exotic space-age industries. Buyers of raw material for such relatively prosaic things as bowling alleys and tenpins must extend their interest forward to the economic stability and planting techniques of the Canadian loggers who supply much of the wood that goes into these products.

Purchasing research on this broad a scale, then, becomes something beyond the scope of the individual buyer's job. He has neither the time nor the special qualifications to collect, interpret, and report the data that should be collected. Recognizing this, the Ford Motor Company set up the first purchasing research department to be formally designated as such. It made research a full-time job in purchasing, to be carried out by specialists trained in economics and analysis. Ford's Purchasing Research Department, headed by a director, was made up of two divisions, each headed by a supervisor: the research section, and the statistics section, which concentrated primarily on the collection and reporting of data.

Research as a purchasing-staff function has developed steadily since that time, although there were scattered instances of organized purchasing research in industry as far back as 1900. The most comprehensive study of the extent and nature of purchasing research [1] yet made shows that the staff purchase research function has been established in a substantial number of the 500 largest United States industrial firms. Almost one-third of the companies responding to Dr. Fearon's mail questionnaire use full-time purchase research personnel.

Although there are no such specific statistics available, a growing number of magazine articles, university seminars, and talks at purchasing association meetings indicate an increasing use of purchasing research by smaller companies. Similarly, many small purchasing departments, in which only one or two people do the buying, have formalized their use of purchasing research to some degree, often without identifying it as such. The approach to purchasing research outlined in this chapter, based generally on larger-company practice, can of course be easily modified and adapted by almost any size purchasing department.

Scope of purchasing research

Current definitions of purchasing or procurement research are extremely broad. This reflects the many ramifications of the buying job and offers the research group almost unlimited opportunities for developing projects within purchasing.

---

[1] Harold Edward Fearon, "Purchasing Research in American Business," thesis for the degree of Ph.D., Michigan State University, 1961.

The manager of purchasing research for American Cyanamid Company, A. A. Kreig, in a talk to the Central Michigan Purchasing Agents Association in April, 1961, described it as "a systematic investigation of any area influencing purchasing performance." Willis Bussard, manager of purchasing research and programs for International Business Machines Corporation, defines it as "a formal, organized and continued investigation of all factors that affect cost of purchased materials, leading to better profit-oriented decisions." Most other definitions offered are as general and all-embracing as these two.

Within the wide-open framework of the above definitions, purchasing research groups carry on an extraordinarily wide range of activities. Some idea of the possible scope of purchasing research activity can be had from this list of typical project areas:

Commodity Studies—Evaluation of company requirements over 1-, 5-, and 10-year periods: long- and short-range supply and demand trends; price trends; technological improvements; outlook for possible substitutes; development of standards and specifications.

Economic Analysis—Effect of business cycles on purchased material requirements; over-all price trends; influence of economic changes on suppliers and competitors.

Vendor Analysis—Qualifications of active and potential vendors; study of vendor facilities; evaluation of vendor performance; analysis of vendors' financial condition.

Cost and Price Analysis—Reasons behind price changes; comparative studies of like parts; analysis of vendor costs and profit margins; investigation of alternate manufacturing methods and of material specifications.

Packaging and Transportation Analysis—Effect of suppliers' plant locations on costs; alternate shipping methods; commodity reclassification; packaging redesign; improved material-handling methods.

Administrative Analysis—Forms control; work simplification; use of electronic data processing; preparation of reports.

Value Analysis—(See Chapter 15.)

The above is only a sampling of the more general types of research work being carried out by staff groups in industrial purchasing departments. The work of some research staffs is more restricted, whereas others are experimenting in relatively new fields. Purchasing research activities at American Cyanamid Company, for example, are concentrated on purchased materials. Research on purchasing systems, training programs, trade relations analysis, and audits of plant purchasing are handled by other staff groups in the general purchasing department.

The procurement research group at Kearfott Division, General Precision, Inc., made up of manufacturing engineers and tool experts, specializes in supplier analysis. They physically check suppliers' plants, analyze vendors' quality performance, and work with them on cost reduction through change in process or method of manufacture.

A specialized activity of purchasing research at Dow Chemical Company is the development of new sources for raw materials for new Dow products. As a new product moves through various laboratory tests, purchasing research is investigating what volume requirements will be when the product hits the market and thereafter; what sources will be able to provide raw materials; and what new sources may have to be brought into being. At all times, they maintain close liaison with Dow's laboratory and product development departments.

A somewhat more diversified approach to purchasing research is taken by the staff group at International Business Machines Corporation. In addition to the type of projects mentioned above, it will take on assignments in personnel testing, preparation of training, and procedures manuals. It also handles all communications—bulletins, instructions on procedure, and so forth—from corporate purchasing headquarters to all IBM plants.

In recent years, purchasing research has been put to a dramatic, if originally unforeseen use. Recurrent political crises and severe international tensions raise the threat of war and the cutting off of normal raw material supply sources. At such times, management will call on purchasing research to provide a quick analysis of the company's materials situation: what the stockpiles of materials are; the effect of hostilities on supply lines; availability of alternate sources; availability of substitute materials; and possible governmental restrictions on the use of certain critical materials. Purchasing research would, of course, be considering these factors among many others as part of its regular job regardless of the international situation. In times of crisis, however, these emergency studies of the materials situation have taken precedence over all other projects.

Organization for purchasing research

The fundamental principles of purchasing research are the same whether it is carried on by a large, separate staff or by the individual buyer as an added responsibility. The amount and nature of the work performed by purchasing research, however, will vary according to the size of the staff and the capabilities of its members. These, in turn, are affected by the size of the company, the nature of its products, and its competitive position.

In this section, and the following on "Techniques of Purchasing Research," we shall assume that purchasing research is a distinct, full-time activity, coordinated with but completely separated from the buying function. Discussion of staff size, organizational relationships, and personnel requirements will be followed by a description of purchasing research methods. The final section will deal with how the individual purchasing agent or buyer can adapt some of the ideas and techniques discussed to his own more or less informal purchasing research program.

Research organizations generally are not large in relation to the purchasing organization as a whole. And, in terms of dollar volume, they are often quite small. Both United States Steel Company and Ford Motor Company, whose purchases run into billions of dollars, pioneered in purchasing research with small staffs. United States Steel had a purchasing research manager with a small clerical staff; Ford had a director, two supervisors (of the statistics and research sections), and the necessary clerical help. In both cases, the purchasing research organization was a staff group reporting directly to top corporate purchasing officers.

Value-analysis projects (designated "purchase analysis" at Ford) were also carried on in the various buying departments. Purchase analysts were assigned and reported directly to assistant purchasing agents heading those departments. They coordinated their efforts with corporate purchasing research as necessary, but were not directly under the supervision of that department.

Ford's purchase research and analysis activity has evolved during a number of corporate organization changes into a 180-man purchase analysis department that reports to the general purchasing agent of the Ford Division. The scope of its responsibility has been broadened to include estimating costs on a new-model automobile as much as three years before its introduction.

Is there any yardstick to determine the number and qualifications of people to be assigned to purchasing research in a company of a given size, with a given volume of purchases? Not any more than there is for determining the size of the purchasing department itself. Buying for a steel company, although by no means simple, is much less complex and subject to fewer competitive pressures than purchasing for the automobile industry. So the attendant research requires fewer people, with greater emphasis on specialists in economic and commodity trends, than in manufacturing processes.

One rough measurement of research personnel needs is that used by Frank Jenkins, director of purchases for Sprague Electric Company. Jenkins holds that a buying group handling minimum annual purchases of $10 million involving at least 100 parts warrants a full-time purchase analyst or researcher. Additional analysts would presumably be added as purchase volume increased, but not necessarily in that proportion—or, at least, not beyond the point of diminishing returns.

The number and nature of purchased parts is undoubtedly the more important factor in any such formula. Where a few basic materials—for example, hides, fibers, minerals, or coffee—account for a large part of the volume, a purchasing research section would probably be superfluous. In such cases, the functions of purchasing and researching should be combined in the buyer, who should be a specialist in one or possibly more commodities. He would, in effect, be carrying on continuous research on the items he was buying.

Where the same amount of money is spent on a larger number of more diversified and complex items—electronic components, for example—the need for specialized purchasing research is more apparent. Products of this kind are subject to all kinds of technological and economic change. The buyer cannot be expected to be an expert on numerous rapidly changing items that he buys in relatively limited quantities.

Educational and training requirements for purchasing research personnel obviously will vary with their responsibilities. Chrysler Corporation's purchase research department uses different specialists in each of three areas of activity: procurement analysis, economic analysis, and comparative analysis.

Procurement analysts are generally technical experts in manufacturing. Typical of the projects they handle are inspection trips to potential vendors' plants to check on facilities, equipment, and labor. They also regularly supply cost data on labor and processing to the economic analysis group. The economic analysts, usually accounting and budgeting specialists, fashion these raw data into detailed cost estimates used by buyers during negotiations.

Comparative analysts study similar parts to see what accounts for differences in prices, and whether or not they are justified. Two pieces of trim made by the same process and finished exactly alike may be priced quite differently by two suppliers. Determining why is often as much a matter of common sense as of technical knowledge, so that the engineering background necessary in procurement analysis is not required in comparative analysis.

Purchasing research becomes broader in scope and less highly specialized in the smaller company. At Sprague Electric Company, responsibilities of the three-man purchasing research staff include such areas as inventory control, paper-work systems, material standards, and value analysis. Sprague prefers to staff the research group with graduate engineers who have had some experience with company shop operations and cost engineering.

Experience has shown that purchasing research is most successful when it is carried on as a staff activity completely removed from the actual buying process. Researchers must also be free of clerical or strictly routine jobs and permitted a free hand in the development of research projects. Limiting them to the mere collection of data or to special or emergency projects forfeits the broad purpose and potential contribution of research to productive purchasing.

Despite its organizational independence, however, purchasing research is only one member of the buying team, and its major objective is to improve the performance of that team.

Purchasing research techniques

How does a purchasing research group decide what its next project will be? Two obvious targets are: (1) important items on which negotiations are being planned, and (2) those items on which the major portion of the purchase dollar is spent (generally speaking, about 20 per cent of the purchased items represent 80 per cent of total purchase cost in representative manufacturing operations).

Even in the most obvious cases, nevertheless, there must be restrictions on the kind and number of projects a researcher takes on; otherwise, he may find himself swamped. Each project should have some chance of success and give promise of substantial results, either short-term or long-term. It should not be beyond the capabilities of the people doing the research. As Frank Jenkins of Sprague Electric Company pointed out at an American Management Association Seminar on purchasing research:

"It may be better to refuse to do projects for which the organizational

---

COMPLETED COST REDUCTION PROJECT
PURCHASING DEPT.   GEN-1479 (4-58)

COMMODITY

Cresylic Acid (meta para feed)

TYPE OF REDUCTION	PROJECT STARTED	PROJECT COMPLETED	LOCATION	PROJECT NUMBER
[x] A ☐ B	Nov., 1958	March, 1959	Point Pleasant Plant	12

DESCRIPTION OF COST REDUCTION

By special arrangement with Productol Company samples of certain mixtures were obtained and evaluated in the plant laboratory. It was found that certain blends would result in a feed equal to that which normally would be priced to us at $1.15 per gal. and that components would be priced so that a savings would be realized. Therefore, 26,000 gals. was purchased for blending and it is hoped this can be repeated once each quarter in the future.

20,392 gals.	Grade 25A (MP) @ $1.15/gal less freight equalization	$20,163.73
5,961 gals.	Grade 2876 (special xvl) @ $0.90/gal less freight equalization	4,413.28
26,353 gals.	Blend equal to Grade 25 (MP) delivered for	$24,577.01
Normal cost @ $1.15/gal. less $4,238.69 (freight equalization) would have been		26,067.26
	One time saving	$ 1,490.25

No extra handling occurred since materials could be mixed either in feed or product tanks.

AMOUNT OF SAVINGS			
ONE TIME SAVINGS	RECURRING SAVINGS		
	ANNUAL VOLUME	UNIT SAVING	ESTIMATED ANNUAL SAVINGS
$1,490.25			$6,000.00

OFFSETTING COSTS			
CAPITAL	EXPENSE	INVENTORY LOSS	TOTAL OFFSETTING COSTS
$	$	$	$ None
DEPARTMENT AFFECTED	OTHER PARTICIPATING DEPARTMENTS		
Production	Laboratory, Central Purchasing, Operations Control (NYO),	Plant Manager.	

AUDITED BY: *Accounting* DEPARTMENT   *βBι* INDIVIDUAL   *QEA*

SUBMITTED BY: *H. O. Frombes,* Mgr. INDIVIDUAL   Operations Service Dept. TITLE   4/22/59 DATE

Fig. 12-2.   Report on Cost Reduction Project of a Research Group.

facilities are inadequate, rather than to spend funds under false pretenses. Some phases of investigation may be best assigned to outside agencies such as consultants, research institutes or universities."

The automobile companies have almost made a science out of the application of purchasing research to high-value purchased items. Using the "key parts" concept of research, they concentrate on the relatively few items that account for most of the purchasing volume. In a Ford car, for example, only 400 to 500 parts of a total of several thousand account for nearly 95 per cent of dollar volume. These parts, plus those subject to frequent style change, regardless of price, are the prime targets of the purchase analysis section.

Purchase analysts keep close watch on these key parts from the inception of a new design until the new model goes into production perhaps two or three years later. Through this time, their technical and economic analysts are used to determine how design changes will affect the price of a new model, how engineering changes will force modification of target prices on parts, and what increases in labor and raw material charges by suppliers will do to the cost of each vehicle.

In contrast, American Cyanamid Company deliberately modifies the high-value concept in selecting materials for study by purchasing research. Its theory is that buyers or researchers can tend to give too much time to products with which they are familiar and neglect others in which there may be a good profit potential. The Cyanamid approach is a good illustration of how purchasing research should be adapted to the particular requirements of a company or industry.

Purchasing research at Cyanamid rates the various materials it buys by "study indicators" in which value is only one of six factors. The others are product profitability, buying position, price-cost characteristics, availability, and quality. Indicators traditionally associated with value analysis (see Chapter 15) are not used, because they are relatively unimportant to or remote from the problem of chemical raw materials. These include use of alternative materials, design changes, combining purchases, and bulk versus non-bulk purchases.

The reasons behind this system are typical, although not necessarily peculiar, to the chemical industry. Most chemical companies have a number of marginal products, in which raw materials make up a high proportion of total cost. For varying reasons, the companies may want to keep these products in their line; therefore, reduction of raw materials cost is a necessity if they are to be made even reasonably profitable.

Further, a study by Cyanamid's purchasing research section showed that surprisingly few of the materials purchased by the company had any significant price change over a period of five years. It was found, also, that price declines were more common among the high-unit-value materials. This indicated that the lower-unit-value items, prices of which had remained relatively stable, were logical targets for research.

Purchasing research totals points for each raw material on the basis of the "indicators" mentioned above—value, product profitability, buying position, price/cost characteristics, availability, and quality. (Each indicator is subdivided into several criteria, for example, under price/cost characteristics are "infrequent price changes," "cost not competitive," and so forth.) High point scorers then are pinpointed as potential projects for purchasing research. In one example cited by Purchasing Research Manager Kreig, a material rated ninth in value scored only a third of the points scored by one in 31st position. Despite the fact that annual purchases of item No. 9 were four times that of the lower-value material, the latter was considered a better subject for a purchasing project.

The emphasis in the projects we have been talking about has been on reducing the cost of purchased parts and raw materials. It should be remembered, however, that these will be only one of the types of projects which an aggressive, imaginative purchasing research department will undertake. The purchasing research department of one of our largest companies, for example, first came into prominence for its work in automating the paper-work system of the corporate purchasing department. Work in this field has been an increasingly important responsibility of most other industrial purchasing research departments.

Research projects should, of course, be carefully planned in advance. The key-parts system used in the automobile industry is the basic plan which the purchase analysis and research organizations, as well as their operations, follow. Smaller-company research sections will ordinarily develop their plans for individual projects as they suggest themselves. The plan may be simply a collection of notes made for his own or his supervisor's use by a researcher, or a somewhat more elaborate written report for management. In either event, it should state clearly the problem or objective for which the research is being undertaken; the general methods to be used in the research; and an approximate target date for completion of the project.

Research in the smaller department

Although the great majority of small and medium companies have neither the money nor the personnel to establish formal purchasing research programs, they have much to learn from the principles and practices described above. A number of them who have encouraged informal purchasing research as a part of the buyers' responsibility, and who have arranged department schedules to

permit time and attention to be directed toward it, have achieved some improvements in purchasing performance.

There is ample evidence that serious research applied to a special project
or product often results in astonishing improvement, with unit savings multiplied many times over in repetitive transactions. So far as time and facilities
permit, the research program should be extended to cover every significant
item in the purchasing list over a period of time. Logically, the items representing greatest physical and dollar volume will receive first attention.

The educational value of such a program and the more intelligent procurement and general alertness resulting from such a policy are far-reaching, even
beyond the tangible improvements or economies that may be effected.

The basic source of commodity and product information for the buyer is
a comprehensive and well-organized library or file of suppliers' catalogs and
descriptive sales literature. In the small company, the catalog file is probably
kept on shelves or bookcases convenient to the buyer's desk, and the familiarity
of constant use enables him to put his finger on the desired catalog without any
great trouble. Under such circumstances, it is probable that the maintenance
of a catalog index is unnecessary and would represent more effort and expense
than would be justified by its use—an ever-present danger in all "systems."

The purchasing department library generally contains a number of general
reference works in addition to the catalog file itself. A comprehensive directory
of manufacturers, national in scope and covering the whole range of products
used in industry, is essential. Details such as the geographical location of
manufacturers and ratings of their size and financial responsibility serve as a
guide to which ones are most likely to be desirable supply sources.

Similar directories of more limited geographical scope are issued by some
state manufacturers' associations, chambers of commerce, and similar organizations. They are of particular value to the purchasing department seeking
nearby sources, and they generally include more detailed information on the
size of the companies, number of employees, annual output, names of key
executives, and the like.

Specialized directories are available covering major industrial fields, such
as paper mills, textile manufacturers, coal mines, foundries, and others. In
specific fields pertinent to the company's supply requirements, these provide
excellent information on the capacity, equipment, and other facilities of the
various units in the industry, special products of each, rail connections, and
other data of value to the buyer.

Many industries, through their respective associations, issue data books
covering trade definitions and customs, standards of quality, and packaging
units, all of which is useful information in planning and placing orders.

Government publications include many books and pamphlets that belong
in every purchasing department's file. Examples are the directory of com-

modity specifications, directory of testing laboratories, census of manufacturers, standardization activities of trade associations, shipping classifications of the Interstate Commerce Commission, and periodical reports on a wide variety of industrial and commercial topics.

Business periodicals

In addition to these permanent and basic reference sources, the purchasing department should have access to selected current business periodicals, for timeliness is of the essence in research. Current conditions and new developments are the ones most applicable and fruitful in helping to direct policies and action. The former quickly become obsolete, and there may be a time lag of months or years before the latter type of information finds its way into the standard reference books.

As a minimum, the purchasing agent's reading should include one periodical (daily or weekly) devoted to general business, one journal devoted to his specific industry or the major material component, and one devoted to his own function of procurement. This combination provides the three essential requirements of economic, technical, and professional news and information—the business climate in which he must buy, the materials he buys, and how best to carry on his buying program.

One or more of the available business, economic, and commodity services will probably have a place in the purchasing library. These are used primarily for their interpretation of current business conditions, but have permanent value in their continuing trade indices, background charts, and indication of trends and cycles. The accumulation of statistical data on many specific fields is also available in annual statistical handbooks. Corresponding to these business services are similar services concerned with such special topics as taxes and governmental regulations.

Sources of information

Although a great deal of the basic information required in purchasing research is available from the above sources, many problems and projects of a special nature call for a knowledge of where to seek specific information.

Trade and scientific associations have intimate contact with their members and can frequently steer the purchasing agent to the proper source of information, even if it is not actually available in their own files.

Trade publications generally maintain a reader service department with well-organized channels of information. The trade press is typically very close to the field it serves and to the interests of that field. It is particularly alert to new developments.

Contacts with other purchasing agents who may have faced the same or similar problems will often provide the desired answers. Such interchange of experience is fostered by purchasing agents associations, which are dedicated to mutual assistance and advancement of the purchasing art.

Manufacturers in supplier industries are another source of information that should not be overlooked, with due regard for the commercial interest that naturally and necessarily directs their activities. Reliable customer service is the foundation of sound business relationships, and mutuality of interest between the buyer and the seller makes many of the technical and research facilities of the latter available to the buyer. The logical contact in such a case is the friendly salesman with whom the buyer regularly has his dealings. Purchasing men generally are agreed that the salesman of a friendly and established supplier, with wide contacts in the field, is one of the most valuable sources of information, which is frequently offered unsolicited.

13

PLANNING AND FORECASTING

SOME SUCCESSFUL BUSINESSES have been launched on a hunch, but few have survived solely on the instinctive genius of their founders or managers. If an enterprise is to continue to be profitable, it must be operated according to some plan. And the plan, in turn, must be based on some estimate of the future—of the demand for the company's products, of the size of its markets, of its requirements for materials, machines, and manpower. Whether this attempt to gauge future conditions is called "forecasting" or, more inelegantly, "educated guessing," it is essential in business. A good manager narrows the range of probabilities he faces and plans what action he will take to meet them.

Purchasing, as a management function, has a responsibility to participate in company planning and forecasting. The scope of its responsibility may vary, depending on the ratio of material cost to finished-product cost, and on the relative position of the purchasing executive in the managerial group. Regardless of the exact position of the purchasing department in the corporate hierarchy, however, the results of purchasing planning or lack of it have a very definite effect on over-all company planning and the realization of company profit objectives.

The importance of purchasing to plan can be seen even in purchasing's most basic activity: forward buying to meet anticipated requirements for a given period. In any continuing manufacturing program, most material needs are reasonably foreseeable. A large part of purchasing can be done in advance of needs, rather than according to individual current requisitions issued when the need arises. But consideration of forward buying immediately calls for some type of planning to allow for certain contingencies. The advantages of forward buying must be weighed against the disadvantages.

On the one hand, goods will be on hand when they are needed; requirements can be lumped together to obtain price concessions through volume buying; economic ordering quantities and other cost-reducing formulas can be applied; special market conditions can be exploited (see the section on Speculative Buying" later in this chapter); and material costs will be stabilized over a stated period. On the other hand are possible disadvantages: the company must increase its financial commitments to cover the cost of the materials; corporate funds are tied up in inventory investment and carrying costs when they might be employed more profitably elsewhere; risks of losses through obsolescence are increased; unless provision is made for periodic review and revision of buying plans, the company may be left with a fixed commitment harmful to its interests if market conditions change drastically.

These points alone would justify the need for the purchasing department to make some organized effort at forecasting and planning. There are others, however. The most important is the value to top management of knowing the probable course of major material prices over a given period. Decisions on how to price manufactured products are much easier to make when material costs can be reasonably estimated. The significance of such information to certain manufacturers is obvious: tire manufacturers must have some indication of the trend of rubber prices (and supply); similarly, soap makers should have a reasonably good forecast on market conditions in fats and oils. But even equipment makers—producers of electric motors and farm machinery, for example—find accurate forecasting of trends in such materials as copper and steel of great value in pricing their products.

Informed estimates of materials supply and availability of substitutes also aid management in its planning. Although studies of substitute materials and other technological developments that may lower costs or improve the quality of manufactured products are logically the concern of other departments, they often are the by-products of purchasing department forecasting.

Purchasing forecasting can be used in setting up departmental plans— setting materials budgets, setting up cost-reduction goals, particularly for the long range; and the establishment of reliable, competitive sources of supply needed for future company expansion and growth. Purchasing in many companies, both large and small, also participates in general forecasts of the general economic situation and their implications both for the purchasing department and for the enterprise as a whole. Each of these applications will be discussed later in the chapter.

Purchasing planning begins with what is essentially a short-term production forecast—the manufacturing schedule. The schedule indicates to the buyer the nature and volume of material requirements and the expected rates of use. In a large and highly organized company, it may come to him in tabulated form from the production control or planning department. In the smaller company, the information may come to him informally from the plant manager or superintendent. The schedule indicates the approximate volume and flow of materials that the purchasing department will be expected to provide. It should be communicated to the purchasing department systematically, for purchasing policies and plans must be keyed to it. Conversely, the purchasing agent should be informed of any changes in the anticipated operations, so that buying plans can be adjusted accordingly.

Regular access to at least a summary report of new orders received is important to good purchasing planning. Trends in this figure often provide a useful indicator of future operating rates in advance of actual changes in manufacturing schedules. For longer-range planning, the purchasing department should be kept informed of company sales quotas and forecasts.

In job shop manufacturing operations, the purchasing department is often called in before the bidding stage to supply cost estimates on parts and materials. This advance knowledge of probable requirements enables buyers to begin planning earlier than would be the case if they had to wait until the business was in the house and bills of material and requisitions all prepared. The collection of cost data in itself is an element in their planning. And without committing the company, they can begin to look for additional sources and alert regular suppliers to the possibility of new orders.

The experience of a well-known chemical company illustrates three important points about purchasing planning: the need for close cooperation between the using and purchasing departments; the variety of techniques available to purchasing in developing a plan; and the benefits that can accrue from good planning.

Forecasts for chemical raw material needs were not given to the purchasing department until after annual budgets were established in November and December. As a result, chemical buying for any year ran into the second quarter of that calendar year. Inevitably, there were delays in delivery, buyers spent much of their time trying to expedite shipments, and there was little time to investigate cost-reduction possibilities, better sources, or supplier and buyer performance.

With the cooperation of the production planning department, purchasing was able to get forecasts of consumption for 12 months at each midyear— from July 1 of the current year to June 30 of the following year. Production planning also agreed to revise the forecast annual rate on a quarterly basis. This gave the buyers at least three months more to complete their planning.

Buyers now use two approaches in planning their purchase. A "plan of purchase" is made up on all raw materials and chemicals with an annual purchase volume above $5,000. The buyer outlines the type of purchase he plans—spot, contract, and so forth—and how the business will be split among various suppliers, both by quantity and by dollars. He indicates the terms and past performance for each supplier, gives a brief description of supply conditions for the item, a price forecast, and data on previous price changes.

A more elaborate approach is used on all production materials costing more than $10,000 annually or on which there is only one supplier. The buyer must follow the following instructions in preparing his plan of purchase for the head of the department:

> Raw Material Significance—State percentage of raw material costs and manufacturing costs for the item and its function in the manufacturing process.
>
> Market Condition—Describe availability, price, economic factors of the market, and significant changes in supply- and-demand relationships which have taken place or are expected to take place in the foreseeable future.
>
> Production—Show total world production, domestic and foreign, broken down by supply company, if possible.
>
> Buying Objectives—What will be done to improve company profits on this item? Show what improvements, if any, can be made in relations with suppliers.
>
> Significant Changes from Previous Plan—Indicate change from previous plan—in price, quantity, business split, suppliers, terms, and so forth, and their effects on supplier relations, profits, and method of purchase.
>
> Reasons for Business Split—Explain the basis for split of business among suppliers and indicate what contributions suppliers have made to improve our profits.
>
> General—Indicate unusual contractual liabilities or advantages and any other information pertinent to buying the particular commodity. When plan does not conform to plant recommendations, explain why.

The immediate results of the planning program were better performance in cost reduction and in service to the operating departments. With more time available, buyers were able to complete twice as many cost-improvement projects during the first year of the program as in the year before. The number of rush orders issued by the purchasing department was cut considerably and relations with other departments improved accordingly. In addition, purchasing managers are now better able to appraise both buyer and supplier performance against the stated objectives of the purchase plan.

Research and forecasting

Forecasting plays an important part in the system described above, although it is not explicitly given that label. In that program, the buyers interpret market conditions and production outlook in their own studies of conditions. In other companies, particularly the larger ones, a research section (see Chapter 12) might develop the necessary data and leave the interpretation of the facts it collected to the buyers and their supervisors. The extent to which research groups make specific forecasts followed by recommendations as to action varies widely. The smaller the company, the more likely it is that the buyer or purchasing agent is his own researcher and forecaster. In the larger organizations, it is generally a joint effort between purchasing research and the buyers.

In at least one large multi-plant organization, the research organization is specifically charged with forecasting and making recommendations. The reports it makes are, of course, the work of large numbers of highly trained specialists and, therefore, outside the scope of the small purchasing department. But the principles on which they are based can be used in modified form even in the smallest purchasing department. In the case of the small department, the reports would be prepared by rather than for the purchasing agent and directed to his management rather than to himself.

Typical reports issued periodically by the group mentioned above are:

Materials Situation Bulletin—An analysis of the current market situation in each of the major materials purchased by the company. This is accompanied by a short-term recommendation as to forward coverage.

Price Information Bulletin—Market-price history of key purchased materials and short-term forecasts of price movements.

PURCHASING DEPT. MONTHLY REPORT _____

Purchase Orders (in 1000$)

SUMMARY	Drug Chem	Pkg Matl	Equip Supp	Total	FORECAST	Drug Chem	Pkg Matl	Equip Supp	Total
Open as of 10-1-	000	0000	000	0000	To be placed in Nov.	000	000	000	0000
Placed in Oct.	0000	0000	000	0000	Deliveries in Nov.	000	000	000	0000
Deliveries in Oct.	000	000	000	0000	" " Dec.	000	000	000	0000
Open as of 11-1-	000	0000	000	0000	" next 6 mos.	0000	0000	0000	00000
COMPARISON									
Total 10 Mos. 19	0000	0000	0000	0000					
Total 10 Mos. 19	0000	0000	0000	0000					

COMMENTS

VOLUME - Chemicals - The value of new orders and deliveries made in October were within 5% of our buyers' prophecy. November is expected to be about 15% less than October.

Packaging Materials - The value of new orders increased sharply over the projection, chiefly due to hedging against shortages that were developing in suppliers inventories as a result of steel and glass strikes. Deliveries were nearly 20% greater than normal thus securing many important raw materials against possible shortage.

INVENTORIES - Current inventories are obviously increased some and normal operations can be expected for some time. However, we recommend continued additions to our inventory of steel items (caps, drums, band and wire) to protect against tight supplies expected for several months after steel production is resumed.

PRICES - In spite of buyers' resistance to price increases, there is no evidence that prices will hold at present levels indefinitely. All indications are that labor costs will continue to contribute to some inflation and reflect in possible increased prices in many of our materials.

Fig. 13-1. Short-term, Informal Monthly Forecast by a Purchasing Department.

Advance Ordering and Inventory Bulletin—A list of suggested ordering lead times and inventory levels in the light of current general economic and market conditions.

The group also issues long-term forecasts—sometimes as far ahead as 10 years—on basic materials such as steel and aluminum. It also maintains price indices on all key materials.

Suppliers and forecasting

Suppliers are involved in any purchasing forecasting and planning operation in two important ways. In the first place, they can provide significant forecasts of their own concerning market outlook, their plans for expansion (or retrenchment), and labor conditions in their industries. Second, they can in many instances help in or interfere with purchasing planning. During the steel shortage of the 1950's, one of the country's most prominent purchasing executives, a vice-president of a large electrical manufacturing firm, spent a great deal of time "selling" his company to the steel companies as a good, long-term customer. The company, which was growing rapidly, was battling to get enough steel to meet its needs. But following custom, the steel companies were allocating their products on the basis of what share of production their customers received in normal years.

In a series of meetings with steel company sales managers, the purchasing executive outlined his case for more steel. He spelled out what his company was going to need in the way of steel for its planned expansion, and what it expected to get from the steel industry. His argument was based on an enormous amount of research on all steel purchases for several years previous. Every procurement factor had been thoroughly analyzed and correlated—types and amounts of steel purchased, mill locations, freight rates, and so forth. On the basis of his forecast, and his own aggressive "sales" approach, the purchasing executive got higher allocations of scarce steel from a large number of steel suppliers.

Suppliers can also be brought into purchasing forecasting and planning in a more positive way as well. As was pointed out in the chapter on purchasing research (see page 176), the purchasing department is often counted on to develop sources of new components and materials that will be required years hence as a company grows and diversifies.

Purchasing forecasting and planning is initially concerned with supply, demand, and price conditions in specific commodities, but it also must consider general business conditions. Industry-wide use of basic materials—steel, for example—fluctuates with the business cycle. Thus, any forecast involving the steel market would inevitably have to include such factors as the outlook for the automobile industry and the construction industry. General business forecasting is a complex and highly specialized activity that most purchasing departments are not equipped to handle. Generally, the purchasing department will call on the company economist or the forecasting group for general economic data that relate to purchased materials for which forecasts are being prepared.

The flow of economic information is not always strictly one-way, however. In a number of companies, staff economists regularly obtain information from purchasing to incorporate in their regular economic reports. The chief economist of a large metals company recently added several sections to his quarterly reports on purchase costs, including an analysis of material costs in relation to the wholesale price index and the effects of material costs on breakeven points during sales rises. In at least one automotive company, a research and forecasting group in purchasing feeds information to a number of other departments. One is the corporate long-range planning office, which is responsible for planning of production facilities, costs of new models, and financial forecasts. The reports include such purchasing information as the outlook for commodity prices, long-range procurement problems, and the effects of wage rates on purchased materials. The purchasing department's forecast of materials and parts prices are also used as a part of the total financial forecast for the company. In a small company with no corporate economist, purchasing might well take over the role on an informal basis if it were already doing a good job in its own forecasting and planning.

Speculative purchasing

Any discussion of forecasting and price fluctuations raises the issue of commodity speculation. This term has an unfortunate connotation. It is frequently argued that speculative buying is in the realm of business ethics rather than of purchasing science, and that it has no place in any legitimate purchasing program. That generalization is not altogether sound. All forward purchasing is speculative to a degree, depending on judgment as to future probabilities. The analysis of these probabilities, and the adjustment of purchasing policies accordingly, are important elements of effective, scientific purchasing. The distinction between speculation and legitimate purchasing action hinges, rather, on the intent of the purchase and the extent of the risk involved.

Keeping material costs at a practicable minimum is one of the functional responsibilities of purchasing. Procurement of goods beyond the immediate need in anticipation of an expected price advance is a means of keeping down material costs. The purchasing agent buys for use, on the basis of reasonably foreseeable requirements. He is not a trader, seeking profits in the resale of what he buys or in the form of inventory appreciation. Most of the accepted methods of inventory valuation figure this asset on the basis of cost or market, whichever is lower. This effectively precludes any claim by purchasing to take credit for speculative profits from this source. The fact of material cost, however, remains, and this is his responsibility. In the event that the price rises as expected, it is of course outside the province of the purchasing department whether management and sales will take advantage of the cost saving to price their own end product for a more favorable competitive position in the current market or for a wider profit margin.

When the price of crude rubber dropped from 15 cents a pound in the early months of 1930 to four cents a pound and finally below three cents a pound during the depression of 1932 and early 1933, real demand was negligible. Yet rubber users not only filled their own storage facilities to capacity but hired outside storage space for the accumulation of three-cent, three-and-a-half-cent, and four-cent rubber. The purchases were made not merely because the price was low—as much too low economically as the artificially held prices up to 1930 had been economically too high—but because it represented a competitive cost level that every user of rubber had to contend with. It was, of course, reasonably certain that the rubber would in time be needed and used and that the price must advance if production were to be profitably continued, but there was little indication of imminent demand or price advance. A great part of this cheap rubber was held for two years or more; for 15 months the price never rose to four cents. After that, price recovery, along with business recovery, was fairly rapid, and rubber prices rose to above 12 cents in 1934 and 1935. No accurate information is available as to what "inventory profit" was realized on the rubber that went from storage into production and use. Such profits doubtless were made, though probably in far smaller degree than the price figures alone would indicate. However, the competitive position of a rubber user who had to depend on the current market when demand reasserted itself, while others in the field were using material purchased at half the price, would have been quite untenable.

Some commodities are much more sensitive than others in respect to price and are subject to considerable fluctuations from day to day. These price movements are of concern to the buyer, for in the large quantities that are characteristic of large-scale industrial operations the difference of a fraction of a cent per pound amounts to substantial sums in the aggregate. Buying on the short price swings is actually more speculative in nature than when the long trend is considered. In the great bulk of purchases making up the industrial procurement program, and in the final evaluation of purchasing competence as a contributing factor to profitable operation, the long trend is the more important. Every transaction is, of course, reflected in the total purchasing record, but the measurement of price performance in a purchasing program is average cost as compared with average market at the time of use, not any single purchase or the difference between the extreme low and the extreme high price.

Responsibility for speculative buying policies

The point at which normal forward-buying policies become speculative purchasing is when the emphasis and motivation change from assurance of adequate supply at lowest practicable cost (the proper function of a purchasing department) to the active seeking of profits from price appreciation of purchased materials, and when greater than normal calculated risks are taken to attain this objective.

Profit and risk are primarily the responsibilities of management. It has already been noted that inventory profits, though resulting from purchasing action, do not customarily accrue to the credit of purchasing in the company audit and accounts. Purchasing science seeks at all points to minimize risk— risk of shortage or surplus, of physical or financial depreciation, of over-extended investment in materials. In many cases, the purchasing agent's authority to take risks is definitely circumscribed by the placing of a monetary limit on the value of orders that may be issued without specific authorization of a superior officer.

Management, however, can and does take risks for profit. In respect to materials procurement, in addition to the routine review and authorization of large purchases, such risks include decisions to risk shortages by deferring purchases in the expectation of lower prices or, at the other extreme, decisions to invest a large proportion of the company's financial resources in materials inventories, perhaps at the expense of other business purposes.

Usually, such decisions are implemented through the purchasing department, but the policy and responsibility lie with management. In some special cases, where one or more key commodities are inherently volatile in price behavior, characterized by short-range fluctuations or wide market swings, where their role in the cost structure of the purchaser's product is significant and correspondingly volatile, speculative purchasing may be indicated as the rule rather than the deviation. It is in such commodities that the greatest problems, opportunities, and hazards of speculative purchasing occur. Because the objectives and techniques of this sort of buying have little in common with the general purchasing program, such procurement is sometimes set up as a separate assignment, handled by a commodity specialist close to management or by an executive in the management group, where the responsibility for speculative risk actually lies.

The most numerous cases, and most pertinent to a study of general purchasing principles, arise in connection with items that would normally be bought in the course of regular purchase procedure. Here a situation may develop which, in the judgment of the purchasing agent, calls for forward buying beyond the scope of his established policy and authority and justifies the additional risk. The common-sense way of handling such a situation is for the purchasing agent to make a recommendation to the general manager or other executive to whom he is responsible, with the reasons why he considers the extraordinary expenditure advisable. If management concurs in this judgment, the purchase is authorized and made through regular purchasing channels. The purchasing agent who is alert to recognize a special situation and does not hesitate to recommend special action to take advantage of it fulfills his function intelligently without arrogating to himself authority beyond the usual scope of his office and without sacrificing sound basic policy. The ultimate decision reflects both purchasing and management judgment and objectives.

For a more comprehensive and continuing control, some companies have established purchasing committees, consisting of the purchasing agent and top executives in general management, sales, and finance. The function of a purchasing committee is not to buy, but to review and set purchasing policies on major requirements. They usually concern themselves with only a dozen or so particular commodities that are the key materials required in the conduct of the business, and they determine the period of coverage that is desirable or make specific purchase authorizations. There are many advantages in this method of coordinating purchasing policies with other phases of company operation and policy; the special advantage to be noted here is that it provides a regular channel for recommendations and decisions as to forward coverage and speculative forward purchasing, with the benefit of several viewpoints that have a direct interest in the matter.

A typical purchasing committee has been successfully functioning for several years in a company that manufactures insulated wire and electrical connections. The 15 key items considered for this operation are: serving cotton, tram silk, copper rod, oil, gum, wire enamel, straits tin, lead, rubber smoked sheets, asbestos, glazed cotton, soft cotton, battery terminals, copper rolls, and lacquer. The committee meets monthly, during the first week of the month. As the basis for discussion and action, the purchasing agent presents a simple summary report on a mimeographed form running lengthwise on a letter-size sheet punched for a ring binder.

The 15 key items are listed down the left-hand side of the sheet, followed by ten columns. The first column shows the previous year's consumption of each of the items; because this figure does not change during any calendar year, it is mimeographed directly on the form when the year's supply is prepared. The second column shows consumption for the current year to date; this is a cumulative figure and is readily derived by adding the consumption of the month just past to the figure shown on the previous report; at the end of the year, the cumulative total is transferred to the first column. The third column shows consumption for the previous month; this is the increment used in arriving at the figure in column two. It is important to segregate this figure as an indicator of whether current rates of use are increasing or decreasing. Columns four, five, six, and seven show, respectively: inventory, quantity due on contract, quantity due on orders, and the total on hand due from suppliers. The first three of these are available from purchasing department records, and the fourth is the sum of the other three. In the eighth and ninth columns, this total is translated into the estimated number of months' supply, or advance coverage, on the basis of the previous year's consumption rate and that of the current year. This, again, is a simple calculation. For column eight, the figure in column seven is divided by one-twelfth of column one; for column nine, column seven is divided by the appropriate fraction of column two—one-fifth for the June 1 report, when five months' consumption has been reported for the current year, one-sixth for the July 1 report, and so on. The tenth column is headed "Purchases Authorized" and is filled in at the committee meeting on the basis of combined judgment after the other figures have been considered, this being the essential purpose of the monthly meeting. The decision as to desirable quantities and forward coverage becomes the purchasing agent's guide for policy and action during the current month.

There has been a distinct tendency in recent years to bring the purchase of key raw materials—cotton, rubber, wool, paper, and similar staples—within the scope of the general procurement program, handled by the purchasing department rather than as a separate executive function and responsibility. It is by no means a general practice as yet, but the trend in that direction is unmistakable. As it works out, specialists in these commodities are developed on the purchasing staff, and the same effect of expert knowledge and attention is attained for the benefit of the company, plus the advantage of putting such purchases under the same guidance of procurement policy and science as the rest of the purchase list. The inference from this trend is that broad-scale speculative buying as a procurement policy is coming into some disfavor and that the basic principles of purchasing science are becoming more universally applicable in respect to all the material requirements involved in an industrial operation.

Cost of speculative buying

Throughout this discussion it has been emphasized that speculative purchasing is really an extension of ordinary forward buying. To what degree it may be carried is determined by the probability of a price advance. It is, therefore, important to weigh the cost of carrying materials in inventory and all the other cost factors beyond the invoice price, as cited in the chapter on purchase quantities, before jumping to a conclusion based on the consideration of price alone.

For example, if a price increase of 10 per cent is anticipated, the inexperienced buyer may reason that there is no easier way to save or "make" 10 per cent for his company than by purchasing an extra year's supply at once. The experienced purchasing man, however, might not see any easy profit in the transaction. If the material were to be held a year before use, he would know that the extra carrying costs would bring his material cost up to the full replacement value at the time of use, so that the net result would be a tying up of working capital over that period and increased risks of depreciation and physical loss, even if the price advance should materialize as expected and be maintained, which is by no means certain.

The success of speculative buying depends on the steepness or rapidity of a price advance, or the recognition of abnormally low price levels, and on the promptness with which materials can be utilized. Investment in materials inventory is not a dividend-paying investment, but an added expense for whatever period it is carried, and no assumption of saving or profit or any comparison of costs is justified until the purchased material actually goes out of stores and into production.

To realize the potential advantages of a speculative purchasing program, therefore, certain special facilities are required in addition to the normal facilities of a business conducted on the basis of current requirements and a regularly scheduled flow of materials. Among these special facilities are the requisite storage space to care for extra quantities of materials over protracted periods and working capital funds for investment in such inventories. As a means of measuring the effectiveness of such purchasing policies, the cost accounting system should be set up to show specifically the total cost of the individual materials at the time of use, with the cost of the extra facilities maintained for this purpose allocated to the pertinent items. A distribution of costs averaged over the entire inventory is likely to be misleading when applied to an unbalanced stock characteristic of specialized forward purchasing.

Minimizing speculative risk

Commodity exchanges, providing facilities for trading in "futures" (contracts calling for the delivery of goods in some specified future month), exist for a number of leading commodities subject to daily price fluctuation. Among these are barley, cocoa, coffee, copper, corn, cotton, cottonseed oil, hides, lard, lead, oats, pepper, rubber, rye, silk, soy beans, sugar, tin, wheat, wool, and zinc. These exchanges serve a useful function, not only in facilitating actual purchases for future deliveries at a firm price, but in minimizing, through the practice of "hedging," the risk of necessary forward purchasing.

Speculative purchasing is sometimes inherent in the nature of a business, particularly when the process of manufacture is a lengthy one or when orders must be taken far in advance, so that there is a possibility or probability of market change between the time of procuring the raw materials and the sale of the product. For example, a cotton textile manufacturer must buy cotton now to start the production of goods to be sold three or four months hence, knowing that the price he can obtain for his product will be in relation to the cost of raw cotton at the time he makes his sale, and not to the cost of his actual purchase, which, for purposes of actual production, cannot be deferred to see what the applicable price will be. If the price of cotton should decline during this period, he may incur a loss not recoverable in the price of his product.

To meet such a condition, the buyer may "hedge" his purchase in the futures market. In its simplest form, such a transaction would be as follows. The buyer purchases the required amount of cotton on the spot, or open market, and at the same time sells an equivalent amount in the futures market, contracting to deliver it at the future date when his own product comes upon the market, at the currently quoted price for that future period. When that time comes, the cotton itself will have been used up in manufacture, but he will make a second purchase at the then current market to satisfy his delivery contract. Thus it makes no difference to him whether the price has advanced or declined, because the two transactions offset each other and leave him in the position of having acquired the cotton at the price level prevailing at the time his goods are sold. If the price has advanced in the meantime, he will have to accept a loss on the hedging operation, but will have a corresponding profit in the market value of his product. If the price has declined, he will have a loss on his manufacturing operation, but an offsetting profit on the hedge. As used for commercial purposes, hedge transactions seek protection rather than profit. The expense of this protection is the relatively small brokerage fee and the use of capital for margin deposits pending the completion of the transaction.

In a large percentage of future sales, actual delivery is not called for, and the transaction is closed by issuing a transfer notice. For this reason, plus the fact that such sales and purchases do not refer to any specific lot of material, the transactions are sometimes referred to as "options." This is inaccurate, for they are *bona fide* contracts, and deliveries may be demanded and taken.

Economic impact of purchasing

It is pertinent to note here the increasing interest of economists in industrial purchasing activity as an indicator of general business conditions. The
monthly Business Survey Committee Report of the National Association of
Purchasing Agents, and regular reports by the N.A.P.A.'s Steel Committee and
Non-Ferrous Metals Committee have received wide attention in the business
press for a number of years. The Business Survey report covers a wide range
of subjects—general business conditions; inventory policy; price outlook, new
orders, and labor conditions. The commodity committees report on market
conditions for specific items and generally offer a short-range price and supply
forecast. In its monthly report, "Business Cycle Developments"—a compilation of economic indicators for analysis and interpretation by specialists in
business-cycle analysis—elements of the Business Survey Report are used as
"leading indicators." (There are 30 indicators of economic activity that usually
reach peaks or troughs before the 15 "coincident indicators" or direct measures
of aggregate economic activity. Employment, industrial production, and retail
sales are among the latter.) The two measurements used from the Business
Survey Report are the buying policy on production materials—per cent reporting commitments for 60 days or longer; and buying policy on capital expenditures—per cent reporting commitments for six months or longer. Another
indicator, vendor performance—per cent reporting slower deliveries, is taken
from the monthly report on business conditions prepared by the Purchasing
Agents Association of Chicago.

Both the Joint Economic Committee of Congress and the authoritative
National Bureau of Economic Research, a private organization, have studied
the influence of changes in stocks of and outstanding orders for purchased
material on the business cycle. One NBER study in progress in 1963 made
extensive use of the monthly report on business conditions by the Purchasing
Agents Association of Chicago, described as a "remarkable pool of information."[1] Purchasing agents participating in the association's monthly survey
provide data not only on their own immediate buying operations, but on a
broad range of activities in their companies. They provide information on
unfilled sales orders, in-process and raw material inventories, status of unfilled
orders, and prices paid for principal materials.

The information, according to the NBER economist making the study, is
essential to understanding how fluctuations in demand are passed backward to
the previous member of the production chain. Her preliminary findings were
that changes in unfilled orders of purchased items appear to move in strong
conformity with, and perhaps earlier than, changes in unfilled orders for the

---

[1] National Bureau of Economic Research, Inc., *43rd Annual Report*, New York, 1963.

products the company sells. Changes in production and in prices of materials reproduce the same movements—the former, very sharply. Changes in inventories of purchased materials follow suit after a delay which is longer than can be explained by the time required for unfilled purchase orders to be shipped. The data "offer some provocative hints about how changes in demand interact with changes in supply to augment instability," according to the preliminary statement of the Bureau.

14

PURCHASED MATERIALS BUDGETS

ONE METHOD OF CORRELATING the great number and variety of forecasting and planning data discussed in the previous chapter is the establishment of a purchased materials budget (as distinct from the departmental budget discussed in Chapter 3). The budget is a planned program for carrying out the purchasing function more intelligently and effectively during a given period of time. The detail of whether advance estimates are scrupulously adhered to is of less importance than having the advantage of a goal and a plan.

Another reason for budgeting purchases is to achieve better control. Expenditures for materials and supplies are correlated with the foreseeable need and probable market trend—not based on generalities or on variables. We have pointed out earlier that avoidable losses may be incurred by buying either too much or too little of a given item, that material costs are substantially increased by overstocking, and that operating losses are sustained when materials are not available as needed. Budgeting minimizes all three factors.

Similarly, budgeting helps keep materials in balance—not only with requirements but with each other. The balance tends to keep inventory turnover high and cuts down on the expense of slow-moving stocks and the danger of loss through obsolescence. And it avoids shutdowns in production caused by parts shortages.

A fourth reason for budgeting is to establish standards of performance. The detailed estimate of materials and supplies to be purchased for a given project or program sets a standard that encourages and requires efficient use and similarly discourages carelessness and waste in the use of materials. Savings and efficiency are revealed quickly and dramatically when balanced against a budgeted estimate, while extravagance and inefficiency are just as apparent on the demerit side.

MATERIAL STATUS REPORT – PURCHASED PARTS

DATE   REQ. INSP. SECTION   REPORT CODE   CRITICAL   PART NUMBER   U/M   AREA   BUYER CODE

REQUIREMENTS

DATE OF REQUISITION	REQUIRED OR PROMISED DATE	REQUIRED OR PROMISED QUANTITY	REQUISITION OR PURCHASE ORDER

VENDOR

RECEIVED

QUANTITY RETURNED TO VENDOR	NET QUANTITY RECEIVED	QUANTITY IN INSPECTION	QUANTITY IN REWORK	QUANTITY IN DPM CRIB

ACCEPTED

QUANTITY ACCEPTED SCRAP	QUANTITY ACCEPTED STORES

OPEN BAL.

QUANTITY

PAST DUE

PER PURCHASE ORDER	PER REQUISITION

1. NEW REPORT
2. INQUIRY
3. CRITICAL PART ACTIVITY
4. REQ. PAST DUE
5. P.O. PAST DUE
6. U/M CHANGE
7. MONTHLY REPORT
8. OTHER

BUYER COPY

Fig. 14-1. Material Status Report of the Type Used in Purchased Materials Budget Programs.

A fifth reason for budgeting of materials, projecting requirements and commitments over a period in advance, is that it permits the adequate and orderly planning of finances to meet the commitments. Budgeting is essentially a financial operation and should be tied into the financial phase of management planning. Normal expense ratios may serve the purpose, but these ratios change with changing markets and costs of material, as well as with changing wage scales and operating rates. The principle of budgeting is recognized in the usual practice of making special appropriations, and special financial arrangements, if necessary, for major equipment purchases and other capital accounts. These purchases may represent large amounts and are typically of a nonrecurring nature; yet the purchased materials and supplies in regular and recurring use, standard items on the purchasing department's list and program, will generally add up to even greater amounts and more significant factors of cost and expenditure.

Sources of budget figures

The basic data upon which material requirements, or a purchase budget, may be calculated have already been indicated. Specifically, these data are the operating schedule, which depends, in turn, upon the summary of orders in hand, the advance estimate of sales for a given period, or the predetermined rate of operations, based on records of past demand and modified by long-term forecasts. Comparable statistics are available for nonmanufacturing service industries, public utility companies, and the like. On standard lines and made-to-order products, this quantitative figure can be translated directly into detailed requirements of the various components by means of the bill of materials. Corresponding figures for the requirements of fuel, expendable tools, and general operating supplies can be derived from previous experience records of the usage of such items for various manufacturing quantities and operating rates. This information, with a suitable allowance for waste and other contingencies, is the foundation of the materials budget. In other companies, where the details of end product are not so specifically predictable, but which follow a generally known type of operation and a general experience pattern, the record of past consumption serves as the guide, modified by such specific information as may be available. This is not as accurate, but it is practicable, provided that those in charge of budgeting will bear in mind that past records are a sound guide only as they are projected into the future, and that changing rates of use must be watched and adjusted with particular care.

Another and diametrically opposed approach to the materials budget should be noted here. It is encountered when specific appropriations are made for a purpose, definitely limiting the amount of permissible expenditures, as in the case of departmental budgets in municipalities, colleges, and public institutions, or, in industrial practice, when appropriations are made for research, for advertising materials, for building maintenance, and for other activities not directly dependent on manufacturing schedules. As in the previous instance, these appropriations start with an estimate of requirements for doing a complete or desirable job; but in setting up the budget, a compromise is frequently made and the extent of the program is determined by the funds appropriated rather than vice versa.

There remains the further step of translating the materials budget into financial terms—an essential one for the purpose of estimating costs. Past purchase prices are not always reliable, although in many cases they are the basis used. From a cost and accounting standpoint, the most satisfactory results are obtained through the use of standard costs, arrived at through a combination of past experience and judgment. Cost-accounting practice has developed the necessary means of handling variations between actual and standard costs, and revisions are made as required, at stated intervals not too frequent to destroy the usefulness and significance of the method.

It should be noted that the materials budget does not originate in the purchasing department, although the translation of the general program into itemized material requirements frequently comes within the purchasing responsibility, and although the estimate of future requirements on standard stock items is even more frequently a matter of purchasing judgment. The purchasing agent does contribute to the making of a budget through his knowledge and records of past requirements and his judgment of business and economic conditions, as well as through his knowledge of costs. Primarily, however, the purchasing officer's responsibility is to administer the budget, to apply it to the act of purchasing, and to provide the needed materials within the pattern set by the approved budget. On occasion, too, it is his responsibility to recommend revisions of the budget or deviations from the original plan, as circumstances make such action advisable. In other words, there must be flexibility, but not to the extent of abandoning or failing to use the guidance of the budget.

Major materials budget

In many companies, a limited list of key production materials embraces the major requirements for continuous operation and also represents the great bulk of financial commitments, and this is where sound purchasing policy has the greatest opportunity for contributing to profitable operation. In such cases, the application of budgeting procedures to the purchase of major materials is highly desirable and may be adequate without extending the practice to all requirements.

The purchasing agent forecasts price changes on these "key parts" by month or by quarter, indicating which are expected from negotiation, design change, material cost, supplier change, or any other factor. Such information is invaluable to management in determining the effect of materials cost on prices and profits for the period. The forecast also enables the purchasing agent to set definite cost reduction targets for his buyers, based on a thorough knowledge of competitive conditions and supplier capabilities.

Unit cost budgets

Another application of the budget system is based on unit product cost. Many product lines are designed and built to strict cost limitations, for competitive or other reasons. Cost of purchased materials and components makes up one factor of this total cost; other elements include cost of manufacturing, sales, administration, and the like. After the original estimates have been carefully made, checked, and tested so that the product can be put into manufacture and on the market, the budgeted standards of cost for each phase of the operation impose a high degree of responsibility on the department heads to keep their several portions of the total cost within the established percentage allotted for their particular cost element.

Probably the most thorough and successful use of the technique has been made in the automotive industry, particularly by the Ford Motor Company.[1] At Ford, purchasing begins its work on a new model as much as three years ahead of its appearance on the market. From even quite general descriptions of a planned new model, purchase analysts can begin to develop fairly accurate cost information. Purchasing continues to guide the new model from a cost standpoint, refining its estimates as the model idea is gradually developed into a marketable product. Costs must be controlled at each stage of design, and a budget is set up (both for parts and for tooling) on each new model. The budget is broken down into sections—so much for the front end, so much for ornamentation, so much for the engine, and so forth.

Purchasing must buy within this budget, but it has the advantage of not being forced to meet targets arbitrarily presented to it. By having purchase analysts estimate design costs at every stage of development of a new model, the purchasing department is given a chance to suggest changes to bring costs into line with the budget.

---

[1] D. S. Ammer, "The Purchasing Department: Ford's Cost Control Center," *Purchasing Magazine,* May 23, 1960, p. 53.

In many respects, this type of operation calls for the highest exemplification of purchasing skill, ingenuity, and executive approach to the procurement function. It likewise provides the most clear-cut opportunity for measuring purchasing performance, with the budget standard as a point of reference, and many of the outstanding examples of constructive purchasing for economy and profit are drawn from departments where such a plan is in effect. Accurate allocation of costs is essential in such a system. For example, skillful purchasing may develop the fact that a given component formerly fabricated in the company's own plant from purchased materials can be more economically procured by purchase of the fabricated part. Obviously, it is in the company's interest to take advantage of this saving, but in the budget plan the saving accrues entirely to the benefit of the manufacturing department, which is relieved of a fabricating operation, whereas the purchasing department is debited with the difference between the cost of the fabricated part, including outside production cost, and that of the materials formerly purchased. A readjustment is then clearly in order. Budgeting on unit cost has great possibilities. The administration of the plan fairly and effectively depends on sound accounting practice, to a greater degree than most other applications of the budget principle to materials and their procurement.

The budget period

Budget procedure applied to purchasing is most effective when a reasonably long term can be projected. On the other hand, flexibility and sensitivity to changing conditions and requirements are likewise essential. This dual requirement is commonly satisfied by combining a relatively long budget period with review and adjustment at frequent intervals. For example, requirements for three months in advance may be set up as the basis of a purchasing budget, with a monthly review and recalculation, so that the program is at all times established for 90 days in advance, corresponding generally with practice in regard to operating schedules. Supplementing this budget, a full year's schedule may be estimated, revised at quarterly intervals for consideration of fluctuations as they develop or may be foreseen. As a matter of fact, advance ordering on many primary lines is customarily limited to the three-month period, so that actual budget purchasing is similarly restricted and the basic control must be exercised through inventory policy, correlated with budgeted requirements of materials. Under such a plan, purchased items involving a longer production cycle, and consequently a longer procurement cycle, may be handled by means of covering contracts on estimated requirements for the more extended period, against which release orders are issued for specific quantities for the shorter period. In many cases, such manufacturing orders serve to bring the desired product up to a certain stage of fabrication, or to secure the allocation of raw materials and fabricating capacity for the buyer's purpose. Then, as budget quantities and precise specifications become known, instructions and orders for cutting, dyeing, finishing, and other similar processes can be accomplished within the period contemplated by the budgeting of purchases.

Adherence to budget

Because purchase budgets are based on estimates of requirements, a considerable margin of error is likely to exist—a risk inherent in all processes of estimating. In respect to materials estimates, it may arise from a number of different reasons, beyond the control of the buyer or of his company and affecting every phase of the estimate. Changes in design or in customers' specifications, or technological developments in the field, may change completely the quality or character requirement of the purchase. On the quantitative side, changing schedules or rates of operation or cancellation of orders are ever-present possibilities, and, in terms of the financial budget, market fluctuations will of course throw the calculation out of balance even though the estimate of physical requirements has been accurate. If errors in budgeting are on the side of deficiency, so that the estimate is not adequate to meet the actual requirement, an additional purchasing problem is presented, but this contingency can ordinarily be met because the requirement will become apparent as the operating program develops. If estimates are in excess of the actual need, and purchasing is done according to budget, the result may be more serious in the way of surplus materials, swollen inventories, additional carrying costs, and increased losses from obsolescence.

In spite of these variables, scientific forecasting and budgeting, supported by continuing and cumulative experience, have shown a reasonably high degree of accuracy. Reports from a representative number of companies where budgeting of purchases is in effect indicate that in two-thirds of the companies the estimate of requirements has come within 10 per cent of actual need, although, in the less successful examples, some of the individual items have varied from the original estimate by as much as 75 per cent. Several of the companies, in types of industry particularly adapted to accurate prediction and stable operating rates, show an error of 5 per cent or less, but the 10 per cent figure is the most representative.

It can be argued to good effect that an error of 10 per cent is a wide margin, tending to discredit the whole budgeting procedure. On the other hand, a review of the functional purposes of both budgeting and purchasing, and the significance of the figure in question, show such a conclusion to fall short of the whole truth. The setting of any standard, such as that established in a purchase budget, implies a comparison of actual performance with the standard; but precise adherence to the standard is not necessarily the measure of good purchasing. Aside from the variables mentioned above, efficient purchasing in itself may improve upon, and thereby vary from, the budget standard. Over a period of time—for example, over the budget period—actual purchases will necessarily be determined by actual requirements. The margin of error is really an error in the estimate, and comparison of the two figures serves to correct the estimate and make it more realistic. For the budget is essentially a guide to probable material requirements, rather than a fixed limitation. A guide that sets a reasonably accurate goal and that permits up to 90 per cent of purchases to be planned and executed according to plan is an important asset to any purchasing program. Furthermore, it provides a standard by which variations from expected performance can be analyzed and explained. Sometimes this results in placing credit where credit is due for superior performance, or it points out those phases of the program where changing conditions or unforeseen factors beyond the buyer's control were responsible for the variation.

This aspect of budgeting as an over-all guide, with expected variations but establishing a substantial zone of safety in anticipated requirements, is well illustrated by the policy of one representative manufacturer who sets up his manufacturing schedule for a period of three months. From this budgeted operation, the total material requirements are calculated. The purchasing agent is authorized to procure up to 75 per cent of the indicated amounts on this schedule at his own discretion. Thus, the bulk of the purchase program is immediately provided for, with complete flexibility in buying and coverage for approximately ten weeks in advance, if this is desirable in the purchasing agent's judgment. At the same time, there is protection against overbuying and a provision for drastic curtailment of the purchases for the quarter if conditions should radically change, thus keeping the hazards of inventory loss at a minimum. If, in the judgment of the purchasing agent, it should be desirable for any reason to purchase up to the full amount of estimated requirements, or even beyond the budgeted three-month period, special authorization is required, and the recommendation comes before the budget committee, where any factors that might support or modify the recommendation are considered. The accuracy of the budget forecast is not left to any one individual opinion.

At the end of each month, the whole situation of manufacturing schedule and materials requirements comes up for review and the budget period is extended by one month in the form of a new three-month forecast. The supply position at this time takes into consideration any quantities purchased in advance of the previous month's actual consumption, as permitted under the

75 per cent limitation. On the basis of the adjusted figure, a new 75 per cent authorization is granted and the budgeted purchase program continues, always retaining a 25 per cent margin of safety for flexibility and possible adjustment without unduly prejudicing or hampering the exercise of good purchasing judgment and practice.

In governmental and institutional purchasing, where budgets are limited by specific appropriations, a comparable measure of flexibility is frequently achieved by means of a revolving fund to be expended at the discretion of the purchasing department for later reconciliation with departmental budgets. On the balance sheet, the purchasing department must account for this fund in the form of cash balance, unissued stores, or debits against other departments. Such a plan has been exceedingly effective in permitting the maintenance of central stores of standard items in use by several departments, in raising purchase quantities into more favorable price and discount brackets, and in the acquisition of governmental surplus property and scarce materials where prompt action is needed and opportunities for desirable purchases might be lost by waiting on the routine of approval and special appropriation. Some of the revolving funds are of modest proportions—a few thousand dollars, for example. In the purchasing department of the State of Michigan, on the other hand, a revolving fund of one million dollars has been made available, and the results have handsomely justified this departure from strict departmental budgeting without any loss of control or accountability.

15

VALUE ANALYSIS

IT HAS ALREADY BEEN SUGGESTED, in the concluding section of Chapter 5, that the value concept breaks across the lines that divide functional responsibility, and prompts a new purchasing activity—value analysis. To measure value, we balance what we get in our purchase against what we must pay. We get from the supplier what we ask him to furnish; thus, we start with the quality definition and apply all our purchasing skills to procure that quality at minimum cost. The essence of the quality definition is suitability. But as soon as we get over into the realm of price analysis and negotiation, we may find that a part of what we are paying goes for quality features that do not contribute substantially or proportionately to suitability of the material or product purchased. To that extent the expenditure is wasteful and value is diminished. This brings us to a study of the purpose or function for which the item is purchased and a review of the specification, looking toward the possible revision of the quality definition that may permit a cost reduction without impairing suitability.

This is a new role for purchasing, because the determination and definition of quality requirements are a responsibility of technical and manufacturing departments, not of purchasing. But value is definitely and importantly a part of purchasing responsibility, therefore, it is a logical and legitimate extension of purchasing activity to make a systematic search for the most economical means of satisfying the requirement.

Value analysis is not in the main stream of the buying process. It takes time, special attention, and special talents. It is essentially a staff service to the buyer. A purchasing agent may undertake the dual role of analyst and buyer, but any full-scale value-analysis program is most effective when provision is made in the departmental organization plan for a staff analyst or analytical section and when organization channels are set up for communication and action with the departments that make final quality decisions.

A second look at the specification

Value analysis is variously defined. One simple definition describes the process as "engineering unnecessary cost factors out of a purchased item." A more elaborate definition states: "Value analysis is the study of the relationship of design, function, and cost of any product, material, or service with the object of reducing its cost through modification of design or material specifications, manufacture by more efficient processes, change in source of supply (external or internal), or possible elimination or incorporation into a related item."

Value analysis by purchasing does not encroach upon the functions or prerogatives of other departments. The cost-reduction possibilities it discloses are initially presented as recommendations—perhaps, only queries—to those who must ultimately define the need. Wherever changes in material, design, or process are involved, approval by engineering or manufacturing departments is essential before a specification can be changed. If a suggestion has merit, the actual changes are often worked out in those departments. If a suggestion is impracticable, or if there are other factors that outweigh the cost consideration, it can be rejected.

The application of value analysis to existing specifications is in no sense a derogation of the engineering skill and judgment represented in the original statement of need. Rather, it adds another criterion in defining right quality. It gives recognition to the fact that, in design and specification, as in every other field, there is an ever-present possibility of improvement, and that the only way to achieve that improvement is through continuous, systematic effort directed toward that end. Characteristically, if any part or material is doing its job satisfactorily, and if the specification satisfies the requirement of suitability, there is no inclination on the part of the user to disturb the situation.

Value analysis also recognizes the fact that, in mass production, no unit saving is too small to merit respectful attention, because small unit savings multiplied thousands of times in the total production program quickly mount up to impressive dollar figures. The Ford Motor Company, a pioneer in promoting value-analysis activities in purchasing, used a slogan pointing out that, with an annual output of a million vehicles, "the difference of one cent per car represents a saving or loss of $10,000 per year." Changing one small component from a forging to an equally serviceable screw-machine product saved 4/10 of a cent per unit, an insignificant figure. But 16 of these parts were used in every car. Annual saving: $64,000.

Typical savings effected through value analysis actually run to many times greater than this very modest example. To anyone unfamiliar with the workings and results of value-analysis techniques, the tangible savings reported may indeed seem fantastic, whether considered as a percentage of previous costs, dollarwise, or in relation to the cost of the activity itself. Where accurate records of savings are maintained, it is almost universal experience that every dollar spent in value-analysis work is returned many times over, and these savings are repeated and multiplied in succeeding years' purchases. In companies where value-analysis programs have been carried on intensively for ten years or longer, there is no indication that the procedure is even approaching the point of diminishing return. Instead, the habits of mind engendered throughout an organization by this approach to value buying give added momentum to the program, with ever-increasing results. Value analysis is an integral, sound, continuing element of scientific purchasing. Such experience, more than any other factor, has brought about the realization that purchasing is, in fact, a profit-making function.

Eliminating unnecessary cost factors

Value analysis is a more fundamental and far-reaching concept than the simple process of price analysis in that it goes to the causes of price. Further, it has the practical objective of applying direct corrective action to minimize these causes and reduce costs, instead of leading only to comparisons and negotiation on the basis of existing costs.

In analyzing a price, with all of the many varied factors that must be included in a supplier's quotation, the hard core of cost is eventually found in the manufacturer's cost of production. This is the irreducible minimum. There may be some flexibility or leeway in other factors, such as overhead charges, the cost of distribution and sales, quantity differentials and quantity manufacturing economies, profit margins, competitive pricing policies, and the like. These have always been considered legitimate areas for purchase inquiry and negotiation, but the cost of production has properly been accepted as inviolate. It is assumed that the buyer will select a supplier whose production methods are efficient and whose costs are competitive. Such suppliers are in a strong position, and it is to the buyer's advantage to keep his sources strong. Any attempt to purchase below the cost of production, quite aside from the ethical and legal considerations that may be involved, merely tends to destroy the buyer's source of supply.

Value analysis recognizes that there is an alternative possibility. The supplier's basic costs of manufacture are largely fixed by the design, materials, and methods specified by the buyer for production of the purchased item. It may be that the item itself, which the buyer is asking his supplier to produce, represents an unnecessarily high cost for the intended purpose. If that is the case, and if it is recognized, the buyer and his associates can attack that hard core of basic production cost, seeking to eliminate or modify the unnecessary features of design and the manufacturing operations that they entail, thus arriving eventually at a part or specification that truly represents the most economical product to satisfy the end-use requirements. It is obvious that this concern for value adds a new and important dimension to the buyer's definition of "right quality."

From the standpoint of economical product cost, it would be difficult to overemphasize the significance and benefits of such an approach. Over a long period of years, the constant trend of economic factors has been to build additional costs into the basic cost structure of manufactured products in the form of higher labor rates, more expensive raw materials, and higher taxes and costs of doing business. Meanwhile, each increment in basic cost of manufacture reduces cost flexibility and tends to perpetuate the higher price plane. Under these circumstances, anything that can be engineered out of basic cost as a direct, item-by-item saving is doubly significant. Such savings permanently eliminate cost factors and conserve productive effort. They are repetitive, multiplied many times over in quantity requirements.

From the standpoint of purchasing practice and supplier relationships, the value-analysis approach also has much to commend it in that it does not attempt in any way to "squeeze" the supplier, to reduce his normal margins of profit, or to exert extraordinary competitive pressure in dealings with him. As a matter of fact, the supplier's own suggestions and cooperation may be enlisted in this effort, to mutual advantage. It is one of those happy situations in which everybody wins.

Check list for value analysis

This approach to the problem of cost is well summarized in the check list of ten "Tests for Value" compiled and used in the purchasing department of the General Electric Company.[1] This code, which has been widely circulated throughout every division of the company, among engineering and manufacturing as well as purchasing personnel, states:

Every material, every part, every operation must pass these tests:
1. Does its use contribute value?
2. Is its cost proportionate to its usefulness?
3. Does it need all of its features?
4. Is there anything better for the intended use?
5. Can a usable part be made by a lower-cost method?
6. Can a standard product be found which will be usable?

---

[1] "Value Analysis," *Purchasing Magazine,* June, 1950, page 94.

7. Is it made on proper tooling, considering quantities used?
8. Do material, reasonable labor, overhead, and profit total its cost?
9. Will another dependable supplier provide it for less?
10. Is anyone buying it for less?

Examples of this type of analysis, with a representative application of each listed test to a purchased component, are cited as follows:

Test 1. (Condenser used across contacts of a relay to provide arc action as contact opens.) When cobalt became available after World War II, an alnico magnet was used to provide snap action. Analysis disclosed that the condenser was no longer necessary with this magnet—it did not add value to the product—and it was eliminated. The saving was 500,000 condensers per year, at 10 cents each.

Test 2. (Spacer hub for mounting light aluminum discs.) Considering the simple function of this part in the assembly, the cost of 90 cents per unit was out of proportion to its usefulness. The cost was high due to undercutting to reduce weight, which was an important factor. Analysis showed that by making the part of aluminum, the undercutting could be eliminated, the weight still further reduced, and identical performance provided at a cost of 20 cents per unit. The saving was 77 per cent.

Test 3. (Stainless steel disc used in dispensing machine.) These washers were formerly chamfered on one side. Analysis revealed that the chamfer made no contribution to value—the part did not need all of its features. Eliminating the chamfer reduced the cost from 18 cents to 5 cents per unit, a saving of 72 per cent.

Test 4. (Mica stack used for insulation.) By changing from sheet mica to molded Micalex, the parts of the assembly were more rigidly mounted, resulting in a better assembly, and cost was reduced from $40 to $34 per M, a saving of 15 per cent.

Test 5. (Hub assembly.) This part was formerly made as a two-part riveted assembly, at a cost of $30 per M. Study showed that it could be made as a one-piece casting, eliminating the assembly operation and simplifying production. At the same time, cost was reduced to $10 per M, a saving of 67 per cent.

Test 6. (Stud contact.) This part had been made to special design, at a cost of $27 per M. Purchasing search discovered a standard-design stud, available at $14 per M, that provided identical performance. The saving was 48 per cent.

Test 7. (Stainless weld nipple.) Because of relatively small quantities required, the former procedure had been to purchase a standard stainless fitting and machine away a part of it to provide the desired weld embossing. Cost by this method was 20 cents each. Value analysis disclosed the fact that production requirements had increased to the point where another process should be considered. It was subsequently produced in quantity on an automatic screw machine at a cost of 5 cents each. The saving was 75 per cent.

Test 8. (Stainless dowel pin.) This part was purchased in large quantities, made to special design and specifications with close tolerances required. The cost of $3 per M seemed out of line with reasonable standards, but was justified by the vendor's costs. The manufacturer was invited to confer on details of the specification, manufacturing process, and inspection. As a result, some wastes of material and labor were eliminated from his operation. The identical part, produced to the same close tolerances, was subsequently produced at $2 per M, a saving of 33 per cent.

Test 9. (Bushing.) Exploration of the market disclosed that this part, purchased from an established source of supply at $18 per M, could be procured from an equally reliable supplier at $13.50 per M, a saving of 25 per cent.

Test 10. (Button.) This part, used by one division in large volume, was being purchased at $2.50 per M. Research within the purchasing department revealed that another division was using a similar button costing $1 per M. The latter was found to be applicable to the use under study, with equally good performance, at a saving of 60 per cent.

The role of purchasing

It will be noted in a review of these representative examples that only the last three are strictly of a purchasing nature; the first seven are primarily concerned with engineering design and manufacturing methods, and the savings achieved through value analysis in these cases were made possible only by working through those other departments. The question naturally arises, then, as to why value analysis is considered primarily as a purchasing function. The first answer to this is that value analysis for cost reduction is everybody's business and is more effective when its principles are applied throughout the organization, wherever requirements and specifications originate. But there are five important reasons why it is logical for the purchasing department to initiate and promote this activity (as in the case of standardization, which is one of the tools of value analysis, indicated in Test 6 of the check list) and why value analysis work is customarily centered in this department.

1. Regardless of how much cost-reduction activity is carried on in other departments of the company, it is still a responsibility of the buyer to seek maximum value when a product requirement comes up to the point of purchase. It is his duty to challenge wasteful and avoidable costs inherent in the things he is asked to buy. Thus, it is inescapable that a large share of whatever value-analysis work is done will be done by the buyer or in the purchasing department in any case.

2. Purchasing, more than any other department, must be cost-conscious in respect to the materials and parts that go into the company's end-product. This is a desirable attribute in every department, but it is an integral part of the buying responsibility. The purchasing agent is brought face to face with the cost factor in every transaction. Even where value analysis is not organized for special consideration, it is practiced to some degree, as a matter of course, in every purchasing comparison and decision.

3. Purchasing is cost-wise through experience in price analysis and comparisons, evaluation of alternative materials and methods, and the handling of many comparable items. The buyer learns why some products cost more than others, and what features in a specification make suppliers' quotations higher. This knowledge is enhanced by his daily exposure to the product offerings and sales presentations of vendors, which can be directly related to his own requirements and often can reveal how cost reductions are being effected in other companies having similar needs.

4. Purchasing is objective in its attention to costs, to a degree that is difficult for the person or department whose first concern is the utility or performance of a product and whose judgment is understandably influenced by established satisfactory usage or by creative pride of design.

5. Purchasing is a natural focal point where each individual requirement and specification, from whatever source in the company, must pass in review. It is therefore in a strategic position to apply the experience gained in connection with one item to other similar items; to recognize the areas in which intensive value analysis gives greatest promise of effective and profitable results; and to carry on such projects as part of a specific, comprehensive, and continuing program.

Thus, beyond its own direct value-analysis activities, the role of purchasing is to initiate and organize; to promote cost-consciousness in all depart ments of the company, keeping this topic in the forefront of their thinking; to point out opportunities or to raise questions as to the possibility of cost reduction in purchased items; to develop practical techniques for product and value analysis; and to train personnel of other departments, upon request, in the application of these techniques, giving whatever assistance may be required.

Technique of product analysis

The techniques of product analysis are as varied as the problems in this field, but particular attention should be directed to one method that has been exceptionally resultful. The examples previously cited have been concerned with individual components or small parts of a larger assembly. The more comprehensive approach starts with the complete assembly, considered as the sum of its parts.

A widely used technique is to take such an assembly, dismantle it, and mount it on a panel board of plywood or other suitable material in such a way that each of the component parts, down to the smallest screw or other fastening device, is shown in relation to all other parts. With this visualization, analysis is facilitated and the pertinent questions are more readily framed, leading to better and more economical practice. The Ford Motor Company

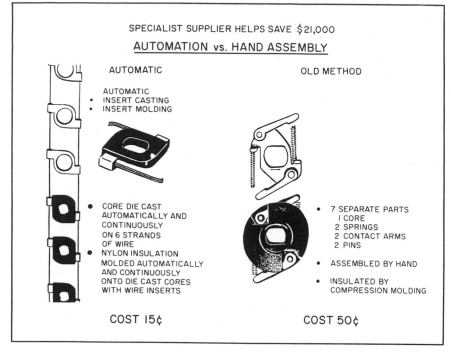

Fig. 15-1. Graphic Presentation of How Value Analysis Cut Product Cost 70 per cent.

used this technique as long ago as 1947 to analyze an automobile radiator. When the radiator was disassembled and mounted as described, certain cost-saving opportunities were immediately obvious:

The overflow tube from the off-center filler spout had been carried down the far side of the radiator. By changing this to the near side, five inches of copper tubing per car were saved.

A rounded indentation in the lower stamped section, originally designed to accommodate the starting crank, had been inadvertently retained in the drawings after the crank arrangement was discontinued. Eliminating this operation resulted in a substantial saving. Coincidentally, the supporting bar, which was a stamping to the same contour, was changed to a straight bar simply cut off to the proper length.

Other changes included the use of tack welding instead of full welding for attaching the overflow tube. It was found that several small parts could be more economically manufactured in quantity by Ford and furnished to vendors than to have each vendor make his own. Clipping the corners of two copper fins for ease in assembly was extended to all five fins, with a resultant saving in metal and in weight. Altogether, a pound and a half of unnecessary metal was designed out of the radiator, at a saving of 45 cents per unit. It is estimated that this one analysis alone, initiated and carried out in the purchasing department, made possible savings of $1,500,000 per year for the Ford Motor Company.

A variation of this technique is to mount adjacently on a panel board, in corresponding position for direct comparison, the disassembled components of competitive or alternative products (for example, dashboard clocks) so that their relative designs and merits and costs may be analyzed, resulting in a revised specification that literally embodies the best and most economical features of each.

The check-list technique, already illustrated in an earlier section of this chapter in connection with the general objectives of value analysis, can be effectively developed in greater detail with specific application to particular classes of products. For example, check lists are prepared covering cost-reduction possibilities to be considered in the specification and purchase of electrical components, or safety equipment, or any other product classification. The virtue of this method is that it pinpoints the problem and insures that no logical line of inquiry and analysis will be overlooked.

Another technique is reference to proven examples of cost reduction. In recent years, because value analysis has gained prominence as an important phase of purchasing, a considerable body of case histories in successful value analysis has become available.[2] These case histories are sometimes directly applicable to comparable problems in the buyer's own company. They are particularly valuable in suggesting areas of potential research, on the principle that what will work in one company can be done equally effectively in another.

Still another technique that has produced excellent results is the "brain-storming" session. A problem or product is presented to a group of people for consideration. They need not be experts in the particular subject. If they represent a variety of special interests and experience, such as purchasing, engineering, and manufacturing, so much the better. The meeting is totally unrehearsed. The group leader presents the problem, stressing the function to be served by the product and showing current design or practice. He then invites suggestions for improvement. Each person makes whatever suggestions come first to mind, however unorthodox or impracticable the ideas may seem to be. These are listed and grouped, and when the first flow of ideas has slowed down, they are explored in greater detail, again in open discussion and with the invitation for further ideas that may have been prompted by some aspect of those already presented.

---

[2] The annual "Value Analysis Issues" of *Purchasing Magazine,* 1949 to date, contain literally thousands of cost-saving case histories, classifield for reference under Materials, Production Tools and Processes, Electrical Equipment, Component Parts, Materials Handling, Office Equipment and Supplies, Maintenance and Safety Items, and Packaging and Shipping.

This technique focuses the working of several minds upon a common problem, with freshness and variety of approach and stimulated by the interplay of contrasting ideas. It rarely fails to produce some tangible and worthwhile results. It is not expected to educe a fully developed answer to the problem in hand, but it does provide one or more starting points, and it frequently happens that the eventual solution has its real origin in some tangential or improbable suggestion. Brainstorming encourages imaginative thinking and provides the germ of many a pregnant idea. In addition to its usefulness as a technique in actual analysis, the method is widely and successfully used as the basis for training seminars in value analysis.

Scope of value analysis

The scope of value analysis is not limited to factors of design and manufacturing method. In chemical manufacturing industries, for example, the product is inherently and rigidly defined in its composition and grade, and variations or alternatives are obviously ruled out of consideration. Nevertheless, value analysis has been effectively applied in this field in respect to reagents, solvents, plasticizers, containers, bulk handling and distribution, and other elements in the process that substantially affect product costs.[3]

The last three items in the General Electric Company's check list for value relate exclusively to purchasing policies and methods and are applicable to any items of use in any company.

The Ford Motor Company study previously cited gives examples of many different phases and methods of approach to value buying. These include financial analysis of a vendor's operation, leading to more accurate allocation of costs to a particular product line and eliminating unwarranted overhead charges; studies of basic raw material markets that helped in formulating buying policies and in keeping product prices stable in a period of wide price fluctuations; and an analysis of components and prices in competitive paint products. In addition, the study considers these points: labor costs in the application of fasteners which justified 40 per cent higher purchase costs to achieve a net saving of 30 per cent in final cost of the operation; vendor locations and the reallocation of orders among these vendors, with resultant savings of 50 per cent in transportation costs on one important item; packaging methods that developed savings of up to 75 per cent on some operations in this area; and the relative efficiency and fuel consumption of various types of welding tools. The scope of profitable value analysis is limited only by the ingenuity and perseverance of the buyer.

---

[3] J. R. Sayers, "Value Analysis in Chemical Buying," *Purchasing Magazine,* June, 1956, page 79.

Because the concept of value is compounded of both quality and cost, the subject is not complete without reference to the criteria of buying at the right price (Chapter 10). Many of the methods used in that determination are properly included in the broad field of value analysis. The same is true of decisions on whether to make or purchase a part or item (Chapter 17) and, as previously noted, the whole field of standardization (Chapter 6).

Setting up a value-analysis program

Value analysis produces best results when it is recognized as a specific responsibility in the buying process and when it is implemented by an adequate staff and facilities to carry on a consistent and continuous program. The important thing is to get started. In small- or medium-size purchasing departments the responsibility is generally assigned directly to the buyers; in that case, it is essential that the purchasing work load be distributed so as to allow time for such work. The preferable arrangement is to have specialized personnel charged with this responsibility and devoting full time to analysis and research. This is most simply accomplished by having a value analyst as a staff assistant to the head of the purchasing department, or by establishing a value-analysis section within the department. In some large companies, an analyst is assigned to each of the major commodity-buying groups. This has the advantage of even greater specialization, and of working closely with the particular buyers concerned.

Value-analysis projects are generally initiated by the buyers. They may be prompted by any number of causes or circumstances: by particular difficulties in satisfactory procurement; by uneven competitive market conditions, by suggestions from vendors' salesmen; by observations in the plant or in a vendor's plant; by discrepancies in departmental usage; by dissatisfaction with a current purchase and the sensing that a cost is too high; by systematic review of items purchased; or by cost-reduction targets set by top management or in the purchasing department itself. The value analyst's job is to take up these suggestions and to follow through with the necessary research, for his primary function is to assist the buyer in obtaining maximum values. So far as time permits, the analyst may initiate additional projects, but always with the knowledge and cooperation of the buyer so that the total effort may be consistent in itself and in relation to the purchasing program. First attention would logically be given to critical items, to those representing substantial volume and dollar expenditures, and to those where repetitive or continuing savings may accrue.

The results of the analyst's work are in the form of reports and recommendations. They are supported in every case by cost comparisons and the projection of anticipated savings, because this is the goal toward which value analysis is directed. The reports are made to the purchasing agent, and only through the purchasing department to other personnel or departments affected. This is the orderly channel of procedure and communication, because decisions based on the recommendations, involving changes in specifications, manufacturing methods, or shop practice must be made at the executive level. To inject a third, independent factor and personality into interdepartmental problems of value and utility tends to confuse the issue, to give the impression of meddling, and in general to weaken the force of the recommendation and the consideration that is given to it. By contrast, a purchasing proposal based on the identical recommendation, and within the buyer's legitimate province of purchase cost reduction, must be weighed on merit even though the proposal may not be adopted for other reasons.

In addition to actual research and analysis projects, an important part of the program is to promote cost-consciousness throughout the entire organization, whether materials are specified and used. The publicizing of improved practice and lowered costs, through bulletins and employee publications, helps toward an understanding of what value analysis tries to accomplish and generates enthusiasm for the program. Cost reduction must be a team effort. When it is accepted that value analysis is not critical of previous decisions but is predicated on the principle that almost everything is capable of improvement, progress is made toward getting everybody on the team. A second step is to make available training in value-analysis techniques. This is best done with small groups, in "workshop"-type sessions. Engineering, manufacturing, and other specifying departments, as well as buyers, should be invited to participate. The mixed group presents various viewpoints on the value and fosters understanding of the common objective.

Chief qualification for a successful value analyst is an imaginative, questioning mind, backed with enthusiasm and perseverance. A knowledge of cost accounting and of manufacturing processes is desirable. The value analyst must have the ability to work with people and the willingness to share credit. Nothing can kill a value-analysis program more quickly than a "credit-grabbing" attitude.

Enlisting vendors' aid

One of the most fruitful sources of information and help in value buying is the cooperation of vendors. Here the buyer has at his disposal the advice of specialists who are expert and experienced in their respective fields to a degree that the buyer, concerned with many different products, can rarely hope to attain. The purchasing agent who can establish a relationship with vendors in which they make his problems their own, and will work with him toward the objectives of cost reduction, enlists the technical resources and manufacturing experience of an entire industry. Such a relationship is, of course, predicated on the assumption that the cooperative vendor will be the preferred vendor and will profit through greater sales. This policy in itself represents a sound concept of value in purchasing.

In organized value-analysis programs, this source of help is cultivated by means of "vendor clinics." A representative group of vendors is invited to come to the buyer's plant, usually for a two-day meeting, at which materials

---

Westinghouse Electric Corporation
Aerospace Electrical Department
Lima, Ohio

Date_____

"COUNTDOWN ON COST" SUPPLIER SUGGESTION

Part Description *Bracket, Connector*   AED Dwg. No. & Item *90PC827-1*

I think Westinghouse could save......
    $ *600 00*   in tooling or development costs...
    $ *.90*   in purchase price... *(24% decrease)*
    ¢_____   in other costs (specify)...

    by adopting this suggestion_____

1. Increase the number of mold cavities from 2 to 6.

2. Eliminate machining stock on the 2 1/4" face dimension and the 1.560" radius by casting to closer tolerances.

3. Permit supplier to belt sand to final dimension, thereby eliminating machining by Westinghouse.

Affects present item ✔ Affects proposed item ___
Financial Objectives shown represent: Actual savings ___ Estimated Savings ✔

Name *W. J. Prestel, President* Representing *OHIO PRECISION CASTINGS, INC.*
Address *P.O. Box 55, Station A, Dayton 3, Ohio*

Assigned to *W. J. Klaruff* for evaluation. Date_____
            Section Mgr.
Note: This form is designed to insure that all suggestions received from suppliers receive prompt attention. Please state your idea clearly, attaching a sketch or outline and using additional sheets as required. Keep one copy. Submit two to the Buyer. Please specify any persons who could facilitate the implementation of this suggestion.

Fig. 15-2. Cost Reduction Suggestion Form Used at a "Vendor Clinic."

requirements, problems, and policies are explained to the group as a whole and sometimes in private conferences. The visitors are not salesmen in the ordinary sense, but are drawn from the higher-ranking management and operating officers of the vendor companies. A focal feature of the clinic is a comprehensive display of the company's important products and the purchased parts that go into them. Here vendors can see at first hand how their own products are used in the buyer's assembly, which is not always clear from the specification or blueprint. It shows the reasons underlying certain terms of the specification, the need for close tolerances at one point or of extra strength at another, and the relationship of each part with other sections that may be procured from other sources. It stresses the idea that the parts manufacturer is in fact a participant in making the end product and that its quality, utility, and cost (and hence, its marketability) are really the concern of all.

This is good education, but the clinics also have a more immediate and practical objective. When the vendors inspect the parts on display, they are invited to indicate those that they are equipped to furnish to best advantage and on which they would like to quote. At the same time it is made clear that the company is receptive to any suggestions as to parts design or manufacturing method that will improve quality or reduce cost, or both. Vendors are furnished with blueprints and specifications sheets on the selected items for further study and estimates. Results of this inspection and study are then reflected in subsequent quotations and proposals. Scores of companies which sponsor such vendor clinics report tangible benefits in the way of better understanding, better-quality deliveries, better vendor relationships, and better procurement.

Reports of savings

A value-analysis program must itself be evaluated in terms of the results achieved. And top management, as well as the purchasing director, should be kept informed.

Most purchasing departments maintain a record of savings. For the record, this should not only show the saving in unit cost on the immediate purchase, but should be projected on the basis of annual usage. A summary of this record, with more detailed information on some of the more significant cases, is often included in periodical reports to management. There are two excellent reasons why this is good practice.

1. It is a significant measure of the purchasing department's alertness and profitable performance.

2. It is a factual justification in support of requests for adequate budgets and personnel for value-analysis work. This is especially valuable in cases

where management takes it for granted that the engineers know what they want and that it is the purchasing agent's job to get best value and to save money in any case, without organization frills.

In making such reports, a brief notation as to how the saving was accomplished is helpful, and the admonition against "credit grabbing" should again be emphasized. When tabulating savings, there may be a natural inclination to claim more than is actually justified, even to taking credit for lower prices available in a generally declining market. If this is done, it discounts the entire report. As a purchasing department report, the tabulation should be restricted to savings actually initiated and achieved by purchasing action. One large company which has a notable record in profitable value analysis goes so far as to have its record of savings audited by the cost accounting department. A sound value-analysis program will stand up and gain increased acceptance through such an audit.

16

NEGOTIATION

NEGOTIATION, BRIEFLY DISCUSSED in Chapter 10, was defined there as "the process of working out a procurement and sales program together, to the point of reaching a mutually satisfactory agreement." Technically, this definition covers almost any transaction between a buyer and a supplier, from a telephone discussion about the price of a few gallons of lubricant to prolonged conferences on the terms of a major equipment purchase.

In practice, the term is generally applied in industrial purchasing to the more complex situations involving buyers and sellers, in which both make a number of proposals and counterproposals before an agreement is reached. The key word in the definition as far as this interpretation goes is *program,* which implies that something more is involved in the transaction than a simple comparison of bids or the acceptance of a catalog price.

Nature of negotiation

The nature of negotiation has been well defined in instructions issued to United States Air Force buying personnel:

> Procurement by negotiation is the art of arriving at a common understanding through bargaining on the essentials of a contract such as delivery, specifications, prices, and terms. Because of the interrelation of these factors with many others, it is a difficult art and requires the exercise of judgment, tact, and common sense. The effective negotiator must be a real shopper, alive to the possibilities of bargaining with the seller. Only through an awareness of relative bargaining strength can a negotiator know where to be firm or where he may make permissive concessions in prices or terms.[1]

The process and techniques of negotiated purchasing deserve special

---

[1] Air Force Procurement Instructions, 3-101.50.

attention for two basic reasons. First, the whole concept of negotiation is widely misunderstood, and in many cases suspect, even by persons engaged in purchasing. Second, technological change has made industrial procurement increasingly complex, particularly in defense-related industries. Simple, rule-of-thumb approaches to buying one-of-a-kind machines or systems, for example, are no longer adequate. Nor are they any longer satisfactory in the purchase of less complicated items like raw materials and maintenance supplies. The trend toward long-term purchase agreements (see "Contract Buying," page 264) on these commodities has placed special emphasis on many aspects of the transaction that are open to negotiation. Responsibility for holding inventory, timing of deliveries, methods of transportation, inspection, and prices are only a few of the factors that must be agreed upon before a purchase is complete.

The confusion over the true meaning of "negotiation" is typified by the attitude of legislators and the general press toward the use of the process in government buying. A few years ago, when regular published Defense Department figures showed that over 90 per cent of the dollar volume of purchases made by the military services was expended in negotiated purchasing, an outcry went up.

Congressmen and editorial writers assailed negotiated purchasing as "secret buying" that all but eliminated competition for government business. A cartoonist in the respected *Washington Post* showed a fat supplier sneaking out from behind a screen near the Pentagon carrying a paper labeled "Negotiated Contracts" under his arm, while a smirking Defense Department buyer waved goodbye. Uncle Sam and the stock figure of an outraged John Q. Public watched angrily. And the cartoon was labeled, "What Happened to that Good Old American Competition?"

Weaknesses of bid system

The opponents of negotiation share an oversimplified view of purchasing: that the government would come out better in any purchase by letting its buyers select the lowest of a number of sealed bids rather than engage in negotiation. This approach is, of course, difficult and even impossible in the purchase of many types of military equipment—sophisticated electronic devices for which there is no existing model, for example, which account for a high percentage of the defense-procurement dollar. Buying by the bid system has its shortcomings even in relatively simple commodities like uniforms and light vehicles. Among those pointed out in a study of defense procurement were:

> —Unless the bid contains airtight specifications, the winning bidder will provide a product that meets specifications but does not always provide the performance the buyer expects.

—The winning bidder often is the one who cuts quality to cut his price. The quality producer cannot afford to be competitive and is driven from the market. The buyer is then stuck with inferior merchandise that wears out or falls apart sooner than expected.

—In industries like aircraft and shipbuilding, which depend heavily on government orders, the bidder good enough to get all or most of the government's business may drive competitors out of the field. He is then in a position to raise prices practically at will.

—Many economists hold that when an industry is dominated by two or three producers, the result can be a monopolistic price structure, even without collusion. Producers behave in a rational manner on price and a follow-the-leader pattern develops. In this case, advertising bidding does not result in competition.[2]

Misunderstanding of negotiation is not limited to those who are unfamiliar with purchasing economics, however. Ironically, some purchasing agents put negotiation in the same category as haggling and consider it unethical or vulgar to bargain over prices. The president of the National Association of Purchasing Agents felt called upon to correct this idea—which is shared by some suppliers—in talks to his own organization.[3] He said:

By negotiation the buyer takes the necessary initiative to optimize his position in any given purchase. Without negotiation, he is merely accepting the best offer given him.

Vigorous price competition is an essential ingredient of the free enterprise system. To refrain from seeking cost advantages through negotiation is to assume that the item price is priced right, that it is best for all concerned.

Much of the criticism of negotiation is directed at the methods used. But within the limits of law and the ethics of good business, the buyer is obligated by his position to aggressively go after the best price that will mean the least cost under the most favorable conditions available to his firm.

The unspoken criticism of negotiation is more likely to be leveled by suppliers who would like to find some haven for price protection where they would be immune to the results of sound, aggressive, and ethical negotiation. They want to protect their weakness of limited sales ability.

Negotiation as we have defined it—"the working out of a procurement and sales program together"—is generally used in the following situations, assuming that a relatively large amount of money is involved:

—Where the purchase involves equipment of a unique or complicated nature which has not been purchased before, and on which there is little cost information. A conveyor line for a new, automated food-processing plant would be a good example. Details of the construction, performance, and cost of such an installation would require involved technical discussions before a purchase was actually made.

---

[2] P. V. Farrell and D. S. Ammer, "The Truth About Military Buying," *Purchasing Magazine,* October, 1957, p. 113.

[3]Russell T. Stark, of Burroughs Corporation, in addresses to local chapters of the National Association of Purchasing Agents during 1962.

—Where prices on an item are fixed, either by custom, "fair trade" laws, or actual collusion among suppliers. If there are many suppliers in the field, good negotiating tactics are generally successful in winning concessions from one producer who is anxious to get the business.

—Where there are few suppliers or only one in the field, but the product in question can be made in the buyer's own plant or bought from abroad or a substitute for it is readily available.

—Where a number of suppliers have bid on an item, but none of the quotations are completely satisfactory. None may meet the buyer's requirements as to price, terms, delivery or specifications. In this situation, the buyer must be sure, before he attempts to negotiate, that all bids are unsatisfactory in terms of the requirements he first placed before the suppliers. It is highly unethical to lead a supplier into committing himself in a quotation merely to put him into a disadvantageous bargaining position. Responsible buyers will notify suppliers in advance that bids may be subject to negotiation.

—Where an existing contract is being changed and the amount of money involved is substantial enough to warrant discussion. Major price changes on high-volume items, for example, are subject to negotiation.

Negotiation strategy

The strategy and tactics used in purchasing negotiations are similar in many ways to those used in labor negotiations. Both types of negotiations have been linked to military campaigns, in which the adversaries first try to out-think, then to out-maneuver, each other.

Once it has been established that negotiation is needed to maximize one's position in a proposed purchase, the basic step is to establish one's own, and the supplier's bargaining strength. The supplier's strength will be affected by how much he wants the business; how sure he is that he will get the sale; and how much time there is to reach an agreement. The buyer's strength will be affected by how much competition there is in the field; how good a price analysis he has made; how much business he has to offer the supplier; and how much time is available to reach an agreement.

A supplier anxious to establish himself with a company or in an industry, for example, may be willing to make price concessions to achieve this end. A buyer under pressure from his shop to have an item on hand at an unreasonable date, on the other hand, is on the defensive and may be willing to pay a premium price for quick delivery.

A seller who is certain that he has no immediate competition (for example, a dealer with an exclusive franchise in a remote area) knows that he will have an advantage in a negotiation. A purchasing agent who has developed an alternate supplier, or who knows that a substitute material can be used, goes into the negotiation in a strong position.

Much of the art of negotiation consists of the ability to determine these strengths and weaknesses in advance and to exploit them to one's own advantage. At the same time, of course, one must try to conceal one's own weaknesses or at least avoid as long as possible having them put to the test.

The first cases—buying a new or complex item, or refusing to take the lowest of a number of bids, or even negotiating a price change on a regularly bought item—supplier costs are a key area for discussion. A negotiator should come into such a discussion with a sound knowledge of costing methods and, if possible, comparative figures from his own cost estimates. Small and medium-sized suppliers particularly—and some of the big ones—do not bother to develop accurate and factual records. Their cost figures are often pulled out of the air—on the safe side, of course. Their sales representatives are given a fairly wide range of prices to submit to prospective customers. Too many purchasing people go into negotiations with the rather vague attitude that the supplier deserves a price that includes cost plus a fair profit. But if they don't go after those costs intelligently and aggressively, they may end up giving the supplier a fair profit and themselves an unfair price.

Just because a supplier has lower costs than the next highest bidder does not mean that his costs are low enough. He may still be using his plant inefficiently. It is the purchasing agent's responsibility to help the supplier bring down his costs to an absolute minimum and still deliver the quality required.

Modern industrial pricing, however, is not based simply on costs. If the purchasing agent is unable to determine specific costs on an item under negotiation, he can always proceed on certain assumptions about the prices quoted to him. They may be based on any one or a combination of the following:

An attempt to get "all the traffic can bear," which is sound economic behavior on the part of a supplier;

Keeping prices just low enough to cut out competition;

Setting a specific rate of return—for example, as a percentage of sales, or of capital invested—and pricing accordingly.

Any one of these areas is fertile ground for a skilled negotiator.

And even in the case of fixed-price or so-called fair-trade items, there is room for maneuvering. A buyer can offer to buy other items, on which prices are not fixed, from the same supplier if he can get a price concession.

The shrewd negotiator can also use the "unique specification" approach, which makes the component or material he buys different from that bought by all other customers. The classic case is that of the automobile companies who buy tailpipes fabricated to their own specifications. The tube from which the tailpipes are made was selling at the same price to all buyers. But bent into special shapes, it is sold at a lower price than the basic product.

Edward M. Krech, of J. M. Huber Corporation, has pointed out a number of fringe benefits that can be negotiated on industry-priced items:

The privilege of bulking orders for quantity discounts;
Split shipments to one destination with the price based on the total quantity;
Make-and-hold agreements which may lower the price and provide inventory
    protection without the cost of carrying it;
Concessions for methods of packaging and palletizing;
Lower shipping costs through a change in carrier;
Terms of payment.

Planning for negotiation

Before the purchasing agent uses any of these general approaches in a specific negotiation, he should plan ahead in order to get a maximum advantage. Indeed, preplanning is as important as the tactics of negotiation, because the tactics are based on plans and objectives established before any meeting.

All good planning begins with the collection of essential data—and in the case of negotiation this includes not only economic but engineering, accounting, legal, and financial information pertinent to the particular matter to be discussed. These should be identified and ranked according to importance.

The collection of facts pertinent to the negotiation may involve several different departments, depending on the complexity of the matter at issue. Similarly, the negotiation itself may require the presence of a team of experts to participate in the discussions accurately and present the company's position and views. An experienced purchasing executive will always assume that the supplier is sending shrewd, well-informed, and skillful representatives into any substantial negotiation, so he will try to match them when he selects his own team.

In an involved negotiation, a team might be made up of representatives from purchasing, engineering, accounting, marketing, industrial engineering, and legal departments. They should be thoroughly briefed on the nature of the negotiation, and the technical and economic questions involved. They should understand, or participate in the establishment of the company's objectives and alternative positions as described below.

It is absolutely necessary to designate a leader when negotiation involves more than one representative. His authority to commit the company, and the limitations on the authority of other team members, should be clearly spelled out. Since the basic authority to commit company funds rests with the purchasing department representative, he is generally considered the best choice to lead a negotiating team.

The next step is to establish the objectives the buyer's company has in the negotiation. The negotiator without clearly defined objectives is put on the defensive, since it must always be assumed that the other participant in the session has entered the negotiation with some definite goal for his company. Uncertainty or confusion over his objectives can lead a negotiator into making damaging concessions.

Defining objectives

Setting generalized objectives like "getting all we can out of the vendor" or attempting to get "the best possible price" are not much better than no objectives at all. A buyer must define his objectives more precisely in terms of what he and his company hope they can get and reasonably expect to get if the negotiation is skillfully conducted. The objective may be a price, or certain concessions on quality, delivery or other factors.

The objective should be expressed in specific terms, such as a certain price, but it must always be subject to modification. Flexibility is at the heart of the negotiating art, and all objectives should be hedged by a minimum and maximum position to which a negotiator can move when he has the opportunity to, in the first case, and when he is forced to, in the second case. A buyer going into a negotiation with an objective, or "ideal" price, of $11,500 for a piece of equipment, for example, should have alternative prices above and below that figure that were deemed acceptable before the negotiation began. In the actual negotiation the buyer might use the minimum price the negotiating team agreed upon—$10,000 for example—as a first proposal without any real hope that the supplier would immediately accept it. Conversely, he would be prepared to go to a maximum position—a $12,500 price, for example—but only as a last resort. The objective, maximum, and minimum prices would, of course, have been determined on the basis of cost analyses, need for the equipment, monopoly position of the supplier, or any of the other factors previously mentioned.

As a corollary to having an established objective and alternative maximum and minimum positions, a negotiator must try to estimate the supplier's objectives and maximum and minimum positions. One or more of these may already be apparent in a bid or proposal already submitted, or they may have to be deduced from the buyer's own cost analysis or from previous experience with the supplier. In any event, a good negotiator will try to guess where a supplier will make concessions, and where he is likely to hold fast to his declared position. The negotiator will then prepare to act accordingly in the light of his own objectives.

Before entering a negotiation it is advisable for both parties—buyer and supplier—to come to some agreement as to what is being negotiated and put the agreement in writing. This tends to cut down on disagreements and arguments once the negotiation is under way, since reference can be made to a written statement or agenda. Similarly, both sides should clearly indicate who has authority to speak for them in the negotiation, and the exact extent of that authority. There is no point in elaborate planning for a negotiation when one side's representative simply does not have the authority to agree on a critical point such as price.

Negotiating tactics

Negotiation is often a highly technical matter, but it is always a very human matter as well. Because the essential element in a negotiation is bargaining between individuals, the process involves personalities, human motives, people's strength and weaknesses, and a great deal of psychology. In numerous addresses to purchasing groups, the authors have stressed these general rules for turning the human element in negotiations to one's own advantage:

Try to have the negotiation carried on on your home ground, according to your own arrangements. There is a psychological advantage to having the other party come to the discussion. It implies that you are in control and already have won one concession. Provide a dignified, comfortable, well-lighted meeting place, free of distractions. Put the leader of your own negotiating team at the head of the table, and try to keep the members of the other team separated.

Let the supplier do most of the talking—at least, in the beginning. Let him give the reasons for his demand first. If you use the proper restraint, he may talk himself into making concessions he never intended to make.

When your time comes to talk, don't fumble over facts and figures. Never send out for vital information in the middle of a discussion. Lack of information or lack of confidence puts you at a strong psychological disadvantage.

Try to avoid emotional reactions to the supplier's arguments, or an emotional approach in presenting your own. Otherwise, you'll obscure the real purposes of the negotiation and possibly endanger your own position. A man who lets pride or anger govern his relations with others usually ends up by giving away more than he intended.

If the supplier has to retreat on a point, let him do it gracefully. If you spot something wrong in a cost estimate, for example, don't accuse the other side of trickery or ineptitude. Suggest that a revision is in order.

Avoid premature showdowns. You have to come to some sort of a show-down ultimately—that's the reason for the negotiation. But if you force a supplier into a position where he feels he has to say, "Here are my terms, take them or leave them," that may end the discussion there. After that kind of an ultimatum it would be difficult for him to give further concessions. So, before you make your final concession, be absolutely sure that it is absolutely final.

Satisfy the emotional needs of the men you're negotiating with. Most suppliers enjoy selling and persuading, but they're somewhat insecure. Give suppliers a chance to persuade rather than trying to head them off brusquely, and they will be better disposed to make concessions to get your business. And give them the impression that, despite your bargaining with them, you respect their position and regard them as members of your corporate team.

Negotiation is not, as often charged, the purchasing department's technique for cutting down the supplier's profits. Nor is it an occult science whose practitioners are exclusively endowed with special gifts. It is the basic process by which competition is furthered in industrial buying and selling. It is the special responsibility of the purchasing agent to negotiate the best possible deal to achieve company objectives—just as it is the special responsibility of a sales representative to negotiate for his company's objectives.

17

MAKE OR BUY

NORMALLY, WHEN INDUSTRIAL requirements arise and are reported to the purchasing department, they are to be satisfied by purchase of the needed product or material from some outside source. However, there is usually the alternative possibility of satisfying the requirement by undertaking the production of a needed part or product within the buyer's own organization, sometimes with potential advantages in cost, convenience, or control. This is a legitimate means of procurement. It is not always feasible, but it should be considered. In a broad sense, the prior question, "Make or buy?" must be answered in advance of every purchase, in the form of company policy if not by special analysis. This question may refer to a particular fabricated part for regular product use, or, on a broader scale, it may involve the decision of whether the company shall operate its own foundry department instead of purchasing castings, or shall have its own printing department or undertake any one of a score of similar operations. It may likewise concern the making of special equipment, such as warehouse shelving, or major construction projects.

These decisions are presumably made before the requirement ever gets to the stage of a purchase requisition, and it is frequently outside the proper scope of purchasing department responsibility to find the answer. On the other hand, it is an ever-present consideration in determining the best method of procurement, even after a requisition has been received and regardless of previous practice. Therefore, purchasing is responsible for analyzing the relative merits and advantages of both procurement methods and of making policy recommendations if a change is indicated. Costs and conditions in the supplier industry may be such as to suggest very strongly the advisability of self-manufacture of products formerly purchased. It may also work in the other direction, when the possibility of advantageous purchase arrangements suggests the adoption of this method, even though such action may mean retirement of equipment and facilities formerly used in production. The whole program of subcontracting, discussed in Chapter 11, is an example of procuring by purchase a wide variety of components, many of which would normally be produced in the purchaser's own plant.

The significance of the question, "Make or buy?" and the amount of study justified in arriving at a decision, depend largely on the dollar volume involved. If it concerns a product representing only a few hundred dollars of annual expenditure, it will not make much difference either way. If the amount runs up into several thousand dollars, it is frequently a matter of utilizing existing equipment balanced against the convenience and cost of procurement from outside sources. If the amount is more substantial, involving investment in new equipment, a full-scale analysis is indicated, going beyond direct cost considerations into matters of company policy, personnel, labor relations, plant layout, scheduling, and the numerous other details incident to any manufacturing program.

A study of several hundred companies using steel stampings shows that 49.8 per cent both make and purchase stamped components; 20.6 per cent procure all their requirements by purchase; and 28.2 per cent make in their own shops all the stampings they use. This almost equal division as to policy indicates that there must be many reasons involved and that the preponderance of these reasons in any given case may lead to directly opposite decisions according to the circumstances.

Cost comparison

The decision whether to "make or buy" involves the consideration of all factors entering into any question of procurement, and the purchasing department—or general management—must approach the question analytically and objectively, viewing the company's own facilities as an alternative source of supply in competition with outside suppliers. All of these factors must be weighed with care before a decision is made, for a change in this policy is not so simple as merely changing from one supply source to another. When it is concerned only with the manufacture of a particular part, utilizing surplus capacity or facilities already on hand, it may not be too serious a matter, and the policy could easily be revoked in case the results proved less advantageous than expected. But in respect to larger and more significant items of supply, and particularly when new facilities are to be added or a new line of operation undertaken, it is likely to involve substantial tooling costs, investment in space and equipment, and enlargement of the organization, all of which represent a continuing problem of cost and efficient operation.

For this reason, a comparison of costs is one of the first considerations, though not necessarily the most important. Cost of purchased goods is ac-

Table I

MAKE	RATING	BUY	RATING
1. Need for		1. Need for	
a) Quantity	_____	a) Quantity	_____
b) Quality	_____	b) Quality	_____
2. Cost of		2. Cost of	
a) Equipment	_____	a) Direct Purchase	_____
b) Plant	_____	b) Leasing	_____
c) Materials	_____	c) Assembly of	_____
d) Labor	_____	Purchased Parts	
e) Time	_____	d) Labor	_____
f) Inventory	_____	e) Shipping	_____
		f) Inventory	_____
3. Supply		3. Supply	
a) Raw Materials	__	a) Limit of Control	___
b) Time	__	b) Quality & Quantity	___
c) Delivery Dependable	__	c) Delivery Reliability	___
d) Labor	__		
4. Manufacturing		4. Manufacturing	
a) Methods & Standards		a) Reduced to Assembly	
b) Production &		b) Decrease of Capital	
Inventory Control		c) Unskilled Labor	
c) Engineering		d) Extent of Plant	
d) Quality & Quantity			
e) Increase of Capital			
f) Skilled Labor			
g) Extent of Plant			
TOTAL: Need	_____	TOTAL: Need	_____
Cost	_____	Cost	_____
Supply	_____	Supply	_____
Manufacturing	_____	Manufacturing	_____

Fig. 17-1. Form for Comparing Costs of Making or Buying an Item.

curately determinable. Complete cost up to the time of use is the significant figure: price, plus transportation charges, plus costs of handling and storage. This cost should be calculated on an annual basis, and on the entire group of products that would be affected by a change in policy. For instance, to follow through with the examples suggested in the opening section of this chapter, it would cover the whole range of castings or of printed forms to be handled in the proposed department.

Against this figure must be balanced the total estimated cost of production. This should include not merely the cost of materials and direct labor, but investment and carrying charges, including depreciation on equipment, and overhead expenses, with due allowance for the possibility of idle time and production at less than capacity, normal waste and spoilage, and the other usual risks of management that are assumed by the supplier when goods are purchased. These costs should be calculated on the standard basis used throughout the company, because the new manufacturing operation will become a part of the company's general activities and must assume its share of the burden. Only when this has been done is a fair and accurate cost comparison possible. The factor of profit, which is necessarily a part of the supplier's price, is not a proper consideration for the buyer, because he is concerned with costs, and the profit to his company accrues only in the sale of the finished product; however, efficient self-manufacture, elimination of sales expense, and consequent lower cost of components do enhance the profit potential in the eventual sale.[1]

Among the cost factors frequently mentioned as favoring the manufacture of parts rather than procurement by purchase is the possibility of spreading overhead charges over a greater volume of operations. This is more than merely an accounting device, but it is not always a complete answer. Where outside and inside costs are close, as they frequently are, other factors may be decisive. If a company is buying an item at, say, $40,000 but decides to make it at $50,000 to spread the overhead burden, a competitor who is still buying it at $40,000 acquires an immediate advantage that may alter the entire marketing situation.

The results of a complete cost comparison may seriously modify estimates of cost and other advantages based on casual judgment. Almost certainly, it will indicate the prudence of a highly selective approach to the question of "make or buy" based on detailed analysis of the individual case.

The quantity factor

Unit cost is not the only factor to be considered. The quantity of a requirement is important for several reasons. In the first place, it will help to determine whether the potential cost saving is sufficient to warrant the undertaking of a special manufacturing project or process. Second, it has an important bearing on actual costs through the economies of mass manufacture and the possibilities of absorbing initial costs. Third, as has already been suggested, it should be sufficiently large to insure that any facilities that may be established or installed for the purpose will be kept reasonably fully occupied, so that overhead costs for idle time will not offset the unit-cost advantage.

A solution for the latter problem has been found in some cases by setting

---

[1] This is a controversial point in accounting. In vertically integrated industries, where one division of a company manufactures components for another division and also sells to other consumers, it is customary to include a profit factor, with or without a differential in favor of the related plant when the product is transferred. In such cases the individual plants are responsible for their own overhead and must individually justify themselves by profitable operation as separate enterprises.

a basic production capacity that is large enough for economical production yet within the limit of minimum expected requirements. This is calculated to keep the facility running at capacity, any deficiencies being supplied by purchases from the outside. Many company printing departments are set up on this basis. The advantages, in addition to those of cost, include the convenience of having such facilities conveniently available, the possibility of producing rush jobs without waiting for an outside supplier to fit them into his schedule or paying premium prices for extra service, and the possibility of handling short runs and other special and commercially uneconomical requirements on a cost basis, where the cost of procuring them from outside sources would be disproportionate to the value received even though not unreasonable from the supplier's cost and pricing viewpoint.

Any system of partial self-manufacture has the disadvantage of decreasing the desirability and the quantity-purchasing appeal of that portion of the business that must still be procured from outside sources. In such a case, the outside vendor is likely to take the position that the buyer's company is a competitor, and to give preference to other customers who purchase their total requirements.

Quality control

The factors considered up to this point have been concerned largely with comparative costs and potential economies. This is not necessarily the determining factor in reaching a decision. It is quite possible that it will be found desirable to undertake, or to retain, the manufacture of a component part in the buyer's own plant when costs under this method are demonstrably and substantially higher than prices obtainable from outside sources.

Among the conditions that justify such high-cost procurement by manufacture, considerations of quality loom large. It is possible to have the assurance of strict quality control when the processing and fabrication of components are performed and supervised by the organization using them. In general, the greater the control required, either in analysis or in dimension, the more significant this consideration becomes. Close coordination and a single responsibility are frequently better than divided responsibility, and the maker's guaranty of the end product means more when control of the entire process and its component parts is in his own hands.

Furthermore, greater interest and effectiveness in quality development and improvement can be expected on the part of a producer who is following through from raw material to end product than from a supplier who is producing to strict specifications furnished by a customer. Such improvements are more promptly utilized and made effective with smaller stocks or commitments for parts made to the original specification to be used up before the improvement can be applied. This is no criticism of the progressiveness or interest of competent suppliers; it is directly a problem of procurement.

Disadvantages of manufacture

On the other side of the balance sheet, there are some disadvantages connected with the self-manufacture of component parts. Once the company is committed to such a policy, and particularly when special tooling or equipment has been installed for the purpose, an element of inflexibility is introduced into procurement. Freedom of selection is sacrificed, despite possible differences in cost or other factors. The assurance of supply that is gained by this additional control must be weighed against the loss of alternative sources.

The hazards of business and changing economic conditions, over which the buyer has no control but which affect markets and procurement, are now assumed by the buyer's company and may seriously alter the calculations upon which the decision was originally based. Such influences include cyclical and long-term trends in the supplier industry, changes in demand for the buyer's product affecting the nature and volume of requirements, technological advances, competitive conditions such as overcapacity in the industry, as well as a variety of unpredictable random factors such as war, government regulations, tax policies, and the like.

From the viewpoint of management, if self-manufacture involves a type of operation foreign to the nature of the principal business or previous plant activities, there will be the necessity of building up a staff with special operating skills, in addition to the normal administrative responsibilities assumed to be incident to the expansion. Efficiency is not merely a matter of equipment, but of production know-how, experience, skilled operators, and supervision; and this new staff must be fitted in with the rest of the organization. Among other considerations, there may be new labor union jurisdiction. All of these are management rather than procurement responsibilities, but they have a direct effect on the cost and satisfaction of supply.

Make-or-buy check list

One company that has made an exhaustive study of this problem as it applies to its own operations has compiled a check list to make sure that no significant factor is overlooked in the final decision. There are six major sections, leading to the conclusion of whether it is advisable to make or to buy on the basis of quality factors, capacity factors, labor factors, scheduling factors, skill factors, and cost comparisons. Every question in each category is weighed with the same question in mind, to arrive at these conclusions. The final step is to recapitulate the six answers, to determine where the preponderance of reason lies, and to make the decision accordingly. The check list asks the following questions:

Quality factors: Adherence to specifications? Quality control setup? Is proper equipment available? Experience in this type of work? Who pays for bad parts?

Capacity factors: Is space available? Is available space obtainable? Is machine time available? Must machinery be bought? Are outside finishing operations required? Is sales relationship a factor? Is stability of supplier relationships a factor? How much working capital is needed for inventory, and so forth? Is new capital investment needed? How much use have we for the new equipment? What return can we expect? Are our costs complete? Is absorption of internal overhead needed? Would total costs, including overhead absorption, be competitive?

Labor factors: Would layoffs be created? Would it help us hold the organization together? Must staff be increased? Is special training necessary? Are there union pressures? Is the labor rate comparative?

Scheduling factors: Can we get all necessary components on time? Have we the capacity to adjust to peaks or slowdowns? Would timing be surer with added sources? Are engineering changes frequent?

Skill factors: Is the best design experience available? Is the part natural to us? Is this the most profitable use of our executives' time? Is design-assistance relationship a factor? Do we have adequate measures of inside efficiency?

Cost comparison, on the basis of 100 pieces: material cost; operations cost (direct labor, overhead, and profit); setup cost; tools repair allowance and spoilage; packing and shipping costs from outside supplier; tool charge (cost of tools per 100 pieces based on two years' run).

This is a very complete and scientific evaluation of the problem, dealing principally with the internal company factors involved. Before leaving this phase of the subject, however, it should be pointed out that make-or-buy decisions also have external effects, and that there are some long-range considerations of this nature that should also have serious attention. The check-list section on capacity factors recognizes this by querying the effect on sales relationships and the stability of supply relationships.

It is not uncommon, in times of business decline, for manufacturers to switch from buying to making certain parts when excess capacity shows up in their own plants. Even if this is done as a temporary measure, rather than as a considered policy based on economy of manufacture, the immediate effect is to leave the suppliers of these parts stranded and to intensify for them the hardships of the business decline. The purchasing agent may well question the wisdom of such use of the make-or-buy alternative, and especially so if the decision is of a temporary nature. For, when business picks up and he once again seeks parts and service from that vendor, he will almost certainly find that the supplier relationship has deteriorated. In extreme cases, he may actually have lost that source of supply.

Authorizing the decision

It is apparent, from the many internal elements affected by the "make or buy" policy, that the decision is not one to be made by the purchasing executive alone, even though it is primarily a question of procurement method. It is within his province to make a recommendation for or against the method in respect to certain requirements of the materials program, and his recommendation should be supported with a detailed analysis of available outside sources, comparative costs, and other factors. His company, like any other supplier, has the privilege of judging the profit potential and other advantages and disadvantages of the proposal, which will determine whether it is advisable to undertake the production or to relinquish it in favor of outside purchase.

Production executives will naturally be in the best position to pass judgment on the equipment and facilities available or needed and on the practicability of the plan. Production and cost departments will check the purchasing agent's cost estimates. Financial officers will consider the advisability of the capital investment involved. Technical and engineering advice will be sought on the advantages of quality control within the organization. Marketing executives are concerned with anything that will enhance the salability of the product, and possibly with finding an outlet for surplus production from the new department. The final decision, after all these viewpoints have been presented, is a matter for top management.

Consequently, although the "make or buy" question may arise in connection with every procurement, it is no ordinary decision as to purchasing policy and source of supply. Even on a minor requirement involving a single item in line with existing facilities, it calls for consultation and cooperation with plant executives. In its larger aspects, as when a considerable manufacturing program is under consideration or when new facilities are to be added, full and formal consultation is in order, with final authorization or adverse decision from the highest company authority.

Importance of review

Inertia is the greatest obstacle to profitable make-or-buy decisions. Many opportunities in this field never come to the point of decision because companies simply continue to make parts or perform operations that have always been handled within the company, when they could be purchased from others more advantageously. And many decisions to make or to buy are put into effect but are never subjected to review to see whether, in the light of actual experience, the decision was a wise one. It is assumed that, with analysis before the change, no evaluation is necessary after it is made. There is a natural tendency on the part of those who make or endorse decisions initially to believe that the projects are successful. Yet this is not always the case. A poll conducted by *Purchasing Magazine* (August, 1955) revealed that, in the opinion of several hundred purchasing agents, one out of every four decisions to make instead of buy a component turns out badly.

This sorry experience may be due to the fact that conditions and costs have changed, or that those making the original analysis were expert in routine fact gathering but deficient in management perspective. In either case, it emphasizes the need for appraisal of the results. This does not mean that the same analysis should be made over and over again. It does mean that an error in judgment should not be perpetuated by inertia. It suggests that decisions of this nature should be under some sort of continuing review by committee action comparable to that of a standardization committee charged with the evaluation of such projects and alert to the changes which might alter or cast doubt upon the wisdom of the original decision.

Vertical integration

The logical development or projection of procurement by manufacture is progressively toward vertical integration of company operations—toward the control, under one management, of the entire process from primary raw materials to finished product, with a minimum of dependence on outside sources. A metal-using industry, for example, may acquire its own rolling mills; then, going back still farther to the source, its own ore deposits, mines, and smelters. Along the way, contributory services such as transportation lines or fleets and facilities for the production of major components are also added.

This was a very popular type of organization policy in the 1920's. The automotive industry, among others, provided several examples of integration on a very complete scale, and smaller industries followed a similar policy to a more limited extent. This organization pattern naturally modifies the procurement problem, but not altogether in the direction of simplification, for the acquisition of each supply source entails also the acquisition of a complete procurement program for that supplier industry. Just so, the decision to procure castings by the establishment of a foundry department instead of by purchase removes one classification of items from the purchase list but adds the whole range of foundry equipment and supplies, gray iron or other metals for casting, sand, and molds.

Where extensive use is made of affiliated or subsidiary companies as major sources of supply, there may be a tendency for the latter to operate inefficiently for lack of competitive incentive. To guard against this tendency, some integrated companies make it a practice to maintain alternative outside sources for price comparison on a portion of total requirements, or insist that the subsidiary shall bid competitively for the parent company's business, or require that a portion of the subsidiary company's output be sold in outside markets where competitive conditions prevail.

More recently, the policy of industrial expansion and development has generally followed a different pattern. Integration of industries in the immediate postwar period was chiefly in the direction of product diversification, the unity of such consolidations lying in centralized functional management control (including purchasing as well as finance, advertising, engineering, and other common functions) rather than in the character of the product.

So far as vertical integration is found in the postwar industrial picture, it has rarely been in the direction of acquiring supply sources. Rather, it has generally taken the form of basic producing industries going into the fabricating field to produce industrial and consumer goods using substantial quantities of their own basic product and, further, into the distribution of those products, financing their sales, and so on. Thus, in a sense, these companies become their own best customers and assure themselves of an outlet for their production. Changes in over-all management policy like this are the indicators of a change in fundamental economic conditions, from a period of competitive procurement to a period of competitive merchandising.

Corporate integration, like the simpler make-or-buy decisions, also has economic implications affecting the public interest on a much broader scale. The federal government has kept a watchful eye, for example, on instances of this sort that might create or foster monopolistic conditions and practices. A large company may acquire one of its supply sources that has also been an important supplier to competing manufacturers. By so doing, he eliminates or controls the supply line on which his competition depends and gains for himself a monopolistic advantage. Some of the recent antitrust decisions banning corporate mergers or forcing the dissolution of such ties have been based on just such circumstances.

18

PURCHASE OF CAPITAL EQUIPMENT

THE PURCHASE OF MACHINERY and other capital equipment is usually differentiated, in policy and procedure, from that of production materials and expendable supplies. It is in the nature of an investment of relatively long duration. Most companies amortize the cost of capital equipment as rapidly as permitted by tax regulations, and many operate on the principle that a new machine must "pay for itself" in an even shorter period, but machines are actually kept in service for many years. As long as they are in use, they are one of the chief governing factors in the company's production methods, capacity, and efficiency, with an importance far beyond the cost of the equipment itself.

The status of expenditures or investments in machinery as a part of the company's capital structure has an important bearing on the purchase of such equipment. It brings financial departments and policies more intimately into the picture than is the case with purchases of production materials and expendable supplies. And it has an important effect on real cost, owing to taxes and the possibility of "write-offs" in the capital account. Many purchases of new equipment, whether for expansion or for replacement and modernization, are approved or disapproved, accelerated or deferred, chiefly on the basis of this factor. Thus, the government's tax policy, which is of minor influence in day-to-day purchasing, is a very substantial consideration where capital purchases are concerned.

Even though the company may have a policy of replacing machines whenever production can be improved by more advanced models, the objective is to acquire equipment that will give maximum useful life. Thus, it is regarded as a one-time or nonrepetitive purchase, which goes beyond the ordinary delegation of responsibility to the purchasing department, though purchasing still has an important role to play in the procurement process.

Purchasing department participation

There is keen competition among manufacturers of machine tools, in the various classifications of lathes, shapers, grinders, milling machines, and the like, but this competition characteristically takes the form of individual features of design and application, so that competing makes are not directly comparable or interchangeable. Consequently, the purchasing devices of alternate sources of supply and approved lists of vendors from which a selection can be made are not applicable. In other respects, the purchasing problems and procedure are substantially parallel to those encountered for any other requirement. However, the selection and purchase of major equipment is by nature a special project rather than a continuing program, and the decision involves the judgment of many persons.

Surveys of buying influences in respect to various types of purchases usually show more different executives participating in the selection of machinery than in the purchases of materials, components, or supplies. The reasons for this have already been indicated. The purchasing department rarely initiates such a purchase and is brought into the transaction at the stage where technical, cost, and delivery data are collected. Assembling these data is more than a routine factor of the purchase, because it provides the factual basis of evaluation. Furthermore, because the original request is likely to be in terms of a particular make and model, the collecting of data requires an intimate knowledge of the work to be performed and the various types of equipment available for this purpose. It is the point at which alternative possibilities are specifically explored for the determination of best value and greatest usefulness.

In large organizations, where much equipment is purchased, there is usually a machinery buyer in the purchasing department specializing in these requirements, just as other buyers have specialized responsibilities for commodity groups. In large companies, which have multiple units of a given type of production equipment, there is likely to be more repetitive buying of machinery, and many such purchases are well defined by standardization in plant practice for simplification of maintenance, uniform training of machine operators, or coordination with other equipment in successive stages of manufacture. For example, once the basic decisions have been made, the replacement or expansion of a battery of identical screw machines or drill presses is distinctly a purchasing procedure.

There is an active trade in used and rebuilt machine equipment of all sorts, which becomes available as entire plants discontinue operations or as individual machines become surplus to a company. Such machines may be bought at auction or through established dealers. Aside from the element of cost saving, this is an important source because the machines so offered are available for spot purchase, whereas orders for new machinery, even of standard models, may take many months for construction and delivery. The purchasing department is familiar with these sources and should be alert to these opportunities as they are applicable to the company's needs.

When the possibility of purchasing used equipment is considered, and when there is no machinery specialist on the buying staff, the equipment is generally inspected prior to purchase by a two-man team, consisting of a buyer and a representative of the production department, to determine the condition of the machine, the tooling and other accessories included, and other details affecting its fitness for the intended purpose. Careful inspection is essential, because used equipment is generally sold "as is," and the original manufacturer's warranty of quality and suitability no longer applies.

As a general rule, the purchasing department also negotiates the actual contract for the purchase of equipment, including the installation, warranties of performance, service, and terms.

Requisition for equipment

The requisition for production equipment originates in the operating division and, at the outset, requires the authorization of the plant manager, superintendent, or other responsible production executive. Similarly, requests for other types of equipment—medical, laboratory, cafeteria, or office machinery—must be presented or certified by the executive in charge of these respective activities.

The requisition alone does not always authorize the purchase. Usually, and almost invariably in the case of major equipment, a special appropriation is required. This serves the double purpose of safeguarding against promiscuous expenditures and major commitments without sanction of the financial department and of keeping management informed of developments that are essentially a part of the company's capital assets. Sometimes these appropriations are made at the time the need is expressed, in which case the requisition and procurement proceed along the normal course for any purchase; more frequently, a specific appropriation is made after the requisition has been translated into a detailed purchase proposal and approved by all those concerned. In companies where a monetary limit is placed upon purchases that can be made without special approval, it is customary for this allowance to be less liberal in respect to capital equipment than for materials and supplies for current use. For example, in one company where a limitation of $1,000 applies to general purchases, capital purchases in excess of $200 require the general manager's approval. This makes it possible to procure a typewriter or a couple of bench grinders in the regular course of business, whereas a request for an elaborate bookkeeping or tabulating machine or a turret lathe would first be scanned by the manager. The logic of such an arrangement is obvious, not because of the money involved, but because any such major equipment would probably affect the capacity and the methods of the company for a long period to come.

For this reason, the requisition for equipment must either be a more detailed form than the ordinary purchase requisition described in the preceding chapter, or it must be supported by additional information to make possible more intelligent analysis of the need and the means by which it is proposed to satisfy that need.

Quality factors

As is the case with all industrial purchases, the requirement fundamentally consists of a purpose to be served or a job to be done, rather than the material or machine to do the job. Quality, in the sense of suitability for the purpose, therefore means the ability of equipment to do a particular job satisfactorily and efficiently over a period of time. The chief factors in selecting heavy machinery include: (1) Economy, (2) Productivity, (3) Dependability, (4) Time or labor saving, and (5) Durability.

These are all ways of expressing slightly different aspects of this same concept of quality; for, in the purchasing sense, quality of equipment is measured primarily in terms of performance and efficiency of operation, ultimately reflected in low cost of product, which is the result that must be balanced against cost of the equipment to arrive at the real value of the purchase.

There are, of course, certain basic descriptions or definitions to be considered first: the type of machine required to perform the desired operation— lathe, grinder, shaper, miller, drill, press, or other. Along with this comes the question of whether the equipment is to be used for a special purpose, continuously employed on a single operation, or for general purposes, adaptable to a greater variety of related operations. Special-purpose machinery may give better performance, and greater efficiency and output under conditions of large-quantity orders and mass production, where a machine is used continuously on one job with a minimum of setup changes. For small companies and for varied production, general-purpose equipment usually affords greater flexibility and a wider range of capacity and consequently offers greater possibilities of full-time utilization.

Within the general type are certain requirements as to precision, speed, power source, and the like. These are minimum requirements in the definition. Superior qualities may be desirable and useful; but, to the extent that extra costs are entailed by building these superior qualities into the equipment, they may represent the purchase of surplus refinements of performance that may rarely if ever be used.

There is also a quantitative requirement in the capacity of the machine. Certain output or productivity is needed to accomplish the purpose for which the equipment is desired. This is also a minimum requirement, a part of the definition.

Up to this point, the statement of the necessary characteristics of the machine is entirely a responsibility of engineering and operating officials. Now the element of competition enters. Whereas machine tools and similar equipment are highly individualized and have specialized features that make them particularly adapted to certain conditions of operation, the basic things that they will do and the purposes for which they are designed are entirely comparable. The issue of value has sometimes been confused and strong prejudices built up in favor of certain designs by stressing the points of difference rather than the fundamental similarity of purpose. It therefore becomes the responsibility of the purchasing department to see that the definition or specification is nonexclusive and to find all sources or makes that will satisfy the requirement. This is directly parallel to the purchasing process in respect to any other requisition. It is only when complete information is at hand regarding possible alternative equipment that will serve the purpose that competent consideration can be given to the points of comparison that lie beyond these minimum requirements and that are summed up in the buying motives listed above.

Ultimate costs

The five buying motives should be analyzed in some greater detail. Economy, productivity, dependability, saving of time or labor, and durability are all operating characteristics, and they are concerned with costs of use after the purchase, not with costs in the purchase price; but because the purpose of this procurement is the use of the machine rather than the machine itself, they constitute a cost increment that must be considered in the ultimate cost of performing the job. As an element of production cost, they frequently outweigh many times over the significance of the purchase price. Therefore, these characteristics of the equipment are constituents of quality and of value, in which the purchasing agent is vitally interested. The final decision is not entirely within his jurisdiction in this case, but it is highly important that these characteristics be interpreted in terms of the buying motives, without which no satisfactory selection can ever be made.

Economy of operation means that the added costs per unit of production will be held to a minimum. This is a generalization covering all sorts of factors that contribute to the end result; and other considerations are more specific.

Productivity or efficiency of equipment means that more units will be produced, or more successive operations performed, within a given period of operation, with the same result of lower cost per unit, plus the advantage of faster production.

Dependability means low maintenance cost and continuity of production, with a minimum of idle productive time due to breakdown. It is the assurance that the requirement will actually be satisfied, and that continuity of use will avoid the increment of overhead charges without corresponding output against which they may be applied. It should be supported with adequate service from the supplier in respect to replacement parts and whatever special mechanical adjustment may be required.

Time- or labor-saving features of equipment point to the fact that important production costs are involved in addition to the cost of the equipment itself and its operation, and that they may vary with different types of equipment. These costs may not be directly allocated to the equipment, but their effect on the over-all cost should be given full consideration. Machines exist primarily to increase the productivity of human labor, and the ability of a machine to operate with a crew of three men instead of four or to increase the output of a single operator 5 per cent or 10 per cent as compared with his production at another machine is perhaps the most significant measure of the machine's efficiency and advantage as an investment.

Durability refers to the service life of equipment at high efficiency. This means a greater total output, a greater return on the investment, and more units of product over which the cost of the machine may be spread. As a matter of cost accounting policy, it is probable that this cost will have been fully depreciated before the useful life of the machine has been exhausted, but this does not alter the basic economy of durable equipment.

The emphasis on operating costs does not imply that initial cost can be disregarded. As a matter of fact, it is highly important in that initial cost is the factor against which productivity, dependability, and durability must be weighed in seeking purchase value. Furthermore, as a capital investment, initial cost has a direct bearing on ultimate costs, because it involves carrying charges, determines the cost chargeable to depreciation, and provides the basis on which profitable operation must be calculated. Just as in figuring the true cost of materials, certain factors such as transportation and handling in and out of stores must be added to the invoice price, the total cost of equipment includes transportation, cost of installation, any extra foundations or other special expenses, and the costs of accessories and tooling.

Joint consideration

On the basis of the requisition and the comparative data and costs assembled by the purchasing department, the problem of selecting the right equipment is a matter for joint consideration by the plant engineer, the chief production executive, the head of the department in which the equipment is to be used, the purchasing agent, and a representative of general management. Expressed in functional terms, these are the individuals responsible for setting up the process, for over-all efficiency of operation, for using the equipment, for economical procurement, and for the company's capital policy.

In the small company, the conference will probably be an informal one, leading directly to the purchase authorization. In the large company, it will lead first to a recommendation, requiring authorization by some designated officer of the company before the purchase can be made. For the purposes of this recommendation, a more formal analysis must be made and put into writing. It is presumed that, if the request is well founded and based on a demonstrable need, the required authorization will be granted; nevertheless, there is a distinct value in going through this procedure. Putting the recommendation and supporting data into writing is evidence that an adequate analysis has been made and that the pertinent questions have been considered and answered. As a record of what the equipment is expected to accomplish, it provides a standard against which actual performance can later be measured. If this later comparison proves disappointing, and it is too late to do anything about the particular purchase, the analysis will still be a guide to judgment in later decisions, indicating whether too much or too little weight has been given to certain factors of selection, or whether excessive optimism or aggressiveness or superior salesmanship on the part of any individual connected with the selection has prejudiced the decision to the disadvantage of the company as a whole. Such circumstances can be guarded against in later selections.

A typical form for analysis and recommendation consists of a letter-sized sheet mimeographed on both sides, with space for such pertinent data as the following:

Operation for which equipment is to be used
Part or product to be produced

Estimated annual requirements of this part
Estimated number of machine-hours that new equipment will be utilized in
  a year
Is equipment to provide additional capacity or for replacement of present
  equipment?
How is the part now being produced?
Present cost of producing part
Cost of procuring part from outside sources
Estimated cost of part produced on the new equipment
Total installed cost of new equipment
Itemized list and cost of accessories required
Age of present equipment
Salvage value of present equipment
Remarks: advantages expected from new equipment
Recommendations for purchase
Signatures of plant manager, chief engineer, purchasing agent, and department
  head

No recommendation requiring such a detailed analysis will be lightly made, and with these data in hand top management can make its decision intelligently and confidently.

In arriving at the recommendation, all parties to the conference are, of course, looking to the same result of satisfaction, efficiency, and ultimate economy. They approach the situation from somewhat different viewpoints and with certain special interests, and because of these special interests each is able to contribute something to the decision. The purpose of the joint analysis is to balance and reconcile these interests, to eliminate those that represent merely preference or prejudice, and to give proper weight to those that appear only when the problem is considered as a whole. In the case of production equipment, the chief production executive will presumably exert the greatest influence, because he is the one ultimately responsible for efficient operation. He is also the one best able to visualize the equipment, and the producing capacity it represents, in relation to the other facilities with which it must be used and in the light of the over-all facilities, flexibility, and balance of the plant as a whole; but the engineers who have planned the process and are intimately familiar with its special requirements, and who may have further developments of a related nature in mind, can best define the basic specification and can recognize and evaluate desirable special characteristics of the equipment under consideration. The head of the department where the equipment is to be used, and which is to be charged with the expenditure and investment, has an important interest in the decision; the enthusiasm or reluctance of his acceptance may have a direct bearing on the efficiency of the equipment in actual use. The purchasing agent, in addition to surveying the market and seeing to it that both initial and ultimate economy are served, has the responsibility of negotiation and procurement once the decision has been made and the purchase authorized.

Equipment records

Most purchasing departments make it a rule not to clutter up their files with reference records on nonrepetitive purchases, but equipment records are an exception to this rule. A detailed inventory should be kept in the purchasing department of all major equipment, whether actively in use or retired. This should include the manufacturer's name and address, the local distributor or other representative, model number, parts list and numbers, references to appropriate catalog data, date of purchase, and date of disposition if the equipment is replaced or retired from service.

This is a record that increases in value with the passage of time by facilitating the identification and procurement of replacement parts. Changes of design in subsequent models frequently make such requirements difficult, as parts have become obsolete from the manufacturer's viewpoint just at the time when the need for new parts arises from the age and long-continued use of equipment. Cases can be cited in which the original manufacturer of the equipment has gone out of business, but, through accurate information, the purchasing agent has been able to trace the original patterns or drawings to the inactive files of some successor organization. One such record going back nearly sixty years is known. Reference to the older entries is not frequent, of course, but they have proved to be of invaluable aid on those occasions when they have been called into use.

The record has current usefulness, too, for replacement and repair purchases, for the procurement of accessory equipment, for interdepartmental transfers in place of purchasing additional capacity, for checking up on later and improved models, for reference in the consideration of subsequent equipment requirements, and, finally, for the eventual disposition of the equipment, which is a responsibility generally assigned to the purchasing department.

19

PURCHASING SYSTEMS

THE WORK OF A PURCHASING DEPARTMENT, dealing with thousands of different items bought from hundreds of different sources under constantly changing conditions, involves a great variety and volume of detail and paper work. Poorly designed systems can submerge the buyer in clerical detail. Efficient systems can help speed and control the routine aspects of purchasing and give the buyer more time for the constructive phases of his job.

In a large and complicated purchasing program, there may be scores of working forms and several intricate systems in daily use. In the first part of this chapter, however, we shall deal with the basic forms and procedures that are common to almost every purchasing operation. In the second part of the chapter, we shall discuss how various mechanical and electronic data-processing equipment, including computers, is being used to eliminate manual clerical work in purchasing and at the same time provide information essential to good planning.

Basic forms and procedures

The procurement cycle, outlined in general terms in Chapter 1, has several distinct phases: requests for materials by the using departments; selection of vendors and issuance of orders; follow-up of outstanding orders; receipt and inspection of materials from suppliers; and checking of suppliers' invoices. Following are brief descriptions, in chronological order, of the usual steps taken in each phase and the forms on which they are recorded.

A using department indicates its need for materials on a *requisition*. It uses a *stores requisition* to obtain materials that are in regular use in the plant and that are carried as normal stock. This goes directly to the stores department, and the requirements are supplied from there. A *purchase requisition* is used for materials that have to be ordered from suppliers. The person who needs the material fills in either type of form with the material name or code identification, the amount needed, and the desired delivery date. Before he sends the requisition to either stores or purchasing, he must have it signed by a supervisor authorized to approve the expenditure.

For items of a repetitive nature, and those for which purchases are normally made to replenish stocks, a *traveling requisition* is used. The form is of heavy card stock so that it may be passed back and forth regularly between the requisitioning department, or stores department, and purchasing. A single card is made up for each item, and identification of the item is entered only once—in the heading of the card. But there is space provided for several (up to 30) requests to purchase. The requisitioner or storeskeeper merely enters the date and the predetermined quantity desired and sends the card to purchasing. When the purchase has been made, it is recorded on the card, which is then returned to stores or the requisitioning department.

Sometimes purchasing is based directly on a *bill of materials,* which lists every item in a company's end product. When a manufacturing schedule is set by production planning, purchasing is notified and can set up its purchasing schedule or program to correspond with production plans. It receives a copy of the bill of materials, on which are indicated those items that are not on hand or ordered. This tabulation serves the same purpose as a whole series of requisitions.

Ordering

The process of negotiation and decision that takes place between the time when a purchase is authorized and the time when the order is issued has been described in Chapters 4 through 14. About the only routine procedure in the process as part of a purchasing system is the invitation to suppliers to bid and the evaluation of bids received, described in Chapter 11. When such invitations are issued prior to ordering, the form used is generally called a *request for quotation.* In most cases, it is almost an exact duplicate of the order form, except that the words "This Is Not An Order" are printed prominently on it.

The *purchase order* is the instrument by which goods are procured to fill a requirement. It expresses in specific language the agreement between the buyer and the vendor. Once accepted, it has the legal force of a binding contract.

The essential information in every purchase order includes: name and address of purchasing company; identifying order number; date; name and address of vendor; general instructions (marking of shipments, number of invoices required, and so forth); delivery date required; shipping instructions; description of materials ordered, and the quantity; price and discounts; and signature. Terms and conditions are generally printed on the back of the form. The purchase order must bear some authorized signature—usually, that of a purchasing agent or buyer.

Many companies try to get written acceptance of the order from the vendor. This is sometimes in the form of an extra copy of the order, known as the *acknowledgment copy;* sometimes it is in the form of a detachable stub on the original copy. It is actually more than an acknowledgment; it should constitute legal acceptance of the order. The law of acceptance is discussed in Chapter 22.

Simple purchase order systems usually require three copies of the order: the original, sent to the vendor; the acknowledgment copy mentioned above; and a purchasing department file copy.

The average number of copies in a typical department, however, is seven. These would include, in addition to the three listed above:

4. Copy to the receiving department as notice that a shipment is expected, and to facilitate identification.
5. Copy to the accounting department as notice of the commitment, to be later reconciled with the invoice and receiving reports as authorization of payment.
6. Copy to the department where the requisition originated, to show that the request has been attended to.
7. Copy for the follow-up or expediting division of the purchasing department.

Clearing the order

In some large companies, the normal responsibility of the purchasing department ends with the issuing of the purchase order. In such cases, the using department or a separate expediting unit follows up for delivery, the inspection department is responsible for acceptance, the stores department takes care of receiving the material, and the accounting department checks invoices and certifies them for payment from its own copy of the order. Usually, however, the purchasing department is involved in all of these duties, on the general principle that procurement responsibility ends only when a satisfactory delivery has been made and materials are actually on hand for use, and when the buyer's obligation to the vendor has likewise been satisfied, completing the contract.

If ordinary expediting methods fail to secure delivery as needed, the buyer who has had contact with the vendor and who made the original agreement is the most effective expediting agent. If materials are not in accordance with specification, the purchasing department must make the adjustment with the vendor. If there are discrepancies in quantity, price, or terms, in the vendor's shipment and billing, it is the purchasing department that has the final responsibility for reconciling the matter.

The first step in follow-up is to secure an acceptance and delivery promise from the vendor. The vendor's promise is recorded, and provision is made for orderly follow-up without waiting for an emergency to develop if the vendor's promise is not kept.

Routine follow-up

Follow-up is selective. A study of prevailing policy shows that less than one-third of all companies follow up every order issued for delivery. An additional one-third follow up orders classified as "important," or production orders as distinguished from orders for stock. In the other companies, follow-up is restricted to those that are actually and seriously overdue, and to special, rush, or emergency orders.

The mechanism for follow-up is a file of open orders arranged in numerical sequence so that those that are longest outstanding are in the front of the file, giving quick visual indication of the oldest ones. This, of course, is not an accurate indicator of the delivery dates requested or promised. Some further coding or signalling device is necessary.

A common method is to print a scale of numbers, from 1 to 31, across the top of the sheet, corresponding to the days of the month. A series of colored tabs, differentiated as to the various calendar months, can then be affixed at the proper point along this scale, on orders for which a positive follow-up schedule is desired. The combination of color and position shows the exact date at which follow-up action is to be taken. The receiving record must be posted against this file daily, and any completed orders must be removed from the file.

Routine follow-up according to such a schedule can ordinarily be effected by simple routine methods. A printed postcard requesting specific delivery information, with reference to date of order and vendor's promise, is the usual first step. A return postcard has been found useful in facilitating the vendor's reply. A somewhat more comprehensive form is sometimes used with provision for asking information on a variety of different points, according to the particular situation.

As the need for expediting becomes more acute, the tone and method of follow-up become stronger and more personalized, the usual sequence being:

personal letter, telegram, telephone call, and personal interview by expediter or buyer at the vendor's plant. The particular action and the amount of pressure brought to bear are adjusted to the circumstances.

Field expediting

In contrast to such routine expediting is the practice of maintaining a staff of expediters in the field, who keep contact with suppliers on important orders. Such expediters are usually made responsible for all orders placed with suppliers in a given territory; oftentimes they operate from the company's branch offices in these territories, but report directly to the general purchasing office. Sometimes this function is combined with inspection of materials at the vendor's plant.

The field expediter makes regular progress reports to the follow-up department at purchasing headquarters during the life of the order or contract, and his reports, checked with the schedule of requirements, show at all times the prospect of satisfactory fulfillment of delivery dates or indicate in advance the likelihood and extent of any delay that may be encountered.

Change orders

It sometimes becomes necessary to make changes in the order originally issued—changes in quantity, scheduling, or specification, changes authorizing some alternative product, or any other of the scores of possible corrections that may arise with changing design and changing conditions of business. Many companies accomplish changes by correspondence. Others make use of a form known as the *change Order* or *change Notice*. It is generally similar to the purchase order in form and is given the same number as the order it revises. In some cases it merely states: "Please change our original order of the above number to read as follows:" and lists the requirements as revised. In other cases, the body of the form is divided into two parts, the first of which restates the order as originally issued, while the second gives the desired revision.

Receiving

The receiving department is usually an adjunct of the stores department, which may or may not be a part of the purchasing department. Its functions are to receive incoming goods, signing the delivery notice presented by the carrier or the supplier in connection with the shipment; to identify and record all incoming materials; to report their receipt to the purchasing department and to the stores, using, or inspection departments as required; and to make prompt disposition of the goods to the appropriate department.

To aid in identification of the materials received, the receiving department is advised of all expected shipments by means of a copy of the purchase order.

All incoming materials are reconciled with the receiving department's copy of the purchase order. A record is kept of every delivery, and receiving reports containing this information go to the purchasing and stock records departments promptly.

Inspection for quality

Not all materials require formal inspection for quality; in a large proportion of deliveries on a normal procurement program, simple visual inspection meets every practical need. But often, where a more detailed examination and certification of quality are required, materials are segregated by the receiving department pending inspection and are not permitted to be placed in stores, or to go into production, until the proper inspection is made. The receiving department notifies the department responsible for inspection that the shipment has arrived, and takes whatever samples may be necessary or otherwise makes the material available for inspection. The *notification* may be accomplished by means of a copy of the receiving slip, or by routing the receiving department's copy of the purchase order through the inspecting department on its way back to purchasing. In the latter case, the *inspection report* may be made on the same copy as the receiving report; otherwise, a separate inspection report is required, certifying that the materials are satisfactory or, if not, giving the reason for rejection

When these two reports are received by purchasing, showing (1) a receipt of materials, including a check on the quantity received, and (2) a certification of quality, they are compared with the purchasing department copy of the order to see that they conform with what was ordered and are attached to it as evidence of a proper delivery.

Checking the invoice

Meanwhile, an invoice for the shipment is, or should be, received from the vendor, and this, too, must be reconciled both with the original order and with the records of receipt. It is important that the invoice be received and processed promptly, in order that the order may be cleared and payment made within the discount period, or that any necessary adjustments may be initiated without delay in case there is any discrepancy. It is customary to ask that invoices be sent in duplicate, one copy to be routed directly to the accounting department and one to the purchasing department, to allow simultaneous processing from both of these viewpoints in the buyer's company, to be correlated later in the accounting or accounts payable division.

Simplified methods

The procurement cycle obviously involves a great deal of paper work and clerical detail. It just as obviously lends itself to simplification and "mechanization" in a number of areas. Where the cost of requisitioning, ordering, receiving, and accounting for an item, for example, is greater than its value, use of complicated systems to procure it is foolish. Following elaborate procedures for every purchase of a part or material in regular use for which prices and vendors are established only once a year is costly and inefficient. As a result, many purchasing departments have set up simplified systems for handling this sort of buying without losing control of it.

One is a "small order" system for the purchase of miscellaneous supplies of low dollar value—usually less than $100. A single, simplified form is used. A typical small-order form will include requisition, purchase order, receiving report, and accounting copy. Most of the items are picked up by a purchasing department representative from local sources. In some systems, the pick-up man pays cash; in others, selected vendors are permitted to bill monthly for all purchases picked up during the period. One company has simplified its small-order procedure to the point where it includes a check drawn on a special revolving fund as a detachable stub on the order form. This eliminates invoices altogether.

This simplified approach to small orders is being carried to its logical conclusion and applied to a wider range of transactions by a number of companies. Perhaps the most outstanding development of this kind in recent years is the Purchase Order Draft system installed in 1961 by Kaiser Aluminum & Chemical Corporation.[1] Under the system, the vendor gets a blank check as part of the purchase order—a detachable portion of the form that is an envelope in addition to being a check. After shipping the order, the vendor puts one copy of his invoice inside the check-envelope, enters the net amount on the face, endorses it on the reverse side, and deposits it in his bank as an

---

[1] "Blank Check Solves Small Order Problem," *Purchasing Magazine,* November 5, 1962, page 70.

immediate cash payment. The check-envelope comes back to Kaiser the same as ordinary checks do.

The Kaiser plan was originally intended to cover orders up to $200 in value. But investigation showed that it could be extended to orders up to $1,000. Thus, it covers 92 per cent of the checks which the company issues for

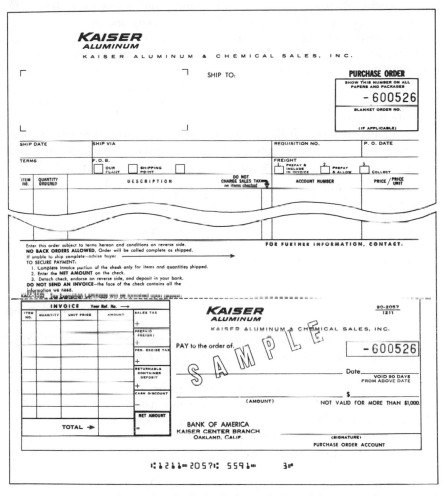

Fig. 19-1. Purchase Order Draft with Blank Check Attached, Used by Kaiser Aluminum Corp.

purchased materials. Success of the system has eliminated an enormous amount of filing, retrieving, posting, check writing, stuffing, mailing, typing, and handwriting.

Another paper-saving order system in use by a number of companies does away with the purchase order and vendor invoices. Requisitioners indicate the type of material and quantity needed by simply filling in a multiple-copy snapout form that serves all purposes in the order cycle. The requisitioner, in a typical case, removes one copy of the form for his records. The rest go to the purchasing department for checking. A buyer selects and calls a vendor, discusses prices and other terms, and places the order orally. No forms are sent to the supplier. The buyer keeps one part of the form as a worksheet and order record, and sends three copies to the receiving department and one to finance. As soon as accounts payable receives a copy indicating that the material has been delivered, it issues a check to the supplier. The system is used on standard shelf items, where the total purchase cost is $500 or less. Price changes, partial or late deliveries, or substitutions of any kind are not permitted.

A significant aspect of the two systems described above is the assumption that both parties to the transaction are trustworthy and reliable, and that both are interested in long-term association with each other. This is further evidence of the maturity of purchasing as an industrial function and refutation of the occasionally heard charge that the buyer-seller relationship is necessarily a dog-eat-dog affair. In the blank check system, the buyer puts full confidence in the supplier; in the no-purchase order system, there is mutual trust, because the purchasing department knows the quality of material it is getting and the vendor knows he will get paid.

Contract buying

One of the most effective purchasing devices for cutting costs is the type of buying agreement variously known as the *blanket order, open-end order,* or *yearly order*. Essentially, it is an expression of the buyer's intention to purchase all or part of his requirements of repetitive items from one supplier during a given period of time. The requirements may be for a certain class of items (the term *blanket order* is generally used when maintenance, repair, and operating supplies are bought this way) or for a specific material or part. Terms are negotiated and an order is issued for a definite period—usually a year.

As the operating departments need materials, they issue simple releases against the order, either through purchasing or directly to the vendor. In the latter case, purchasing is kept informed of what releases are issued. A refinement of the blanket-order release system is the use of Bell System's Data-Phone, an electronic transmission device, for ordering material from suppliers. Transmission units are installed in both supplier's and customer's offices. Items under contract are listed on punched cards, which are maintained in the purchasing office and which are fed into the Data-Phone instrument, as

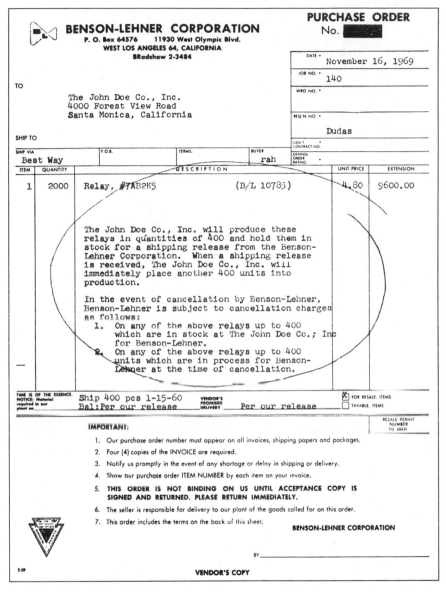

BENSON-LEHNER CORPORATION
P. O. Box 64576   11930 West Olympic Blvd.
WEST LOS ANGELES 64, CALIFORNIA
BRadshaw 2-3484

PURCHASE ORDER
No.

DATE • November 16, 1969

JOB NO. • 140

WRO NO. •

TO

The John Doe Co., Inc.
4000 Forest View Road
Santa Monica, California

REQ'N NO. •

Dudas

SHIP TO

GOV'T CONTRACT NO. •

| SHIP VIA | F.O.B. | TERMS: | BUYER | DEFENSE ORDER RATING • |
| Best Way | | | rah | |

ITEM	QUANTITY	DESCRIPTION	UNIT PRICE	EXTENSION
1	2000	Relay, #7AB2K5 (B/L 10785)	4.80	9600.00

The John Doe Co., Inc. will produce these
relays in quantities of 400 and hold them in
stock for a shipping release from the Benson-
Lehner Corporation. When a shipping release
is received, The John Doe Co., Inc. will
immediately place another 400 units into
production.

In the event of cancellation by Benson-Lehner,
Benson-Lehner is subject to cancellation charges
as follows:
1. On any of the above relays up to 400
   which are in stock at The John Doe Co.; Inc
   for Benson-Lehner.
2. On any of the above relays up to 400
   units which are in process for Benson-
   Lehner at the time of cancellation.

TIME IS OF THE ESSENCE. NOTICE: Material required in our plant on

Ship 400 pcs 1-15-60
Bal:Per our release

VENDOR'S PROMISED DELIVERY   Per our release

☒ FOR RESALE, ITEMS
☐ TAXABLE, ITEMS

RESALE PERMIT NUMBER

IMPORTANT:

1. Our purchase order number must appear on all invoices, shipping papers and packages.
2. Four (4) copies of the INVOICE are required.
3. Notify us promptly in the event of any shortage or delay in shipping or delivery.
4. Show our purchase order ITEM NUMBER by each item on your invoice.
5. **THIS ORDER IS NOT BINDING ON US UNTIL ACCEPTANCE COPY IS SIGNED AND RETURNED. PLEASE RETURN IMMEDIATELY.**
6. The seller is responsible for delivery to our plant of the goods called for on this order.
7. This order includes the terms on the back of this sheet.

BENSON-LEHNER CORPORATION

BY _____

5-59

VENDOR'S COPY

Fig. 19-2. Typical "Stockless" Purchasing Agreement in Which Vendor Is Responsible for Carrying Inventory.

requirements arise. As price, quantity and similar data are transmitted to the supplier, similar cards are produced on his unit, from which he can fill the order.

This type of order generally carries no guarantee that the buyer will

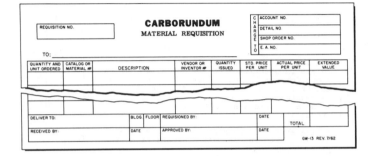

TALLY SHEET

SHEET____ OF____

TO: THE CARBORUNDUM COMPANY

VCHR. NO. _____
PAYEE NO. _____
TERMS _____
PRICE CHECKED _____
EXT'N CHECKED _____

PERIOD ENDING _____ DATE _____

REQUISITION NUMBER	DOLLAR EXTENSION	REQUISITION NUMBER	DOLLAR EXTENSION	REQUISITION NUMBER	DOLLAR EXTENSION

							TOTAL	

CARBORUNDUM
MATERIAL REQUISITION

REQUISITION NO.

CHARGE TO: ACCOUNT NO. / DETAIL NO. / SHOP ORDER NO. / E. A. NO.

TO: _____

QUANTITY AND UNIT ORDERED	CATALOG OR MATERIAL #	DESCRIPTION	VENDOR OR INVENTOR #	QUANTITY ISSUED	STD. PRICE PER UNIT	ACTUAL PRICE PER UNIT	EXTENDED VALUE

| DELIVER TO: | BLDG | FLOOR | REQUISIONED BY: | | DATE | TOTAL | |
| RECEIVED BY: | | DATE | APPROVED BY: | | DATE | | |

GW-13 REV. 7/62

Catalog No.	Description and Size
	Flat Head Brass Machine
551	6-32 x 1
552	6-32 x 1/2
553	10-24 x 3/8
	Round Head Stove Bolts
561	3/16 x 3/8
	3/16 x 1/2

	Flat Head Stove Bolts
591	3/16 x 1
592	1/4 x 3/4
593	1/4 x 1
594	1/4 x 1-1/2

Fig. 19-3. Systems Contracting Procedure Includes a Catalog of All Items Bought Under Contract (top); Material Requisitions Which Take the Place of Releases and Are Sent Directly By Plants to Vendors (center); and Tally Sheet Sent to Accounts Payable By Supplier.

purchase a given amount of material during the term of the contract. It simply designates one company as the supplier for a class of purchased items, for example, plant supplies or office supplies. The order is usually revocable at the will of the buyer, although in practice this rarely occurs. Blanket orders are negotiated only after careful consideration and only when there is some assurance that they will be maintained until the end of the agreement.

Some orders, however, notably those of the open-end type used in the automobile industry, authorize the supplier to produce a certain number of items at various times during the life of the contract (for example, 10,000 crankshafts in the first two months, 15,000 the second month, and so forth). Such instructions then obligate the buyer to pay for the items produced in the specified time, whether or not he is able to use them.

A more advanced form of blanket, or "stockless" purchasing, is used by the Carborundum Corporation and is known as "systems contracting." The company's headquarters buying staff draws up contracts or purchase agreements with suppliers covering large groups of materials or supplies generally bought from distributors. These would include office supplies, bearings, steel, mill supplies, and tools. Part of every contract is a detailed catalog of the items covered (see Fig. 19-3). Suppliers are required to stock sufficient quantities of all items in the catalog.

Requisitioners in the company's plants are allowed to requisition items directly against the contracts. Material requisitions go directly to the supplier holding a contract, rather than to the purchasing department. No invoices are required from the supplier, who simply mails a tally sheet (see Fig. 19-3) to Carborundum's accounts payable department every ten days.

The blanket order and similar plans do a lot more than eliminate much of the paper work involved in requisitioning, buying, and invoicing. They enable the purchaser to get more favorable discount items on the basis of the increased volume he is able to offer the supplier. And the buyer can get this discount without incurring the heavy carrying charges he would be faced with if the whole order were brought into the plant at one time. By having material shipped in as needed, he transfers some of the carrying cost to the vendor. This is not so burdensome or inequitable as it seems at first, however. The vendor, with some knowledge of what his customer will need over a given period, is in a better position to plan his own stocks or production and to eliminate the peaks and valleys in supply that often occur otherwise.

Data processing

Office machines and data-processing equipment, like their counterparts in the factory, have made tremendous advances in the past decade and a half.

The automated office is becoming as much a reality as the automated plant. Applied to purchasing operations, this equipment has resulted in greater speed, efficiency, and accuracy. It has helped to reduce paper-handling costs and to free buyers from routine clerical work. In the case of the computer, it has also given the purchasing executive a continuing source of significant data not previously available to him without an enormous amount of hand calculation. The statistical information which the computer produces helps him in long-range planning, in rating the performance of his vendors and his own personnel, in analyzing price trends, and in reporting to management.

The most widely used system of purchasing automation is known as integrated (IDP) or automated (ADP) data processing. It employs electro-mechanical devices, as distinct from the electronic machines (computers) used in the more sophisticated systems known as *electronic data processing* (EDP).

The basic elements in an integrated data-processing system are paper tapes, or cards, into which repetitive data are punched, and machines that accept the tapes and cards and automatically reproduce the information they carry on various forms.

The data may be any appearing in the forms used in the procurement cycle already described—requisition, purchase order, change order, or receiving slip.

The tapes are then fed into electric machines—specially designed typewriters or teletypewriters which automatically produce the required documents on continuous-feed forms. Only the information on the tape is typed automatically. Variable information, such as quantity, price, or vendor, may be manually typed in by the operator. The machines can also produce new tapes during the operation, which carry both the constant and the variable data. When the teletypewriter is used, a copy of the form can be printed and a new tape punched out at some remote location on another machine linked to the master machine in the purchasing department. The second tape may then be used to print receiving reports as material is delivered.

Tapes are used effectively with the traveling requisition system (see page 257). The requisition form is made up as an envelope, with all basic information printed on the outside. A punched tape carrying most of the data needed on a quotation request or purchase order is kept in the envelope. The tape was originally made up the first time that the required part was bought or submitted to suppliers for bid. Once it has been made up, it can be used many times over in the sequences described above.

Punched cards are used in basically the same way in many integrated data-processing systems, and often both tapes and cards are used, particularly when the system is tied into a computer. At International Telephone and Telegraph Corporation's Federal Division, bills of material (see page 257) are "exploded" into punched cards, one for each item in the product. These cards are sent to purchasing, where a buyer selects the vendors. The cards are fed into Flexowriter machines, along with other punched cards containing vendors' names and addresses. As the operator runs the cards through the machine, it prints the purchase order. At the same time, it turns out a punched tape containing selected information, which is sent to the data-processing department. There the tape is converted into punched cards which in turn become "input" for the computer. (Use of the computer in the purchasing cycle will be described in the next section.)

An unusual application of the punched card-punched tape system is found in the commercial airline industry, where the airlines must necessarily buy standardized parts for their huge aircraft from one supplier. Called *ATA* (Air Transport Association) Specification 200, it involves an exchange of basic data between purchaser and supplier, all of which is contained on punched cards or punched tapes. All purchase orders and related documents are exchanged via wire transmission systems in special code. The system is widely used by both United States and foreign airlines.

Computers in purchasing

Mechanization of the clerical work in purchasing is most advanced where computers are used to process data. The electronic computer is, in effect, a huge file, a calculating machine, and a printer rolled into one. It stores basic data in its "memory"—either on reels of magnetic tape or on magnetic discs—and translates that data for procurement action. A typical machine used in purchasing operations can produce requisitions, write purchase orders (in most cases, hundreds per hour if necessary), initiate follow-up of orders, audit supplier invoices, and prepare payment vouchers and checks. In addition, it can turn out a wide variety of operating reports significant to purchasing and corporate management— such as status of open orders, commitments, and amount of expenditures. It can be used to analyze price trends, vendor performance, and buyer performance.

No machine can replace personal judgment and decision in purchasing. But the electronic computer is a potent new tool for eliminating drudgery and for improving performance in purchasing. It gives added authority to the purchasing agent's decision on what and how much to buy, and it reduces the possibility of error in reference and calculation.

The computer mechanizes several basic steps of the materials cycle. It can automatically:

—Calculate parts requirements for a given production run.

—Calculate proper inventory levels and reorder points for stores items.

—Calculate economic purchase quantities, that is, that quantity of a part or material that results in minimum annual total cost consistent with adequate inventory (see page 105).

—Write purchase requisitions, purchase orders, and follow-up documents.

—Produce statistical reports on buyer performance, vendor performance, purchase orders by commodity, open purchase requisitions, and numerous other reports important to purchasing and general management.

Before it can perform these operations, of course, the machine must be fed raw data—in computer language, "input." The data are accumulated from previous transactions that were handled manually. This is punched into tapes or cards and fed into the computer, where it is stored on magnetic tapes or discs, ready for use when new transactions involving the same data are to be carried out.

Economic purchase quantities are computed in a matter of seconds from a number of empirical data: for example, annual usage, cost of issuing an order for it, inventory-carrying charges, quantity discounts available, and variable tool charges if they are involved.

The strictly purchasing part of a computerized materials operation has three phases: the requisition or requirements phase; the purchase order phase; and the report phase.

In a typical system, three types of requisitions come to purchasing. One is produced from a punched tape or card that is itself the product of a computer breakdown of a new production job. When a new customer's order comes into the shop, the computer is used to analyze the parts requirements and to separate "make" items from those that are to be bought. The machine turns out "order release" tapes for the "buy" items.

A second material request is a tape that is the output of a daily inventory check of stores items, that is, all those parts and materials that are in regular use in the plant and do not have to be bought specially for a new job. The machine, which records all material receipts and stock issues, calculates the daily stock balance for all stores items. Whenever the stock level falls below established reorder points, the computer turns out a tape into which basic reordering information has been punched. One tape may contain data for all stocked parts and materials that have reached their reorder points on that day.

The third type of requisition that comes to purchasing is a handwritten request from the shop or engineering department for items that are neither stocked nor used on regular production runs.

The two tapes mentioned above—the order release on production parts and the reorder notice on stores—are fed into the computer to produce requisitions to purchasing. This is generally a two-step process: the computer

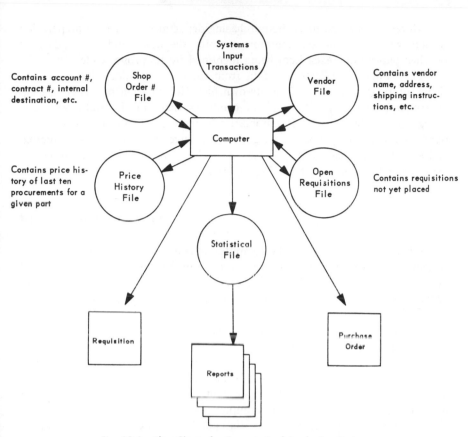

Fig. 19-4. Flow Chart of a Computerized Purchasing System.

takes information from the input tape—part numbers, quantities, due dates, and so forth—and combines it with buying data already stored in the magnetic file. The result is a requisition tape that goes into the printing unit of the system to write the purchase requisitions. These go back to the requisitioners, who check them, attach drawings or specifications of the part, and forward them to the purchasing department.

After the buyers receive the requisitions (both those printed on the machine and the manually written ones), they check the requisitions and start the purchase order phase. They select sources and negotiate prices and terms when necessary. Once they make their decisions, they need add only several numbers to the almost complete requisitions: vendor code, buyer code, promise date, prices, and discounts. The computer relieves buyers entirely of making price extensions or calculating net prices. It does this automatically from the figures which the buyer enters on the requisition form.

All requisitions go from the purchasing department to a tape-preparation section, where Flexowriter operators transfer the new handwritten data to punched paper tape, each item being identified by its proper code.

The computer collects the data from these tapes, adds whatever additional information it needs from its own files (information on vendors, shop orders, and open requisitions), and combines them in the right sequence. Using this combined data, it automatically instructs a printer to print the purchase order. The printed order goes to the buyer for checking and signing, and a hectograph master that is part of the document goes to the receiving department for preparing receiving reports.

Purchase data compiled

While processing orders, the computer adds all new purchase data to the statistical file. Receiving reports are also fed into the file by means of punched tapes. From all this material the computer produces important statistical reports for purchasing management. By giving the purchasing department and company management more information about the department's work, they help provide better control and improve efficiency.

One good example is the monthly buyer analysis, run off from the statistical magnetic tape in just two minutes. This lists each buyer's purchase volume for the month. Beside his code number appears the total number of items purchased, the amount of money spent, and a breakdown of his orders by dollar size—for example, $0-24, $25-49, and so forth.

The report immediately gives the purchasing executive useful information about his department that otherwise could be obtained only by time-consuming and therefore expensive calculation. It indicates buyer work load by number of orders and dollar amount. By breaking orders down into dollar size groups, it reveals buying patterns not usually apparent in a manually controlled system. If, for example, the computer shows a high percentage of small or low-value orders, the purchasing department is alerted to seek ways to reduce the number: for example, put frequently ordered parts in inventory; or try to consolidate requisitions that duplicate each other.

Another report that gives the purchasing department better control over materials is the part-number procurement report. In the system described here, the computer runs off a numerical tabulation of all purchased items. It consists of the part number and name, and lists all purchase orders on which the part has been ordered during the year to date, including order numbers, order date and quantity of each purchase. If a part is being ordered too often, the buyer or purchasing agent can spot the fact immediately and recommend that it be made a stock item.

Commodity code analysis is another report produced by the computer. It lists purchases by part numbers and groups them according to commodity codes; thus, related items, like many different types of drills, are listed as a group. The report is made up in the same form as the buyer analysis. The data give the buyer an idea of the buying volume on important items and serve as a basis for negotiation when he sets up blanket orders or long-term buying contracts.

These are just a few of the by-products to the basic buying process that a computerized system can offer. Others include reports on volume of purchases by vendor; purchases placed with each vendor by each buyer; number of open orders with a given vendor. At the Endicott, New York plant of International Business Machines Corporation, this type of vendor performance analysis has been extended to develop a performance index for key parts, each vendor, and each buyer. Ratings are based on quality and delivery and price factors, measured against the previous year's record. Purchasing management receives a quarterly summary which gives an over-all view of purchasing performance. The report shows total dollar commitments for the quarter, and average price, quality, and delivery indexes. The index numbers indicate immediately whether over-all performance, or performance in a specific area, is better or worse than it was in the previous period.[2]

There are a number of variations of the system described above, but most of them are based on different mechanical techniques or different sequences of computer operations. Punched cards, for example, are used as "inputs" as much and perhaps more than the punched tapes mentioned. In a number of installations where stores items make up the bulk of purchased commodities (in oil refining companies, for example), the computer is programmed to issue the purchase order automatically without the intermediate step of producing a requisition tape.

These and other methods are merely a matter of technique, however, and do not alter the basic concept of handling constant, repetitive information electronically rather than manually.

Values of automation

Automated purchasing procedure follows, in general, the very same steps and procedures that make up the standard procedures described in the previous chapter in terms of a manual operation. It does not change the function of a procurement department, and it is necessarily based on

---

[2] John Van de Water, "Tomorrow's Purchasing Today," *Purchasing Magazine,* Feb. 27, 1961, page 71.

exactly the same data for each purchase transaction and record. The special characteristics of the automated procedure are speed, the elimination of tedious and costly paper work, and the quick availability of information for almost any purpose desired, including some types of information and calculation that have heretofore been so difficult to obtain by clerical means that they have never been fully utilized in purchasing science.

This greater efficiency is in itself a tremendous asset. But even more important than the improvement in procedures is the improvement in management of the purchasing activity that this makes possible. The additional information gives the purchasing officer more tools to work with, a basis for better and faster policy decisions, and the means for extending the constructive aspects of materials and purchasing management. For the abilities of the computer are by no means limited to the procedural operations. At least one automobile manufacturer uses the computer to take care of the almost infinite variations of color combinations and accessories that are encountered in purchasing and production for today's highly individualized "standard" models. The appraisal of vendor performance, studies of stock obsolescence, and the preparation of reports to management are other applications that come readily to mind. The possibilities of this sort are limited only by the amounts of computer time and printing time on the machine that are allotted to purchasing department use, and the ingenuity of purchasing and computer personnel in programming the operations to produce new types of information from existing data.

Further, automation of all routing and repetitive activities makes possible what is sometimes called "management by exception." It has been pointed out in the sections dealing with automated stock control, follow-up, and invoice checking, for example, that it is only the unusual situation, the emergency, the discrepancy of error, that comes to the attention of the buyer once the basic decision has been made. When the routine transactions proceed according to schedule—in perhaps as many as 95 per cent of all cases, once the system has been properly installed and adjusted—the buyers' time, ability, and judgment can be concentrated on the research, negotiating, policy, and special projects phases of procurement free from the burden and intrusion of routine details.

20

PURCHASING POLICIES

THROUGHOUT THIS DISCUSSION, frequent reference has been made to a variety of purchasing decisions as matters of policy. The decision to cover forward requirements for a period of 30 or 60 or 90 days becomes a purchasing policy; it is subject to revision, to be sure, according to changing conditions, but so long as it is in effect it determines and controls purchasing action. The decision to maintain alternative sources of supply for purchased items sets a policy of a somewhat more permanent nature; it is expressed in instructions to buyers and in the working records and procedures of the purchasing department.

Every purchasing department has policies, whether or not they are put into writing. They are one of the administrative tools of departmental management. The advantages of establishing specific policies, and recording them, are threefold:

1. An established policy eliminates the necessity for making a new decision every time a comparable situation arises.

2. A written policy assures understanding; it assures that decisions and actions will be consistent, and in accordance with the judgment of the responsible department head.

3. An approved policy gives authority to the indicated course of action.

Internal relationships

The establishment of centralized purchasing is in itself a policy of company management. It immediately entails a whole series of internal, interdepartmental policies relating to lines of authority, channels of procedure, and departmental relationships in general. These policies should be promptly clarified and made a matter of record, for they define the scope and responsibilities of the purchasing function in any particular organization and determine to a considerable extent the effectiveness of the purchasing operation. The principles underlying these relationships have already been set forth in Chapter 2, but they cannot be assumed. Neither can they be set by the purchasing agent alone, because they affect the responsibilities and actions of other departments as well. The purchasing agent can suggest and try to persuade; but to have valid force, such decisions must have the stamp of management approval.

Policies in this category include such matters as the authorizations required on requisitions to purchase, permissions for vendors' salesmen to contact plant personnel, the final responsibility for specifications, the procedures to be followed in standardization and value-analysis recommendations involving engineering changes, and similar points on which conflicts of function and authority may arise.

To be effective, a policy must be clear and definitive, but it need not be arbitrary. Consequently, many policies set up criteria for decisions, or methods of handling situations, or conditions of action. For example, it is obviously undesirable to grant free access to plant personnel for all vendors' salesmen, either at their own initiative or at the request of the plant man, for such a policy would negate the principles of centralized purchasing. Yet there are many situations in which such a contact is mutually desirable and is, in fact, an aid to intelligent procurement. A sensible and commonly accepted policy on this point is to require that such contacts be made through the purchasing department and that in such interviews no commitments are to be made by plant personnel as to preference for products or sources, which might weaken the position of the purchasing department in subsequent negotiations.

Vendor relationships

Relationships with vendors and their representatives, too, are subject to policy control. Should the purchasing agent's door be open to every business caller, and is every salesman entitled to the chance to tell his story? Perhaps so, on the first visit; after that it is for the buyer to decide whether the proposal is pertinent and timely from the viewpoint of the company's needs and whether the interview time is warranted. Should specific, limited hours be set for interviewing salesmen? That question can be argued endlessly. Departmental policy often compromises by "suggesting" fixed calling hours and making provision for exceptions in the case of the out-of-town caller and special appointments.

THE CLEVELAND GRAPH

RELATIONS WITH OTHER DEPARTMENTS

1. It must be recognized that the Purchasing Department is the primary point of contact between the company and its suppliers.

2. The Purchasing Department has a primary purpose of conserving the time of operating, engineering, and other personnel whose responsibilities and specialties lie elsewhere.

3. All requests for price information, demonstrations, samples, and trial lots are made through Purchasing.

4. There are certain instances where Purchasing acts in a liaison capacity in the original contact with an outside supplier and does not wish to participate in subsequent discussions. In such cases, Purchasing is kept fully informed of progress by the parties involved.

5. Negotiations, commitments, and expressions of opinion of a binding nature on merit and acceptability of a product are not considered in discussions between other departments and vendors without prior concurrence and discussion with Purchasing.

6. No person outside the Purchasing Department will divulge information regarding the source of supply for any products, competitive performance, or past prices paid for products and services.

7. It is recognized that Purchasing will receive and interview all supplier representatives. Personnel from other departments requiring information from supplier representatives will so notify the Purchasing Department. Purchasing, in turn, will make necessary arrangements or authorize the requester to contact the source directly.

8. Purchasing retains full authority to question the quality and type of material requested in order that the best interests of the company may be served.

9. Purchasing retains full authority to check quantities ordered for conformance to manufacturers' standard packages and quantity discounts.

10. Embarrassment to the company is prevented by having a single management source, namely the Purchasing Department, present all opinions on the merits and acceptability of any purchased product. The company recognizes the importance of centralization with respect to purchasing.

Fig. 20-1. Statement of Purchasing Policy Endorsed By Company President.

Should price information be kept confidential? In industrial purchasing, yes. (The governmental buyer, with a mandatory system of sealed bids and a public bid opening, has no such option. That is another policy, characteristic of a particular field.) Should vendors be permitted to revise their bids? Only in case of obvious error, or in a subsequent negotiating stage if terms, quantities, or specifications are modified so as to warrant a price adjustment. If the stated requirement is changed, should all bidders be given a chance to make a new quotation? Not necessarily. If it becomes a new proposal on the buyer's part, a new request for bids may be in order. But if he has selected a vendor on merit, on the basis of the original proposal, and the terms are altered in negotiation, he will probably stand on the original choice. If the cost-saving changes come at the vendor's suggestion, fair purchasing policy demands that the vendor retain the patronage, with the status of a preferred supplier on succeeding orders. Should unsuccessful bidders be notified? Yes, and with the reasons for the adverse decision, if feasible.

Policies in this category have their roots in ethical considerations as well as in economics and "good business." The ethical aspects are discussed in greater detail in Chapter 21.

Should orders ever be issued on the vendor's contract form rather than on a standard purchase order? This is a point on which purchasing policy and sales policy frequently come into conflict. Ordinarily, purchasing policy favors the use of the buyer's standard order form and terms in all cases. But sometimes, when installations and special warranties are involved, the vendor's form that is specifically designed for these situations is more appropriate and obviates the need for writing in a lot of special clauses and conditions on the buyer's form. For such cases, purchasing policy can set up certain criteria for the acceptability of a seller's form—criteria that will safeguard the rights of the buyer and avoid conflict with other basic company and purchasing policies. The policy may include getting approval of the contract by the company's legal department.

To what extent should personal contacts with vendors be cultivated, including visits to vendors' plants? It may be good policy to put this on a systematic basis, and to extend it with a policy of inviting vendors periodically, individually or as a group, to acquire a personal knowledge of the buyer's plant operations.

Policies on supply source

Another group of purchasing decisions that lend themselves to the guidance of a consistent and considered policy concerns the selection of supply sources. The policy of maintaining multiple or alternative sources is almost universal. But this does not answer the question of what kind of sources should be chosen.

Should any preference be given to local suppliers? In theory, the local supplier offers natural advantages of convenience, faster deliveries, and lower transportation expense. There are factors that weigh in his favor in any source consideration. However, the objective appraisal of supply sources may show others to be equally or more desirable, and a more distant competitor may underbid him sufficiently to offset his initial advantage. At this point another set of factors comes into play. How much is it worth to foster good community relations by patronizing local sources, to help maintain local prosperity by keeping business in the local area, to develop and maintain strong supply sources nearby? These factors have enough validity and importance to make some companies go so far as to establish a small percentage cost differential that is considered acceptable in dealing with local sources, all other things being equal. Such a policy is usually permissive rather than mandatory.

Assuming that facilities are adequate and prices are competitive, should any preference be given, as a matter of policy, to dealing with either large or small companies as such? The case for the small company as a supplier usually hinges upon the mathematical fact that an order or account of given size looms proportionately larger in the operations of a small supplier, and it is logical to expect that he will give it closer individual attention and service than it might receive in the larger organization, where it is of relatively minor importance. Another argument cited in favor of the small company is the rather pardoxical one that the buyer's patronage helps the small company to grow larger; the inference in this case is that the buyer will get greater loyalty and cooperation from the small supplier. Both arguments are probably unfair to the many efficient and conscientious large supplier companies that have attained their present stature through high standards of service. Be that as it may, many large companies take pains to point out in their annual reports and public relations releases that a considerable part of their material needs are supplied by companies in the category of small business. This condition may be merely a reflection of the interdependence of all elements in the total economy, in which both big business and small business have a place.

Should an effort be made, as a matter of policy, to deal, so far as possible, directly with primary manufacturing sources rather than through distributors and other middlemen? If quantity warrants, there may be some price advantage on direct mill shipments. If the distribution system and price structure are such that there is no saving on direct purchases, as is often the case, there may be advantages in the distributor's services. The reputable manufacturer will support his product and warranties, and will usually provide essential technical services in either case.

Reciprocal purchasing policy

The most persistently troublesome and controversial question of policy regarding supply sources is that of reciprocity. The urge to select vendors on the basis of their status as actual or potential customers may come either from the supplier's representative or from within the buyer's own organization, usually from the sales department; of the two, the latter is likely to be the more potent and insistent. The onus for pressure on this point cannot be placed entirely on the vendor. The problem is never altogether absent in a purchasing program; it is a permanent factor, and it is greatly intensified in periods of depressed business activity when every means of leverage is exerted to get orders.

Purchasing agents generally resent the pressures of reciprocity, which is a negation of the principles of scientific value buying, a tacit admission that a sale could not otherwise be made on the basis of merit of product, service, or price. It is discriminatory, and it is an intrusion on the buyer's authority to make buying decisions. Few purchasing agents can rationalize or would espouse a policy of reciprocal buying on their own initiative. But it may be an approved company policy of marketing. Realistically, then, purchasing must adjust buying policies to come within the framework of company policy and to make company policy as effective as possible, even if it involves some compromise with normal purchasing principles. In the competition for market outlets, reciprocity may be considered a legitimate argument, provided that all the implications are faced squarely and weighed in the final decision. It was pointed out earlier that sound procurement decisions sometimes sacrifice purchasing advantages to secure greater offsetting economies in the production department, or vice versa. The same reasoning is applicable in arriving at a favorable economic balance between purchasing and sales factors.

When reciprocity is used as a vendor's sales argument, it is largely a matter of pressure. As a buying argument, it is a matter of scientific and factual evaluation. It requires a knowledge of just what is to be sacrificed, if anything, and what is to be gained. Purchasing power and patronage become bargaining tools, negotiation factors of known quantitative and dollar value, applied to the sales program. The procedure does not imply the abdication of purchasing responsibility, but rather imposes the responsibility of seeking full value in another direction, different from the purchasing agent's usual concern with tangible materials and their application. This calls for greater sales-mindedness on the purchasing agent's part, and an appreciation of the company's distribution objectives and opportunities, in order that he may be of maximum assistance to his sales department in effecting advantageous reciprocal agreements.

It is this factual and scientific approach that gives reasonableness and effectiveness to the elaborate three-way and four-way reciprocity arguments that would otherwise lapse into utter ridiculousness. Simple two-way reciprocity is easy to understand and relatively easy to handle. A manufacturer of office machines uses steel, available from many sources; steel mills use office machinery, also procurable from a variety of sources. A petroleum company uses compressors and pumps; the machinery manufacturer uses petroleum products as factory lubricants and for the operation of its automotive equipment. In each of these cases, although there is a great disparity in the volume and value of the products involved, both companies appear in the dual role of supplier and customer, and the opportunity for a reciprocal claim for patronage is obvious.

The relationship, however, may not be so direct. Let us say, for example, that Company A manufactures a control mechanism applicable to heavy machinery. It purchases large quantities of steel, but the steelmaker is not a prospect for its product. It seeks business from Company B, which manufactures heavy machinery of a type not used in A's operation. But steelmaker C is one of B's important customers. Company C may induce B to purchase its accessories from its customer A, at the latter's suggestion or on its own initiative. Or Company B may induce A to purchase its steel from its customer C. Thus a three-way reciprocal relationship is developed, with the purchasing power and patronage of the respective companies used as the inducement in each successive stage for sales purposes. The primary objective for each of the companies concerned is greater volume or assurance of sales. It is accomplished with the consent or the active cooperation of the purchasing executive, for in this case reciprocity has become a buying argument. Presumably it has been accomplished without the sacrifice of any significant purchasing advantage, or at least it has provided compensating sales advantages to offset and justify any purchasing compromise involved. It has been made possible through an intimate knowledge of material requirements and purchasing policies. The same process may be followed through still more devious and extensive series of buyer-seller contacts to achieve four-way reciprocity or even more complicated stages. The fact that such agreements do exist and are maintained is evidence that the principle is a practicable one, whatever its merits or demerits may be.

The practice of reciprocity

Realistic acceptance of reciprocity as a factor in purchasing should not blind either the buyer or his top management to the limitations and the positive disadvantages that are inherent in this policy. It is only by facing these aspects of the situation honestly and analytically that reciprocity can be intelligently applied in either buying or selling, or with any assurance that its advantages are real rather than apparent.

The inherent advantages of reciprocity accrue to sales rather than to purchasing. It may result in greater volume of sales for the individual company or in holding a greater proportion of sales under buyers'-market conditions. It does not create new demand or increase total sales or consumption of a product, because it is strictly a competitive device. Consequently, reciprocity has more to offer for the high-cost producer and the inefficient or incompetent distributor, using the purchasing power and patronage of the company to compensate for the lack of other competitive advantages or for the weakness of the sales plan and organization. The correction of these shortcomings, if that can be accomplished, is obviously the more constructive and permanent way to greater sales, without handicapping purchasing with the obligation to patronize sources that may be in a similarly uneconomic position.

The effectiveness of the reciprocity argument is strictly limited by the size of the purchasing expenditure. The value of the patronage that is offered in reciprocal purchasing can be no more than the dollars-and-cents volume of purchasing power in a given material or product classification. The disparity between what is offered and what is sought in many cases is one of the factors that frequently reduces the attempt at reciprocity to an absurdity. Even this limited force of reciprocity may be further diluted by the necessity of dividing patronage among several customer-suppliers if the policy is consistently carried out.

Under any form of reciprocal buying policy, purchasing becomes less selective because freedom of choice among suppliers is limited. To this extent it is a general negation of scientific considerations that would normally indicate the selection of the most favorable supplier. Furthermore, it discourages competition among suppliers, who quickly become aware of the negligible opportunities to share the market, and without such competition the purchasing agent is stripped of his negotiating or bargaining power. These factors are difficult to measure in terms of purchase cost, but it is safe to state that their effect and implications go considerably beyond the measurable cost features.

Reciprocity does not necessarily entail additional unit cost on purchased items, although, because price may be one of the factors that is compromised in making a reciprocal agreement, this is frequently the case. The theory of reciprocity is that any such additional cost will be more than offset by the sales advantages. In justice to purchasing, as well as to management, which ought to know the cost of reciprocity in order to evaluate the effectiveness of the policy, and ought also to know accurately the performance of each of the several departments, any additional purchase costs should be meticulously recorded and allocated. If they are in fact incurred as items of sales expense, the fact should be made known.

Once a course of reciprocity has been decided upon, the purchasing department will naturally strive to operate within the policy as efficiently and effectively as possible. It can contribute not only by making the purchases that are called for from the agreed sources, but by a continuing factual study and record of everything that is entailed. With this specific information at hand, including not only comparative costs, qualities, and service, but a clear-cut reason for every choice of supplier (including reasons of reciprocity), the purchasing agent is in a position (1) to substantiate or refute the theoretical advantages of reciprocity in any given case, (2) to direct reciprocity negotiations and agreements toward customer sources that promise greater purchase advantages for the same volume of sales or greater sales volume for the same purchasing compromise, (3) to resist, for good and demonstrable reasons, reciprocity pressure that is outside the official policy, whether it comes from the supplier's representative or from one of his own company's salesmen, (4) to avoid making an issue of reciprocity where it makes no difference either way, and (5) to make an equitable distribution of business among suppliers having legitimate claims upon his patronage under the reciprocity policy. In other words, in the administration of such a policy, it is a responsibility of the purchasing department to make the most effective use of the buying power that it directs, within the limitations which the policy imposes.

The ramifications of a reciprocity program are so complex and extensive that specialized attention must be given to it if the expected opportunities are to be fully realized. Large companies operating on this principle generally set up a central point of responsibility generally designated as the "trade relations" manager or department.

It is the duty of such officers or divisions to determine where the opportunities for reciprocity exist, for obviously this policy cannot apply to the entire purchasing or sales program. They must weigh the advantages of the policy in each case, negotiate the arrangement with the other company—either through the purchasing and sales officers or the corresponding "customer relations" division or through top management—and watch carefully the results of the policy on company sales and purchases.

To carry out such a program requires, first of all, a complete and detailed knowledge of the company's own purchase requirements—the potential patronage that the company has to sell—and where the business is currently being placed. This information comes from the purchasing department files and current records. To facilitate its use in reciprocity, it must be carefully organized for ready analysis according to individual items, commodity groups, and sources of supply. In companies where this is a major policy, it is customary for purchase records to be carried on machine tabulating cards that can be quickly sorted by mechanical means to produce the required data.

Second, it requires a knowledge of sales outlets for the company's product, representing the possible sales advantages that may accrue to the company through reciprocal dealings. This information is obtainable from sales and sales prospect records, the companies involved being rated quantitatively as to the potential total of their business, estimated as accurately as possible from the volume of their operations, business known to be placed with competitors, and similar miscellaneous information current in the trade. This information, too, is checked against purchasing department records to identify those potential customers who are also actual or potential suppliers. Their desirability or acceptability as sources, their eagerness to do business, as evidenced by sales effort expended, and the like, should be considered.

To evaluate these data properly, the purchasing department should be able to demonstrate clearly why current purchases are being made from the selected sources. It is presumed, of course, that there is a reason for every purchase decision; but, aside from the tabulation of competitive bids on purchases that are made under this procedure, few purchasing departments make their reasons a matter of record as a normal policy, except where this practice may be required in purchasing for governmental agencies or on contracts for the government's account, or in some types of mutual or cooperative organizations where records are constantly open to the scrutiny and criticism of shareholders. Thus, for purposes of reciprocity, an additional responsibility of record keeping accrues to the purchasing department.

To explore and exploit the fully possibilities of reciprocity, these primary records or information are supplemented by a knowledge of corporate relationships—affiliated companies, subsidiaries, and interlocking directorates. Each of the companies thus brought under study is subjected to the same two-way analysis as to sales or purchase potentials, or both, and how these may be related either directly or indirectly to reciprocal trade opportunities.

Personal purchases

One other question that should be decided by established policy is the matter of making personal purchases for employees through the facilities of the purchasing department and with the advantages of the company's purchasing power. Sometimes these requests are predicated merely on the convenience of utilizing an established buying facility familiar with sources of supply and having contacts with suppliers that are not ordinarily available to the individual buyer. More frequently, they are prompted by the desire to make personal purchases at wholesale prices. Sometimes the practice is actively sanctioned as a fringe benefit in the company's employee relations policy.

Against the possible employee relations benefits, there are a number of important disadvantages to be considered:

1. Ethically, it is open to question whether any purchasing department is justified in extending to individuals trade discounts that are based on an industrial-use classification.

2. Economically, the practice tends to undermine a supplier's distribution system.

3. Most suppliers resent the practice, even though they may grudgingly comply as a courtesy to a valued industrial customer. Thus, it is inimical to the maintenance of good vendor relations. (The exception, of course, is distributing houses that are specifically organized to sell to employee groups under a variety of plans involving the company purchasing department as a clearing house for orders and credit.)

4. The small-order problem is magnified to the point where a purchasing department may find itself spending a disproportionate part of its time and effort on a lot of miscellaneous personal purchases to the neglect and detriment of the company purchasing program which is its primary function and responsibility.

5. If a nominal service charge is added to cover the direct costs of making and accounting for personal purchases, much of the psychological value of the service is lost. Furthermore, if the purchase is in any way disappointing, the employee's resentment is directed upon the company purchasing department, and employee relations are actually impaired.

On the other hand, there are some circumstances and some items for which it is entirely legitimate, and even essential, for the purchasing department to do the buying even though the items are ultimately paid for by the individual and become his personal property. The usual criterion is that such items are used in the worker's employment or are prescribed by the company. Included in these categories are uniforms, certain types of work clothing, safety equipment, and small tools used by pattern and die makers.

For example, the company sets safety standards. If these are to be effective, they may entail the use of specified types of safety shoes, or of prescription goggles, and the quality of such equipment must be kept up to standard. The only positive means of control is to procure such items through the purchasing department and furnish them to the workers at cost. The company has an ethical responsibility to the worker to keep cost at a minimum, because the purchases are made in conformance with a company regulation and requirement. Negotiation for such purchases by the purchasing agent on the basis of the total quantity and using the company's status as an industrial buyer usually results in a substantial saving. Either the items may be purchased outright by the company and issued from stock with a corresponding charge against the employee, or a blanket contract may be negotiated with specified suppliers who become the official outfitters for those items. In the latter case, the worker may be given a card or order signed by the purchasing agent, entitling him to buy the specified equipment at contract price, or purchases may be charged to the company, which is later reimbursed through some form of payroll deduction.

Policy manuals

At the beginning of this chapter, emphasis was placed on putting policies into written form. For policies that affect only the internal activities of the purchasing department, this may be in the form of standard-practice instructions. When policies affect activities outside the department, as in the case of interdepartmental relations and vendor relations, a more formal statement is desirable for purposes both of record and of communication. The most comprehensive and effective means of presentation is a purchasing department policy manual. The very act of compiling such a manual and committing it to writing is a useful project in itself, because it frequently clarifies ambiguities and points of issue; it may also reveal discrepancies or shortcomings in current policy, thus serving to improve departmental standards.

Because departmental policy reflects and is a part of general company policy, the manual must be approved by management authority. To secure that approval, the stated policies must be developed and agreed upon in consultation with those in charge of other phases of company operations who are affected by the rulings. Arrival at this stage of agreement is the most important part of the compilation of a policy statement and is essential to the workability and effectiveness of the policy. These consultations are on the plane of the best interests of the company as a whole, and they involve the whole management philosophy of centralized purchasing. They may call for a high degree of salesmanship on the part of the purchasing officer in presenting his views on points at issue, as well as the art of compromise and adaptability to meet particular conditions.

The process of arriving at a satisfactory agreement, or compromise, on purchasing policy may take months and represent several successive revisions. During this period, the purchasing executive has the opportunity not only of persuading, but of demonstrating his points and earning their acceptance by other department heads. In the last analysis, it is the responsibility of top management to reconcile any differences of opinion and conflicts of authority, and to make the final policy decisions.

The scope of the policy manual depends largely on the distribution that is contemplated and the ways in which it is to be used. Some companies have found it advantageous to supply copies to their entire list of vendors, and it has proved to be a potent means of developing good business relationships and cooperation. One representative manual designed for such widespread distribution consists of the following sections:

I. Foreword by the company president, giving authority to the manual as a statement of company policy.

II. Objectives of the purchasing department.

III. Scope and responsibilities of the purchasing department.

IV. Organization charts, showing the position of the purchasing department in the complete company organization and the detailed setup of the department itself.

V. Limitations (requirements of authorization to purchase; final determination of quality reserved to manufacturing and sales departments; certain classifications of purchases exempted, for example, food, insurance, rentals, advertising art and media, style and design sketches).

VI. Policies of selecting sources of supply (dealing only with reliable vendors, requirements of competitive bids, criteria used in evaluating sources, reciprocity).

VII. Policies on making commitments, placing purchase orders and contracts (all negotiations to be conducted and concluded by the purchasing department; no commitments to be made as to preference for products or sources by anyone outside the purchasing department; no commitments to be valid except as authorized by the purchasing department; conditions for acceptance of vendors' own sales contract forms).

VIII. Policies on vendor contacts (prompt reception of business callers; opportunity for complete sales presentation on initial call; arrangements for interviews with other departments to be made through purchasing; all correspondence, requests for catalogs and samples, and so on, to be cleared through the purchasing department; acceptance, trial, and report on free samples; price quotations held confidential; gifts and excessive entertainment forbidden; handling of complaints and adjustments).

IX. Relations of purchasing with other divisions and departments (reference to VI and VII above; buyers to be alert in passing on to interested personnel in other departments all potentially useful information gained through sales contacts; purchasing department authorized to ask reconsideration of specifications or quantities, in the best interests of the company; purchasing department to consult with traffic, legal, tax, insurance, and credit departments on all pertinent problems; purchasing records to be available to the controller, treasurer, president, or any auditor delegated by them).

X. Policy on centralized verses decentralized buying (Director of Purchases has authority to allocate responsibility for specific purchases or types of purchases in the best interests of the company; criteria used).

XI. Policy on buying for employees (limited to tools used in company activities that are customarily supplied at employee's expense).

The statements of policy are supported by an explanation of the principles upon which they are based, and of the objectives toward which they are aimed.

In addressing the manual to other departments and to suppliers, it becomes more effective when such reasons are briefly given as a background for the policies stated, which seem less arbitrary when thus presented.

For intradepartmental use, in training work, for indoctrination, and as an administrative guide, this is equally valid. Instructions are better received and better observed when the "why," as well as the "what" and "how," is included. Representative short-form manuals customarily include sections on customer and interdepartmental relationships, ethical considerations, and the like, emphasizing teamwork and cooperation in practical terms. Some of the more extensive manuals contain chapters discussing the principles of proper quality, quantity, price, and value, with applicable criteria, the use of specifications, and the fundamentals of purchase law, contracts, and patent rights. Some of them go so far as to instruct the staff in the principles of acceptable business letter writing and reports, with "right and wrong" examples and a list of phrases to be avoided.

This type of material is distinctly of a training nature and clearly indicates one of the purposes for which such a manual is intended. It is of particular value in the smaller organization where formal training courses are not practicable. In the larger companies, where training may be highly developed, the manual may well become the textbook for a basic training program and for later use as reference or refresher material.

Of particular importance in any policy manual is the statement from top management that establishes departmental policy as company policy and thus gives the entire code an authority which would otherwise be lacking. Quoting from the president's foreword in one effective manual that has been widely distributed:

> This manual states the Company policies on which our purchasing practice and procedures are based. The Purchasing Division administers these policies as a separate division on the same management level as the other major business functions of Finance, Manufacturing, Sales, and so on.
>
> This manual is for the guidance of the Purchasing Division and the information of other divisions, as well as our suppliers. These policies have been reviewed by all Division Heads, and the Plant Managers and I have approved them. . . . I recommend careful study of this manual by all concerned.
>
> These purchasing policies and principles are in furtherance of the basic objectives of the company.[1]

---

[1] *Purchasing Policies and Principles of Bigelow-Sanford Carpet Company, Inc.* Revision dated July 1, 1950.

21

ETHICS OF PURCHASING

ALTHOUGH PURCHASING has developed the methods of a science, its decisions remain largely a matter of personal judgment, and it is necessarily carried on, to a great extent, through personal contacts and relationships. The purchasing agent is the custodian of company funds, responsible for their conservation and wise expenditure. Moreover, through his contacts and dealings with vendors, he is a custodian of the company's reputation for courtesy and fair dealing. The ultimate act of selecting a vendor and awarding the order is essentially a matter of patronage. For all these reasons, a high ethical standard of conduct is essential. The purchasing agent not only must act ethically, but he should be above the suspicion of unethical behavior. Just as standard principles and patterns of procedure have evolved in the development of this function, so a code of conduct has also been formulated. The best statement of this code is embodied in the "Principles and Standards of Purchasing Practice" advocated by the National Association of Purchasing Agents:

1. To consider, first, the interests of his company in all transactions and to carry out and believe in its established policies.
2. To be receptive to competent counsel from his colleagues and to be guided by such counsel without impairing the dignity and responsibility of his office.
3. To buy without prejudice, seeking to obtain the maximum ultimate value for each dollar of expenditure.
4. To strive consistently for knowledge of the materials and processes of manufacture and to establish practical methods for the conduct of his office.
5. To subscribe to and work for honesty and truth in buying and selling and to denounce all forms and manifestations of commercial bribery.
6. To accord a prompt and courteous reception, so far as conditions will permit, to all who call on a legitimate business mission.
7. To respect his obligations and to require that obligations to him and to his concern be respected, consistent with good business practice.

8. To avoid sharp practice.
9. To counsel and assist fellow purchasing agents in the performance of their duties, whenever occasion permits.
10. To cooperate with all organizations and individuals engaged in activities designed to enhance the development and standing of purchasing.

Ethical obligations

The above code is necessarily of a general nature and requires some further elaboration or interpretation as to its application to specific circumstances. As a generalization, it is an exceedingly practical code, like a great deal of our folk wisdom on the theme that "Honesty is the best policy." Hard-headed business moralizing is not predicated on the principle that virtue is its own reward, but recognizes much more tangible dividends. It is certainly true in purchasing that courtesy and fair dealing begets confidence and cooperation on the part of the supplier—assets that frequently spell the difference between a merely adequate purchasing performance and a major contribution to operating efficiency and sound profits, and without which ordinary purchasing problems can readily become serious supply emergencies, particularly in times of economic change or stress. There are opportunists and "sharpshooters" in purchasing as in every other field, but they are rarely successful over any extended period of time. Any going concern that expects to be in business a year or ten years hence will do well to insist upon and to support high ethical standards in its procurement policies and practices.

Obligations to the company

The purchasing agent's obligations to his own company, covered by the first four points of the code, and in part by the seventh, essentially consist of the responsibility for doing a complete and conscientious job in the function to which he has been assigned. Such terms as "the interests of his company" and "maximum ultimate value" are basic and self-explanatory; they summarize, in effect, the objectives of this entire study and discussion of the procurement function. "Knowledge of materials" and "practical methods for the conduct of his office" are the means of implementing these aims.

The code wisely goes beyond this, however, in emphasizing the obligation to buy without prejudice, which implies the obligation to maintain an open mind on purchasing matters. Prejudice is usually interpreted in terms of its manifestation, as discrimination against particular suppliers, their representatives, or their product, usually on personal or irrelevant grounds. Basically, however, prejudice concerns an attitude of mind on the purchasing agent's part that has implications far beyond this relatively simple and elementary example. Prejudice is not altogether a negative concept. A good part of all sales effort consists of the attempt to prejudice a buyer in favor of a product or supplier. There is nothing remotely unethical about this. Often it succeeds only too well. There are probably more orders placed because of the inertia that comes from habit, reinforced by relatively trouble-free experience with an established source of supply, than are withheld because of annoyance with a salesman's mannerisms or dislike for his taste in neckties.

Freedom from prejudice implies a thoroughly objective approach to the purchasing problem. It means that propositions are not to be prejudged, or decisions predetermined, because the purchasing agent has closed his mind to facts and considerations that might modify or change previously held opinions. It means that irrelevant and superficial details, including personalities, should not be permitted to influence the just evaluation of a product or source in the light of its value to the company. It means that prejudices on the part of technical or operating personnel are to be combated just as consistently as those of vendors, with the same objective of maximum ultimate value.

The open mind, receptive to new ideas and capable of clear and objective judgment, is one of the outstanding characteristics of the successful buyer. Frequently it represents the difference between a merely competent job of buying and truly constructive and profitable procurement. Its ethical force is that it accomplishes in practical terms of daily conduct what ponderous legislation has attempted with but indifferent success to establish in law—equality of business opportunity, based on merit.

The purchasing agent has an ethical responsibility to his company not to place himself under special obligation to any supplier by the acceptance of excessive entertainment or by permitting salesmen consistently to buy his lunches, even though this may be done in the spirit of ordinary business courtesy and with the truthful and persuasive argument that it is a legitimate use of the salesman's expense account. It is highly desirable that such relationships be kept upon a thoroughly equitable basis, with the purchasing agent contributing his full share of the expense over a period of time. For this reason, progressive companies recognize the legitimacy and desirability of a purchasing expense account, thus helping to avoid the abuses of a common, pleasant, and generally desirable business custom and encouraging friendly and informal contacts.

The problem of Christmas gifts

A special case arises in connection with the subject of Christmas remembrances. It is a farily common business practice for a company to distribute some sort of gift to its customers at the Christmas season, and frequently, through the natural sales contact, this may be addressed to some member of the purchasing staff. In the great majority of cases, this practice has no ulterior motive; it is general in its application, a genuine expression of appreciation and good will, and often prompted by personal friendship that has developed naturally in the course of mutual dealings and relationships over a period of time. But because of the possible implication of commercial bribery, and on the grounds that such extra "sales expense" must eventually be reflected in some small way in the cost of goods sold and purchased, many purchasing departments have established a definite policy and regulation against the acceptance of such favors. Some weeks before the holiday season, vendors are apprised or reminded of this policy by means of a printed card or form letter, and any gifts which are received contrary to this policy are returned with an explanation. Items of small value or distinctly of an advertising nature may be exceptions to such a rule, but there is danger in the haphazard interpretation that "two cigars are acceptable, but a box of cigars must be returned."

There are many cases where the meticulous observation of such a rule may verge on the ridiculous, but it is one of the penalties of this particular function that the standards cannot be relaxed. There is a further point in this regard, in that the practice extends down the line to persons in subordinate purchasing positions, where the possibilities of insidious effect are greater. A department head, concerned with prestige and efficiency and freedom of choice in the buying operation, will avoid placing himself or his department under any obligation to a supplier, as a matter of ordinary good business sense, but buyers farther down the line in the organization scale may not be so strongly motivated by such considerations and may be in an economic position where favors of this nature seem more attractive. Therefore, the over-all policy is in the best interests of the company. It may be pertinent here to call attention to the tremendous responsibility of even a junior buyer in the allocation and disbursement of large sums in the form of purchase orders, and to suggest that a most effective incentive or implementation of high ethical standards is a salary scale commensurate with that responsibility.

Finally, as was suggested in the introduction to this chapter, the purchasing agent has an ethical responsibility to his company to see that the company not only deserves, but actually enjoys in the trade, a reputation for scrupulously fair dealing. As the point of contact in dealing with vendors, he holds the company's reputation in this respect largely in his own hands. He may be very sure that his actions and conduct are critically judged and that this judgment, for better or worse, is quickly and widely disseminated among the sales fraternity at large. Frequently these impressions are based on incomplete knowledge or understanding of the facts, as seen from the outside, and they may be colored by disappointment and pique on the part of individuals. But whether or not the criticism is justified, the purchasing agent cannot afford to ignore it. He cannot rest with satisfying his own conscience as to the conduct of the purchasing office; he must use every reasonable effort to make it clear to all that courtesy and integrity are fundamental and spontaneous in the purchasing policy, even if doing so means "leaning over backward" in extending courtesy and observing technicalities so as to avoid any possible misunderstanding.

Vendor relations

The latter point naturally revolves chiefly around personal relationships with vendors and their representatives. Interviews with salesmen are among the most important of these contacts in establishing or losing a favorable reputation. The purchasing agent is under no moral obligation to see every salesman, putting his time absolutely and indiscriminately at the disposal of any and all comers, however frequently or at whatever time or on whatever mission they may be calling. To do so would effectively destroy the possibility of organizing his work schedule efficiently and of accomplishing the work of his office, in which sales interviews are but one of many activities. To accept this statement is not contradictory to the policy of receptiveness and open-mindedness stressed in the preceding section. Some matters are patently not appropriate to the company's needs, or are not timely for consideration at the particular moment that the salesman elects to present or press them. Some salesmen are inconsiderate in making frequent calls with nothing new to contribute regarding their product and its application to the buyer's needs. The purchasing agent, and not the salesman, is the proper judge of when the calls become too frequent, but this does not relieve the buyer of his obligation of courtesy—a prompt acknowledgement of the call and a reason for not granting an interview. Every salesman should be seen on his first call and be given an opportunity to tell his story; subsequent policy will depend on the particular circumstances. There is no justification for keeping any caller waiting for a protracted period if the interview is to be denied. And in any event, waiting time should be kept at a minimum.

Accomplishing this may be primarily a matter of organizing the reception procedure. Callers should be announced to the buyer on arrival. If there is an immediate answer, it can be given at that time. If there is to be any appreciable delay before the interview can be granted, for any reason, the salesman should be apprised of the approximate waiting time that will be necessary, so that he can utilize that time to other advantage if he wishes, making a definite future appointment. If the waiting time exceeds the estimate, the receptionist should make it a point to remind the buyer and give an explanation to the caller. All this may appear to be a matter of etiquette rather than of ethics, but it does involve a basic policy of conserving time, which is an important factor in the salesman's stock in trade, his means of productive effort and earning a livelihood.

Similar courtesy should prompt the purchasing agent to inform unsuccessful bidders when a proposition has been closed, as well as to inform the one who receives the order. Small companies, particularly, cannot afford to have a number of proposals outstanding, which would overtax their capacity should all bids be successful. They should therefore be relieved of these tentative commitments of capacity promptly. Furthermore, if the notification indicates in what respect the proposal fell short of the buyer's requirements, it will help the vendor in future negotiations and may lead to the development of a useful source of supply for the buyer. At the same time, it will temper the disappointment of an unsuccessful bidder to know that there was a real reason for the adverse decision.

When a sample is accepted for test, it entails an obligation on the buyer's part to make a fair trial, and it is a courteous gesture to inform the vendor of the outcome of that test, at least in general terms. Some buyers find it easy to terminate an interview by accepting a sample, even if they have no serious intention of giving it a trial. Such practice verges on misrepresentation and in the long run undermines the confidence that is essential to sound business relationships. It is avoided in many companies by a policy requiring that all sample lots for trial be bought and paid for by the buyer's company. This procedure works both ways: it incurs no obligation to the vendor, express or implied, beyond the transaction itself, and it gives the company a definite interest in completing the trial and making a fair evaluation of the product or material thus acquired.

Well-considered policies of this nature build confidence and respect and strengthen the personal relationships between buyer and vendor.

Obligations to vendors

In the large sense of obligations incurred in the course of doing business, the law is rather explicit, but there are many cases of interpretation and procedure that involve ethical concepts of this relationship, beyond the strict letter of the law. For example, if business is to be awarded on the basis of bids, the buyer should insist on receiving firm bids within a stated time. If he permits or encourages revisions, particularly at the last moment, he opens the way for sharp dealing on the part of vendors and is not free from suspicion of the same fault on his own side. If revisions are to be permitted, the same opportunity should be frankly offered to all bidders, and, if the specifications are changed because of an alternative product offered by one of the bidders, all should be invited to bid on the new specification.

The purchasing agent is not responsible for a vendor's error in calculating a bid. But if one of the proposals seems excessively low, indicating that an error may be responsible for the discrepancy, it is good practice to ask for a recalculation. If it happens that some item has been omitted from the estimate, or that a mathematical error has been made, the purchasing agent is not in the position of taking advantage of such an inadvertent slip to the detriment of the seller. On the other hand, it frequently happens that such a recalculation results in an even lower bid, although this possibility may have been far from the buyer's mind. Naturally, if the bid is accompanied by a detailed breakdown of costs, and the error is patent, it would be unethical to hold the vendor to such a proposal, which obviously does not represent his real intention.

Once an order or contract has been placed on the basis of a legitimate bid, the buyer is not responsible for assuring the bidder a profit on the transaction. Sellers occasionally appeal for relief from a contract which turns out contrary to their expectations, but the buyer is under no obligation to surrender or modify his own contractual rights if the agreement has been made in good faith. There is an ethical responsibility to his own company and to competitive bidders in cases of this sort. If an adjustment can be made, or an alternative source found, without sacrifice of the buyer's position, it may be the part of wisdom to take such action on the grounds that service and satisfaction will be greater under the new arrangement. But the whole purpose of the contractual agreement is to provide for carrying out the transaction as planned, with a definite allocation of responsibility to both parties, including the risk of unforeseen developments. As a general rule, sellers respect the buyer who stands firmly on his rights, and prefer to do business on this basis, having the corresponding assurance that he will observe his responsibilities under the contract just as conscientiously.

Confidential information

The buyer is under no ethical compulsion to answer questions other than those that relate directly to the proposal. Competitive price information is regarded as confidential and should not be disclosed under any circumstances. And although it is generally true that full and frank discussion leads to a better mutual understanding and perhaps to a better purchase, there are circumstances where factors other than price are also of a confidential nature.

For example, some sellers decline to bid unless they know the use to which their product is to be put. They argue that unsatisfactory performance on a job for which the product was never intended might react unfavorably and unfairly against the reputation of the product and the producer, and they prefer to forego a sale rather than risk this unjustified demerit. They point out, quite logically, that with a knowledge of what is to be required, they can recommend or prescribe the best materials for the purpose. But sometimes, also, they have a sliding price scale according to the application of identical material, a marketing practice that can be plausibly explained on the basis of special concessions to capture new markets or applications, but for which the logic of purchasing value is somewhat more obscure when one ingot or roll is exactly the same as the other.

However, we are here concerned with buying reasons and policy. Although trade secrets are much less a factor in industry today than they were a generation ago, there are still a number of things that a company may wish to keep strictly "within the family"—little kinks of manufacture that make for the individuality of their product, or short cuts that give them a slight advantage in competitive costs. All buyers are well aware that suppliers rarely know the full extent of the uses that their product serves. They have no desire to broadcast the direction of their experimental program or to have the vendor's salesmen scurry around to their competitors with the "new idea." The buyer who is reticent about the proposed uses of the things he purchases need not be concerned over the implication that his reticence is unethical. On the other hand, he must recognize that under such circumstances he waives the benefit of any implied warranty on the seller's part and has no basis for later expressing dissatisfaction or pressing a claim for unsuitability in his purchase. The seller who is not informed as to the intended use is bound only to the extent of conformance with any specifications that may be set forth in the order.

Engineering services

One question of ethics that is frequently raised is the proprietary interest of a supplier in business that he has originally earned through valuable and expensive preliminary development and engineering services to evolve a design or formula or product best adapted to the buyer's need. Is the buyer justified in sending out blueprints of such designs, product samples, or formula specifications for competitive bids, or does the supplier who originated them have a continuing claim upon the business? It is obvious that the seller must recoup these expenses, and is legitimately entitled to do so. In the typical case, the service is not of a sort that can be protected by a basic or design patent. It is not a cost that he can pass along as a special charge, for he is not in the business of consulting engineering except as a means of making sales for his production facilities. It is a cost that will normally be reflected in his quotation, preferably spread over a reasonable manufacturing quantity, lest the original lot cost be excessively high for the buyer's purpose. Consequently, the distribution and absorption of this cost item frequently contemplate repeat orders to justify the quoted price, and the price is calculated in the expectation or hope of continuing business.

However thoroughly the buyer may recognize the implications of such a position and sympathize with the claims of the seller, the prospect of accepting and maintaining a monopolistic supply situation is contrary to the principles of good purchasing, and he cannot conscientiously accede to this solution. There will probably always be controversy as to the fairness of any compromise, but the logical answer, and the one in most common usage, is usually worked out in the form of a liberal term contract, with the vendor originating the design or product, covering requirements for a year, or more or less, depending on the quantities involved, during which time the vendor is expected to recoup his experimental and development costs in addition to normal production profits. At the end of this period, the business is opened to more general competition, and it is expected that cost to the buyer will be reduced, for he cannot reasonably be expected to accept these development costs as a permanent factor of price. The original supplier, having already profited from his superior skill and from being a step ahead of the field, is still in a preferred position and has a substantial competitive advantage in a year's manufacturing experience as well as, perhaps, in patterns, dies, and tooling, which have been totally depreciated as a cost factor. Except in some very unusual cases, such an arrangement satisfies the buyer's ethical obligation to the vendor.

Sharp practice

The term "sharp practice," as condemned in the buyer's code, is best defined by some typical illustrations of evasion and indirect misrepresentation just short of actual fraud. They belong to the old school of unscrupulous shrewdness, when buying was concerned with the immediate transaction rather than the long-range program. These examples would have been commonplace among an older generation of buyers, and sellers in that period were habitually on their guard against such possibilities. In modern procurement and marketing, which are based on mutual confidence and integrity, such practices are frowned upon just as severely by the buyers themselves as by the sales organizations with which they deal.

It is sharp practice for a buyer to talk in terms of large quantities, encouraging the seller to expect a large volume of business and to quote on a quantity basis, when in fact the actual requirement and order are to be in relatively small volume that would not legitimately earn the quantity consideration.

It is sharp practice to call for a large number of bids merely in the hope that some supplier will make an error in his estimate, of which the buyer can take advantage.

It is sharp practice to invite bids from suppliers whom the buyer will not patronize in any case, using these quotations only for the purpose of playing them against the proposals of those who are really acceptable sources of supply. It costs money, time, and effort to prepare estimates and bids. Sellers are glad to undertake the expense in the hope of securing a contract, but the buyer has no right to impose these costs on a seller when he has no intention of giving the seller an opportunity to get the business.

It is sharp practice to misrepresent a market by placing the price of job lots, seconds, or other distress merchandise in ostensible competition with real market prices.

It is sharp practice to leave copies of competitors' bids or other confidential correspondence in open view on the desk while negotiating with a seller, in the knowledge that the latter can scarcely fail to notice them.

It is sharp practice to deal only with "hungry" suppliers and to try and keep them hungry so as to force concessions. More generally stated, this applies to any abuse of purchasing power to the detriment of the seller. Although it is legitimately expected of a purchasing agent to make full use of his company's purchasing power, this factor should normally operate to mutual benefit, with the buyer's position strengthened by virtue of being a more desirable customer, offering greater volume, steadier flow of orders, more prompt payment, or similar considerations of value to the seller.

Combating unethical practices

The subject of business ethics is not one-sided. Purchasing men are faced from time to time with unethical sales practices, although these are no more representative of selling policy in general than are the occasional instances of unethical buying. There is sharp practice in selling: collusive bidding, restrictive conditions in specifications, artificial stimulation of demand and prejudice among shop operatives, sabotage of competitive products, padding of orders and shipments, the use of unfamiliar trade terms and metric measurements, supposedly sample orders that are magnified into excessive quantities, obscure contract clauses buried in small type, and many others. In most cases these can be avoided by proper selection of vendors, but perhaps only after unfortunate experience has indicated the disreputable sources of supply. In dealing with some of the practices, such as collusive bidding, more direct and aggressive action is called for as a corrective measure.

The best defense is competent, objective buying, supported by the necessary follow-through in insistence on contract performance, acceptance testing, and the like. The purchase order or contract in itself constitutes a legally enforceable document. All supplementary agreements, specifications, and special terms should likewise be reduced to writing, using care to see that no ambiguity exists in respect to what is expected of the seller. Reputable sellers respect the buyer who is alert, thorough, and conscientious in the conduct of his office, and they respond in kind.

Confidence in a supplier is an essential of any sound purchasing department, but confidence need not be blind. It must be earned, and the reputable supplier welcomes the opportunity to show that he is worthy of confidence. The purchasing agent is grossly neglectful of his own responsibility who unquestioningly accepts the oft-heard advice: "Select a reliable vendor, then trust him to supply the right material and to charge a fair price." The classic admonition, *"Caveat emptor—*Let the buyer beware!" was coined for him. No honest buyer apologizes for checking a delivery, making an acceptance test, or analyzing a quotation. These precautions are a test of his own judgment and performance as well as of his supplier, and the responsibility cannot be delegated.

22

LEGAL ASPECTS OF PURCHASING

THE CONTRACTUAL RELATIONSHIP between a purchaser and a seller is a legal relationship. The commitments made by the buyer are legally binding upon his company. The purchase orders issued or contracts signed are legal documents. Many governmental regulations—both those of a permanent nature, directed primarily to labor conditions in the production of goods or to insuring fair competition, and those of a temporary emergency nature governing the price and distribution of goods—have a direct bearing on purchasing practice. It is not enough that a purchase be economically sound; it must be legally sound as well, both in the act or agreement itself and in the way it is carried out.

Law is a highly technical and complicated subject; its application and interpretation are a matter for those professionally trained in its practice. The old adage that the layman who tries to be his own lawyer has a fool for a client is nowhere more true than in respect to business transactions and contracts. A primary rule for every purchasing man is to consult competent legal counsel on any doubtful or controversial points, in the analysis of unusual or obscure terms in sellers' contract forms, and in the phraseology of the clauses and conditions that are to be incorporated in purchase agreements. If the company has an established legal department, or retains legal counsel for advice on its corporate affairs, the purchasing department should avail itself of these facilities to whatever extent may be necessary. On the other hand, there are certain basic principles of business law applicable to all the common conditions of doing business, and the purchasing man should be familiar with these as general guides to the conduct of his office. The objective in all cases should be to avoid misunderstandings and controversy, and particularly to avoid litigation. If litigation should arise, however, the probability of getting a favorable court decision will be greatly enhanced if the purchasing agent is reasonably familiar with the legal principles involved in a contract and has consistently applied these principles in the exercise of his responsibility.

This chapter is not intended as a complete legalistic treatise. Rather, it sets forth the more important legal principles applicable to purchase transactions, as interpreted in recent cases, to serve both as a guide and as a warning against the more common pitfalls.

Law of agency

Contracts of purchase and sale in industrial practice are intended to be binding on the principals (the respective companies involved), but they are negotiated and signed by employees or agents of the companies. One of the first points to be considered, therefore, is the relationship of principal and agent, and the authority of an agent to act for his principal.

The purchasing agent, as indicated by his title, is an agent authorized to make valid contracts of purchase for his company, and to obligate his company thereby. A seller has the right to rely on the validity of an agreement when the title "purchasing agent" is used. In general, the status of agency is established by direct authorization of the employer, empowering the employee to perform certain functions, as in this case. The customary approval of the employer for the performance of similar functions in the past is also construed to constitute the agency relationship, and the performance of any act or series of acts by the employer, which would lead a reasonably experienced seller to believe that such authority existed, either expressed or implied, would be accepted by a court as evidence of agency.

The purchasing agent is particularly interested in knowing that the salesmen with whom he deals are also authorized agents. The principles outlined in the preceding paragraph apply with equal force to this question, but there is a further consideration as to the extent of a salesman's authority as the agent of his company. He is presumably authorized to solicit orders, but in most cases these orders do not become binding until specifically accepted at the main offices of the company. Likewise, his authority as agent may be limited in respect to modifying price schedules or contract terms or making binding promises regarding time of delivery. This is especially important in respect to verbal promises and modifications that are not included in the written order or contract accepted by the salesman's principal. No legal reliance may be placed upon such representations, for ordinarily the purchaser's contentions, even when sustained by evidence that the salesman did make such promises, will not stand up in a court of law because the salesman lacked authority to so bind his company. On the other hand, there have been decisions in favor of the purchaser when such promises or modifications of terms were agreed to by a sales manager, even though the latter's employer refused to approve the contract, because a sales manager is assumed to have broad authority to make terms of sale binding upon his employer.

Brokers are recognized as having the status of an agent when the companies involved customarily do business through such channels. However, contracts made with companies whose business is to act as "selling agents" are usually not enforceable against the principals who are the selling agents' suppliers.

What is a contract?

The definition of agency has a direct bearing on the validity of purchase agreements, for an enforceable contract requires both an offer and an acceptance, in identical terms. A formal contract of purchase is signed by authorized agents of both the buyer and the seller. Unless a purchase order is issued in acceptance of a specific bid or offer by a vendor, it is not a contract; it is an offer, and becomes a contract only when it is accepted by the seller. This is the reason for "acknowledgement copies" of purchase orders, sent with the original order, to be signed and returned by the vendor. Such copies should be identical, including the same clauses as the original, and any modifications thereof should be indicated on both copies. The term "acknowledgement" is not a particularly happy one, though in common use, for a vendor may acknowledge receipt of an order, or offer, without legally accepting it. It is better practice to phrase the acknowledgement as "We acknowledge *and accept* this order." Nevertheless, if a shipping promise is included, as requested on most acknowledgement forms, legal acceptance is implied. Also, in the absence of a formal acceptance, shipment of any part of the order by the vendor implies acceptance of the whole.

It has been held in various courts that a signed order given to an ordinary traveling salesman is not an enforceable contract until his employer sends his acceptance of the order, because the salesman's implied authority is merely to solicit orders and submit them to his employer for acceptance. Consequently, either the buyer or the seller may rescind or cancel an order given to a salesman if such cancellation is made prior to acceptance of the order.

If acknowledgement is made by the vendor on his own form, differing in any respect from the buyer's purchase order, or by letter noting any variation from the terms of the original order, this constitutes, not an acceptance, but a counteroffer that must be accepted by the buyer to make a valid contract. Subsequent correspondence relating to the order and indicating mutual agreement on points not in the written agreement itself is construed to be a part of the agreement in law. Deviation from printed terms can be indicated on order or contract forms. When this occurs, typewritten matter has precedence over the printed terms, and handwritten matter has precedence over both, on the principle that these revisions represent the latest intention and agreement of the contracting parties.

The second requirement of a valid contract is that it impose an obligation on both parties. A one-way or unilateral agreement, by which one party is bound to do something without a corresponding consideration or obligation on the part of the other party, is not enforceable. In an ordinary contract of purchase or sale, the seller agrees to sell and deliver *and the buyer agrees to purchase* certain goods or services on certain terms and conditions. Default by either party then becomes a cause for litigation and damages.

The obligation should be a specific one. If quantity requirements are not definitely known, the best approximate estimate should be noted as such; contracts calling for "all our requirements" of a given item for a specific purpose or over a specified period of time have been held valid inasmuch as the total requirements for a purpose or period can be determined eventually (with the completion of the contract or contract period) even if they are not exactly predictable in advance. Because of the ambiguities in such an arrangement, some "requirements" contracts are qualified by stating a minimum quantity that shall be bought and a maximum quantity for which delivery can be demanded.

However, an indefinite contract for future delivery of merchandise may be void (1) when there is no obligation on the buyer's part, (2) when the demand in question is purely hypothetical, or (3) when the quantity to be delivered is conditioned solely by the will of one of the contracting parties. Such a contract is invalid for want of consideration and mutuality.

The buyer's obligation under a contract is also measured by the quantity specified on the order. A court action involving this point of law brought out the following facts.[1] The buyer in this instance, a building contractor, ordered a specified quantity of roofing tile to be specially manufactured, the order amounting to $2,526, for completing certain of his projects. The vendor's quotation, on which the order was based, was good for 30 days, but with the stipulation that the order was to be "subject to the approval of our Executive Office at Chicago." The vendor acknowledged the order, saying, "We are passing this to our Executive Department for consideration and attention"; no formal acceptance, however, was issued. Nevertheless, the vendor started manufacturing the tile and made several partial shipments, which were accepted and paid for by the buyer. During the course of the contract, after $1,431.56 worth of tile had been delivered and paid for, it became evident to

---

[1] *Ludowici-Celadon Company* v. *McKinley,* 11 N. W. (2d) 839, reported January, 1944.

the buyer that he had overestimated his requirements, and he refused to accept further shipments, whereupon the vendor filed suit to collect for the full amount of the order. The buyer contended that no valid contract existed because of the vendor's failure to make a formal acceptance of the order, and the lower court ruled in his favor. The case was carried to a higher court, however, and this decision was reversed. In holding the buyer liable for payment, the court cited the principles that the shipment itself indicated acceptance, and that shipment of part of the order is acceptance of the whole. "In the instant case," said the court, "plaintiff [seller] manufactured the tile, delivered a part thereof, and tendered the remainder. Had the seller refused to deliver the remainder, the buyer could have recovered damages for the breach of the contract. It must follow, therefore, that the seller is likewise entitled to recover damages because of the buyer's refusal to accept the remainder of the tile." In other words, the obligation is a mutual one. A reasonable variation from the specified quantity, plus or minus, due to manufacturing conditions, is recognized as coming within the meaning of the contract and satisfying its obligations, but this allowable variation is generally limited to a fixed percentage of the specified amount. Trade customs in the various producing industries are usually clear on this point and are accepted as governing in the legal interpretation of a contract.

As to price, the custom of issuing unpriced purchase orders, as is done in some purchasing departments, is not good practice unless it is clearly understood and specified that shipments are not to be billed at higher prices than those prevailing on the previous order without first notifying the buyer of the change and securing his assent.

Time of delivery is another factor that should be clearly specified, becoming a part of the contract agreement. Acceptance of an order with a specified delivery date or schedule, or acceptance with a definite delivery promise named by the vendor, places on the vendor an obligation to meet this schedule, failing in which he may be held in default. Where this schedule is particularly important to the buyer, so that the value of the goods in his operation will be impaired by failure to receive them as promised, it is customary to call attention to this phase by inserting a clause stating that time is "of the essence" of the agreement, and relieving the buyer of his obligation to accept deliveries that do not come within the specified time.

A third requirement of a valid contract is that it shall not be in conflict with existing federal or local laws and regulations, so that performance of the contract would in itself be an unlawful act. Examples of this would involve agreements embodying discrimination in violation of the Robinson-Patman Act, transportation charges either higher or lower than those established by the proper regulatory commissions, agreements based on production under conditions in violation of wage and hour laws, assumption of tax charges by either party in violation of Revenue Department ruling on tax liabilities, and many others.

A fourth requirement of a valid contract is that no fraud shall be practiced by either the buyer or seller in arriving at the agreement.

Conditional sale contracts

Conditional sale contracts are those relating to merchandise that is purchased under the "condition" that the purchaser agrees to pay for it in accordance with prearranged terms. The characteristic feature of such contracts is that the seller retains title to the merchandise until payment is completed, although the term is also applied to transactions in which the purchaser takes legal title but assumes an obligation toward the seller in the form of a chattel mortgage. Conditional sale contracts and chattel mortgages are valid in all states of the United States if they are recorded according to the laws of the state where the merchandise or property is situated. They are also valid and enforceable with respect to all persons who know of the existence of such an agreement, whether it is recorded or not. This is true because the legal object of recording such instruments is to give constructive notice to all persons that another holds a first and valid lien on the merchandise or property specified. In industrial purchasing, such transactions generally concern industrial equipment.

Conditional contracts of sale are designed to protect the interests of the seller. This protection can be defined by specific clauses in the agreement as to the use and disposition of the equipment, which may forbid its sale or the assignment of the contract. But the buyer is also protected to the extent that the contract cannot be rescinded and the merchandise repossessed merely because the seller becomes dissatisfied with the arrangement, but only in the event that the contract is breached, which circumstance would usually come about through a default on the buyer's part in meeting the due payments.

Under ordinary circumstances, it is not necessary for the vendor to give notice to the purchaser of his intention to invoke his privileges of repossession in the event of default in payments. But if a precedent has been established by the vendor in accepting delinquent payments or in issuing a notice of his intent to repossess and then subsequently accepting late payments, the courts have construed such a course of action as a forfeiture by the vendor of his right to stand squarely on this feature of his contract, and in such cases the purchaser is entitled to a formal notification of the seller's intention to terminate the contract on a specified date, and is further entitled to the opportunity of making the required payment before that date and keeping the contract in force.

One circumstance that is sometimes encountered and that introduces serious complications into transactions of this nature arises when equipment purchased under conditional contracts is permanently attached to a building in such a way that it becomes a fixture of the building or that it cannot be removed without damage to the premises. Among the decisions on file where this situation has occurred and where mortgages have been given on the building even *after* chattel mortgages have been duly recorded covering the specific pieces of equipment, there are several in which the building mortgage was ruled to have precedence over the chattel mortgage and the vendor was denied his right to repossess and remove the equipment.

Law of warranty

Warranties are of two sorts: express and implied. If, in the absence of express warranties of quality, fitness, or performance of a product given by the seller, the buyer makes known to the seller the particular purposes for which the goods or equipment are required, relying on the seller's judgment and skill, there is an implied warranty that the goods shall be reasonably fit for that purpose. The inclusion of an expressed warranty covering any of these points renders the implied warranty void, because the latter cannot exist when the seller expressly guarantees his merchandise.

Statements made by a salesman are not enforceable as guarantees. Courts have repeatedly recognized the natural tendency of salesmen to "puff" the virtues of their products for the purposes of making a sale, without imputing to such enthusiastic claims the status of a formal guarantee. An employer is not bound by guarantees made by salesmen unless (1) the guarantee is confirmed by the employer or someone in his organization authorized to do so, (2) the employer has notified the purchaser that he will be bound by guarantees made by the salesmen, (3) the employer has in the past, without such notification, accepted responsibility for such guarantees, thereby implying that the salesman has this authority, or (4) the guarantee constitutes actual fraud, in which case the employer is responsible for the action of his employee even though he did not authorize the salesman to make the fraudulent statement or guarantee, either expressly or by implication.

In invoking the warranty clauses of a contract, the purchaser is under obligation to take action as soon as the deficiency of the goods or the breach of warranty is determined. Many claims based on inferior quality of merchandise delivered under a contract have been thrown out of court because of unreasonable delay in ascertaining that such a condition does exist. Many sales contracts, for goods that are capable of inspection on receipt, place a limit on the time within which such claims may be made—usually 30 days—and these limiting clauses have been adjudged valid. There are other types of defects or deficiencies that are not ascertainable until goods have been put into use or until equipment has been installed and started in operation. In such cases, "reasonable" promptness is a matter of interpretation, and the buyer must be in a position to prove his alertness and promptness in discovering the alleged breach of warranty and taking action to recover. Furthermore, the buyer is not entitled to retain merchandise or to continue to use equipment at the same time that he refuses to make payment because of alleged breach of warranty.

The measure of damages for breach of warranty depends upon the circumstances and the nature of the warranty. It may be limited to releasing the buyer from his obligation to pay the purchase price, upon rejecting the merchandise, or it may be the cost of replacing the defective merchandise by purchases from another source. In the case of equipment bought under a specific guarantee of performance, it may include damages based upon lost time and profits for the period during which replacement equipment is being built. This was the case in a litigation[2] involving a lamp manufacturer and an oven manufacturer, on a contract with implied guarantee of performance. The lamp manufacturer explained to the supplier that he required a pass oven that would maintain a uniform temperature, one suitable for use with a certain type of synthetic enamel, which was not a new product but one whose properties were known. An official of the oven manufacturer stated that he knew all about the enamel in question and could make a pass oven that would meet all the requirements. After the equipment was installed, the purchaser found that the oven that had been furnished did not in fact comply with the guarantee and was not adapted for heating the specified enamel efficiently. Countersuits were filed, the seller suing to collect a balance of $903.50 due on the purchase price, which the purchaser refused to pay, and the buyer suing for $5,293, representing lost time and profits over the period while another manufacturer was building a suitable oven. Both suits were decided in favor of the buyer. The court held that an implied guarantee existed because the purpose for which the oven was intended was known to both parties and because the buyer relied on the seller to supply an oven that could be depended on to operate efficiently for this purpose. Because the seller had failed to supply an oven that fulfilled the guarantee, the buyer was entitled to recover full damages resulting from the seller's breach of the implied guarantee.

Sale of merchandise or equipment "as is" cancels and invalidates any implied guarantee as to quality or performance. Higher courts have held that an "as is" clause in a contract is equivalent to a full statement that no guarantee whatever is given by the seller. A leading case involving this point[3] illustrates a number of basic principles in contract law. A scrap metal dealer had pur-

---

[2] *Hover* v. *Colonial-Premier Company,* 45 N. E. (2d) 201, reported January, 1943.
[3] *Johnson* v. *Waisman Bros.,* 36 Atl. (2d) 634, reported May, 1944.

chased an old steam shovel for $25. Soon afterward he made a contract to sell it to a contractor for $225, the written contract containing a clause providing that the shovel was being sold "as is." The purchaser paid $25 down and agreed to pay the balance when he came to get the shovel. The contractor then entered into a contract with a construction company to do certain excavation work. When he came to get the shovel and offered to pay the due balance of $200, the scrap dealer reconsidered his agreement, refusing to accept the money and to turn over the steam shovel. The contractor decided to enter suit, and claimed damages based on the profits he would have earned on the construction job if the scrap dealer had completed the contract and delivered the shovel to him. But the courts refused to hold the dealer liable on the grounds that no guarantee existed to assure that the machinery in question would have enabled him to fulfill his own construction contract. This suit was based upon improper legal grounds. Had the purchaser asked the court to compel the seller to deliver the machine upon payment of the $200 balance due, he could have won his suit, for the seller could have been compelled to fulfill the exact terms of his contract of sale. But the "as is" clause invalidated the implied warranty and enabled the seller to avoid liability either for failure of the machinery to operate with reasonable efficiency or for alleged loss of profits based upon the inefficiency of the machinery. In rendering it verdict, the court said: "The plaintiff [purchaser] was not entitled to assume that the shovel would do the work in question. The seller sold it 'as is' and this term, when contained in a memorandum of purchase and sale, means that the seller sells and the purchaser buys the specific chattel in its then existing physical and mechanical condition and without warranty as to quality or fitness for a particular purpose."

Title to purchased goods

Making a purchase involves a transfer of title to the merchandise from the seller to the buyer. It must be assumed—or ascertained, if any doubt exists—that the seller has a clear title to the goods in the first place. The time and place of the actual transfer of title are important, for ownership entails responsibilities and risks, and this point is the source of frequent legal controversy. Thus, the designation of an f.o.b. (free on board) point has a much more far-reaching effect than indicating whether the seller or the buyer is responsible for paying the transportation charges.

If goods are sold and shipped f.o.b. the seller's location, the purchaser automatically takes legal title to the goods at the moment the shipment is delivered to the carrier. By doing so, he assumes full responsibility for all accidents, contingencies, damage, loss, delays, and the like, occasioned by the carrier. He is responsible for seeing to it that suitable insurance is carried on the goods while in transit and for recovering from the carrier any damages for which the latter may be liable through its negligence or other reason. (It has been ruled contrary to public interest for a shipper to agree to relieve the carrier from liability for loss or destruction of goods through negligence of the carrier, and such contracts have been held invalid.) The buyer or consignee is responsible for payment of the transportation charges to the carrier and for payment for the merchandise to the shipper even though the shipment is lost or destroyed in transit.

In shipping f.o.b. seller's location, the title having passed, the seller cannot regain possession of the goods during transit even though he receives definite information that the buyer is insolvent before the goods have reached their destination. On the other hand, the seller is obliged to exercise ordinary prudence and good judgment in protection of the purchaser. In one leading case[4] a buyer was adjudged to be not liable for payment for a shipment lost in transit, even though the terms of the contract were f.o.b. seller's city, because the seller had used poor judgment in making a nominal declaration of value ($50) to the carrier, when for a few cents additional he could have listed the true value ($500) of the merchandise. Similarly, a seller defaults and assumes liability if he fails to follow the buyer's shipping instructions regarding the route, the carrier, packing equipment, date of shipment, or other reasonable instructions issued by the buyer. This law is applicable irrespective of the usual law pertaining to shipments ordered f.o.b. the seller's location. When the testimony shows that a seller breached any competent clause or element in a valid contract, the buyer is relieved of his responsibilities, including those arising under f.o.b.-shipment rules of law.

If goods are sold and shipped f.o.b. buyer's location, title passes to the buyer at the time when goods are delivered to him by the carrier. Under these circumstances, he does not assume the responsibilities outlined above, but they are for the account of the seller so long as the latter retains title to the merchandise.

One of the important implications of f.o.b. terms concerns the liability for sales and use taxes, and for the determination of whether transactions are in fact interstate or intrastate commerce. Such questions arise, for example, when the contracting offices of both buyer and seller are located within the same state but shipments are made from seller's plants outside the state or purchaser reconsigns purchased materials to his own plants outside the state. Because the tax structures of individual states vary widely, generalizations are likely to be misleading, beyond stating that the mere juggling of f.o.b. terms and freight payments is not a basis for evading tax liability. When such controversies arise,

---

[4] *Semler* v. *Schmicker*, 38 Atl. (2d) 831, reported October, 1944.

the courts endeavor to ascertain the real intentions of the contracting parties and the real nature of the transactions, to determine the taxability of the sale. On the other hand, carelessness in defining the point at which title passes may needlessly incur a tax liability, and obviously the avoidance of such taxation is advantageous when enforcement of taxation laws on a given transaction is in itself illegal. The record of litigations on issues of this sort shows numerous cases in which verdicts were made against such bodies as the United States Treasury Department and the California Tax Board and in which were recovered important sums—in one case amounting to $120,196—that had been improperly assessed as taxes.

Fraud

Legal fraud has been defined as any act, deed, or statement, made by either a buyer or a seller *before* the purchase contract is signed or completed, that is likely to deceive the other party. A seller is not liable for fraud if the evidence proves (1) that the seller or his salesman made a false statement *after* the contract was signed, (2) that the seller or his salesman actually did not know that the quality of the merchandise was not as claimed in the sales contract but merely expressed an opinion that he believed the quality to be as represented, or (3) that the purchaser did not believe or rely upon the statements made by the seller or his agent. If a purchaser inspects merchandise before entering into the contract, he is put upon his guard and is expected by the law to use his own good judgment in respect to the quality and characteristics of the goods; but if a purchaser is not sufficiently experienced to judge the quality of the merchandise he inspects, and relies upon a fraudulent statement made by the seller, the latter is liable.

If a contract agreement is made on the basis of fraudulent acts or statements, the contract is not valid. The buyer is not bound to accept and pay for the goods, and he may rescind the contract when he discovers the fraud at any time later, but he will forfeit these privileges if he fails to act promptly. A delay in claiming fraud, or making a payment after having discovered the fraud, may destroy the basis for rescission and damages.

Law of patents

A United States patent is a monopoly created by law. There are five classifications or bases for patents: mechanical, process, composition, articles of manufacture, and design. The rights of the patentee are summed up as follows: "The patentee has the sole right of making, using, and selling the patented articles, and he may prevent anybody from dealing with them at all. Inasmuch as he has the right to prevent people from using them, or dealing in them at all, he has the right to do the lesser thing, that is to say, to impose his own conditions. It does not matter how unreasonable or how absurd the conditions are." [5]

A patent can be extended by improvements on the original device, but after the expiration of a patent (and an expired patent cannot be renewed) the patentee loses all of his former rights in the patent. Then anyone can make, sell, purchase, or use the invention without any chance of liability. A patentee may obtain another, new patent on some improvement of the original patent when the latter has expired, but this protection covers only the improvement; the original invention is unprotected after the patent period of 17 years (or a maximum of 14 years in the case of a design patent).

A person or a company may be liable for infringement of a patent (1) if he uses it, (2) if he makes it for his own use, (3) if he purchases a part and combines it with other parts, comprising an infringing device, (4) if he conspires purposely or unintentionally with another and contributes in any manner to an infringement, or (5) if he purchases and resells an infringing device, although the purchase is made in the belief that the seller had a license from the patentee to sell or use the device.

The owner of a valid patent is privileged to sue for infringement either the manufacturer, the seller, or the user of the invention, or all of them. Or he may sue only the maker, and, after infringement is established by the court, he may obtain an injunction to prevent the continuation of the infringement by other parties. All parties are liable in damages to the patentee. The measure of liability is equal to all profits earned by sale or use of the invention, plus any and all damages that may have been sustained by the patentee. If the infringement is proved to be willful and intentional, the damages allowable may be three times the actual damages.

A phase of the law of particular importance in industrial practice relates to the repair and replacement of parts on patented machinery. Such parts may be separately covered by patents, in which case they can be made, sold, or used only by authorization of the patentee. However, the owner of a patented machine has the right to make repairs to keep it in usable condition, purchasing ordinary parts for repairs on such a machine, provided the parts so replaced are not separately covered by a patent. But if the machine as a whole is worn out and useless, the owner cannot practically rebuild and make a new machine under the guise of repairing it.

In view of the heavy liability that may be incurred through patent infringement, without knowledge or intention on the part of a purchaser, a

---

[5] *Cantelo,* 12 Pat. Law R. 262.

precautionary protective clause is desirable in contracts whereby the patentee or seller agrees to assume full responsibility for losses sustained by purchasers as a result of infringement suits. Such clauses are valid, and they are effective provided the patentee or seller is financially able to fulfill his agreement to hold the purchaser safe. They do not cancel, but merely transfer, the liability. A clause of this nature is cited in Chapter 15.

One more point should be clarified in this connection. The marks "Patent Pending" and "Patent Applied For" imprinted on a manufactured product have no meaning beyond the fact that the inventor has applied for a patent. Unless and until the patent is granted, he has no right to sue and recover damages for infringement. The imprint does serve notice on purchasers and users that he is endeavoring to obtain a patent and that later infringement may be involved. Many inventors, however, continue to use such imprints on their products long after they have been notified by the Patent Office that no patent can or will be granted. By this means they may lead persons to believe that some protection against infringement of their right exists, when in fact they have no patent right to protect.

Conclusion

There are many more aspects of law that have a bearing on purchase transactions and purchasing practice. This chapter has merely summarized the points that are most commonly encountered and that should be observed in order to keep free of litigation or to enhance the prospect of a favorable verdict when litigation cannot be avoided. The cardinal rule of law should be remembered: that no one should come into a court of law "with unclean hands," that is, without being sure that his own action and intent are lawful and that the breach of legal obligation is not on his own part. When the controversy concerns interpretation of an agreement, the court will endeavor to determine the real intent of the parties in making that agreement. But, on the whole, the legal principles and requirements are clear and well established, although their interpretation may be modified by the particular circumstances of their application in a given case.

It is important for the purchaser to read carefully and to know what he is signing, for this is the evidence of the agreement. Although the courts have in some cases ruled in favor of a buyer who failed to notice some contract clause that was inconspicuously placed or printed in excessively fine type or faint ink, or when he had definitely been led to believe that no such condition was incorporated in the agreement, these are the rare exceptions to the general rule of responsibility for knowing what the contract contains.

Finally, by mutual consent, arbitration can be substituted for litigation.

Contract clauses are valid by which contracting parties agree not to enter suit but rather to abide by a decision rendered by a disinterested arbitrator. Under such an agreement, the decision of the arbitrator is final and conclusive (unless in making the decision the arbitrator himself is guilty of fraud, misconduct, or such gross mistake as would imply bad faith or failure to exercise honest judgment). Arbitration of contract disputes is encourages in business practice and is supported by modern higher-court decisions; its legal effect is the practical elimination of litigations.

23

CONTRACT CANCELLATIONS

THE PRIMARY OBJECTIVE of purchasing is the procurement of materials, a positive goal and action. The whole purchasing procedure is directed to this end, and the consideration of legal principles has likewise been chiefly from the viewpoint of developing a contractual relationship to implement such procurement and of placing the supplier under the obligation of making a satisfactory delivery. However, the point cannot be overlooked that, after such commitments have been made and such contractual relationships have been established, requirements may change so that it becomes desirable or necessary to cancel all or part of a purchase contract that has not yet been completed. The largest and most dramatic example of this situation came with the abrupt cessation of hostilities at the end of World War II, when requirements for military equipment and supplies were immediately curtailed. To have continued their manufacture in accordance with contracts, or even to complete the manufacture of goods in various stages of completion when this occcurred, would have represented sheer waste and needless expense to the government. Consequently, government contracts amounting to billions of dollars were summarily cancelled, in turn calling for the cancellation of thousands of contracts, which had been made on the basis of the prime requirement, with suppliers and subcontractors who were furnishing the raw materials and component parts for the military items. On a smaller scale, similar situations are constantly arising in the everyday conduct of business. It should be remembered, too, that an accepted purchase order has the same legal standing as the more formal or long-term agreement to which the word "contract" is generally applied.

The confidence and orderliness needed to do business satisfactorily depends on the sanctity of the contractual relationship, backed up with legal force. A good contract protects the interests and rights of both the buyer and the seller, and its obligations are equally binding upon both parties to the contract. Cancellations and defaults in respect to contract agreements cannot be made arbitrarily by either party to the detriment of the other. Therefore, to meet the exigencies of a situation involving contract cancellations, a fair and orderly procedure and adjustment must be provided, with the same legal force as in the making of a contract. Although it is probably true that no contract is actually "noncancellable," this statement does not mean that the existence of the contract in question can be ignored, or that the obligation to hold the other party harmless from the consequences of such cancellation can be avoided.

Liability under contract cancellation

An important point to bear in mind in respect to contract cancellations is the financial liability that may accrue, for a cancellation is in effect a repudiation of obligations that have been assumed under the contract. The general rule of equity is that the innocent party shall not be made to suffer a loss. However, it is the rules of law that decide which party is responsible and that determine the extent of the liability, if any; and these decisions depend on the specific circumstances in each individual case. Therefore, both the circumstances and the manner of cancellation should be carefully considered before this step is taken, so that rights which seem perfectly clear as a matter of equity will not be legally forfeited or unintentionally waived. If there is any considerable sum involved, or if there is any shadow of doubt as to the liability that may be incurred, it is a prudent precaution to secure competent legal advice in advance of issuing a cancellation.

In general, cancellations come within three classifications: cancellations for default by the seller, for the convenience of the buyer, or by mutual consent. These are separately discussed in the following sections. It should be noted also that, as a general rule, contracts which are indefinite as to quantity or duration of time can be terminated at will by either party, unilaterally, without penalty, upon due notice to the other party.

The very indefiniteness of the terms, in such a case, is construed in law as evidence of mutual consent for termination.

Cancellation for default

The simplest case is that of a default by the vendor in failing to perform as agreed in the contract, in making deliveries that do not come up to specifications, or in failing to meet the specified delivery dates. All of the essential factors should be so clearly and definitely incorporated in the terms of the contract as to become a part of the seller's obligation. Then any failure on his part to fulfill the terms is a default on the contract, giving the buyer a cause for redress.

A seller's default may be willful (that is, he may be unwilling to make delivery at the agreed price because of an advance in market prices), or it may be due to inability to perform (he may have been unable to secure necessary equipment or materials, or may inadvertently have made overoptimistic promises and oversold his production), or it may be due to causes beyond his control—strikes, fires, floods, or "acts of God." The latter contingencies are generally noted specifically in a seller's quotation as exempting him from blame and penalty. Whatever the cause, the contract is naturally inoperative in the event of failure to perform. A definite cancellation should nevertheless be issued by the buyer, as formal notice that he is no longer bound by his part of the mutual obligation and to clear the way for procuring the needed materials from another source without finding himself in the position of having made a dual commitment in case the original seller should later attempt to fill the contract. Furthermore, because the buyer has the right to rely upon the seller's promise, he should not incur any loss by reason of the seller's default. Thus, if he is forced to buy the materials from another source at a price higher than that stipulated in the contract, he has a legitimate ground for legal action against the original contracting party to recover the added cost, or for other demonstrable damages that are directly attributable to the breach of contract.

Convenience of the buyer

On the other hand, it may become necessary for the buyer to cancel a contract even though the seller is able and willing to perform his part of the agreement, as was noted in the government's case in the introductory section of this chapter. In such cases of contract cancellation for the convenience of the buyer, the similar principle holds that the seller should not be called upon to incur any loss through the buyer's default.

In this case, the situation may be complicated by certain expenditures made prior to the time of cancellation for such items as engineering design and special tooling, raw materials and components purchased specifically for the purpose of the contract, for which no alternative use or outlet may be immediately apparent, and some part or all of the manufacturing process which may have been completed. All of these expenditures have presumably been made in good faith upon the assurances contained in the contract, and, because they are properly for the account of the buyer under his contract responsibility, some equitable adjustment is clearly in order. Even without such special considerations, as in the case of standard products that are allocated to the buyer and ready for delivery in full accord with contract terms, a cancellation may result in hardship to the seller. The outside market may have dropped below the contract price, so that the seller's potential return for selling them elsewhere would be less than that stipulated in the contract; indeed, this may be the reason for the cancellation.

Under any of these circumstances, if the buyer refuses to accept delivery of the goods for which he has contracted and he orders work on the contract stopped, whereas the seller has fulfilled his obligations up to that point, the latter has grounds for legal action against the buyer to recover his loss in the event that no satisfactory adjustment can be reached out of court. If he is forced to find another buyer for the goods manufactured on the contract and ready for delivery, at a price lower than that stipulated, he may sue the original purchaser to recover the difference. Or, if the products are not otherwise salable, he may sue to secure reimbursement for purchases made and work done toward fulfilling the contract, as well as for anticipated profits. It is quite conceivable that such an adjustment may still be to the advantage of the buyer if the need for the contract items no longer exists and, even though an economic loss may be involved in scrapping the material and labor already applied, a further useless expenditure may be avoided.

Where the possible or probable necessity of cancelling a contract commitment can be foreseen, it is good policy to take cognizance of this in the conditions of the contract and to have an agreement with the seller as to the manner and terms of the termination. But in any case, the buyer should be prepared to handle cancellations promptly and effectively if the necessity should arise, for these circumstances often come with startling suddenness. A sharp, unforeseen curtailment in production rates and requirements, a quick decision involving radical changes in product design, the prospect of a prolonged strike, and fire or flood damage that temporarily incapacitates the plant are examples of the hazards that may call for peremptory mass cancellation of outstanding orders. There is not only the financial aspect to be considered. Where the flow of incoming materials is large, the physical storage facilities, even to the space for accommodating cars on rail sidings and unloading docks, could quickly become hopelessly clogged if the flow were not halted.

Cancellation by mutual consent

Cancellation of a contract is not necessarily a cause for legal action. Just as the making of a contract represents a meeting of minds resulting in an agreement between the buyer and the seller to undertake certain mutual responsibilities, so there may be a meeting of minds in respect to the termination of that agreement without invoking a penalty on either side. There are many instances in the course of business when requirements change, so that a contract or open order is no longer appropriate to the buyer's need. A cancellation is indicated, for the convenience of the buyer. But if no particular hardship to the seller is involved, for example, if the item concerned is so standard that another outlet can be found, or if it is of such a nature that materials and work-in-process can be diverted without loss to the orders of some other buyer, the seller may be quite willing to accept a cancellation in good faith as a normal risk of doing business. If an adjustment is in order because of special materials purchased or work done on the contract, a reasonable agreement can be reached through negotiation rather than litigation, based on the equity of the situation.

Change orders, which are fairly common in purchasing practice, in line with changing requirements, actually constitute a cancellation of the original agreement and the substitution of a new contract agreement. Yet this question rarely arises. Change orders are quite generally accepted by both buyers and sellers as a natural and necessary part of procurement and supply, carrying no implication of bad faith or breach of contract. Any necessary adjustment of terms is negotiated just as in the first instance. In this case there is, of course, the consideration of contract continuity under the new terms, and the vendor has a new order to take the place of the unfilled portion of the original order.

Conversely, a vendor may find himself unable to fulfill his part of the agreement owing to circumstances beyond his control, despite his best efforts to do so. If he brings this condition to the buyer's attention before it gets to the point of actual default and emergency, and if the goods can be procured from another supplier in time and without additional cost, it is probable that a cancellation by mutual consent can be agreed upon.

The importance of a good business relationship, and of mutual confidence between buyer and seller, can scarcely be overestimated in situations of this sort. The important intangible asset of good will, the value of friendly supply sources to the buyer and of desirable customers to the seller, are factors that frequently outweigh the legalities of a situation. And most business concerns wisely prefer to stay out of court if an equitable settlement can be made by mutual agreement.

Waiver of right

Nevertheless, a contract is a binding legal document designed to protect both parties, and the legal rights inherent in the contract agreement should be meticulously safeguarded, for they can easily be forfeited by careless action. For example, time of delivery or performance is an integral part of the contract if it is stated, as it should be, in the purchase order or contract. Yet it is a point upon which many buyers are inclined to be lenient, within reasonable limits, so long as systematic expediting is successful in getting deliveries made before the absolute deadline. Now suppose that a certain vendor is chronically tardy with his shipments on a continuing contract, requiring an undue amount of expediting effort, until the patient buyer eventually decides to terminate the agreement. The buyer claims breach of contract, and has an imposing lot of evidence in the form of late shipments to support his claim. But if he has consistently condoned the lateness of deliveries in the past, and has continued to accept overdue shipments, he may find that he has waived his rights for legal action upon this point. He can still cancel the contract, but he has forfeited his claim for any redress on the basis of the vendor's default.

Cancellation clauses

Some purchasing departments include a special clause in their purchase orders and contracts, on the subject of cancellation. For the most part, such general clauses add nothing whatever to the rights or protection afforded by the contractual relationship itself. In fact, they may actually destroy the force of the entire contract by making the contract obligations or promises "illusory" in the eyes of the law. For example, the following clause appears in one purchase order, ostensibly to relieve the purchaser of continuing responsibility under a contractual agreement and to reserve the privilege of rescinding or cancelling any portion of the order without liability:

The buyer reserves the right to cancel any unshipped portion of this order.

The broad effect, in court, of such a general disclaimer of responsibility for carrying out his part of the agreement, however, would probably be a decision that the document is unilateral and that no contract legally exists under such a condition.

On the other hand, some practical advantage may be obtained by specifically stressing a particular phase of delinquency that is to be interpreted by mutual consent as cause for cancellation of an order by the buyer, without penalty. In most cases, clauses of this nature are based on the fact that time of delivery is "of the essence" of the contract and that failure to make delivery as promised relieves the buyer of his responsibility to accept and pay for goods furnished tardily under the contract. An example of such a clause is the following:

Should any portion of this order be unfilled at the expiration of 60 days from its date, we reserve the right (notifying you) to cancel said unfilled portion without liability other than to make payments for that portion of the order that has been delivered.

Although it may be argued that this gives the buyer no rights that could not be equally accomplished by specifying a definite delivery date among the terms on the face of the order, it could be invoked in cases where previous leniency in accepting delinquent deliveries (which would be a normal policy for occasional infractions and if the urgency of the requirement did not require rigid enforcement) was cited as precedent to diminish the force of a delivery agreement. It does serve notice on the seller that the time element is an essential part of the agreement and will be so interpreted. At the same time, it provides the means for clearing open-order files with reasonable promptness and for avoiding the accumulation of miscellaneous outstanding commitments.

A third representative clause may be quoted:

> Either party may cancel any portion of this order affected by failure of the other to comply with terms and conditions hereof.

This statement is thoroughly innocuous and superfluous. It neither grants, defines, nor modifies any right that is not inherent in the contract itself. Unlike the first example cited above, it does not tend to vitiate the contract; neither does it serve any useful purpose. If a contract is breached by either party, the second party is relieved of its obligation to carry out its respective part of the agreement, which is predicated on mutual performance. The quoted clause is merely a restatement of this fact.

Termination agreements

It may be accepted as a basic thesis that a contract is made with the expectation of carrying it through to completion on both sides. But under certain circumstances there may be a strong probability that the buyer may wish to cancel at some stage prior to completion because of contingencies that can be foreseen in principle but not in detail. If ordinary forms of conditional contracts are not appropriate to cover these circumstances, it is highly desirable to have an understanding with the seller as to the procedure to be followed in the event of such cancellation. This agreement may be embodied in a termination clause that is made a part of the contract. Sellers are naturally reluctant to accept termination clauses, and there is no obligation on their part to do so; they are fully entitled to stand on their contractual rights under the principles of cancellation for the convenience of the buyer, as outlined above. But if a good, continuing relationship has been established between the contracting companies, and if the contract is an advantageous one so far as it goes, the agreement may frequently be worked out as a part of the negotiation in such a way as to relieve the buyer of the extreme penalties or obligations involved in an ordinary cancellation, without calling upon the seller to sustain any loss by reason of the cancellation. It is important that the principle of equity and mutual interest be observed in any such clause, for, as already pointed out, a condition phrased to relieve the buyer of all responsibility for carrying out his part of the contract would probably rob the entire contract of its binding force.

The situation in respect to termination of government war contracts, cited in the introductory section of this chapter, illustrates the general principles that may well apply. The example is not altogether typical, because the wartime powers of government as a contracting party made possible a mandatory termination clause, which the seller had no alternative but to accept in his contract. The buyer for private industry has no such power to dictate the terms of the agreement. However, the general outline of procedure as to termination settlements, proved in the experience of thousands of cancellations in which this clause was invoked at the war's end, provides a useful guide, for the negotiation of prior agreements, as to the method of adjustment.

Broadly, the government's termination clause required the contractor (vendor) to stop work on the contract immediately upon receipt of notification of a cancellation, and to cancel his own outstanding contracts pertaining to the project, so that no further obligations would be incurred. The government (buyer) assumed full responsibility for all completed work, at full contract price; for partially completed work, at cost plus a profit percentage scaled according to the progress of the job and how much work had been done, but not to exceed eight per cent in any case; for raw materials and purchased components, at cost plus a lesser percentage to cover the expenses of handling (two per cent); for engineering, tooling, and other direct expenses attributable to the contract that had not been absorbed in the contract price; and for termination costs entailed in the contractor's settlement with his own suppliers. At every stage of this adjustment, provision was made for special negotiation. For example, if work-in-process was at an advanced stage, so that a relatively small amount of additional work would bring it to completion and commercial value, whereas there was no recoverable value in the incomplete product, that portion of the contract might be reinstated to avoid a complete economic loss of the labor already applied. Or, in the case of standard products, materials, and components, the contractor could take title by omitting them from his claim and diverting them to use on other contracts, or he could submit a bid for such items to the government contracting agency. In a substantial number of cases, no termination claims were entered, a fact that argues well for the equity of this arrangement.

To make such a plan workable, two factors are imperative, in addition to having a prior agreement. One of these is the maintenance of accurate records and costs, which is fundamental to good management and control in any case. The other is the necessity of physical segregation and identification of the materials and work-in-process involved in the adjustment, which would not normally be found in industrial practice.

There were two major shortcomings to the practical operation of the plan. One was the necessity for audit by the government contracting agency, which involved considerable delays in settlement owing to the magnitude of the situation. As a matter of fact, however, the records indicate that the greater part of the delay was attributable to contractors' tardiness in submitting complete claims. This slowness was due largely to difficulties in arriving at settlements with their own suppliers, necessary in the compilation of their claims, and points to the second major shortcoming. To be completely satisfactory, this settlement formula should be predicated on similar agreement between the contractor and the next tier of his suppliers, and so on down the line. The termination clause, however, was effective only in the prime contract of which it was a part, and in which the government was one of the contracting parties. The mandatory provision could be extended only one step beyond, by requiring the contractor to incorporate a similar clause in his own contracts with suppliers. Beyond that—and the stream of supply frequently ran down through several successive tiers of subcontractors and suppliers—no such control existed, and cancellation adjustments were a matter of negotiation or litigation, or the contractor had to accept the goods he had contracted for and include this expense in his own termination claim.

The importance of some such arrangement can be visualized by remembering that, in the tremendous war program, the majority of manufacturers had necessarily made contract commitments that exceeded their capital resources many times over. There are many cases on record where, if a manufacturer had been obliged to accept all the materials for which contract commitments had been issued, and had then been obliged to liquidate this material in distress sales representing even a conservative loss of 10 per cent, the transaction would have wiped out his entire capitalization at a single stroke. To the thousands of companies in this position, the privilege of including a reasonable termination clause in their purchase agreements meant their very existence.

In the normal conduct of business, prudent management and purchasing would not permit the assumption of such a dangerous and disproportionate risk; but even in the lesser degree to which such hazards may apply in every contractual agreement, the probability of cancellation should be considered, and if this probability is a strong one, such provision as is possible in the way of an agreement for settlement or adjustment should be made, consistent with the volume and value of the business to the supplier and with his rights under the contract relationship.

Contract cancellation is distinctly a matter of interest to the purchasing department, not only because it is involved in the negotiation of the contract, but because the settlement itself, like all vendor contracts, is a purchasing responsibility.

Renegotiated prices

Somewhat related to cancellation agreements, in that it involves possible changes in original contract terms, is the renegotiation of prices after a contract has been partially or completely filled. Government negotiated contracts, particularly in the military programs, contain a provision for review and adjustment of prices at the conclusion of the contract. This is prompted by the fact that such contracts typically involve large areas of cost that cannot be accurately estimated in advance, such as developmental expense and manufacturing operations for which there is no suitable precedent or experience, yet the urgency of the requirement demands that the work go forward immediately. The stipulation for renegotiation extends to major subcontractors as well as to the prime contractor. The renegotiating process audits actual costs and explores the reasonableness of profits and management charges; allowable expense items are defined in advance, and maximum profit margins are established. Although actual ultimate price is not fixed under such arrangements, renegotiation is considered to be a better procurement method than the various forms of cost-plus pricing in that the supplier assumes normal business risks, he has an incentive for efficient performance, and the buyer shares in any cost savings that may be accomplished.

The buyer in private industry has no such statutory and enforceable privilege of negotiating for a better price after the contract has been completed, although there may frequently be instances where the problem is comparable. His closest approach to remedial pricing is to include a provision in the contract for reopening it, for price review and adjustment, either at stated intervals or at the option of either party. This possibility has already been suggested in Chapter 10. In many well-established, continuing source relationships, where a high degree of mutuality exists, formalized in term or blanket contracts, price review and renegotiation by mutual consent are a part of the agreement. Such revisions or adjustments, of course, are not retroactive; they merely set a new price basis for the balance of the contract term or until the next revision.

Any procedure of this sort requires the consent of the seller, who can otherwise stand on the terms of the contract as written. Therefore, if the desirability of future price review for any reason is foreseeable, this provision must be included in the original contract. Also, to be effective, the basis of price revision should be tied to specific factors and standards of cost, as in the case of escalator clauses. If a contract is to have meaning, the privilege of price review is not merely a license to start bargaining all over again. If renegotiation is prompted only by the fact that the buyer has received a lower offer from another vendor, the present supplier is under no obligation to reduce his price to meet competition. If he elects not to do so, and the buyer still wishes to avail himself of the lower price, the buyer's only recourse is to terminate the contract, accepting whatever costs and penalties are entailed by the cancellation, and to make a new contract with the second vendor.

24

EVALUATING PURCHASING PERFORMANCE

PURCHASING AND MANAGEMENT executives alike would welcome some reliable yardstick for the measurement of efficiency in purchasing, and, consequently, a great deal of serious thought has been given to the problem. It has been the subject of continuing study for several years by the National Association of Purchasing Agents. At one stage of the study, the cooperation of the National Association of Cost Accountants was enlisted, with liberal cash awards offered for the best papers submitted. Although such research has not resulted in any formula or method capable of general application, it has developed a number of principles that are helpful and worthy of consideration in approaching the problem as it affects the individual company operation.

Some common fallacies

It is easy to fall into the error of oversimplification in measuring purchasing performance. Probably the most common fallacy in this direction is to set a standard of efficiency by expressing departmental operating cost as a percentage of total purchase expenditures. This percentage is necessarily an average figure, for it is obvious that there is a wide disparity between the purchasing cost in respect to orders of relatively small value, for hard-to-find items and those that are required only occasionally so that procurement must start with the most elementary considerations of quality, source, and value, and the cost of procuring standard and familiar materials from established sources in substantial volume. Examples can be found of purchasing costs ranging all the way from $\frac{3}{4}$ of 1 per cent of expenditures to 2 per cent or more, each of which could conscientiously be described as an efficient performance for the particular company and conditions concerned. Independent purchasing services operate on percentages ranging from $2\frac{1}{2}$ per cent to 5 per cent and are able to demonstrate savings as compared with unorganized and inexpert

325

purchasing. A reasonable average figure would be in the neighborhood of $1\frac{1}{2}$ per cent to 2 per cent, but this is the broadest sort of generalization and has little meaning for the individual company; a variation of $\frac{1}{2}$ of 1 per cent on any substantial purchasing program runs into significant dollar figures.

The fallacy of such a standard of measurement is readily demonstrable on a simple mathematical basis, for the percentage can be reduced to any desired level by the expedient of paying more for the materials purchased, which would represent highly expensive and inefficient purchasing.

Another method sometimes advocated is the measurement of cost per order. This has the virtue of being tied to actual operations performed, rather than to the incidental (though highly important) factor of funds expended. It is subject to the same sort of criticism, however, because cost per order can be reduced by issuing more orders for smaller quantities, whereas real purchasing efficiency may lie in the other direction.

The positive principle to be deduced from these analyses is that there is a dual job of measurement to be done—efficiency in departmental administration, and efficiency in procurement. There is the cost of operation and the cost of materials to be considered before performance can be truly evaluated. This principle has already been indicated in the chapter on purchase budgets. The first factor, administrative cost, presents a relatively simple problem; management science has developed standards and measures for such performance that can readily be applied. The second factor is more difficult; the approach has been suggested in the type of information included in purchasing department reports to management—inventory ratios, material costs related to current market levels, savings effected through good purchasing practice, adherence to material budgets, and the like, all tending to demonstrate specific accomplishments or performance in the actual procurement function.

The most satisfactory measurements are those in which the two phases are separately considered. For convenience, they may be designated as efficiency and proficiency, both of which are important to the company. Of the two, the second is the more characteristically related to specific professional skill in procurement, which is the functional purpose of the department. Furthermore, it is the phase that embraces total expenditures and product costs, whereas departmental administration represents only a small percentage of total cost. No really useful purpose is served by trying to force a relationship between the two, much less by trying to measure the greater and more fundamental performance in terms of the minor factor.

Variables in purchase standards

One of the basic difficulties in devising a standard method of measuring purchasing performance is that so many variables are involved. This fact is apparent in the widely differing scope and character of requirements in various types of operations, where the value of purchased materials may range all the way from 20 per cent to 80 per cent of total expenditures, with a corresponding variation in the relative importance of the purchasing function to profitable operation and its potential contribution to such operation in any particular enterprise. Thus, the first principle of evaluation is that it must be done on an individual-company basis. Comparisons are significant only to the extent that the type of industry and the size of the unit are comparable.

There is a further variation in the functional organization of individual companies and the responsibilities assigned to the purchasing department, which may range all the way from simple clerical detail to complete materials management, in companies of similar size within the same industry. The logical method of measurement, therefore, is some form of job-evaluation technique applicable to the particular company, rather than a general functional analysis when the function itself is not definitively classified in industry as a whole.

Purchasing itself deals in variables. Price is a variable. Price alone is not a proper measure of performance, because it is frequently subordinated to other considerations, so that better procurement may be effected by paying more for materials. It is, however, an important factor. In evaluating price performance, it must be considered against the variable standard of changing market levels or against adjustable standard costs as established in cost accounting procedure.

Purchasing problems and effort vary with market conditions. Costs rise rapidly under circumstances where intensive expediting is required to assure delivery, or where constant research is needed to develop satisfactory sources of supply.

Inventory ratios and turnover are widely and understandably accepted as an indication of the efficiency of the purchasing policy and program. Here, again, standards will vary according to conditions, as noted in the discussion of proper purchase quantities, for good purchasing policy calls for the accumulation of greater material reserves and greater advance coverage in times of advancing prices, which would result in less favorable turnover for the time being. In using such a yardstick, therefore, the condition at any given time could be seriously misleading, but the average of a month-to-month record over the period of a year would give a reasonably fair measure of accomplishment.

The functional approach

No attempt will be made here to propose a formula capable of application in every case to measure the efficiency and proficiency of purchasing. But an approach to such a solution can be outlined. Throughout this study, emphasis has been placed upon the functional considerations of procurement. That is also a sound basis upon which to measure purchasing performance.

The functional responsibility of a purchasing department is to provide a steady flow of materials as needed, at lowest ultimate cost. This involves many factors—the right material, the right quantity, the right time, the right source, and the right price—which interact upon one another so that each decision of what is "right" in a given case depends upon what is "right" in respect to some or all of the other factors. A compromise or balance must be achieved to arrive at the best end result. In the same way, the measure of accomplishment is to be found in terms of the end result, in which these various measurable factors are contributory elements, to be reconciled in the final accounting.

The system of measurement should be such as to focus attention and effort upon performance rather than upon the details of rating, and the department head should have confidence that it will fairly reflect his accomplishments.

The system should conscientiously segregate the factors for which each department is directly responsible, in order that the credits and demerits may be equitably applied. It should never be permitted to set up the type of interdepartmental competition that might discourage fullest cooperation toward the common aim of the most economical and profitable over-all operation.

The end result of purchasing is product cost, and the measurement of purchasing performance can logically be based on that consideration. The direct responsibility of the purchasing department is the net cost of product materials up to the point of use, excluding the cost of maintenance and operating supplies. The standard of measurement is standard cost, arrived at by careful and detailed analysis of the complete bill of materials, with normal margins for waste and spoilage, corresponding to the standard costs used in accounting and in sales price estimates, and adjusted monthly to market fluctuations with the assistance of the purchasing executive, whose business it is to be informed concerning these markets. These standard costs will take into account the quality specifications representing the grade of material required to satisfy the company's standards of product and operation. The standard cost is expressed as one over-all figure, either cost of purchased materials per unit of product or a percentage of total product cost, although the figure is made up of carefully itemized elements. This is done partly to simplify accounting and evaluation, but even more as recognition of the facts that flexibility is essential in working out the purchasing program and that attention should be focused on the end result rather than on the details. And the end result is total product cost.

Besides being adjusted periodically to market conditions, the standard

cost is revised for any changes in product design, bills of material, or manufacturing policies at the time these changes are made. For example, if it is
decided to purchase a component part in fabricated form rather than manufacture it in the plant, in the interest of greater ultimate economy or for
better utilization of facilities, a cost adjustment is in order. For the purchase
cost will necessarily be higher, because outside manufacturing services are
now being purchased, and at the same time the company's own manufacturing
operations are reduced. The same principle would apply if the decision were
reversed. The object at all times is to reflect fairly the specific cost responsibility of both departments.

Such standard costs, which are in effect a purchase budget for product
materials, provide a practical and significant basis for the measurement of
purchasing performance in respect to the largest and most important phase of
the procurement function. Adherence to the standard cost may be taken as
100. If the purchasing department succeeds in bettering this figure, the rating
of performance is raised by a percentage corresponding to the saving; if costs
are higher, the rating is proportionately reduced. In other words, performance
is rated on a percentage basis, inversely to the costs actually incurred, as compared with total standard cost.

Modifying factors

In many cases, this basic rating will be sufficient for the purpose. There
are, however, a number of other factors involved in the complete operation
and responsibility of purchasing, affecting full evaluation of performance.
These can be separately considered and the results, properly weighted, applied
as a credit or demerit to the rating above. The more important of these are
as follows:

1. *Inventory performance.* Continuity of operation, to the extent of having materials on hand when needed, is a purchasing responsibility. It is recognized that this requires the maintenance of working inventory, entailing
certain carrying charges that are a legitimate cost of business as production
insurance. The size of this inventory, in relation to current operating rates,
is a matter of company policy. If the approved policy is to carry a 60-day
supply, the inventory should amount to one-sixth of the amount of annual
expenditures; if it is a 90-day supply, the inventory would be one-fourth of
annual expenditures. This variable standard should be adjusted according to
prevailing policy, and it should be measured in total dollar value. The cost of
carrying inventory is calculated upon experience, by standard cost accounting
methods. For purposes of illustration, a cost of 10 per cent annually may be
assumed.

If, by efficient planning, scheduling of purchases, and stores management, continuity of operation is maintained with a turnover of inventory every 45 days instead of 60 days, average inventory is reduced by 25 per cent, and purchasing performance should be credited with the carrying cost of 10 per cent on that amount. If the inventory runs high because of overbuying or inefficient materials control, resulting in a slower turnover, a corresponding debit should be applied.

Turnover is not the only measure of inventory performance. Demerits may accrue through losses due to the obsolescence (unless due to change in design or other causes outside of purchasing's jurisdiction and control), production delays due to lack of standard materials that should have been in stock when needed, and extra transportation charges incurred for faster and more expensive means of delivery, provided that the requirement should have been foreseen in time to permit utilization of the normal, economical means of transportation. Obsolescence losses may be offset by credit for salvage operations and sales of scrap and surplus items. This group of factors does not lend itself to evaluation on a strictly quantitative or percentage basis and may call for a prorating with other departments, because the delays and emergency shipments may be caused by rush requisitions, changes in specifications, or abnormal and unforeseen demand. They should be noted, however, and a point rating assigned to fit the circumstances. It should also be kept in mind that such demerits are not a serious reflection on purchasing performance unless they occur too frequently and run into large amounts. Few enterprises expect to operate without any losses for surplus or without occasional emergency requirements.

No credit is contemplated for appreciation in inventory values, because this benefit is reflected in production cost as compared with standard cost at time of use. Nor is there any adjustment for heavier-than-normal inventories accumulated in anticipation of a price rise, for similar reasons; if the ultimate saving in cost does not offset the carrying charges involved, the advance purchase is not justified. The whole effort in devising a system of measurement is to focus attention on good purchasing practice, not on the formula of evaluation. The purchasing executive and staff should be able to concentrate on their function of procurement, with confidence that their actual accomplishment will be fairly recognized and reflected in the measurement.

2. *Quality factors.* The purchasing department is responsible for procuring materials of adequate quality, in accordance with approved specifications. Failure to do so is an indication either of faulty buying or of selection of the wrong supplier. In respect to most fabricated products, a certain percentage of rejects is recognized in trade practice and in purchase transactions as allowable. In evaluating purchasing performance, demerits are in order for rejects in excess of the allowable margin, and for the cost of reworking substandard items to make them usable and up to specification.

3. *Maintenance and factory supplies.* This part of the purchase program is segregated from product materials because it is an indirect cost, allocable to the operating expense of other departments. For example, the quantity of supplies and expendable tools used for a given volume of production primarily reflects the efficiency of production departments; the quantity of fuel used reflects the efficiency of the power plant department; and so on. It would be illogical to attribute excesses or economies to the purchasing division, even though purchases in these classifications make up a substantial part of the purchasing program. In companies where a specific control is exercised over the purchase and use of supply items, the usual procedure is to budget such requirements as an amount or percentage based on current rates of operation or volume of production, as indicated by past experience, but without a detailed breakdown by individual items; adherence to the budget then becomes a measure of the efficiency of using departments. Evaluation of purchasing performance on such items should be made on the basis of standard cost per unit of the purchased item rather than cost per unit of product. The figure can be correlated with the purchase rating on product cost in a ratio corresponding to the relative value of the two parts of the purchase program. Credit for purchasing accomplishment in procuring more efficient or more durable products in the maintenance and supply categories would be noted in the consideration of specific savings, as indicated below.

4. *Savings other than price.* Savings due to buying at favorable prices, whether on product or maintenance and supply items, are taken into account in the basic evaluation of purchasing performance and in the supplementary rating suggested in the preceding paragraph. Consequently, they are not separately considered. But savings from other sources—substitution, standardization, specification changes, packing and transportation costs, and the like, as detailed in the chapter on purchasing department reports—are separately listed and totaled and are credited on a point scale. Credit given for such developments should be liberal rather than on a strictly quantitative or percentage basis, for not only are they repetitive in nature, but they represent the qualities of initiative that are the foundation of both efficiency and proficiency in purchasing. Furthermore, as such developments are accepted in standard company practice, they make the basic yardstick of product cost more exacting, so that at the same time that these benefits accrue to the company in the regular course of its operations from that time on, each further source of saving becomes more difficult and represents a superior accomplishment on the part of the purchasing officer. These factors are all on the credit side, for prevailing company practice is the starting point in this phase of evaluation, and errors or demerits are already reflected in the cost ratings.

5. *Administrative cost.* In discussing purchase budgets, it was noted that purchase expenditures and administrative costs must be separately considered.

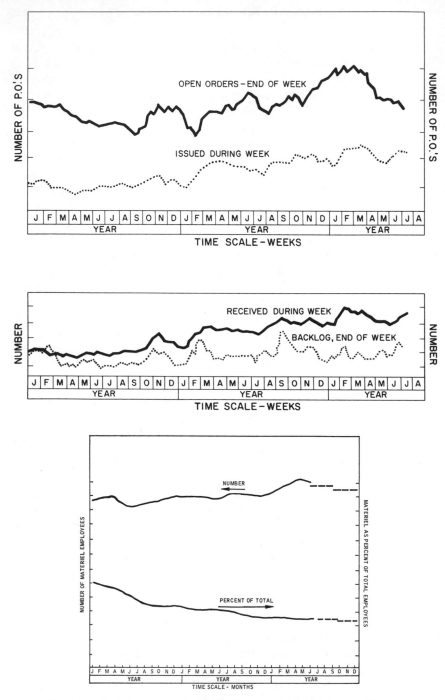

Fig. 24-1.   Typical Measures of a Purchasing Department's Activity and Efficiency.

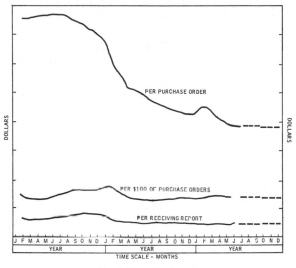

Fig. 24 1.   Continued.

In the over-all evaluation of purchasing department effectiveness, both factors must be included, for purchasing, like every other department, has the responsibility of planning and carrying out its function at the minimum cost consistent with proper performance. As previously stated, administrative cost cannot logically be used as the measure of effectiveness, and it does not necessarily bear any fixed ratio to the amount of purchase expenditures. Another point to be kept in mind is that, although the effort should be made to keep department expenses at the practical minimum, this attitude should not be emphasized to a degree that would suggest or encourage doing without such departmental activities as research, training, cost analysis, field work by buyers at the company's plants and those of suppliers, and similar activities that may not be reflected in immediate price advantage but are essential in the long run to proficiency, soundness, and ultimate economy in the purchasing program.

The measure of departmental costs should, therefore, be made against a budgeted standard cost developed by an analysis of activities, the volume of specific operations such as the number of requisitions handled and purchase orders issued, an allowance for incidental functions and special projects, recommendations and budget requests of the department head, and a proportionate share of general administrative overhead. This budget should be liberal enough to include personnel and facilities for carrying on a complete and progressive program of procurement, "spending money to save money." It should be close enough to represent prudent management, efficient work production on clerical and other processing operations, and good administrative control. In short, it should be a realistic appraisal of the job to be done. It should be adjusted from time to time as conditions change and as the department head can demonstrate the need for such adjustment. Evaluation of this phase is based on adherence to budget, with proportionate credit for keeping expenses below the estimate and proportionate debit for expenses above this figure.

In weighing this factor as it affects the general rating, a fair proportion would be the ratio that general company overhead bears to total manufacturing cost, because this is essentially what the figure represents.

Using the ratings

Under such a plan, the total evaluation of purchasing department performance consists of a basic rating on product cost, which is the real test of the department's performance, and five modifying factors representing various phases of departmental responsibility and accomplishment. Three of these factors—inventory ratios, cost of maintenance and supply items, and administrative cost—are measurable on a scale comparable to the basic rating and can be applied directly to that figure by giving them weight commensurate with their importance on a logical mathematical basis. The other two—errors in quality of purchased items and savings due to causes other than price—require a somewhat arbitrary point evaluation in applying them to the scale. The whole calculation can, however, be put in mathematical terms, arriving at a figure that may be either more or less than 100.

What does this figure mean? In the first place, although the 100-point standard in the various sections of the measurement and in the total rating represents an objective to be attained, it does not necessarily follow that it is attainable under all conditions or that a lower rating is the indication of incompetence, any more than it is true that a baseball player's batting average is expected to be perfect or that a sales department is expected at all times to provide orders equal to the company's total production capacity. Rather, it is an index of performance that can be interpreted as showing that the department is falling short of expectations and not making its fair contribution to profitable company operation, so that some specific attention should be given to this department by management, or that it is coming close to the standards of performance that the company can reasonably expect in this phase of its business and is, thus, doing a competent job, or that it is making an exceptional record of accomplishment deserving of appropriate recognition.

In the second place, it must be recognized that the standards in each case are based on judgment that may or may not be accurate and realistic in its expectations. An index of this sort measures both the performance and the standards against which it is rated. A record that is consistently above or below the stated standards may show that management is expecting too much or too little of its purchasing division, and this discovery in itself is highly important; it may suggest and demonstrate that the estimates of material costs, or administrative costs, or policies of procurement, should be revised to conform more closely with actual performance, but the competitive and profit factors of doing business must be based on actual performance. And for purposes of the rating itself, the standards and the expectation must be reasonable in relation to the conditions, both internal and external, under which purchasing is done.

Third, the ultimate rating provides a comparison of performance not only in relation to the stated standards, but also in relation to performance in previous periods, which ratio it is important for management to know. However, the rating is not a measure of comparison with purchasing performance in other companies or a definitive percentage measurement of excellence. There are too many variables in the type of materials purchased, the volume of purchases, and the specific organization responsibility, as well as variables of judgment in setting standards, to permit any such general interpretation.

These qualifications do not imply that the measurement and rating are inaccurate or of little value; rather, they constitute a warning against too superficial or arbitrary acceptance of the numerical result as the significant figure, and especially against the psychological inference of "100 per cent" performance. Systematic measurement of performance is a highly desirable guide to intelligent management, and to intelligent functional and administrative policy; the method outlined above covers the essentials so far as purchasing activities are concerned and is believed to provide as accurate an evaluation as possible in this field where judgment and adjustment to changing conditions play such an important part—where so much depends on what is *not* done as well as on positive decisions and on timing.

It is recommended that, in using this scale, all of the several factors and their respective ratings be shown, as well as the composite figure; for each of these phases has a significance of its own as an indicator of efficiency and proficiency, and the breakdown is the surest guide as to where attention and effort should be concentrated for improved performance. In particular, the basic rating on cost of product materials should be shown both before and after the modifying factors have been applied, because this is the figure that reflects the functional accomplishment of purchasing. A good record on this one essential point justifies the purchasing operation. Also, it is an important factor—sometimes the determining factor—in respect to policies of design, pricing, and marketing; it may well be the key to the company's competitive and profit position. In companies where it is impracticable to undertake a complete and detailed measurement of departmental performance, this analysis of the materials factor of product cost may in itself serve the purpose.

Job analysis and evaluation

Many experienced purchasing executives who are convinced that no practicable performance-rating system can be applied to the purchasing operation, but who are nevertheless aware of the desirability of having some measurement, have turned to the techniques of job analysis and evaluation, a method developed from the viewpoint of personnel administration. It takes the form of an itemized definition setting forth the specific responsibilities of the function and the minimum qualifications of education, training, experience, personality, and ability to fulfill the requirements of the position. On this basis, with suitable relative weights assigned to the various items, a rating of individual competence and performance can be made. It is a workable method, and it can be applied to all grades of personnel in a purchasing department, as in other departments. It has serious limitations, however, in that its significance depends entirely on the adequacy of the basic definitions. These definitions are necessarily couched in terms of minimum requirements, and there is a real danger that these minimum requirements may tend not only to become the maximum opportunities permitted to purchasing department personnel, especially in the higher grades, but also to limit the scope of what management expects of its purchasing department, thereby limiting the potential achievement. The greatest values of good purchasing performance as a contributing factor to efficient company operation and profits lie in the superior field of performance that is broadly indicated by the term "proficiency," involving those attributes of imagination and resourcefulness that are outside of any definition. The desirable objective viewpoint implied by such a system of analysis may also be a limiting factor to truly proficient performance. This is so because the able purchasing officer himself is not only the best qualified, but he may be the only person in the organization qualified to recognize the full potential of his function and its service to the company.

A somewhat similar approach involves the use of a series of check points for evaluating performance. Included would be such inquiries as:

1. What are the personal characteristics, ability, and organizing skill of the department head that have a particular bearing upon his competence in the performance of his function and his value in serving the over-all company interests? This question recognizes the principle that departmental efficiency largely reflects the competence of the department head. The evaluation would necessarily be made by a superior management executive or by a professional management engineer.
2. Does the purchasing department have a broad statement of policy, pref-

erably in written form? Is it a good policy? Is the policy observed in practice?

3. Does the purchasing department have a standard procedure, preferably in the form of a written manual? Is it a good procedure? Is it efficiently carried out in practice?

4. Is the performance of the purchasing department satisfactory in securing the delivery of material in quality and at the time needed?

5. Are materials secured at the right price? Measurement of this factor may be against the standard of market price for buyers in a comparable industrial position and for a comparable volume of purchases, or against "standard cost" prices as established in the accounting procedure of the company. The most practicable method of determining this point is by a systematic spot check or audit of the more substantial purchases, including an examination of the method of inquiry and choice of supplier as supporting evidence of whether or not the right prices are being obtained.

6. What is the cost of operating the department? It may be judged in relation to the departmental administrative budget, or measured by the cost of placing an order, or by what it costs to spend a dollar in purchasing.

7. To what extent does the purchasing department create or dissipate good will for the company? The general reputation of the purchasing department in the trade and among its suppliers has a bearing on this point. On a more specific basis, the statistics of reciprocal business obtained may serve as an indicator, although they are neither complete nor accurate.

An analysis of this sort, giving proper weight to the relative importance of the various points checked, will not provide a numerical rating of efficiency, but it should establish with a reasonable degree of certainty whether the purchasing department is operating satisfactorily in respect to its major responsibilities. This sort of information is valuable both to the purchasing executive and to the company management.

Record of performance

An effective system of recording, analyzing, and gauging the performance of the purchasing department has been developed in one large eastern manufacturing company with notably beneficial results. It has the unique and significant feature of considering the important factor of the time required for proficient purchasing, and the selection of key data in this report is such as to indicate not merely the "what" but the "why" of purchasing performance in any given period. Furthermore, the form of the record is such that the comparison of actual performance with standard and normal performance is immediately apparent and the necessary steps for correction or improvement can be promptly taken.

A simple form has been prepared for use in the system. It is separately filled out by each of the several branch or divisional purchasing offices of the organization. It is ruled in parallel columns for entering (a) standard figure for each item, numerically, by dollar value, or percentage as the case may be; (b) actual record for each of the 13 four-week accounting periods of the calendar year; and (c) annual total and average. The items making up the record are:

1. *Number of orders placed.*
2. *Number of invoices passed.*
3. *Dollar value of invoices passed.*
   These first three items, routine entries to show the volume of work handled, both in buying and in clerical operation, have the dual value of indicating the work burden of the department for any given period—in the light of which performance may be more intelligently judged—and showing business and company trends, which have a bearing on personnel requirements and on purchasing policies.
4. *Cost of purchase order.* This is derived by dividing the total cost of operating the department (including all salaries, traveling expense, telephone expense, supplies, miscellaneous charges such as legal, magazine, and periodical subscriptions, association membership dues, and repairs and charges on furniture, office machines, and fixtures) by the number of orders placed during the period. It is the most direct measure of departmental efficiency included in this evaluation.
5. *Percentage of cash discount.* This factor is not within the control of the purchasing department, but it is deemed significant as a modifying factor of the dollar value of invoices listed above, as an indicator of the department's accomplishment in securing the most favorable terms, and as evidence of prompt processing of the receiving and invoice documents.
6. *Percentage of orders less than five dollars.* In the company in question, all requirements, however small, are procured through the purchasing department. Although small orders cannot be avoided altogether, they should be held to a minimum by foresight in requisitioning and by consolidation of requirements. The number of such excessively small orders is, of course, reflected directly in the ratio of the cost per order to dollar volume of purchases. More significantly, it reflects conditions that are not conducive to good purchasing.
7. *Percentage of rush orders.* A basic concept in this purchasing department is that time is of the essence for competent procurement and for satisfactory delivery. To this end, a "purchase time" is set for each item, indicating the minimum time that should reasonably be allowed between the date of the requisition and the required delivery. It includes the necessary time for processing the requisition and order, negotiating the purchase, lead time in ordering, and the manufacture, transportation, and receipt of the materials, and it is subject to revision according to market supply conditions. Using departments are informed of the length of time allowance and are expected to anticipate their requirements to this extent. For the purposes of this analysis, a rush order is defined as one that allows less than the stated purchase time, one on which subsequent requests to speed delivery curtail allowable time to less than the standard, or one in which special purchase requirements are shown to be unreasonable as to the delivery demanded. A rush order does not relieve the pur-

chasing department of its responsibility to get materials as and when needed, but the effect of this practice on purchasing cost and efficiency is noted. As in the case of small orders, this is a factor which should be held to the practicable minimum.

8. *Percentage of overdue orders.* An overdue order is reported as overdue only once. Subsequent follow-ups of the same order are not included in this figure. Consequently, a true ratio is maintained between shortcomings in delivery and the total number of orders placed.

9. *Number of changes in purchase time.* This is a numerical count, without distinction as to whether the change calls for a longer or shorter purchase time. It is an indication of changing market conditions and is evidence that the purchasing department is conscientiously aware of these conditions and is adjusting its own standards of performance and keeping the Balance of Stores records adjusted to current conditions as a means of effectuating the minimum inventory policy.

10. *Number of notifications held.* At the end of each period, the purchasing department receives a list of "Notification of Goods Received" slips that are being held waiting for invoices that are more than ten days old. These are counted and the figure is inserted in the report.

11. *Number of people* in the purchasing department, classified as buyers, clerks, or stenographic. The number should bear a logical relationship to the volume of work handled in each category.

When this system was first instituted, there was no attempt to set performance standards, but the month-to-month comparison was both significant and helpful. For example, in one month, when the cost per order jumped to $2.17 as against a previous average of $1.77, the explanation was readily apparent in the fact that the percentage of rush orders had nearly doubled in that period, and steps were promptly taken to correct the condition. Another fact that became evident was that no numerical standard was generally applicable to all manufacturing divisions, although a standard or norm might be set individually for each division according to the nature of the purchasing program. In one division, for example, the cost per order was consistently around $1.28, or roughly 27½ per cent below the normal cost in the division cited above.

During the second year of operation, it was possible to set a tentative standard for each of the items, using the norm of the previous year's experience, and thus provide a means of comparison with what might reasonably be expected as well as with actual performance in other months. After the second year, it was possible to set a standard that represented an objective to be attained.

It will be noted that this evaluation takes no account of the prices paid for materials. It is the assumption in this company, accepted by management, that the price performance of the purchasing will be satisfactory, provided that the conditions of operation, the demands made upon purchasing, and the time allowed for purchasing are reasonable. The outstanding contribution of

this plan to purchasing thought and science lies in its consideration of the
time factor. The Director of Purchases states:

> It is assumed in this purchasing department, and by management gen-
> erally, that purchasing will fullfill its responsibility of procuring the needed
> materials on time, and within the purchase time allotted. The test of efficiency
> in purchasing lies in the variations from that standard schedule, whether these
> variations are occasioned by failure to meet the schedule, whether that failure
> is due to conditions beyond the control of the department, or whether the de-
> mand on purchasing has not allowed sufficient time for normal performance.
>
> In every purchasing department, there are many operations or transac-
> tions that consume time, and these operations are taken into consideration in
> setting the standard purchase time for an item. If every transaction were
> handled correctly *once*, that would consume less time, but unfortunately there
> are many complications. Orders have to be followed, invoices are late in
> coming in, partial shipments entail additional operations in which time is
> consumed without any corresponding benefit in the way of more efficient pur-
> chasing performance. The time that is spent on these operations may properly
> be characterized as nonproductive time, and the burden imposed by these
> extra operations is largely what determines the efficiency of the department.
>
> Consequently, this analysis seeks to gauge nonproductive time in its pur-
> chasing operations. More important, it seeks to find out *why* this condition
> exists, so that the responsible purchasing agent in each of the several purchas-
> ing divisions may know where to put emphasis in correcting the difficulty and
> thereby improve the efficiency of operation.[1]

Just how effective this plan has been in improving conditions, and thereby
improving efficiency, may be judged by the fact that in one division the percentage of rush orders has been reduced from 20 per cent to less than 3 per
cent, and the percentage of small orders from 5 per cent to less than 2 per cent.

Whatever system and whatever standards may be adopted for measuring
purchasing performance, management owes it to itself to be informed about it.
Purchasing is the first step in production, it is responsible for the expenditure
of a significant proportion of company funds, and it represents a major item
of product cost. Too frequently regarded solely as an expense or a nonproduc-
tive factor in the company operation, it embodies potential savings at the
source and prospective accomplishments proportionately greater in net profits
than the more obvious accomplishments of production and sales. The very act
of setting standards and measuring purchasing performance should bring
forcibly to management's attention and consciousness the vast potential advantages of competent procurement. The corollary to this fact is that management will look to purchasing for the realization of these possibilities, demanding scientific, proficient performance, recognizing the accomplishment, and
implementing the function with the necessary organization, facilities, and
authority to attain the possible ends.

---

[1] "The Time Factor in Purchasing," *Purchasing Magazine,* March, 1947, page 105.

CASE STUDIES

1. BERGMAN'S SONS FURNITURE COMPANY

The Purchasing Function

Harold Bergman had built up a relatively small but thriving furniture-manufacturing business in the two decades before World War II. The basic products were various types of wooden garden furniture. To supplement this business, which was somewhat seasonal, Bergman took contracts or subcontracts for such items as home workbenches and hotel and institutional furniture. As a matter of policy (Mr. Bergman's personal decision), the market was limited to a rather small geographical area. He felt that this enhanced the company's local business relationships and to some extent relieved him from the pressures of strong outside competition.

The company's profit position was good. The principal raw material was lumber, for which several reliable supply sources had been developed over the years. This item represented about 40 per cent of product cost. Other materials and supplies represented an additional 15 per cent. Because sales and administrative costs were low, Bergman was able to add a comfortable 40 per cent markup on the standard lines. One of his business axioms was that, so long as lumber was bought right, the company had no cause for worry. On contract business, generally more competitive, the margin was not so great, but it was still satisfactory because he was highly selective in the type of contracts he accepted.

During the war years, the company received a good deal of business from military installations in the area, and the contract business grew to represent a major portion of total sales.

After the war, Mr. Bergman decided to retire and turn the business over to his two sons, now in their thirties. Both had worked for him for a few years before entering military service.

When George and Edward Bergman returned and took over the business from their father, they found it in excellent shape. The cash balance was large and materials inventories high in asset value. Plant and office were staffed with experienced older employees. The sales slack caused by the decline in military contract business was substantially offset as the postwar vogue for "outdoor living" brought more orders for garden furniture. Also, the growing popularity of "do-it-yourself" projects was creating a steady and promising market for home workbenches. The brothers decided to add these items to the regular line, and their hardware and department store customers showed good interest in the new numbers. This gave better diversification and balance to the company's operations. The younger Bergmans gradually went a little farther afield to extend their market. At the same time, they continued the policy of seeking some contract work to keep manufacturing volume at a high level.

As the business grew, they leaned heavily on Fred Wilt, who had been general manager under their father. They left all procurement and production responsibilities to Wilt, while George took charge of sales and Edward concentrated on finance and personnel. Wilt was a competent, conservative executive, as the older Mr. Bergman had been, and was completely loyal. He was considered an expert in all types of lumber and woodworking processes. He took pride in quality of product and in high standards of service. To maintain these principles, he believed in dealing only with established suppliers whom he considered loyal, and in having "plenty of materials" on hand at all times. And he tolerated no slipshod methods of workmanship in the plant.

In his search for contract business, George Bergman took a small order to do some laminating of plywood and plastic panels for an aircraft parts company. The project was experimental for both companies, but turned out very satisfactorily. Within a year additional orders came in steadily, and this phase of the business boomed until it accounted for nearly 25 per cent of all Bergman sales. This meant a rapid increase in plant personnel, a build-up in inventories, and an expansion in purchasing, both in money volume and in the number and diversity of items purchased. Plastics, adhesives, and metal trim were a few of the new items added to the buying list.

With expanding business, the Bergmans realized that a larger executive staff was needed. Among other things, they saw the need for a purchasing agent to relieve Wilt of the growing burden of procurement details. Wilt felt that this could be accomplished more simply by adding one or two persons to his own staff. The brothers, however, aware that manufacturing problems, too, were becoming more complex and demanding, and looking ahead to further growth, decided to follow out their plan for a separate purchasing department. Temporarily, at least, the new purchasing agent would double as office manager, a responsibility heretofore carried by Edward Bergman. For this position, they settled on Frank Parvis—like themselves, in his thirties. Parvis was currently employed as purchasing agent for a book publishing concern. He knew the Bergmans only slightly, but came to their company highly recommended by close mutual friends.

In a general way, the Bergmans looked upon Parvis as one of a small group of "comers" who could help build the company into a substantial enterprise. He was given a good salary and assurances that he would receive generous bonuses based on annual profits. He was told that he had a free rein in organizing and running a complete purchasing department—except that "for the time being" Fred Wilt would continue to purchase the major raw material, lumber.

Parvis set up the new department and procedures on the basis of his experience in his previous purchasing position. He took on two young men from within the company as buyers. One had been a clerk under Mr. Wilt and had handled the routine buying of shop supplies. The other had served in various positions in the plant, with a consistent record of promotions in recognition of his capacity to accept additional responsibility. Both men had been with the company for upwards of five years. Both had two years of college education, and the first one was attending evening classes to complete his work for a degree in business administration.

Except for the normal problems encountered in building any organization from scratch, Parvis had no great difficulties. Mr. Wilt seemed quite cooperative, even to the point of expressing relief that the detail of buying had been lifted from his shoulders and gratification that two of "his boys" were to be in the buying positions. At the same time, he made it clear that he considered lumber buying to be his prerogative and had no intention of surrendering it, for two reasons: his expert knowledge of the material, and his continuing responsibility for quality of product. Although, nominally, he turned over the rest of the buying to Parvis, he continued to see most of the regular suppliers who called at the plant, and occasionally he would call Parvis or send him a memo requesting favorable treatment for a certain supplier. Early in his experience at Bergman's, Parvis learned the expediency of tending toward liberal margins of safety in ordering and inventory, merely to forestall Wilt's outspoken anxiety over possible shortages of "minor" non-lumber materials, and he took pains to see that no actual shortages developed. The implied criticism, he felt, was of policy rather than of fact.

The situation was not intolerable for Parvis, but he did feel frustrated by having to share a divided buying responsibility. He felt that neither his personal nor his departmental performance could be fairly evaluated on the basis of a partial purchasing program, especially because the material excluded from his control was, in terms of dollar expenditure, the largest single factor of total purchases. Personally, he got along well enough with Wilt and had no desire to raise the issue of organization on personal or theoretical grounds. Objectively, he considered Wilt's position to be a roadblock to good, professional purchasing. He realized, too, that he had his own position to establish and prove before he could effectively challenge management's organization plan. The Bergman brothers, with complete confidence in Wilt, were not aware of any shortcoming or conflict. Meanwhile, Parvis was so occupied with other details, both of purchasing and of office management, that he tried to live with the situation until he should have his own organization fully developed and could talk with the Bergmans about centralizing all purchasing in his department.

In preparation for such a proposal, Parvis made an intensive study of the entire materials and procurement situation, documented so far as possible by actual purchase records and specifically related to the criteria of product cost and over-all company interest. Among the points he noted were the following:

A. With extended markets and the introduction of new products, the company was meeting with harder competition, so that the markup and profit margin were narrowed. To date, increased volume had maintained total profits and had enabled Wilt to effect some manufacturing economies. The materials factor of product cost had not changed significantly. The profit squeeze was intensifying, and the point of breakeven volume was steadily rising.

B. With diversification of product beyond the simple garden furniture line, lumber was no longer the unique and dominant item of purchased material cost in the same degree that it had previously been. The company was buying more lumber than before; but instead of the previous 40:15 ratio, it was now just about equal in dollar expenditure to the sum of other materials.

C. In view of both the above-mentioned factors, the theory that "right buying" of lumber is the answer to all materials cost problems must be discarded. Query: What is "right buying" of lumber?

D. Prices paid for lumber have risen by seven per cent over the past year, corresponding to the general advance in the lumber market. On new materials purchased since product diversification, there is no basis for comparison, but contracts now in force assure that the present level will hold for another six months. On materials previously used, and now bought by the purchasing department, a modest saving of three per cent over all can be shown, despite rising markets. There are a variety of reasons in respect to individual items; in general, the saving can be attributed to the closer attention given to these so-called "minor" items. Query: Is it reasonable to assume that similar savings could be made on lumber through specialized purchasing attention?

E. On non-lumber items, economical order quantities, scientifically calculated, average a 45-day supply; inventory quantities average three-weeks' supply. On lumber, order quantities are usually dictated by the carload unit, and inventories are maintained at 60 days' supply. This adds a substantial carrying cost at time of use. Query: Could scientific methods of determining order quantities, closer scheduling of deliveries, and inventory control be applied to reduce carrying cost by half? Could broadening the base of supply provide the assurance of ample material now provided by reserve stocks?

F. Concede Wilt's expert knowledge of lumber and Parvis' lack of experience with this material. Buyer No. 2, with excellent experience in working with lumber in varied shop operations, is (or can become) well qualified for lumber procurement. Standards set by Wilt or with his approval, and observed in purchasing, can give the needed assurances of quality.

G. The company now has no consistent purchasing policy. It has two policies, independently developed and administered. There should be a single policy, with the authority of executive approval.

Before Parvis had the opportunity of presenting this brief and argument to his management, the Bergmans announced plans to acquire a small electronics company in a nearby city. This concern produced control mechanisms in small lots. Its annual sales volume was about half as great as the Bergmans'. The company was highly engineering-oriented. It had two buyers, both graduate engineers, working under a vice-president responsible for product development as well as for procurement. The Bergmans had come to know the company through their contacts in the aircraft industry.

They called in Parvis, explained the new venture, and asked him to submit a report covering three points:

1. *What kind of purchasing organization do you recommend for the company, including the furniture, laminating, and electronics divisions? How should present personnel be assigned? Will more people be needed?*
2. *Write a statement of purchasing policy applicable to the entire organization.*
3. *How would you evaluate purchasing performance for all divisions, and how can we, as owners and managers, be kept informed?*

2. LUND STAGELITE CORP.

Purchasing and Management

Bart Dawson was the intelligent, ambitious, and highly articulate purchasing manager for Lund Stagelite Corp., manufacturer of theatrical lighting equipment for commercial and institutional use. Sales of the company's products, about two-thirds of which were made to order, and about one-third produced for stock, averaged $18 million annually.

Approximately 55 per cent of that figure was spent every year on purchased material and supplies.

Before coming into purchasing ten years ago, Mr. Dawson had spent close to eight years in various positions in the manufacturing and production control departments of the company. He was well-known in the company, respected for the competence he displayed in every job he had held, but was considered by many to be motivated solely by a desire for personal advancement. In the course of his career, he developed an immunity to what others thought of him and concentrated on certain goals he believed were in his own and his company's interest.

One of these goals was the establishment of a materials management system for the Stagelite Company. Mr. Dawson had developed a strong and very efficient purchasing department in the company. But his own experience and his regular study of other industrial purchasing departments had convinced him that a broader type of organization was needed to handle the materials cycle in his company. He made no secret of his view that there should be a materials department with jurisdiction over all activities involved with the acquisition, handling, and storage of raw materials. The department would, of course, be headed by a materials manager.

"Put your proposals down on paper," his executive vice-president said one day following a conversation on the subject. "I'm interested, but I'd like something a little more concrete on which to base my judgment."

Mr. Dawson immediately prepared a memorandum to the executive vice-president. Following a general description of the materials management concept, he outlined the objectives of such a program, using a list adapted from a definitive article on materials management he had read in a trade magazine. The list of objectives was as follows:

1. To provide materials at the lowest possible over-all cost.
2. To keep investment in raw material inventories at the lowest level consistent with sales and production objectives.
3. To maintain lowest storage and carrying costs and develop optimum turnover rates.
4. To improve interdepartmental communication and thereby reduce administrative costs.
5. To develop and maintain favorable relations with suppliers.
6. To maintain continuity of supply.
7. To keep down acquisition and possession costs and minimize obsolescence and deterioration of inventories.
8. To improve techniques of purchasing and inventory control.

Specifically, he suggested that these objectives could be achieved by the Stagelite Company if the purchasing, inventory and material control, and traffic functions were combined into one department. The three groups would balance one another, he said: purchasing would buy materials against a planned program; inventory control and material control would maintain stocks at desired inventory levels (against known production requirements) and establish proper turnover rates; traffic would certify receipt of materials and be responsible for storing and disbursing them to the production department. Buyers and material control planners would act as teams in determining timing and amount of raw material purchases.

Mr. Dawson listed these advantages as accruing to the company under a materials management organization:

—Responsibility for materials would be centralized and clearly defined.
—Fewer people would be needed than in individual departments. Duplication of files would be eliminated; fewer copies of purchase orders and receiving reports would be needed.
—Buyers could schedule deliveries from vendors on a much more rational basis when they had up-to-date knowledge of present inventory levels and anticipated production requirements. The time lag involved in getting this information would be eliminated. Therefore "peak-and-valley" ordering, frequent rescheduling of open orders, and short-lead-time ordering would be reduced and relations with vendors greatly improved. Close cooperation with vendors to match production requirements with their capabilities would help prevent emergencies.
—There would be less repackaging and material handling, because packaging would be specified to meet production requirements.
—More opportunities for advancement would be offered to personnel in all affected departments. The experience that inventory and material control personnel would receive would make them natural candidates for promotion to buying positions.

The executive vice-president passed a copy of the purchasing manager's memorandum to Sid Scofield, production manager of the company and asked for his comments. Part of Mr. Scofield's reply was as follows:

The materials management organization suggested is more to the advantage of the purchasing department than to that of the Stagelite Company. It would eliminate the material control function and build up the purchasing

function, but without the benefits claimed. Material planners would be dominated by higher-paid buyers, who would buy when and as much as they pleased
without reference to others.

Responsibility is clearly defined now. Production control has responsibility for inventories. Purchasing has responsibility for getting material in on
time. Material control has responsibility for maintaining stocks of raw materials at optimum levels. That's the way it should be.

Inventory turnover would not be any better than it is now. Turnover depends on amounts purchased and amounts used. Sales, then schedules, determine usage, and variations in these two elements are great. A combined
buyer-specifier team wouldn't improve the situation.

The alleged improvement in vendor relations is more of a device to improve purchasing's position. A buyer's success is measured by the relations he
builds up with his vendors and the job his vendor does. The more he can
claim "better vendor relations," the more he inflates his own importance.

Promotion opportunities exist for everyone in the Stagelite Company
through our regular merit system. The material planner would be dependent
on the buyer for advancement—again strengthening the purchasing department at others' expense.

The executive vice-president studied the two memorandums, and a week later
prepared his own answer to Mr. Dawson and Mr. Scofield.

*Write a memorandum analyzing Mr. Dawson's and Mr. Scofield's positions.
Make and explain in detail your decision as to whether Lund Stagelite Company
will consider establishing a materials management organization.*

3. NEARFRANK ROLLER COMPANY

Organization for Purchasing

Nearfrank Roller Company manufactures a wide variety of steel rolls used on
industrial machinery, ranging from small printing presses to large food-processing
equipment. Its purchasing department buys a relatively small number of items—
quality steels, several types of components, and maintenance supplies—but the
critical nature of the materials requires a high degree of skill in the buying staff.

Harry Fenlon, the director of purchases, had reorganized his department two
or three times in the 15 years he had held the position. In the last reorganization,
eight years ago, he had settled on an arrangement that paired a buyer and a clerk-
typist in a "buying team." The clerk-typist's responsibilities under this arrangement were quite broad. In addition to typing orders, she acted as the buyer's secretary. She handled all routine follow-up of orders, answered requests for delivery
information from operating departments, and occasionally handled the purchase of
nontechnical, noncritical items such as office supplies, janitorial equipment, and so
forth. Several of the more competent clerk-typists were recognized unofficially as
"assistant buyers" and were considered capable of handling many of the buyer's
responsibilities in his absence. There were six buyer-clerk-typist teams in the de-

partment, one receptionist-file clerk, an accounts-payable clerk, and a part-time clerk who helped check invoices and handle overload work of the other girls.

Mr. Fenlon was quite satisfied with the arrangement and had no reason to believe that his department's performance was considered anything but good by the company's management. When the president called in a management consulting firm to study the operations of major departments of the company, he cooperated wholeheartedly in the project. He instructed his departmental personnel to provide the consultants with information on their jobs, work habits, allocation of time, and so forth. He discussed the activity of the department and its individual members with the consultants.

To Mr. Fenlon's surprise, the management consulting firm's final report included a strong criticism of the purchasing department organization and recommended a drastic change. Excerpts from the section dealing with the purchasing department follow:

> The team basis for buying is not acceptable, as within my knowledge no other company of comparable size is using it. . . . In the team arrangement, the clerk-typist acts as a crutch for the buyer, thus weakening him to a point where he delivers less in the way of productive effort rather than more.
>
> Many purchasing departments are handling your ratio of orders-per-buyer without the use of a buying team.
>
> Under the team setup, each clerical member of a team reports to the director of purchases, but organizationally they are well removed from his direct supervision. As a consequence, each member sets her own pace.
>
> The entire clerical group is a functional one, as distinct from the line group of buyers. Their function is to handle all paper work and record-keeping. This function should be handled separately from the line group in a centralized arrangement.
>
> Labor is a commodity. You are paying too high a price for it in the purchasing department. There is not enough awareness of the productive capacity a dollar will buy.
>
> We recommend that the department be reorganized, with all clerical help grouped together under a clerical supervisor who should be appointed immediately. At least two and possibly three members of the clerical force could then be let go or moved to other departments, because workloads would be more evenly distributed and more efficiently handled.

The president called Mr. Fenlon in and handed him a copy of the section of the management consulting firm's report that dealt with the purchasing department. "They're pretty outspoken in their comments, Harry," he said. "And I want you to be the same in your answer—which I'd like to have right away."

Mr. Fenlon dictated a point-by-point reply to the criticisms listed above. Then he wrote the following general memorandum, and sent both documents to the president:

"The consultants support the concept of a strictly functional approach. I still support a combination functional-line approach.

"Every company designs its own purchasing facility to fit its own needs, with the objective of developing a strong, well-trained profit-making group. Therefore, broad statements about what should be done about reduction of clerical costs or changes in organization must be considered along with their effect on our ability to carry out major objectives.

"The consultants are well qualified to determine practical clerical workloads. But they seem unwilling to give our buyers the assistance they need to perform their functions—that is, to give good service to the shop, save the company's money, and continually increase his knowledge of the products he buys. Buyers have to have time to review requirements, get the most out of sales interviews, and make visits to suppliers' plants. They have to be free to attend conferences away from their desks and to take on another buyer's responsibilities in case of sickness or absence for some other reason. And above all they must have plenty of time for the preparation and conduct of negotiations.

"We must not reduce our clerical personnel until we are able to reduce the clerical work accordingly. We are adopting some changes, considering others, and expect to effect other improvements as we go along. Some of these will require the cooperation of other departments.

"Our present organization and clerical procedure were adopted owing to the shortcomings of the functional-type operation previously followed. I believe we have made good progress and would resist any backward steps in this respect. We have no intention of making any changes that would hinder the buyer or his ability to perform his proper function."

Write a point-by-point answer of the management consultants' criticisms and recommendations based on your understanding of the nature and scope of the purchasing function. List specific changes and improvements that could be carried out to improve the efficiency of the purchasing department. Describe and explain the need for each.

4. JACKSON CORPORATION

Personnel for Purchasing

The Jackson Corporation specializes in electronic communications equipment. Founded in 1947 to supply the Air Force with certain highly specialized items, it is still primarily a supplier to the military departments. The company has, however, steadily sought to develop some less complex commercial business as a hedge against technological change or a sharp cutback in defense spending.

Jackson Corporation's purchasing department had grown along with the company, adapting itself to expansion and changing conditions. At the beginning, purchasing decisions were made by the engineer-owners, and the administrative operations of ordering were carried out by clerks. Gradually, a full-scale purchasing organization developed to handle the rapidly increasing material requirements resulting from military orders during the Korean War. Production was limited to a few important items, and the four buyers brought into the purchasing department soon became familiar with the relatively complex parts and materials they were buying. With only slight assistance from the engineering department, they were able to handle all procurement efficiently.

Jackson Corporation's business dropped off following the Korean War but picked up considerably in a few years as the space-exploration program got under way. By the late 1950's, Purchasing Agent Archer Dix was expanding his department and adding buyers. By 1960 the department was staffed by Mr. Dix and eight buyers. Four of the buyers were college graduates, three of whom had business administration degrees, and one of whom had an undergraduate engineering degree and a master's degree in business administration. Four of the buyers had been with the company from the start and had been brought into purchasing from the manufacturing and stores departments. Two trainees, both with B.S. degrees in electrical engineering, joined the department a couple of years later and were used as expediters and general backup men for the buyers.

Space-age production and procurement problems were quite different from those faced in a war, however, and the Jackson Corporation purchasing department felt the difference. Most of the products ordered for use in spacecraft were custom-built for a particular mission, and output was in terms of one to five units, in contrast to the hundreds and thousands turned out during the war. Technological change was much more rapid. Components and materials satisfactory for one satellite were obsolete a few months later. Designers increasingly called for patented or proprietary items or highly specialized products available from single sources.

Under these complex, swiftly changing conditions, the buyers were not so quick to learn as previously, and their dependence on the components engineering department was much greater. The components engineers had responsibility for analyzing customer requirements, acting as liaison between customers and the design engineering department, and testing. They set the specifications for all purchased products that went into Jackson products. Increasingly, vendors with new ideas or suggestions for changing specifications would find themselves referred to the components engineering department after pleasant but unproductive visits with purchasing department personnel.

When the contradictions in the organization became apparent, General Manager Walter Walsh asked his operations manager to make a careful analysis of the situation. It showed that the components engineers were making more and more actual buying decisions although they had no clearly defined authority to purchase. They were also providing special services—testing, collecting technical data, and making recommendations on design—yet they had no direct responsibility for cost reduction. Further, they were spending as much time with vendors as the buyers were, with the result that salesmen were obligingly making two calls—one to the buyer, one to the engineer—and wasting everyone's time.

Mr. Walsh decided that a revamping of the whole procurement operation was needed. He was able to get Sam Harmin, manager of materials of a recently acquired Jackson Corporation subsidiary, temporarily attached to his staff to undertake the job. Mr. Harmin was a brilliant young executive with broad experience in manufacturing and cost accounting and a master's degree in business administration. He was considered one of the bright lights of the Jackson organization.

After six weeks' study, Mr. Harmin came up with the following recommendations: The entire components engineering group should be moved into purchasing, because they are in effect already selecting vendors as well as specifying components. They should be called *procurement engineers,* or *materials engineers,* to indicate that they have buying authority as well as responsibility.

One of the present buyers (with the engineering degree) should be retained as a procurement engineer. One buyer should be given a special assignment as a packaging specialist, working with packaging vendors and with components suppliers on packing of Jackson purchases. Two buyers should be assigned to buying other nontechnical, nonproduction items.

The four younger buyers should be grouped into an inventory control-buying group with responsibility for determining inventory levels and order quantities, handling all administrative details of ordering and expediting. The trainees should be transferred to another department, preferably manufacturing. The clerical help should be absorbed elsewhere in the company.

He made no recommendation concerning Mr. Dix.

Do Mr. Harmin's recommendations offer a solution to the basic procurement problems of the Jackson Corporation? Explain your answer. As manufactured products grow more complex, should there be a corresponding increase in the technical knowledge required of buyers? Is there a risk of wasting or misapplying engineering talent by giving technically trained people buying responsibilities? Conversely, would sound purchasing experience not be wasted under the organization suggested by Mr. Harmin? What effect, if any, does the difference between defense-oriented purchasing and standard commercial purchasing have on a situation such as the one that existed at Jackson Corporation? If you were Mr. Dix, what would you reply to Mr. Harmin's recommendation?

5. TEMPLE DRUG COMPANY

Buying the Right Quality

Temple Drug Company is a relatively small drug company, but it enjoys a good reputation for several of its proprietary items. Temple Toothpaste, for example, has had good sales for many years at a premium price. Much of its success has been due to a distinctive flavor that appeals to many people, and to an aggressive merchandising campaign among dentists.

About two years ago, Purchasing Agent Arthur Kaplan had worked out a highly successful program for improving the quality performance of suppliers of packaging materials. The Temple Company buys several hundred different packaging items, including over a dozen varieties of collapsible tubes for its toothpaste and other extrudable products. The production department had complained that it was having trouble with various shipments of tubes: off sizes would cause machinery breakdowns, spillage, and general disruption on the packaging line. There were also other complaints of faulty packaging, but the problem of the tubes was the most troublesome one. Mr. Kaplan decided that a complete review of the company's procurement and use of packaging materials was needed.

He sought the cooperation of the company's package-development section, representatives from the production department, and quality control engineers. Together they reviewed the company's packaging requirements, its packaging specifications, and the performance of packaging suppliers. At Mr. Kaplan's suggestion, they invited supplier representatives to a number of their meetings and frankly discussed their problems with them. Several of the committee members just as frankly expressed their suspicions that the suppliers were completely at fault for the quality problems the company was facing.

Ultimately the facts came to light and, as usual, indicated that blame for poor quality performance could be shared by both sides. In its growth from a two-man manufacturing operation in one corner of a warehouse to a good-sized manufacturing company, the Temple Company had been satisfied with an informal approach to a number of functions. Its packaging department, for example, was a relatively recent development. Over the years, the company had relied on suppliers' suggestions and drawings in buying its packaging materials instead of developing its own.

In the case of collapsible tubes, existing suppliers had changed manufacturing methods, and new suppliers had taken their own approach to design. As a result, little "gimmicks" or variations in size or shape had gradually crept into the designs of the tubes. Instead of buying a standard tube from a number of suppliers, the company was in effect purchasing a large number of specials. Eventually these variations began causing trouble on the highly automated packaging line, which requires a high degree of standardization.

With the help of its suppliers, the company's package-development group worked out a program for supplying its own drawings and set up acceptable quality levels for all major items. An interesting phase of the cooperative effort between buyer and suppliers was the program of reciprocal visits to permit representatives from the Temple Company and its packaging suppliers to see each other's manufacturing plants in operation. In one of the first visits arranged under the plan, the production manager of a bottle manufacturer was able to suggest a change that immediately cleared up a problem that had existed on the Temple Company bottling line.

A year later, Mr. Kaplan decided to try a slightly different approach to the problem posed by the rising number of complaints from the processing department about the quality of raw materials. He thought he would do some of the basic research himself in advance, rather than take the valuable time of a whole group of executives. He began by calling in vendors, discussing complaints about the quality of their products, and asking their advice. Several of the suppliers indicated that the problems were caused by the casual approach taken to specifications by Temple Company operating and procurement personnel. They pointed out that the company assumed too much knowledge on their part as to what was required; that specifications were often vague or incomplete. As a result, the suppliers would occasionally take advantage (consciously or unconsciously) of the general specifications to ship off-quality material.

On the basis of his own findings, and the comments and recommendations of major raw materials vendors, Mr. Kaplan drew up a memorandum to Fred Schulte, superintendent of the processing plant, and Morton Dunn, the chief chemist. In it he suggested that his chemical buyer, a chemical engineer, be named coordinator of a program to review and organize the company's raw materials specifications. The buyer could work with the laboratory and the using departments, as well as with suppliers in this project. As a start, he suggested taking U.S.P. (United States Pharmacopeia) minimum requirements as the basic Temple Company specifications.

"Up to now," he wrote, "different suppliers have practically been using the trial-and-error method to meet our requirements. I think we'll all agree that it's time to change this situation." He asked Mr. Schulte and Mr. Dunn to call him.

Instead of a call, he received an answering memorandum from Mr. Dunn the following day, indicating that a carbon copy had also gone to the president, Mr. Baker. In summary, it read:

> Any program of this type will only lead to further deterioration of quality. Vendors will try to get us to lower our standards, so that they can sell us standard or lower-quality items they are making in volume for other suppliers, at greater profit to themselves. We must force them to meet our specifications, or we run grave danger of losing the small but loyal market for such products as our toothpaste, one of the big features of which is its distinctive flavor.
>
> U.S.P. standards are inadequate for us, since they specify chemical purity. We make no compromise with purity, of course, but we do have special processes and special ingredients that differentiate our products from others— in color, taste, and texture. I believe we need more crackdowns and less cooperation with suppliers in this matter.

A short while later, Mr. Kaplan had a call from Mr. Baker asking him to come into his office to discuss the situation.

Assess Mr. Kaplan's handling of the raw materials quality problem. Was his failure to get immediate cooperation from Mr. Dunn the result of a fundamental mistake on his part? Or was it merely a matter of timing and handling? Outline an approach that might have produced a more favorable reaction from Mr. Dunn. If Mr. Kaplan's plan is essentially sound, how should he attempt to salvage it? How can he get Mr Baker's support for it?

6. ASPINWALL, INC.

Standardization of Product Components

Aspinwall, Inc., manufactures industrial, automotive, and domestic space heaters. The industrial line consists of six models, essentially the same in design and construction, but differing in size to provide a range in unit heating capacity. The bulk of sales volume (about 80 per cent) is in three of these sizes. Each heater consists of about 200 parts, including fasteners. Within each size there are minor electrical variations to adapt the equipment for use with direct or alternating current, 110 or 220 volts. In addition, because each installation must be individually adapted to specific conditions of location and mounting, there is for each model a variety of alternative accessory items such as hangers and brackets. Aspinwall produces in its own plant the heating elements, fan blades and hubs, outer casings, grilles, and shafting; raw materials for these manufactured items include wire, sheet steel, and bar stock in a variety of sizes, gauges, and specifications. Other components, purchased from outside suppliers, include castings, couplings, flexible tubing, bearings, manifolds, oil seals, switches, fuses, motors, ceramic cores for the heating elements, rivets, and machine screws.

The automotive heaters are generally made in larger quantities on contracts with automobile manufacturers. They are specially designed to fit available space and dashboard arrangements on each model of car or truck. At any given time there may be as many as 18 different models in current production. One of the problems is that these heaters have to be completely redesigned each year, corresponding to automobile model changes. Corollary to this is the problem of balancing out special parts and components toward the end of each model year to avoid the accumulation of obsolete items. This business is highly competitive, so that cost is an important factor.

Between these two major lines, plus domestic heaters, the stock list of production materials and parts numbers 4,100 items, including all different sizes. A few more are added with each change of design. It is only rarely that items are deleted from the list. Once a model is approved in the automotive line, the design and parts list are "frozen" for the duration of the model year; if a part is superseded in the next model, it is nevertheless kept in stock as a replacement part for heaters in service.

Aspinwall's policy is to maintain a 30-day supply of materials and parts to support the manufacturing program. Actually, turnover of production items is only about four times a year. This is partly due to the long lead times required in procuring special items, typically longer than 30 days. It is partly due to production scheduling; slower-moving models in the industrial and domestic heater lines are manufactured only two or three times a year, so that materials may be held four months or longer before actually going into production or assembly.

The purchasing agent had been quite successful, working with the maintenance manager, in standardizing maintenance and supply requirements—lubricants, cleaners, paints, small tools, and hardware—with a substantial inventory reduction, as to both variety and volume. He had been unable to make similar headway in respect to production items.

With increasing costs of materials and labor, and a moderate decline in sales volume in 1962, the company made a determined effort to cut costs. The general manager called a meeting of all department heads and announced a target of 15 per cent over-all cost reduction. He was not critical of past performance and he did not expect miracles. He believed that each department could contribute something; with a little here and a little there, the goal seemed reasonable. He promised to talk it over with the department heads individually within the next few days, looking for suggestions.

When he came to the purchasing agent's office, he said:

"I know that material prices have been going up, and I'm sure you have tried to make the best possible buys. We've just got to try a little harder. Maybe it means looking for new and better sources, or asking our present ones to sharpen their pencils. Aspinwall is a pretty good account, you know."

"Most suppliers are in the same position as we are," said the purchasing agent. "I haven't much hope of price reductions. However, I have three suggestions on how we might do better. There's just one catch. This is nothing I can do by myself. I can only ask the questions."

Exhibit 1 was a blueprint of the manifold coupling used on all sizes of industrial heaters. Attached was a memo: *Annual use, 114,000; lead time, 3 weeks; cost 29 cents each in 5 M lots.* Along with this was a page from a supplier's catalog with a penciled circle around one of the items, and another memo: *Standard coupling. Variation from our spec. ⅛" i.d., 5/16" length. Immediate delivery in any quantity. Price, 19 cents each, less 5 per cent in 5 M lots. This example can be multiplied by 12 to 20 items in the industrial line alone.*

Exhibit 2 was a sheaf of six blueprints, the special manifolds for the industrial

heater line, differing only slightly as to size. Attached was an itemized price list:

	Annual usage	30 days' supply	Unit price, min. quantity of 500	Less 5% in lots of 2,000	Less 10% in lots of 5,000*
No. 1	40,000	3,333	.92	.877	.828
No. 2	6,000	500	.95		
No. 3	8,500	710	.98		
No. 4	30,000	2,500	1.01	.96	.909
No. 5	25,000	2,083	1.04	.988	
No. 6	4,500	375	1.07		

* Orders for 5 M units can be split into two shipments. Underlined figures show best quantity price obtainable without going beyond 30 days' supply in stock.

A second memo stated: *This has to be a special item. Does it have to be six special items? If No. 4 manifold could be used on smaller sizes 2 and 3, and No. 5 manifold could be used on 6, inventory would be cut in half, with about a 20-day turnover. The price list would look like this:*

	Annual usage	30 days' supply	Unit price	Less 10% in lots of 5,000	Annual saving
No. 1	40,000	3,333	.92	.828	—
No. 2 ⎫					.041 × 6,000
No. 3 ⎬	44,500	3,700	1.01	.909	.071 × 8,500
No. 4 ⎭					—
No. 5 ⎫	29,500	2,460	1.04	.936	.052 × 25,000
No. 6 ⎭					.134 × 4,500

"I think we should have the chief engineer in to have a look at this," said the manager, reaching for the telephone.

"The dollar saving is only about 2½ per cent," said the purchasing agent, "but there are fringe benefits, and there's a principle involved. I'd like to see what he thinks of my third proposal."

The engineer agreed that both of the purchasing agent's suggestions were practicable and might be applied to other design parts after suitable investigation. "Anything else?" he asked.

Exhibit 3 was a bulky document, the latest IBM run-off of the parts inventory. The attached memo stated: *This is a list of 4,100 production items now carried in stock. We are already working on heater specifications for the 1963 automobile lines. Would it be possible to make these designs using only components already in use for similar applications, without extending the present stock list? Would it be possible to eliminate any items from this list without detriment to design or service? (There are 134 different types and sizes of rivets, bolts, and screws alone.)*

"On your first question, I won't promise," said the engineer. "I don't want to put any restrictions on our designers that would hamper them in working out the best possible heaters for the job. But I get the idea. We can try. On your second question, perhaps you and I could go over the list together and do a weeding job."

In making his standardization proposals, the purchasing agent is concerned primarily with the cost factor. How would such standardization affect manufacturing and design departments? Is purchasing overstepping its proper functions in questioning the design of the manifolds? Insofar as his suggestions concern steps that should have been taken earlier, is this not chiefly a criticism of past performance in other departments? Will it help to improve performance in the future?

The engineer's presence at the conference sets a basis for joint action in standardization. What other persons or departments should participate? What would be the most suitable organization for a standardization committee at Aspinwall? What should be the scope of its objectives and activities?

Formulate a policy and agenda for a standardization committee in respect to all three phases mentioned: (a) commercial standards, (b) company standards, and (c) simplification.

What criteria should be used in setting up a standard stock catalog on the basis of the present parts list? How valid is the engineer's argument against restricting designers' freedom of choice? What procedures or regulations could be established to resolve this problem within the framework of a standardization policy?

7. THE WASH-RITE COMPANY

Quality Control and Inspection

Since its founding early in the 1920's, the Wash-Rite Company had enjoyed a substantial position in the domestic washing-machine market. By 1929, when the industry began its first great expansion, Wash-Rite held about 30 per cent of all the electric washing-machine business in the country. Wash-Rite was literally a household word and the product was a standard of quality for consumers and competitors alike. In its merchandising and advertising, the company carefully promoted brand loyalty through emphasis on Wash-Rite quality and performance.

The success of these efforts, and the demonstrated superiority of the machine, were reflected in the price Wash-Rite was able to command. Despite the entrance of numerous competitors into the field from 1929 to 1939 (when industry output tripled, and machine prices dropped by more than half), Wash-Rite was still able to sell its product at a premium price.

The founders and owners of the company, both engineers, were justifiably proud of the Wash-Rite reputation, and they impressed the entire organization with the need for maintaining it. It was not unusual for purchasing, for example, to pay premium prices to parts suppliers who had been selling to the company since it started, and who had good quality records. With a high-priced product, steady consumer demand, and a good profit margin, Wash-Rite management appeared content to take the same attitude toward its suppliers that it expected from its customers: as long as we're getting the quality we want, we're willing to pay the price.

In the late 1940's the home appliance market changed profoundly. Sales of washing machines, ranges, refrigerators, and similar "big ticket" household items rose rapidly as the end of the war released pent-up demand. Concurrently, however, the "discount house" made its appearance in the retailing world. List prices, which had been relatively stable up to and during the war, suffered severe cutting as dealers accepted lower margins to get greater volume. The Wash-Rite Company, which had carefully policed its distribution and tried to discourage price-cutting, began to feel the effects of heavy competition. The pressure increased when major electric firms pressed hard for a larger share of the market and expressed little opposition to the discounters. Wash-Rite Company's share of the washing-machine business steadily declined.

Unwilling to stay in what they now considered a cutthroat business, the Wash-Rite owners decided to sell out to the giant Cullen Electric Company. Cullen had been making electric washing machines for several years but wanted a higher-quality product to round out its line. Acquisition of Wash-Rite offered a good opportunity to promote a highly regarded product profitably, using the mass-merchandising techniques that had been so successful on other Cullen appliances.

Cullen began an aggressive campaign to re-establish the Wash-Rite machine's position in the market. Its plan was to offer the machine at a price competitive with that of any other high-quality, premium-price washer on the market. The marketing department of the division set as its target for the following year a 15 per cent reduction in the current price (from $279.50 to $239.50) and a 40 per cent increase in production to meet anticipated sales. The engineering, design, production, and purchasing departments had participated in the planning that led to the establishment of the price and production goals, and each began to set its own goals to meet the over-all corporate objectives.

Purchasing Agent Jack Booner had already begun a major change in the Wash-Rite purchasing policy. When he moved from another Cullen division to succeed the Wash-Rite Company's original purchasing agent, Booner had recognized immediately the need for a broader, more competitive base of supply for the division. It was clear that Wash-Rite's dependence on relatively few high-priced sources for the bulk of its parts and raw materials requirements had hurt its ability to compete.

The setting of price and production targets made the development of new and more competitive sources a necessity as well as a matter of sound purchasing practice. Additional sources for major components—castings, metal and plastic parts, motors, belts, switches, and so forth—were brought in. Target prices set for purchased items, based on the finished-product target price, were negotiated.

As Wash-Rite's expanded program gathered speed, problems arose. Despite the fact that the division had relaxed its Acceptable Quality Level (AQL) on a number of parts, rejection rates were rising. At the same time, customer complaints of breakdowns and malfunction of parts increased out of proportion to the increase in sales of Wash-Rite machines.

Booner and the division's quality control manager, Henry Nelson, had discussed the problem of rejects a number of times, but had come to no definite conclusion as to how it should be resolved. Nelson, a long-time employee who had been retained when the Wash-Rite Company was acquired, enjoyed good relations with Booner. But he was firm in his stand that Wash-Rite's original approach to controlling supplier quality was sound.

Under the system then in effect, the quality control department:

—Was responsible for inspection and rejection or acceptance of incoming material. It decided when out-of-specification material could be accepted for limited use or reworking.
—Regularly and systematically reported to purchasing on vendor quality performance, both good and bad.
—Provided purchasing with various information on Wash-Rite's quality requirements and expectations. This information was to be passed on to the vendor by purchasing. It included data on current AQLs, explanation of Wash-Rite's inspection procedures, and suggestions to vendors on the use of special inspection tooling and methods.

The purchasing department, in turn, was responsible for all contacts with vendors on any question of quality performance. Its responsibility included:

—Informing suppliers of Wash-Rite quality requirements;
—Return of all rejects to suppliers;
—Negotiations with suppliers on refunds or rework charges;
—Consultation with suppliers on their quality performance records and award or withdrawal of Wash-Rite business on the basis of those records.

"Our job," Nelson declared at one point, "is to make sure the stuff coming into the plant is up to Wash-Rite standards. We have a special responsibility to our customers, both old and new, to give them the best. It's up to purchasing to police our suppliers and to put the pressure on them when they fall down on quality. If a supplier can't or won't give us the quality we want, then it's purchasing's job to drop him and go out and get another that will. If we can get an O.K. to enlarge the quality control department to handle the increased volume of incoming materials, and if purchasing will get tougher with suppliers, we can begin to lick this problem."

Booner felt that this was too simplified a view of the three-cornered relationship of quality control, purchasing, and company suppliers. He was certain that there was room for greater cooperation and coordination of effort between the two Wash-Rite departments without either surrendering any of its prerogatives. He also believed that purchasing had a greater responsibility to the company and to suppliers than to reject a vendor solely on the basis of a poor quality record, without investigating the conditions that led to it.

"If we consider the supplier an extension of our production facilities," he said, "we ought to consider his quality problems our own. Good procurement isn't simply a matter of dropping one supplier and picking up another (assuming there are that many to draw on). There are too many other factors to consider—the vendor's record in other areas, such as price and delivery, and his potential worth to us in the future. I think there should be some kind of joint purchasing-quality control effort to start the control of quality before the order is placed."

Meanwhile, the number of complaints from dissatisfied Wash-Rite customers increased. It was obvious that some strong action had to be taken soon. The general manager of the division instructed all members of the planning group—including the purchasing agent and the quality control manager—to come to the next meeting with specific, detailed recommendations on how the quality problem could be met.

Who is basically responsible for Wash-Rite's quality problem? The new division management? Purchasing? Quality control? Suppliers? Explain.

Assume you are either Booner or Nelson. Outline and defend the recommendations for solving the problem that you would make to the general manager and the planning group.

List and explain the specific changes you recommend in departmental organization, quality control procedures in the Wash-Rite plant, handling of rejects by quality control and purchasing, and quality discussions with the vendor.

Do you agree with Booner that "the supplier is an extension of our production facilities" and "we should consider his quality problem our own"? What are the implications of such an attitude?

8. WILLISTON MILLS

Buying the Right Quantity

Williston Mills is a family-owned woodworking and specialty shop. The company normally employs about 80 men. Mr. Williston, the present principal owner and manager, came up through the mill. Long first-hand familiarity with materials and with every phase of plant operations has given him an intuitive knowledge of quantities and costs; he prides himself on his ability to estimate a job quickly and accurately. The business has grown in volume and profits under his leadership. He is impatient with details and paper work, and has developed numerous rules of thumb to guide his decisions and action. "Practical results"—his only measure of performance—have been generally satisfactory. In addition to his general management and supervisory activities, he had done most of the purchasing. With increasing shop demands on his time, he decided to break in an assistant to take over the buying.

His choice for this assignment was Mr. Jarvis, a young man presently in charge of the stock room, who had shown considerable aptitude and interest in the business. Jarvis was not altogether inexperienced in buying, for he had the responsibility of keeping the supply inventory replenished. The system was a very simple one. Arbitrary minimum stock limits had been placed on each item, based on experience as to average usage and on Mr. Williston's judgment. When the supply was down to this minimum quantity, restocking orders were placed in the quantity of the convenient commercial unit—nails by the keg, glue by the barrel, jig-saw blades by the gross, and so forth. Sometimes this entailed reordering every week. On the rare occasions when an item came uncomfortably close to running out of stock, the minimum-quantity limit was revised upward to forestall a recurrence of this condition.

Mr. Williston was a firm believer in "learning by doing." Consequently, Jarvis was introduced to his new duties by being handed a copy of the latest job order. It called for 12,000 instrument carrying cases, 12 x 6 x 6 inches in size, to be made and delivered at the rate of 1,000 per month, with the option of continuing the contract for a longer period. There were eight items of purchased material: plywood for the body of the case, leatherette covering, cloth lining, locks, handles, name plates, brass corner reinforcements, and carrying straps. Nails and glue would be furnished from general supply stock. Mr. Williston estimated that the material bill would amount to about $25,000.

"I want you to buy the materials for this job and keep them coming in as we need them," he said. "On the plywood and yard goods, allow 10 per cent for waste in cutting; the rest are all counted out for you. We figure on keeping two weeks ahead at all times; that's for insurance. Anything you can buy in carload lots, do so; that's the cheapest way. On everything else, find out how long it takes to get the stuff delivered, and how much we would be using in that length of time. Buying in those quantities will get the shipments coming in just about when the old shipment is used up. We don't want a lot of stock hanging around here waiting until we're ready to use it; that ties up money for no good purpose—we want to keep our money working, too. You can stretch an order a little to bring it to even quantities, but don't do it just to get a quantity discount; that's a sales trick to pad the order."

Jarvis calculated total requirements on the job, checked the files to see where Mr. Williston bought the various items, and phoned the suppliers to get prices and delivery time. He then made a preliminary analysis (Exhibit 1) to set up the buying schedule according to the manager's instructions.

Jarvis respected Mr. Williston's judgment, and was generally in agreement with the policy of maintaining a flow of materials to correspond with the rate of use. However, he questioned the efficiency of a buying schedule that involved issuing upwards of 200 purchase orders a year on such relatively simple requirements. He noted that more than half of these orders would be for amounts of less than $100, which seemed uneconomical in view of the total amount to be spent. Despite Mr. Williston's warning on quantity discounts, it disturbed him to see that, except for

EXHIBIT 1

	Annual usage	Price	Annual cost	Weekly usage	Delivery time	Order quantity
Plywood	1,100 sheets 4' x 8'	15¢ sq. ft., less 5% in carloads of 400 sheets	$ 5,026	22 sheets	1 wk.	carload (18-week supply)
Leatherette	4,000 yds. 36" wide in 50-yd. rolls	70¢ yd., less 5% in lots of 25 rolls	2,800	80 yds.	3 wks.	5 rolls
Lining	3,000 yds. 42" wide in 50-yd. rolls	44¢ yd., less 5% in lots of 25 rolls	1,320	60 yds.	1 wk.	2 rolls
Locks	12,000	60¢ each, less 5% in lots of 1 M; less 10% in lots of 5 M	7,200	240	3 wks.	750
Name plates	12,000	12¢ each, less 3% in lots of 1 M	1,440	240	2 wks.	500
Handles	12,000	14¢ each	1,680	240	2 wks.	500
Straps	12,000	22¢ each	2,640	240	1 wk.	240
Corner pieces	96,000	3¢ each, less 5% in lots of 10 M	2,880	1,920	2 wks.	4,000
			$24,986			

the single instance of plywood, which could be purchased in carload quantity, the discount privilege on five other items was sacrificed even though total requirements were large enough to come into the quantity discount brackets if ordering quantities were increased beyond the stipulated two weeks' supply. He felt that there was a serious discrepancy in this policy, too, for his experience in storeskeeping made him conscious that plywood, the one item to be purchased in quantity, was by far the bulkiest and most difficult to store, and the heaviest to handle in and out of stock.

Jarvis was anxious to make a good record on his first major purchasing assignment. At the same time he realized that his own conclusions, like Mr. Williston's buying policies, were only a matter of judgment, and that he had no comparable background of experience to support his judgment. Before making an issue of the matter, or making a recommendation to change the buying schedule, he needed more tangible reasons. He had done some reading on the principles of storeskeeping and had in his possession a copy of the Westinghouse best-order-quantity table. (See Chapter 8.) Such procedures had not seemed particularly important in a relatively small stores operation like that at Williston Mills, but he decided to make a second calculation on that basis to see whether it would confirm his own thinking.

Using the figures of annual usage on the various items, and assuming the lowest rate of inventory-carrying cost, he checked the indicated best-order quantities and made a second tabulation (Exhibit 2).

EXHIBIT 2

	Annual usage	Weeks supply to order		
		Williston policy	Best order quantity	
Plywood	$5,026	18 weeks	5.6 weeks—125 sheets	
Leatherette	2,800	3 "	7.2 "	12 rolls
Lining	1,320	1 "	11.1 "	14 "
Locks	7,200	3 "	4.8 "	1,200*
Name plates	1,440	2 "	10.6 "	2,500*
Handles	1,680	2 "	9.7 "	2,400
Straps	2,640	1 "	8.0 "	1,920
Corner pieces	2,880	2 "	7.2 "	14,000*

* On these three items, best-order quantity automatically brings purchases into the quantity-discount bracket and reduces annual cost by $360, $43, and $144, respectively.

This entire purchasing program could be carried out with only about one-forth as many purchase orders, receiving operations, and invoice payments as under Mr. Williston's proposal. As to material cost itself, the quantity-discount savings of $547 were offset nearly half by failure to take a $254 discount on the plywood by buying in smaller quantities. Before presenting any recommendation to Mr. Williston, he made a further calculation to appraise the real effect of this in relation to the purchase investment in plywood, and the potential effect in respect to purchases of leatherette and lining cloth. He tabulated these figures in Exhibit 3.

EXHIBIT 3

Plywood

Net saving on 4,000 sheets bought in one lot	$ 96.00
Extra initial investment required	1,224.00

Return on extra investment—7.8% in 18 weeks.

Leatherette

Net saving on 25 rolls bought in one lot	$ 41.87
Extra initial investment required	410.13

Return on extra investment—10.2% in 15½ weeks.

Lining Cloth

Net saving on 25 rolls bought in one lot	$ 27.50
Extra initial investment required	214.50

Return on extra investment—12.8% in 21 weeks.

From this standpoint, Mr. Williston's instructions to buy plywood in carload lots seemed well justified, for the best-order-quantity table did not take variable prices into consideration. The advantage was even more pronounced on the other two items. By the same reasoning, therefore, the indicated buying policy was to increase the order quantity on leatherette and lining cloth to 25 rolls of each, at the quantity-discount price. Jarvis revised the order quantities noted in Exhibit 2 accordingly.

Mr. Williston examined Jarvis' figures with interest. He was skeptical of

Exhibit 2, but could take no exception to Exhibit 3 even though it was in conflict with his theory of quantity discounts.

"We can afford to tie up $600 to save $70 twice a year," he said, "but remember, you're asking me to triple the investment, as you call it, on the rest of the materials as well. If we did that all along the line, I might have trouble meeting the payroll every Friday, or in keeping our suppliers happy so that they will continue to send along the smaller quantities we need to keep the plant running."

Mr. Williston's quantity buying policies logically consider many important factors—lead time, rapid turnover, and minimum idle investment. The discrepancy between his conclusions and those of the scientifically derived table suggest that other factors have been overlooked. What are some of the hidden factors? What additional cost information must he have to calculate best-order quantity more effectively?

Is the Westinghouse order-quantity table necessarily applicable in a business like Williston Mills? Is Jarvis right in accepting this as a standard? To what extent should he use it? Can he verify it for his own purposes?

Jarvis stresses the smaller number of orders to be written. Because these are routine and repetitive, just how important is this factor? Because suppliers' prices take quantity brackets into account, should Jarvis be concerned about quantity per order?

Williston links order-quantity policy with problems of working capital. Would he do better to borrow for working capital, if necessary, to take advantage of the purchase savings and maintain his credit rating with suppliers? Is investment in materials actually idle, as he assumes?

Assuming that Jarvis takes over all purchasing for Williston Mills, what steps should he take toward formulating an order-quantity policy? How would it affect the present system on supply items? What circumstances and what specific characteristics of materials should he recognize as limiting or modifying application of a general policy?

9. TRIGSON & HOWELL

Inventory and Stores Control

Trigson & Howell specializes in the production of processing equipment for the petroleum, food, and pharmaceutical industries. The company does most of its own work in the fabrication of equipment sections requiring piping and metal sheet or plate. Accessories, such as meters, controls, and other components, are purchased from outside suppliers. Units vary greatly in size, and short-run demand from the company's customers is unpredictable. Of 20 orders in the shop at one time, more than half may be for petroleum plants. When these are complete, there may be a period of six months or more in which no orders are received from that industry, and most of the company's production is scheduled for the food industry. As a result, there is unevenness in the use of raw materials, and management is particularly concerned that there be a reasonable supply of all major items on hand to meet the varying demands of customers.

The materials cycle on a given project begins when a bill of materials goes to the stores department, which is under purchasing jurisdiction. The storeskeeper checks off all items that are available in stock and allocates the necessary quantities to the job on his record, subtracting this amount from the balance-of-stock figures. The bill of materials then goes to the purchasing agent, who places orders for the unchecked items. He also issues orders for special parts not ordinarily carried in stock. In ordering stock items—materials and components used regularly in most T & H products—the purchasing agent uses a table of economic ordering quantities based on annual usage. Orders are placed in these quantities or multiples thereof, and any excess over the amount of the immediate need is added to the reserve stock, to be applied against the next requirement.

By this system, the supply of unallocated stock is constantly, though unevenly, replenished. Also, because the allocation is made on the records but physical stocks are not assigned until they are issued from stores against an order, there is a further cushion for immediate shop demands. The presumption is that materials on order, which cover the total needs for work-in-process, will be delivered in ample time to replace quantities that have been "borrowed" from preceding deliveries. On materials that are in current demand, there may be from two to half a dozen purchase orders outstanding or in transit. Thus, although orders are placed on what amounts to individual job requisitions, materials are actually received and put into production on a flow basis, with rapid turnover.

The purchasing agent does not see the bill of materials until the engineering drawings and calculations have been completed. Manufacturing time ranges from three to four weeks on simpler jobs to four months on more complex units. Ordinarily, this provides enough lead time for procurement of purchased parts such as meters. But there are times when the shop wishes to take advantage of open time and begin work on the assemblies T & H fabricates itself. When this happens, as it has with increasing frequency, the pressure on purchasing mounts.

The company bid on a number of pieces of equipment for a large food concern in late August, 1964, and received the orders during the first week of October. Requirements of ½″ stainless steel tubing for the orders totaled 1,200 feet, somewhat higher than the normal monthly usage of that item. Average annual requirements were about 10,000 feet, and the normal order quantity was 500 feet. As the work orders were received, three purchase orders for that quantity were issued. Normal delivery time per order is about 2½ weeks. Two shipments of 500 feet each were expected by the end of the month, and 500 feet by the 10th of November.

Two weeks after the orders were in the house, the production manager stopped the purchasing agent in the hall. "Look," he said, "I have people sitting around out there in the shop twiddling their thumbs. I want to get to work on these Consolidated Food orders right now, then hold the units for final assembly. But we're all held up because you haven't gotten us enough stainless tubing. What kind of a deal is this?" The purchasing agent answered that his figures indicated that there was enough reserve stock on hand. They checked the situation together.

They found that on the first of October there were 1,100 feet of tubing on hand, but all of it allocated to other orders. In fact, total allocation amounted to 1,550 feet; but, against this additional requirement, two orders of 500 feet each had been placed in September for early October delivery. Total supply on hand and on order was, therefore, 2,100, or 550 feet more than was needed at that time. The average unit of demand, or quantity called for on a single work order, was 450 feet. On the basis of annual usage of 10,000 feet, usage during the lead time of $2\frac{1}{2}$ weeks would amount to 500 feet. Looking at it either way, the purchasing agent said, there was ample safety stock on hand.

He pointed out that the orders for the October jobs would add another 300 feet to the reserve, making it 850 feet in all. This, he said, was almost equal to a full month's normal usage, 70 per cent over average usage during a lead-time period, and almost two average unit demands.

The production manager wanted tubing, not explanations. The fact remained that there was not enough in stock for his immediate need, despite the theoretical reserve. He rejected the purchasing agent's reasoning that the safety factor had been appreciably increased by the three latest orders. A reserve equal to "almost two" unit demands still covers only one demand adequately, he argued, so the situation was really no better than before.

He held that stock policy must be set in the stores department and not as a corollary to purchasing policy; that it must be measured in terms of actual physical, unallocated stock, not in purchase commitments; and that the predetermined minimum stock quantity should have as much force in initiating a purchase for replenishment as a work order or a requisition for actual use.

"The trouble with your system," he said, "is that you really make no provision at all for safety stock. When these new deliveries come in, you will claim to show a reserve of 850 feet of tubing, but it will actually be working inventory, not reserve. Your stock clerk will allocate it against the next order. You won't know about it, and won't buy again until he has too little on hand to fill an order. In other words, there is no safety factor at all—only a succession of stock-out failures, which you may or may not be lucky enough to cover up before they become production failures."

The purchasing agent defended his policy on the ground that the determination of best ordering quantities necessarily took inventory needs and costs into consideration; that minimum stock quantities would have to be calculated as a function of lead time and usage, which were inherent in the purchasing formula; that any scientific method (that is, formula) must be based on averages, particularly average usage, and not on exceptional rates of usage such as those experienced in the October orders.

The production manager disagreed on two basic points. In his opinion, lead time was wholly irrelevant to the size of safety stock, being of concern only as a matter of procurement in the timing and size of purchase orders. Second, he said, average usage broken down to anything less than the full-year period was mathematically bound to be wrong as often as it was right; the only dependable criterion for safety in stock was maximum demand or usage within the shorter period.

Is the production manager justified in his emphasis on the importance of having inventory in advance of need? What would be the effect of his proposals on the size and cost of inventory? What could he do specifically to help purchasing provide better service on materials?

Does the purchasing agent give enough importance to the safety factor in inventory? Does the reserve stock he cites actually constitute a safety stock, or is it working inventory, as the production manager charges? Stock items are consistently purchased in quantities greater than the immediate need; is this a good policy? How could it be improved? Because the purchasing agent is in charge of inventory and stores, what factors other than stock-outs must he consider?

Does the purchasing agent place too much reliance on order-quantity tables as a means of solving inventory problems? Is he making proper use of the order-quantity formula? What elements in the T & H operation tend to limit the effectiveness of this method?

Does purchasing lead time have any significance in respect to safety stocks? Can purchasing and inventory policies be separately determined? Is average usage an adequate guide to the amount of protective stock needed?

10. RUPERT METAL GOODS COMPANY

Buying at the Right Price

In its manufacture of steel furniture, cabinets, and shelving, the Rupert Metal Goods Company uses large quantities of dipping primer as an undercoat applied to the products before spray painting. For several years, up to 1960, the business was divided evenly among three suppliers. At that time their prices were, respectively, 78 cents, 79 cents, and 83 cents per gallon. The higher-priced Vendor C was retained in this arrangement because he was also an important supplier of other essential finishing products, and the purchasing agent wished to maintain the best possible relationship with this source.

During the period of material shortages following the invasion of South Korea, the price of dipping primer advanced sharply from an average of $.80 to an average of $1.18 per gallon. However, the purchasing agent was less concerned about the higher prices (which were now frozen at the higher level by governmental price controls) than about the material shortages that had caused the rise, for the three established sources were now able to supply only 75 per cent of his total requirements. His confidence in Vendor C was doubly justified in this period. Vendor C was the only one to maintain its full quota of deliveries. Pricewise, although Vendors A and B had raised their quotations by 48 cents and 35 cents per gallon, respectively, Vendor C's price had gone up only 32 cents.

Two more sources were added to supply the needed quantities of dipping primer. One of these was a small concern, a relatively low-cost producer but with very limited capacity equivalent to only 8 per cent of Rupert's requirements; this small available quantity had not been considered significant in the normal purchasing program, despite possible price advantages, and had eliminated Vendor D from previous consideration. The balance of Rupert's requirements, 17 per cent of the total, were procured from Vendor *E*, a large company that had previously bid for the business.

When price controls were lifted in 1956, there was another sharp advance in the cost of dipping primer. With greater freedom of supply and the renewed opportunity for negotiation, the purchasing agent reviewed the price situation, tabulating the results in Exhibit 1. The purpose of this analysis was not only to compare prices from the various sources, but to note trends in price performance with reference to each vendor. The ultimate objective was to reallocate the business on the most favorable cost basis, returning, if possible, to the established policy of procurement from three sources.

EXHIBIT 1

Comparative Costs, Dipping Primer

	1950		October, 1952			August, 1953		
	Price per gallon	Per cent of total purchases	Price per gallon	Per cent increase	Per cent of total purchases	Price per gallon	Per cent increase	Per cent of total purchases
Vendor A	$.78	33%	$1.26	61.5%	22%	$1.53	21.4%	?
Vendor B	.79	33	1.14	44.9	20	1.75	53.5	?
Vendor C	.83	33	1.15	38.5	33	1.60	39.1	?
Vendor D	—	—	1.01	—	8	1.15	13.9	?
Vendor E	—	—	1.12	—	17	1.52	35.7	?
Average	.80		1.16	45.0		1.57*	34.9	

* Based on current (1952) distribution of purchases.

A second tabulation was made, Exhibit 2, based on prevailing costs of the principal raw materials entering into the composition of the dipping primer for the corresponding periods. This provided an indication of the trend in actual cost as a justification of the price increases and the "rightness" of present quotations.

EXHIBIT 2

Cost of Raw Materials
(per gallon of dipping primer)

	1950	October 1952	Per cent increase	August 1953	Per cent increase
Linseed oil	12¢	21¢	75.0%	36¢	71.4%
Hydrocarbons	12	14	16.7	14	—
Glycerine	6	8	33.3	13	62.5
East India nubs & chips	5	10	100.0	13	30.0
Pigments	7	9	28.6	9	—
Total	42¢	62¢	47.6%	85¢	37.1%

Further, it made possible an evaluation of manufacturing costs and pricing margins in respect to the various sources beyond the simple comparison of competitive prices. With a generally higher price level, it was important to Rupert to reduce the average cost of $1.57 per gallon paid for dipping primer, if possible, within the bounds of currently available quotations and a sound distribution of business to provide alternative sources and reliable supply. The cost information would be valuable in reopening negotiations.

A comparison of Exhibits 1 and 2 showed that vendors' price increases had been generally in line with the rise in material costs. Of the three original vendors, C had been most consistent in this respect. Vendor A, who had been the highest-cost supplier during the 1950-1952 period, had re-established his position as low bidder of the three following decontrol of prices. Vendor B's price was now high by a considerable margin. This might be responsive to negotiation; if not, there was a possibility of dropping B in favor of Vendor E, who was in an excellent competitive price position. Assuming an even distribution of business among Vendors A, C, and E, at current quotations, the average price of $1.57 per gallon would be reduced to $1.55.

Vendor D presented a special case. He was clearly the lowest cost producer, and his relatively modest price increase in 1952-1953 reflected his low operating costs, outweighing the material cost factor. His product and service had been satisfactory, and he was apparently satisfied with his profit margin on Rupert business. The difficulty in his situation was still the very limited capacity which kept him from consideration as a major supplier. Rupert's purchasing agent approached him with a proposal assuring him of increased orders, roughly four times as great as the eight per cent he was presently supplying, provided that D would install additional capacity to take care of the larger volume. Vendor D was receptive to this proposal, but he estimated that it would take from six to eight months to install the new equipment and get it into operation. Further, he was unwilling to guarantee that his present price would be maintained under those circumstances; with the cost of new equipment and financing, the added overhead, and business risks, he felt it would be necessary to increase his price by 5 to 15 cents per gallon.

Meanwhile, Rupert reopened price negotiations with Vendors B and C in an effort to bring these quotations more nearly into line with the others.

The analysis of raw materials prices also opened another line of approach. The biggest factor in the price increase had been the cost of linseed oil, which had tripled from 1950 to 1952 and represented more than half of the total increase in material costs. The purchasing agent suggested changing the specification from an oil-base primer to one of the newly developed synthetic-base types that were gaining acceptance in the industry. Vendors A, C, and E were already equipped to furnish the new type of primer, and a number of additional sources would be available if needed. This could reduce raw material costs by six to eight cents per gallon. His suggestion was referred to the company's engineering and laboratory departments for consideration.

Suggest a suitable basis for allocating Rupert's dipping primer orders (a) pending the completion of Vendor D's new facilities; (b) assuming the availability of Vendor D as a full-scale supplier. Is Rupert's purchasing agent justified in committing himself to place increased orders with Vendor D? Should he insist on a firm price commitment by the vendor? Would he have done better to take advantage of D's lower price simply to the extent of the vendor's capacity, without a specific commitment, even though this would be a relatively small part of total purchases?

If D's price is "right," isn't Rupert paying too much for the greater part of its primer requirements? At each stage of the study there are quotations (including the median) that are very close—.78 and .79; 1.12, 1.14, and 1.15; and 1.52 and 1.53. Does this suggest that the "right" price may lie in these areas rather than at some lower point?

Could the purchasing agent have reached the same conclusions, for practical purchasing purposes, by simple comparison of current quotations, rather than by going through an elaborate analysis? What significant additional information does this study give him? How can he use this information (a) in negotiating with Vendors B and C? (b) in formulating his own purchasing program?

In his relationship with Vendor C, Rupert's purchasing agent makes price a secondary consideration, whereas he is keenly price-conscious in respect to other vendors. Is this unfair to other vendors? Is it good purchasing? Should Vendor E, as second lowest bidder, have a place on any list of three sources for this item?

Is it within the purchasing agent's province to suggest the change in specifications? If the change is adopted, will the present price and cost study on oil-base primer have any further value? Will it be necessary to start all over, getting and analyzing new bids on the synthetic-base primer? How will this affect the commitment made to Vendor D?

11. DUBIN CORPORATION

Selecting Sources of Supply

After many successful years in the electrical contracting field, the Dubin Corporation decided to go into the business of manufacturing and installing air diffusers in commercial and industrial buildings. The move was logical in view of the company's long experience in the fabrication and installation of electrical systems. Production problems would be few because of the relative simplicity of the product. Procurement could be handled by an expansion of the present buying department, which already had considerable experience with many components similar to those used in the ventilating system—sheet metal, ducting, fasteners, and so forth. Art Berlin, who had been Dubin's purchasing agent, was named Director of Purchases and given responsibility for getting the new division's purchasing program under way immediately.

Dubin Corporation's shop force was also expanded to handle assembly and installation of the diffusers. Several experienced machine operators and an additional foreman were added, all under the supervision of Ed Anderson, general superintendent.

Because of its early establishment in the industrial area in which it was operated, the high quality of its work, and its record of on-time performance, Dubin Corporation had had little effective competition in the electrical field. As a result, the purchasing department, although not indifferent to price, had concentrated on quality and assurance of prompt delivery in dealing with vendors. Prospects for competition in the air distribution field were different, however, both from equipment manufacturers and from contractors already well established.

Berlin took personal charge of establishing new supply sources for major items that the company had not previously bought. The most important of these were the production stampings used in the diffusion unit placed in the ceilings of buildings. Special requirements called for in specifications for stampings included smoothness and cleanliness to expedite further finishing in the Dubin plant, and close adherence to tolerances to permit tight fit in installation. Berlin had had no buying experience with stampings of this type and determined to make a careful study of suppliers before making any major commitment.

Berlin also had a number of discussions with Anderson, with whom he had had an excellent relationship for a number of years. Both were aware of their limited experience with the special type of stampings to be bought for the new line, and agreed that they would, at least initially, depend heavily on vendors for advice and assistance.

After a concentrated study of the technical aspects of stamping (including an analysis of the components of a competitor's unit), Berlin began calling in suppliers. Several of them were helpful in offering suggestions when Berlin frankly told them of his lack of experience. Berlin reviewed the quotations of about six of the suppliers, considered their willingness to offer technical advice and service, and decided to narrow the field to three. The bids were not far apart, and all were within reasonable competitive range.

Following his custom with major suppliers to the electrical division, Berlin decided to visit each of the three stamping plants, in company with the superintendent and new foreman. Because he wished to see the plants in normal operation, Berlin made arrangements for his visits by telephone, only one day in advance. This, he felt, would give the suppliers little or no time to cover up major deficiencies in their facilities. None of the three companies seemed to resent this tactic, however, and all welcomed his visits.

Berlin was somewhat surprised on his visit to Company *A,* acknowledged as one of the leaders in the field, to find a rather old building and a number of old presses among the many new machines. Building and machines were, however, clean and well kept and, despite obvious high production, there were no signs of sloppiness, poor maintenance, or slowdowns because of inefficient equipment. During the tour of the plant, the company's sales engineer was joined by two men from the technical staff. They pointed out new deep-drawing equipment that produced better finishes on the stampings and an elaborate inspection setup for controlling quality. Throughout, they demonstrated an alert, progressive attitude and an interest in helping Dubin with its technical and procurement problems. Company *A*'s bid was slightly higher than those of the other two suppliers.

Company *B* was in a brand-new plant, laid out for straight-line production. It was clean, well-lighted, and almost completely equipped with new presses and other machinery. Berlin noticed that it apparently was not operating at full capacity. He was impressed by the skill of the machine operators and foremen and their willingness and ability to answer his and the superintendent's technical questions promptly. Company *B*'s purchasing agent was in the executive group that welcomed Berlin. He showed them the equipment that would be used on Dubin's order if the business were placed with his company. Just before the entire party was ready to leave for lunch at a nearby restaurant, the purchasing agent asked Berlin and the superintendent to examine the raw material stockroom. It was spacious, well-stocked, and well-equipped with a variety of materials-handling devices. A carload of steel sheet was being unloaded at the time, and he showed them the receiving procedure, which included sampling for standard acceptance tests applied to each lot.

Company *C* was the low bidder. It had a mixture of both old and new equipment, all of which appeared to be working at top speed. Both men and materials seemed to be moving at a very rapid pace, and the foreman who took the party through was polite but preoccupied. Several times he was called away to answer telephone calls or to discuss various matters with machine operators. He did, however, spend a good deal of time explaining the company's inspection and quality-control procedure, a feature of which was 100 per cent inspection of all parts. At the end of the tour, he turned Berlin and the superintendent over to the general manager, who invited them out to lunch.

Do you think Berlin's approach to selection of suppliers was adequate, considering the nature of Dubin Corporation's problem? What other steps might he have taken before visiting the three stamping plants? What do you think of his technique of visiting plants with only short notice?

Based on the plant inspections, which company would seem to be the most desirable supplier in the long run, bearing in mind the price differentials?

Would the director of purchases and the superintendent agree in their judgments of the supplying companies? What factors would most strongly influence the decision of each? Would you have added anyone else in the Dubin Corporation to the inspecting team?

12. LASSITER & COMPANY

Purchasing Research

Lassiter & Company, an Ohio corporation, manufactures popular-priced toiletries. The formulas for Lassiter products contain a number of the less common fine chemicals and essential oils, whose markets are as volatile as the materials themselves. They are the kind of materials whose price movements frequently run counter to or far in advance of general market trends, and so they must be studied and followed individually. This is particularly important in view of the fact that the company's own products are not only marketed in a highly competitive field, but must be made and packaged to fit conventional price brackets for resale. Any sharp or unforeseen price change in any one of a score of critical materials could quickly throw Lassiter's costs and profit calculations out of balance.

Mr. Newman, the purchasing agent, keeps a price record on some thirty of the major ingredients purchased. This record is kept in a loose-leaf notebook with a separate page for each of the commodities. His secretary posts to this record each day the latest price information available; if there is any change in price, she brings this to Mr. Newman's attention for whatever further investigation or action may be indicated. For a few of the more common items, such as alcohol, glycerine, and talc, daily prices are readily available. For others, weekly price reports in drug and chemical trade journals are consulted. Government commercial statistics, released monthly, showing tonnage and dollar value of imports, are the source of price information on some materials of foreign origin. It required considerable searching to find these information sources; once established, maintenance of the price records became routine. For a few special items, on which no regularly published price information could be found, Mr. Newman relied on special commodity reports from a reliable economic service. He spent about $700 per year in subscribing to such services and periodicals to keep himself fully and currently informed.

When price changes were reported, Mr. Newman tried to analyze the causes and to project a trend in terms of both the probable extent of the price change and its probable duration. He tried to verify his own judgment by comparison with general trends and the forecasts of industrial economists, by conversations with salesmen, and by reference to the futures market quotations on related products where such information existed. As a result of these continuing studies, he was frequently able to anticipate market changes and to adjust his purchasing policies accordingly.

In 1948, Lassiter & Company decided to add to its line a new fluoride toothpaste, capitalizing on the wide public interest in this theory of dental hygiene. The key ingredient in the formula developed by the company chemists was a substance known as FL-3.

In setting up the purchasing program for the new product, Mr. Newman found that FL-3 was a proprietary item, produced only by Windham Chemical Company, of Birmingham, Alabama. Windham, however, made no direct sales to users. FL-3 was a highly unstable substance, requiring skilled chemical treatment to make it suitable for commercial usage. Therefore, Windham had entered into franchise agreements with a limited number of other chemical houses, who compounded it with various types of inert stabilizing materials adapted to particular applications and distributed it in that form. Mr. Newman called in representatives of two of these companies. In consultation with Lassiter's chemists, an appropriate formulation was agreed upon, and Mr. Newman negotiated identical contracts with both suppliers for monthly deliveries of this compound.

The price in these contracts was a firm quotation, predicated on the current cost of FL-3, 66 cents per pound. There was no extensive price history for this material, which was a relatively new development, but Mr. Newman believed it quite likely that, as in the case of many other new materials, there might be a price shakedown as a result of further manufacturing experience and with the development and stabilization of logical market outlets. The representatives of the processing houses conceded that this was a possibility, but thought it unlikely in view of the fact that Windham had a proprietary monopoly on FL-3; further, although relatively new, that product was well past the experimental stage. Mr. Newman pressed the point that he was primarily concerned with procuring FL-3, or the FL-3 content of their compounds, and that this should govern his costs. Neither vendor was willing to make a price automatically adjustable in accordance with possible fluctuations in the price of FL-3. With distribution only through franchise, there was no "market price," they pointed out; their own costs, and their dealings with Windham, were, after all, confidential information. They were, however, willing to include a provision for the review of the contract price, at the initiation of either party, on thirty days' notice.

Mr. Newman immediately requested his economic service to add FL-3 to the list of items included in his special commodity price report, and shortly thereafter he began to receive this information regularly. For three years there was no change in the monthly quotations reported. The price was, indeed, being firmly held. By this time, Lassiter's purchases were twice as great as when the original contracts had been made, for the fluoride toothpaste had been a very successful product. Windham had expanded its production because of the broadening acceptance and demand in this and other fields.

In April, 1951, Mr. Newman's secretary called his attention to the fact that the reported price of FL-3 had declined one cent, to 65 cents. Mr. Newman investigated and learned that Paulus Chemical Company had developed a product of similar characteristics, known as PFL, and was making inroads on Windham's business. Windham was feeling the pressure of competition. Mr. Newman had no means of knowing how serious this situation was; but, when the price dropped to 60 cents the following month, he asked his vendors to review the price on his contracts.

This negotiation took place in June. The competition between PFL and FL-3 was now a matter of common knowledge. The first vendor, in his interview, conceded that there had been some decline but intimated that Mr. Newman's figures were not entirely accurate; his company, at least, had not felt the effect of any such cost reduction. It was his considered opinion that the price war was a temporary condition and that the price would stabilize in the neighborhood of 64 cents. He proposed a price revision on that basis. Mr. Newman's argument, meanwhile, had been strengthened by the June report of a further reduction to 58 cents per pound. He was not able to effect an agreement reflecting the entire price decline, but he did secure a compromise price revision on the basis of 62-cent FL-3. His negotiation with the second vendor followed the same pattern, with the same result.

In July and August, the price of FL-3 turned moderately upward but was still under 62 cents. In September, the price jumped to 64 cents. Mr. Newman wrote to a business friend in Birmingham asking him what was happening at the Windham Company. At the same time he asked his banker to write to the correspondent bank in Birmingham with the same inquiry. The two reports confirmed each other in general: Windham had found it unprofitable to operate at the depressed price for its product and had curtailed production very drastically, even though there was an active demand for FL-3 and shortages were developing. The businessman added that Paulus was apparently unable to supply the demand, and he predicted that Windham would be back in full production as soon as the price had been restored to a profitable level. Mr. Newman's best estimate of what that price would be, based on his previous conversations with the vendors' representatives, was 64 cents.

As he had anticipated, he received a request for price review from both vendors as soon as the price went to 64 cents. This negotiation took place in October. Meanwhile, the price for that month went up to 67 cents. In preparation for that interview, Mr. Newman made a tabulation of price history over the past several months and projected it for the months ahead. (See Exhibit 1.)

EXHIIBT 1

		Average Monthly Price of FL-3 (cents)	Basis of Contract Price (cents)	Differential: Actual Price to Contract Basis
ACTUAL	March	66	66	—
	April	65	66	— 1
	May	60	66	— 6
	June	58	62	— 4
	July	58.5	62	— 3.5
	August	60	62	— 2
				—16.5
	September	64	62	+ 2
	October	67	62	+ 5
PROJECTED	November	64	62	+ 2
	December	64	62	+ 2
	January	64	62	+ 2
	February	64	62	+ 2
				+15

The vendors asked for a price revision to the 67-cent basis. Mr. Newman showed them his tabulation, which was predicated on stabilization of the price of FL-3 at 64 cents, which was their own forecast, not his own. He pointed out that for five months, during which the contract had been priced on the basis of 66 and 62 cents, the vendors had procured FL-3 at substantially lower costs. If the price now held at 64 cents, as seemed likely, the present contract could be continued without adjustment through the following February and they would still have a slight advantage on the year's business as a whole. They protested that it was unreasonable to ask for a contract under which they would show a loss for several months to come. Mr. Newman said that this was not his proposal. He believed it was just as unreasonable to ask for a contract based on 67-cent FL-3. The equitable basis, in his opinion, was to adjust to the 64-cent price, effective with October deliveries; even though this would show an apparent loss for the vendors for the current month, there was a minimum risk involved, in the light of the previous history and the projection. The 67-cent price quotation presumably reflected a temporary shortage which would be promptly corrected, probably before the end of the month. Mr. Newman strongly suspected that neither vendor had bought any substantial quantity of FL-3, if any at all, at the 67-cent price; it was more likely that they had filled Lassister's September and October orders with 60-cent FL-3 procured in the depressed market of May-August.

Paulus Chemical Company offered to sell PFL to Lassiter & Company at 61 cents per pound in the uncompounded state. The chemists were willing to accept this substitution, but the manufacturing department did not believe it was economical to undertake the extra compounding operation.

At what price basis should the contract for FL-3 compound be set in October, bearing in mind the possibility of further price reviews? Is Mr. Newman's proposal, based on probability rather than actual quotations, an equitable one? How does his commodity and price research improve his bargaining power? Compare the effectiveness of this method with his first request for price adjustment by formula, tied directly to the price of FL-3.

Does Mr. Newman make maximum use of his price information? For example, should he have pressed for more frequent and larger price reductions in the May-August period? Should he have increased the quantity of his purchases during this period, in anticipation of the September price advance?

What advantage, if any, did Mr. Newman gain by dealing with two suppliers of FL-3 compound when both were dependent on Windham Chemical Company as to supply and cost and both quoted identical prices and terms? When the competitive situation developed, should he have changed his purchasing strategy? If so, how?

Should greater consideration be given to Paulus' offer, as a means of maintaining competition? Should Lassiter & Company try to secure a franchise from Windham, for the advantage of direct dealing?

13. CASTAIN BATTERY COMPANY

Planning and Forecasting

The Castain Battery Company, prior to 1948, was using about 5,000 short tons of lead annually in the manufacture of storage batteries. The business was a very stable one. Castain had a steady outlet for more than half of its total production, sold to Logan Motor Company, a manufacturer of trucks and tractors. The price of batteries on this contract was tied in with the current market price of lead. On the supply side, the company had contracts with two primary metal producers for weekly carload deliveries, to be billed at the average published market price for the month. This not only provided a steady flow of material, but protected Castain against the effect of short-term price fluctuations. Altogether, the price and quantity risks of buying and selling seemed to be minimized under these arrangements, and the company fared well. A reserve inventory was maintained at about six weeks' supply.

In the slight recession of the late 1940s, the price of lead dropped from 18 cents to 13.5 cents per pound, and Castain Company was caught in a squeeze. It took a substantial inventory loss on metal stocks in hand. In addition, during the decline, end-of-month prices were below the average for the month, so that prices paid were consistently higher than replacement value. Further, under the price agreement with Logan, batteries were sold at a loss for several months as lead bought at higher prices went into batteries priced at the current lower-cost basis. Meanwhile, Logan's requirements were cut in half, so that the normal six-week inventory represented almost three months' supply. The purchasing agent was able to curtail his supply contracts to a twice-a-month schedule, as the low price was not attractive to producers and they were willing to cut production.

A policy meeting was called at this time to consider the situation from all angles. It was impracticable to approach Logan seeking a revision of contract terms. Competing batteries were being offered at the same depressed prices, and Logan would have little trouble finding a new supplier; in all likelihood, that was what they would do to protect their own cost position. This would put Castain in the very difficult position of trying to find new outlets for half of its production in a period of generally depressed business, and of probably losing Logan permanently as a customer. On the brighter side, it was the consensus that lead prices had reached bottom; whatever happened, the next price move could only be upward. If and when that move came, with rising prices the company would begin to recoup some of the losses incurred on the downward cycle. Meanwhile, because there was no immediate prospect of improvement, the company decided to work off its inventory, and the purchasing agent was instructed to keep reserve stocks to the absolute minimum consistent with production requirements, to conserve working capital, and to continue that policy until there was definite evidence of business recovery.

This situation prevailed for nearly two years. In 1950, the purchasing agent asked and received permission to resume buying lead for inventory. Logan's orders had picked up again and the business outlook in general was far more cheerful. The price of lead was then 14.5 cents per pound. The purchasing agent predicted that it would rise to its former levels as fast as demand warranted. Within the next two years, the price advanced 20 per cent, to 17.5 cents, which was still substantially under the 1948 price, but further advances seemed imminent with the introduction of a new factor—the prospect of defense production demands. During this period of expanding business and rising prices, Castain maintained a consistently favorable cost position, but the purchasing agent had not had much success in accumulating reserve stocks. Even at 17.5 cents, the price was not very attractive to the mining and smelting industries, and they were reluctant to push production. Castain's battery production was now approximately equal to the volume of five years earlier, but the company had not been able to restore its contract purchases to the former quantities, and it was now buying a large part of its requirements on the open market. Like some other companies in the field, Castain had to turn down some business for lack of the raw material. Logan Motors alone would have increased its orders by 25 per cent if Castain could have accepted them. The company decided, however, that it would not be good policy to commit so large a proportion of its business to a single outlet. Logan was forced to divide its orders, placing some with another battery manufacturer.

Following the Korean War, government contracts were being cut back or cancelled. Inventory restrictions were relaxed, and normal civilian product uses once more became the major concern. Castain's supply of lead, procured for government orders, placed the company in a fairly comfortable position. Nevertheless, the purchasing agent again asked for permission to buy more aggressively for inventory. The former policy of maintaining a six-week supply was not sufficient protection, in his opinion. He expected that lead would be in short supply for at least another year. Furthermore, he saw no financial risk involved, for it was probable that the price would increase sharply. From his conversations with lead producers, he expected that the price would go to 20 cents a pound, or even higher. On the strength of these representations, he was authorized to extend the inventory as rapidly as possible to a four-month supply.

At this time, the purchasing director of Logan Motors came to Castain and inquired as to the supply situation and policy. He was well aware of the situation in lead. He estimated that Logan's requirements would increase by another 25 per cent in the year ahead and was anxious to safeguard both his supply and his costs. He proposed that his company would finance the purchase and carrying costs of sufficient lead to make a year's supply of batteries, at the present price or the best price obtainable to complete the purchase. In consideration of this, he asked for a firm price contract on batteries for the year, to be determined after the average price of the lead was known. He pointed out that this would not materially change the present pricing basis, except that Logan would assume the entire risk and cost of forward buying to cover a year's requirements.

Castain declined this proposal on two grounds. The purchasing agent doubted that he would be able to obtain any such quantity in addition to other current requirements. The sales manager felt that he would be in a poor competitive position if all or the bulk of low-cost lead were allocated to a single customer; he foresaw serious complications in customer relations, even if it were possible to procure the lead, in maintaining a dual price in the event that costs should rise as anticipated. Logan renewed its contract with Castain on the former price basis.

Logan made the same proposal to its alternative supplier, who also rejected it. However, in this negotiation the supplier agreed to make batteries at a fixed manufacturing fee, provided that Logan would purchase lead for its own account and provide the material to cover its battery orders. Logan's purchasing director agreed to this and promptly set about buying lead wherever he could find it. The price of lead went up to 18.5 cents per pound. More metal became available at the higher price and, by acting quickly, Logan covered its year's requirements on the second contract within the range of 18.5 to 20.5 cents.

At the time of the first price advance, Castain had accumulated slightly more than a two-month reserve stock. The purchasing agent reported that, with the higher price return, the acute shortage in mine and smelter production would be relieved. Nevertheless, he advised continuing to buy for stock, up to the four-month supply level, until the price reached 22.5 cents, which now seemed probable. Meanwhile, business quickened faster than the company had anticipated, and his reserve stocks were drawn upon several times for current manufacturing needs before he was able to achieve the desired ratio at the end of the year. By that time, the price had gone over 22.5 cents. Castain's purchases of lead in 1955 averaged 21.5 cents in cost. In calculating prices on Logan's battery orders, based on current market price, the cost averaged 21 cents over the year, but on all this business Castain made a reasonable profit on material through forward purchasing on the rising market.

Before the end of 1957, the price of lead had gone up to more than 28 cents per pound.

In the 1948-1950 period, the average-current price policy worked well for Logan Motors, but it caused a loss for Castain Company. How is this linked with forward-buying policy? Does it imply any difference in skill in forecasting business conditions?

Was Castain Company right in curtailing forward purchases when lead prices were at their lowest point? More liberal forward purchasing would have eased problems of supply, protected product cost, and afforded the opportunity of profits through inventory appreciation. Which of these was most immediate and most important? When lead was most difficult to obtain, owing to depressed prices, should Castain's purchasing agent have offered premium prices to procure his requirements?

Castain and Logan agreed as to the probable course of supply and price trends, but Logan was the more aggressive in action to meet them. Was Logan's proposal a legitimate method of procurement? Would Castain have benefited by accepting the proposal? Should Castain have considered the purchasing and sales phases separately, and would this have made any difference in the decision? Is the action any more, or less, speculative, depending on whether Logan or his supplier purchases a year's material in advance?

In the light of previous experience, and assuming that the price advance from 22.5 cents to 28 cents was predictable in trend if not in actual extent, suggest a two year forward-buying policy for Castain Company. For Logan Motors.

14. JARMAN PRODUCTS, INC.

Working under a Purchase Budget

About two-thirds of the business of Jarman Products, Inc., consists of zinc die castings and extruded parts sold to automotive manufacturers. These include grilles, radiator ornaments, and inside trim. They are bought on the basis of annual contracts, with monthly release orders; the release order specifies the quantity to be shipped during the current month and an estimate of the quantity that will be required in the following month. The other one-third consists of accessories, including horns, rear-view mirrors, directional signals, and spot and fog lights, which are sold under Jarman's own trade name to wholesale and retail automotive supply dealers. These products are manufactured for finished goods inventory, and sales orders are filled from stock. Work orders are issued by the production planning department, based chiefly on the volume of new sales orders, with some consideration also for available machine capacity, to keep production at a generally even rate. Materials for the accessory manufacturing business are drawn from stores, which issues purchase requisitions to maintain supplies at predetermined stock levels.

Jarman's volume and distribution of business had been fairly steady over a period of several years. Sales outlets on both lines were well established. Sales volume expanded moderately, at a rate of about five per cent a year. The general inventory policy was to keep sufficient materials on hand to support six weeks' production. Stock limits were adjusted from time to time to keep pace with expanded sales.

In 1961, though the company was financially sound, it had to negotiate several short-term bank loans to supplement working capital. The comptroller analyzed the situation and attributed it (a) to excessively high and unbalanced finished goods inventories, without any compensating reduction in production stores; (b) to forward buying of raw materials, particularly zinc. He felt that existing inventory control methods should be strengthened by budgetary procedure, and that the most effective place to apply budget controls was at the purchasing stage.

For budget purposes, purchases were divided into the following categories:

1. Major raw materials for automobile manufacturing orders.
2. Other raw materials for automobile and accessory lines.
3. Purchased components, including lenses and mirrors.
4. Plating materials and supplies.
5. Packing and shipping supplies.
6. Miscellaneous maintenance and operating supplies.
7. Fuel.

For production materials, groups 1, 2, and 3, an annual budget figure was set for each group, predicated on expenditure and usage for the past 12 months, and adjusted to the volume of anticipated sales; these figures were not itemized within the respective groups. Similar budget figures were set for groups 4, 5, and 6, calculated as a percentage of production material cost, from past-experience ratios. The conventional method of budgeting operating supplies as a percentage of productive payroll was not followed, for the reason that a single basic figure of reference was desired, and it was felt that the conversion of payroll expense to the proportionate production-volume figure was sufficiently accurate for control purposes. Fuel—in this case, natural gas—was handled in the same way, except that requirements for heating, as distinguished from power, were separately budgeted and allocated specifically to the months during which the heating plant was operated.

In group 1, where materials did not pass through general stores, the purchasing department was directly responsible for budget performance. The purchasing agent was permitted to buy one-twelfth of the annual requirement in any given month without further authorization. If actual usage exceeded this amount during the month, so that reserve stocks were depleted, the allotment for the following month was increased by the budget committee to provide for replenishment. If the purchasing agent wished additional funds for forward buying, he had to get a special appropriation, which was carried as a debit against the budget allowance until offset by underbuying in succeeding months.

In groups 2 through 6, where materials were purchased for and disbursed from general stores, the procedure was somewhat different. The monthly budget amounts were related directly to actual sales volume. Sales for the current month were calculated as a percentage of anticipated annual volume, and the budget figures in each group were set proportionately. Meanwhile, monthly records were accumulated from the purchasing department showing total orders placed in each category of materials or supplies, and from the stores department showing total disbursements. At the end of the month, differences in purchases versus budget and in purchases versus disbursements were noted in a cumulative variance record. Whenever such variances amounted to 10 per cent (plus or minus) of the cumulative budget figure based on sales to date, they were investigated with a view to corrective action.

For example, if purchases exceeded budgets and disbursements, it indicated that inventories were being increased disproportionately to current business. If purchases were in line with budgets but exceeded disbursements, the probability was that production was lagging, and the comptroller could expect a corresponding lag in accounts receivable.

If purchases were less than budgets and disbursements, it could mean that inventories had been excessively high, or that they were being depleted below the safety point, or that purchases were being deferred for some reason. In the latter case, a situation was being built up that would call for future purchases in larger volume to satisfy requirements, and the comptroller could anticipate unusual demands against his cash position. It was the lack of such information that had prompted the budgetary procedure in the first place.

Because the budget was set realistically, based as closely as possible on anticipated requirements and expenditures, it was expected to balance out closely over the period of the year. If the trend in actual sales was substantially greater or less than the original estimate, the total budget figures were adjusted accordingly. The month-to-month check of variances was primarily a control designed to regulate the flow of expenditures in accordance with current requirements, to correlate purchase commitments with the company's cash position, and to keep the investment in materials at an economical level consistent with demand and safety. If the variances were large, or persisted over any extended period of time, it indicated either that sales estimates were faulty, or that supply cost ratios were out of line, or that inventory policies needed adjustment. Correction of any of these factors, as needed, was in the direction of better planning and management, for better profits.

During the first six months of 1963, sales to automobile manufacturers were at a high rate, and raw materials requirements consistently exceeded the budgeted amount of one-twelfth of the projected total for the year. The purchasing agent received and spent an additional budget allotment for this account in four successive months. About half of this requirement was for zinc, which, like most metals at that time, was in very tight supply. The purchasing agent was under constant pressure to procure the additional quantities needed. In July, orders from manufacturers began to taper off seasonally, corresponding with the lull in production during redesign and retooling for the new-car models. Release orders indicated that August and September volume would be at only about half the rate of the first six months. This was not unexpected, for Jarman's business was always drastically affected. The products that Jarman furnished, grilles and trim, were highly stylized; if anything in car design were changed, it was almost certain to include these items. Consequently, for a period of several weeks production schedules were limited to balancing out the old lines and building up such stocks of the parts as might be needed for service and replacement after the present models had been discontinued. Jarman generally took advantage of this period to build up its finished goods inventory on the accessory lines.

Although actual requirements of raw materials were well under budgeted quantities for these two months, the purchasing agent continued to buy up to the full budget allowance, spending the funds that were in excess of current need chiefly for zinc. He was prompted to do this because of the continuing scarcity. He saw an opportunity to build up his inventory of the metal against the expected heavier demand of the fourth quarter, when the new models would come into production. He could do this within the regularly budgeted allowance without incurring a budget debit for forward buying. He estimated that by October 1st he could double his normal six weeks' reserve stock. This would carry the company safely through the balance of the year, even though zinc should become increasingly hard to get, as seemed likely.

Midway through September, the company was informed that it had lost one of its two largest automobile accounts to a competitor. In October the second large customer was obliged to curtail car production by 25 per cent owing to the shortage of steel, and cut back its parts orders correspondingly. The quantity of zinc that had been regarded as a prudent 12 weeks' supply suddenly loomed as a 30 weeks' supply.

When the comptroller revised the raw materials budget to fit reduced sales for the fourth quarter, this situation led to a heated argument. The comptroller charged that the purchasing agent had violated the clear intent of the budget plan in stockpiling zinc; that he should have curtailed his third-quarter purchases of zinc in proportion to demand, and in balance with other materials; and that he should have come to the budget committee for specific authorization before making forward purchases. His overbuying had made the whole control procedure futile and had placed the company in a very bad position. The purchasing agent defended his action on the ground that he had made these purchases within the materials budget set for him; that the budget system in itself recognized a basic difference between buying raw materials and buying parts and supplies; that he had used the flexibility of the plan expressly to avoid variances such as had occurred in four months of the first half-year, when the budget was inadequate. He argued that the excess and imbalance of stock resulting from this action were not due to faulty purchasing judgment, but to the breakdown of the budget estimate and the failure to maintain sales.

Did the purchasing agent make improper use of the materials budget as an express or implied authorization for forward buying? Would the argument as to budget conformance have arisen if Jarman had not lost the orders from its two largest customers? Does this suggest that the failure of budget control in this instance was due to (a) weakness in the budget system, (b) purchasing policy, (c) lack of coordination, or (d) unforeseeable circumstances?

Should the raw materials budget control be placed on the same basis as used for other materials and supplies? How could raw materials control be made more effective? For example, by using information on release orders to set the factor of current demand? By itemizing the budget, particularly on such an important material as zinc? By using a shorter budget period? By making allowance for seasonal variations, as in the case of the fuel budget?

Would the changes you recommend have avoided Jarman's problem in respect to zinc purchases? Would they unduly restrict the exercise of purchasing judgment? Would they give the comptroller the information he is seeking?

Is Jarman's budget period of one year too long to be successfully used for control of materials inventory and purchasing? When a specific budget figure is set in any category, would you consider this an invitation (or temptation) to spend up to the full budgeted amount?

Should greater emphasis be placed on conformance to budget as a measure of performance, rather than merely analyzing variances after the fact?

15. HAWLEY & BROTHERS

Value Analysis

After several years of pleasant but in many ways frustrating experience as purchasing agent for Hawley & Brothers, Dan Dinnock was getting restless. He had no complaints about his personal treatment from the company, an old, conservative manufacturer of toys and games. But the management was strictly engineering-oriented and gave other departments, including purchasing, very little chance to use initiative, to innovate, or to depart very far from established ways of doing things. Mr. Dinnock, who made it a point to stay abreast of the latest procurement techniques through reading in trade magazines and attending educational sessions of his local purchasing association, felt stifled every time one of his suggestions for improvement was politely rebuffed.

He took a new lease on life, however, when Hawley & Brothers bought out a small firm, in the same city, that made baby furniture, wagons, and bicycles. His department was given a bigger buying job (the smaller firm's purchasing had been done by the two partners), and he gladly accepted the challenge of increased responsibility. The very fact that Hawley & Brothers was expanding, he reasoned, indicated that management might be more receptive to new ideas than they had been in the past.

One of the new concepts in purchasing that intrigued Mr. Dinnock was value analysis. Here, he thought, was a technique that could help make purchasing a scientific, profit-producing function. Still a little gun-shy from previous resistance to his suggestions by management, he determined to build a strong case for value analysis—prove its worth beyond doubt—before proposing the idea of a formal value-analysis program to his superiors.

Without mentioning it outside his department, he set up a small, informal value-analysis program with his buyers. They met once every week, for two hours on Friday afternoon, to review components they purchased for both divisions of the company. They submitted each of the parts selected for analysis to the "Ten Tests for Value" made famous by the General Electric Company. When a promising project appeared to be developing, one person was given the job of accumulating cost data on the part, estimating savings through substitution, capabilities of various vendors of the part, projected savings over a given period, and similar data. This extra activity was burdensome in terms of time and effort, but the entire group was enthusiastic about its possibilities.

After half a dozen inconclusive meetings, the group finally came up with a project that showed promise. Studying the function of four threaded rods used on a line of express wagons, they questioned the special design of the rod and the fact that the thread was cut on a screw machine. Buyer Jack Bolton, follow-up man on this project, ultimately came up with the following information:

> The holding function of the rod was not critical, could just as easily be performed if the thread were rolled (a much cheaper process than screw machining). The special bend in the rod had been designed in during the manufacture of an earlier-model wagon, was no longer necessary in the current streamlined design. A standard rod widely used in the automotive industry would do the job just as well. A specialty supplier, now making similar parts, could supply the rolled-thread, standard rods to Hawley & Brothers for approximately two cents each. The company was currently paying ten cents each for the specially designed part.

In his enthusiasm over coming up with a substantial potential saving, Mr. Dinnock lost some of his caution. He went directly to the president. "T.J.," he said, "just look at this. An 80 per cent reduction in part cost on just this one item. And we use thousands of them. Our group came up with this almost in their spare time. Think what we could do with a real value-analysis program—with a full-time value analyst." He went on to explain the basic principles of the technique.

The president listened attentively and complimented the purchasing agent on an excellent "cost-reduction suggestion." But he seemed unimpressed by Mr. Dinnock's proposal to establish a formal value-analysis program. "Our engineers will get around to these things eventually," he said, apparently assuming that the products of the toy and game division were already so well-engineered that value analysis of them was unnecessary. "You can be a good stimulus to them by this approach—which is really only good buying to begin with, isn't it? Go and talk to the engineers about what you're doing, and the two of you can probably work out a good cost-reduction program."

Mr. Dinnock quickly realized that he had made a mistake. "Should have value-analyzed my own approach to value analysis," he ruefully told his buyers at their next meeting. They took him literally and began to suggest alternative approaches. Among their suggestions were these:

> Develop and document more than one value-analysis project and present them as a "package" to the president, detailing in dollar figures the total savings to be achieved in one year.

Present savings on a given product—the express wagon, for example—in cumulative form and show, if possible, their effects on the profit margin on that product. Or, if the product is a highly competitive one, show how value-analysis savings would make more competitive pricing possible.

Using the kind of figures developed above, make a formal presentation to the president, asking for an organized value-analysis program in the plant. Show the potential "payoff" on value analysis as compared with the cost of setting up a value-analysis organization.

Alternatively, suggest that purchasing be allowed to "borrow" an engineer from design engineering for a few half-days a week to work on value-analysis projects developed in conjunction with buyers and vendors.

Go around management for the time being, and try to expand the informal program by bringing the production and engineering departments into it. Later, with concrete results obtained by this method, present a united front to management and ask for a formal value-analysis program.

Was Mr. Dinnock's initial "secret" approach to value analysis sound? How else might he have run his campaign to get a value-analysis program going? Wouldn't engineers consider purchasing's efforts at value analysis interference in their affairs? Do you agree with Mr. Dinnock's own estimate that he had "made a mistake" in taking his first value-analysis project to the president? Explain.

Would you agree that the president's reaction is fairly common in industry? How much justification is there for it? Which of the alternative approaches suggested would you support? Discuss.

16. ALBREE MOTOR PARTS

Negotiation

The vice-president of Albree Motor Parts was much impressed by the conveyor system in a new plant erected by one of its customers. The installation, he learned, had cost $110,000. It had been specially designed for that plant and was an integral part of the operating plan. The customer was well pleased with it. He had no breakdown of operating costs specifically applicable to this equipment but considered it the key to over-all plant efficiency.

Materials handling was a major item of expense in Albree's own operation, amounting to nearly 30 per cent of total manufacturing cost, or about $3 million a year. This included the movement of raw materials in and out of stores to the machines, through several fabricating processes, and delivery of fabricated parts to the production assembly line and thence to finished stores. The plant was well laid out for sequence of operations and had been extensively mechanized; but, because the handling equipment had been acquired piecemeal as the company expanded and new needs arose, it was not completely coordinated. Considerable rehandling was required at and between work stations. By means of power-lift trucks, manual handling was kept at a minimum. Total investment in materials-handling equipment was carried on the company's books at the depreciated value of $130,000. Replacement cost at current prices was estimated at $300,000. There was $90,000 available in the capital equipment reserve account, accumulated on depreciation schedules.

The vice-president sent the chief engineer and the general superintendent to inspect the installation at the customer's plant. At the same time, he asked Northeastern Equipment Company, makers of that equipment, to survey Albree's situation and make recommendations. Northeastern's proposal, after this study, was to retain about half the present equipment, with minor changes, replacing the rest with an overhead-conveyor installation similar to the one that had appealed to the vice-president in the first place, but tailored to Albree's special requirements. The cost was estimated at $140,000. It seemed probable that savings of double that amount would be effected in materials-handling costs each year. The superintendent felt that certain modifications and additions to this plan would be necessary to obtain maximum benefit. With these changes, $8,500 was added to the bid.

A conference was called, including the president, treasurer, and director of purchases, to consider the proposal. The discussion centered largely around the extra charge. The president and treasurer held the view that Northeastern, a specialist in the field, was best qualified to tell what was needed; they felt that only the original proposal should be considered. The superintendent contended that the problem at this point was to find the best possible solution to the materials-handling needs, and that those who were to use the equipment could make a practical contribution to that decision. It would still be possible to make any necessary compromise, for cost or any other reason, but it seemed more logical to him to have an optimum goal as the starting point. In the present instance, the indicated saving was more than ample to provide the complete installation.

The engineer agreed that the suggested changes were desirable, if not absolutely necessary, but recommended that cost studies be made to see whether the added investment would be justified economically. As a matter of fact, he pointed out, their cost information on the whole project was not only meager but hypothetical. It seemed fairly certain that substantial savings could be made, but he felt that these should be verified and calculated more accurately before the money was invested.

The director of purchases had two suggestions. He proposed, first, that Newell Company, which had installed most of the present conveyor equipment, should be asked for advice and costs of modernizing the existing installation, if possible, to achieve the same result. Second, he believed that competition should be invited on systems comparable to Northeastern's, so that results and costs could be better evaluated. The engineer supported this view. The vice-president was cool to both suggestions. As to the first, plant efficiency was already suffering from a patchwork policy on materials handling. As for alternative sources for new equipment, he had great confidence in Northeastern due to the installation he had inspected, and he felt under some obligation to that company on account of the survey they had made. The director of purchases felt no such obligation to Northeastern. He did feel a responsibility to his own company to explore the alternative possibilities. He could at least secure descriptive literature from a number of manufacturers, without committing the company in any way; if any of these products seemed appropriate, the group could then decide which manufacturers, if any, should be invited to make a proposal.

The chief engineer mentioned that he was planning to attend the annual Materials Handling Show in Cleveland some weeks hence. He suggested that the others also attend this exhibit to see at first hand what types of equipment were being shown, and to judge how they might fit Albree's needs. The vice-president, superintendent, and director of purchases also made the trip. They found several systems that were interesting, ranging all the way to full automation, and noted some new developments that could be incorporated to advantage in their own specification. By process of elimination, their preference was narrowed to two firms, Fitch Corporation and Merritt Conveyors, whose product was basically similar to Northeastern's. Bids were invited from each of these companies.

When these quotations were received, Albree had four proposals to consider:

Newell Company offered supplementary equipment amounting to $22,000, expanding the present installation to take care of increased volume, without any significant change in present methods or flow.

Northeastern, as previously noted, proposed to replace half of the present equipment with a new overhead system that was considerably faster and more efficient. The cost was $148,500. The director of purchases believed that he would be able to dispose of the replaced equipment, within a reasonable time, for about $45,000, or 70 percent of its current book value.

Fitch's proposal was substantially the same as Northeastern's, on a bid of $144,000.

Merritt bid on a completely new system, costing $275,000. Certain features of their equipment, they believed, were so far superior to the present installation that a fully integrated system would show much greater efficiency. In this case, the disposal of old equipment would bring up to $75,000.

In tabulating these several proposals, the director of purchases found it very difficult to evaluate relative performance and efficiency, because there was no direct factor of productivity that could be measured and applied against cost as in the case of production machinery. In consultation with the manufacturing and cost acccounting departments, he listed three factors that might serve as useful indicators.

1. Direct maintenance charges of five per cent annually on total cost of equipment.

2. Estimated savings in manpower for materials-handling operations. With Newell's additional equipment, four of the present employees could be dispensed with or transferred to other duties. Northeastern's and Fitch's installations could be operated with nine fewer employees. Merritt's system, more completely mechanized and coordinated, would require 14 fewer men than the present system.

3. As a measure of improvement in over-all manufacturing efficiency and cost saving, a cost study was projected as accurately as possible for each of the proposed systems. Under present conditions, materials handling represented 30 per cent of total manufacturing cost. With the additional Newell equipment, this would be reduced to 28 per cent. With the Northeastern or Fitch equipment, it would be

further reduced to 25 per cent. With the completely new Merritt system, it would be only 22 per cent.

The cost department further applied standard overhead and depreciation schedules for the new investment.

Technically, the engineer believed that any one of the four proposed systems would be adequate. In order of excellence of the completed installations planned, he rated them: (1) Merritt; (2) Northeastern; (3) Fitch; (4) Newell. He stressed that this did not include any economic factors. It did give some weight to the newness of the equipment. This gave the edge to Merritt in the immediate evaluation, an advantage that might be modified if all bids contemplated a wholly new installation.

As a matter of personal preference, the vice-president and superintendent were still favorably disposed toward Northeastern, largely on the basis of the successful installation they had inspected.

Evaluate the four proposals on the basis of information gathered and judgments expressed. Which factors should prevail in the final decision—management's concern with capital expenditure, the superintendent's preference as user of the equipment, the engineer's technical appraisal, or the purchasing director's economic analysis? How, and by whom, should the final decision be made?

Could the problem be solved more expeditiously, and just as competently, without the conference method? Should the director of purchases have been called into conference at an earlier stage of the project, that is, before Northeastern's original proposal was invited and received? The vice-president and superintendent retained their original preference for Northeastern's equipment in spite of the elaborate studies; what are the advantages, if any, in making this additional investigation?

Is the vice-president correct in feeling an obligation toward Northeastern that would make this company a preferred supplier? Does any comparable obligation exist in respect to Newell Company? Could a satisfactory solution be found by negotiation with either of these companies independently?

Should competition be invited on this project? Did Albree go about getting competition in the most effective way? For a fair evaluation, should all proposals be placed on a more comparable basis?

Is the purchasing director's method of evaluation sound? Are there any other factors that should have been considered? Can you suggest a more direct approach to the determination of cost and value?

17. HOOKER & METCALF, INC.

Make-or-Buy

Hooker & Metcalf had manufactured industrial pumps in the relatively isolated, rural town of Glenglade for more than half a century. The company had the only plant in the area and enjoyed the most cordial relations with the community as the largest employer and taxpayer. As a matter of necessity in its early years, the company had tried to be as self-sufficient as possible. One of its earliest moves in this direction was the establishment of a foundry for casting pump housings and similar parts. Although in the intervening years Hooker & Metcalf had turned more and more to outside suppliers for materials and services, it had kept the foundry operating. As a result, only a small percentage of castings requirements were purchased on the outside.

As industrial expansion outward from the great metropolitan centers continued during the late 1950's and early 1960's, the company found itself closer to the main stream of business activities. More and more salesmen were calling on the purchasing department every day, many of them from foundries that had proliferated in the tristate area surrounding Glenglade. The intense competition among the foundries and the attractive prices they were offering interested General Purchasing Agent Glenn Howard. Howard, a competent, aggressive newcomer, had been brought in a year earlier as an understudy to Director of Purchases Harold Amber, who was due for retirement.

"Have we ever gone deeply into the question of buying more of our castings on the outside?" he asked Mr. Amber. "We seem to be incurring a lot of overhead to make parts we can buy cheaper from dozens of suppliers around here. And we could be using some of the space we save for factory expansion—something we can make real money with."

"Take it easy, Glenn," Mr. Amber said. "There are a lot of factors that have to be considered before you go yanking out what has been part of our business for 50 years. In the first place, don't build your case on generalities. What do you mean when you say a 'lot' of overhead? And how do you know what 'cheaper' is? You've got to come up with real cost figures—and then you'll have Joe Ewell to battle. He's been superintendent of this plant for many years, and he doesn't give up any plant operation very easily. He'll give you all kinds of arguments—that he doesn't trust other foundries, that he wants his castings coming from a place where he can keep an eye on how they're made and how their quality is assured, and that he wants to keep the plant filled up with work."

Mr. Ewell used just those arguments when Mr. Howard discussed the idea with him—and added a couple more. The company's relations with the community might be disturbed, he said, if a large group of skilled and unskilled workers employed in the Hooker & Metcalf foundry were let go because of work going to outsiders. "I have no other place to put anyone from our foundry," he said, "and these new foundries won't hire them. We'd only be adding to the unemployment problem." A better move, he added, would be to try to develop some outside casting business among the many industries springing up in the area and expand the Hooker & Metcalf foundry.

Mr. Howard realized that a more factual approach to the problem was needed. He decided to work out a make-or-buy savings comparison on a specific casting, using a formula on which make-or-buy decisions had been based in his former company. In the formula, vendor price and shop cost are compared for a year's usage of the part. Differences in tooling cost are considered, when applicable. The combined difference is the X factor. The X factor is compared to the Y factor, which is the burden, or overhead, that would be charged to the shop whether it made the part or not. When X is greater than Y, it pays to buy rather than to make. When Y is greater, it pays to make.

Mr. Howard called in several foundry representatives who had been calling on him and asked for quotations on a part that Hooker & Metcalf had been making in its foundry for a number of years. No new patterns were required, and each of the foundries was equipped to handle the job with existing equipment. All quotations were within a few cents of each other.

Using cost figures agreed to by both manufacturing and purchasing, this is the comparison he came up with:

Description: Part No. 6-2379, Chamber, Model T-31 pump

A—Annual usage	10,000
B—Additional tool cost, in-plant	None
C—Additional tool cost, vendor's	None
D—Unit cost, in-plant	$5.00
E—Unit cost, purchase	$1.65
F—Unit overhead cost, in-plant	$3.00

CALCULATIONS:

X—Annual apparent savings by purchasing
A times $(D-E)$ plus $\dfrac{B-C}{2}$ $33,500

Y—Annual overhead absorbed in-plant, or A times F $30,000

According to the formula, because X was greater than Y, the most economic choice would be to buy.

Mr. Ewell remained unconvinced. He repeated his previous objections to taking any substantial production out of the plant. He placed particular emphasis on the quality problem involved in going to new suppliers. "You haven't even figured in there what defective castings from these other foundries would cost us in terms of downtime, rework of parts, and rejects."

"Well," replied Mr. Howard, "can you give me any figures on what our own quality problems are costing us? How many defective castings do we turn out? What's our total rework expense for a year? Perhaps I can work a comparison of our actual costs versus estimated costs from vendor defects into our formula."

"We don't have any specific figures on that," Mr. Ewell said, "but I know they'd be much lower than what we'd have if we depended on some of those foundries on the outside. I've been around here long enough to know we've got our quality under pretty good control. You never know how much trouble you'll run into with those other fellows, so your estimates wouldn't be very realistic in this case."

Should any substantial portion of Hooker & Metcalf's castings requirements be purchased? How much weight should be given to noneconomic factors in this case? In make-or-buy decisions generally? Is the formula used by Mr. Howard an adequate guide to make-or-buy decisions? Who is more "realistic" in his approach to the problem, Mr. Ewell or Mr. Howard? Explain.

18. GRASSER DRUG COMPANY

Purchase of Capital Equipment

Grasser Drug Company is a small but progressive pharmaceutical firm specializing in antibiotics in various forms. Major equipment purchases, which have been steadily rising, had been almost exclusively made by Nils Jensen, the chief engineer. Major raw material purchases were handled by Dr. Hal Forman, chief chemist. The president, Mr. Grasser, who was the son of the physician who had founded the firm, was by inclination and education more interested in the financial aspects of the business and had complete faith in the technical competence of his department heads.

As the company grew, so did the clerical group handling the routine purchasing, until it became obvious that a formal organization with a qualified department head was needed to process requisitions, place orders, and negotiate with vendors. After initial interviews at lower levels, a selected group of three applicants was personally interviewed by Mr. Grasser, who finally decided on William Walsh. Mr. Jensen had sat in on the final interviews and had concurred in the selection of Mr. Walsh.

Mr. Walsh came to Grasser Drug from a slightly larger company that produced molded and bonded rubber parts. In that position he had supervised the work of two buyers and had handled the raw material purchases himself. He was also a member of the committee (which also included the plant manager, the chief engineer, and the vice-president in charge of operations) that passed on all major equipment purchases. Mr. Walsh did not have an engineering degree, but had a good technical background, including a few years in manufacturing.

The chief engineer and the new purchasing agent got along well from the start. Mr. Jensen made it clear that he was delighted to have a professional purchasing department to handle the buying of certain types of equipment like pumps, compressors, blowers, storage tanks, piping, and valves. He made it clear to operating personnel that, although they were free to recommend suppliers of items like these, the purchasing department should be allowed to make its own selection if this appeared justified on a cost basis and no impairment of quality or performance was indicated. He emphasized that requisitions should be properly prepared and as complete as possible to give the purchasing department the latitude it needed in developing suitable supply sources. He made himself available to both requisitioners and the purchasing agent to resolve any technical problems that might develop in the requisitioning and purchasing of such equipment.

Mr. Jensen made it equally clear, however, that on major equipment he was to have the final word. He freely expressed the opinion that any effort on the purchasing agent's part to change the established procedure for buying such equipment was unnecessary and potentially dangerous. "Bill," he told Mr. Walsh, "we simply can't afford the risk of shopping around among unknown suppliers to save a couple of thousand dollars. One big breakdown on a machine, or a long delay in getting delivery on a unit, would put us behind the eight ball in this market. We've got a strong competitive position because we can handle our own customers' small orders promptly. I don't want to take chances with that capability now. I prefer to stick with the suppliers who have done the best for us in the past. And I honestly think I'm the only one in this plant capable of evaluating their reliability and technical competence."

"Look," replied Walsh. "I'm not questioning your judgment or the reliability of our equipment suppliers. You should have the final say on technical aspects. But there are a lot of gray areas in equipment purchasing that are part technical, part commercial. If I had your O.K. to take a closer look at some of them, I think I could come up with some ideas that might save the company money while giving you the equipment you want."

"For example?" said Mr. Jensen.

"Well, look at that extractor we bought last month," said Mr. Walsh. "We paid close to $38,000 for a machine after getting only two bids on it. I know there are other shops that could have handled that job and would have been delighted to bid fairly low on it just to get their foot in the door of this company. Yet we string along with the highest bidder—just because he's a good old loyal supplier. That's not good purchasing, in my opinion."

To Mr. Walsh's surprise, Mr. Jensen seemed rather annoyed and abruptly ended the discussion by saying, "Well, that's the way it is and that's the way it's going to be." After lunch in the plant dining room that day, Mr. Grasser called Mr. Walsh over to sit with him and Mr. Jensen. "I heard from Jensen here that you've been criticizing our purchasing," he said with a smile. "I was in on that extractor deal, too, you know." Before Mr. Walsh could reply, he went on: "I understand your point of view on this matter, Bill. But the way we stand now, I have to go along with Nils. We just can't afford to take chances. If we were a big company that could afford an equipment engineer in the purchasing department, maybe I'd think differently. But we're not, so I'm not going to change our policy now. You can handle all the paper work and strictly commercial aspects of these big purchases, but I don't want you getting involved in anything technical with our own people or with vendors." There was no further discussion on the matter.

Although he accepted Mr. Grasser's decision in principle, Mr. Walsh could not easily change his basic attitudes on what he considered sound procurement. When the next requisition for a piece of major equipment came through—with a request that only two specified suppliers be asked to quote, he decided to go further than he had been authorized to do.

The equipment in question was a special type of stainless steel filter press that would eliminate the need for two operators per shift. The unit would enable Grasser Drug to save (including shift differentials, overtime pay, and so forth) about $8,400 a month or more than $100,000 a year. Delivery date sent to firms quoting on the job had been a vague "Soon as possible."

Mr. Walsh took a long chance and invited another equipment maker in to make an informal bid on the filter press. Aside from the well-established name and the good credit rating listed for it in business directories, Mr. Walsh knew very little about the company. But it was the only other manufacturer in the area capable of making the equipment, and he felt he should experiment, at least to the extent of getting another quotation to match against those of the specified bidders.

In analyzing both the formal and informal quotations, Mr. Walsh determined the following factors:

Vendor *A*—A long-time supplier to Grasser Drug Company. Delivery time on the filter press would be four months because of difficulty in accumulating special sizes of stainless steel bars required. Price quoted: $16,000.

Vendor *B*—Occasional supplier to Grasser Drug Company. Delivery time on the equipment—8-10 weeks because of special stainless components needed. Price quoted: $15,800.

Vendor *C*—No experience as supplier to Grasser Drug Company. Delivery on filter press as described in specifications would be approximately same as that quoted by other bidders, for same reason. Informal quotation: $18,000.

Mr. Walsh called in Vendor *C* again, expressed his disappointment with the quote, and, without revealing anything from the other vendors' data, asked the sales manager if he couldn't improve on the quotation.

"There's not much we can do on the price," the sales manager said, "but we may be able to help you on delivery. If you can get engineering's O.K. to let us buy heavier stock and machine it down to the size you need in those stainless bars, we can deliver the unit at the same price in two months, or about half the time we first talked about."

A quick calculation showed Mr. Walsh that the more expensive equipment, assuming it was up to quality standards, could mean a real saving to Grasser Drug Company: that is, a two-month earlier delivery would mean a saving of $8,400 x 2, or $16,800, less the $2,000 additional cost of Vendor *C*'s equipment, or a net saving of $14,800.

Mr. Walsh pondered his next move.

Discuss and evaluate the two points of view toward capital-equipment buying represented by Mr. Jensen and Mr. Walsh. On the basis of what you know about Mr. Walsh and about the Grasser Company, do you feel that the purchasing agent should be given more voice in equipment buying in the company? What are the "gray areas" in equipment buying that should be the concern of the purchasing department? What do you think of Mr. Grasser's atttiude?

Do you think Mr. Walsh's evaluation of Vendor C's *bid is sound? Was he justified in calling Vendor* C *in after Mr. Grasser's comments about his role in equipment buying? What alternative approach could he have taken? What should Mr. Walsh's next move be? Why?*

19. CHARLTON MANUFACTURING COMPANY

Purchasing Systems

Charlton Manufacturing Company, in the electronics industry, grew very rapidly in the period 1957-1962. The purchasing department expanded along with other phases of the business. With increasing diversity and volume of requirements, the department successfully maintained an excellent record of service in meeting the company's needs. It was handling a program that had doubled in magnitude with only a 70 per cent increase in staff. Nevertheless, the purchasing director was disturbed to find that the cost of purchasing was steadily mounting, whether calculated in relation to total purchase expenditures or as the cost per order issued. He concluded that the system which had been efficient for the smaller operation was somehow not so well adapted to the larger program. He had made several changes in equipment and methods to speed up the procedure, but he was unwilling to sacrifice the close controls that were established in the system. He strongly felt that controls must be maintained to avoid lapses in service and leaks in expenditures. The larger volume of materials and dollars now involved made this responsibility all the greater.

About 2,000 purchase orders per week were now being issued. The system in effect, for both production and nonproduction items, was as follows:

All purchases were made against requisitions, which originated either in operating departments or in stores. The majority of requisitions came from stores and were based upon predetermined maximum and minimum stock quantities. The requisition form was in duplicate, a carbon copy being retained by the issuer for his own record and to avoid a duplication of requests to buy. The information on the form was quite complete. It included an identifying part number or ordering description of the material wanted. On stock items, the quantity issued during the past 30 days was also entered; this gave a quick indication of usage rates, so that stock quantities could be revised if volume requirements changed. If the name of the supplier of the previous lot was known from package markings or other identification, this was also noted as a guide to the buyer. On requisitions from operating departments, the job number was shown to aid in the distribution of costs. Altogether, the requisition provided a comprehensive work sheet for the buyer. All requisitions were signed by the appropriate department head or storeskeeper and were filed with the corresponding purchase order to show authorization for the purchase.

This, in conjunction with the purchase record card that was kept on each item regularly purchased, which showed the past history of purchases by quantity, date, price, and vendor, usually gave the buyer all the information he needed to issue the order.

It was the policy to price all purchase orders. A request for a quotation form was used in getting bids on new items. On repetitive and stock items, prices were checked every six months, by phone in the case of local suppliers and using the form for out-of-town suppliers. Otherwise, the price on the previous order was used; if a vendor revised his price, new bids were taken.

The heart of the system was the purchase order itself, a 12-part form that served many purposes by the distribution of copies made at a single writing. Consideration had been given to the preparation of orders from hectograph master copies and by other methods, but the final decision was to use continuous forms with snap-out carbons, filled in on electric typewriters that gave a clear impression throughout the entire set. This was a rapid method. Distinctive colors of paper for the various copies facilitated distribution. When the system was first adopted, it eliminated two separate forms formerly used in the receiving department.

The original and the acknowledgment copy were sent to the vendor. The copy, signed by the vendor, was returned to Charlton as evidence that the order was accepted and with a promised delivery date. It was then filed with the purchasing department's working copy.

Three copies were retained in the purchasing department. One of these was placed in a folder with the requisition and tabulation of bids and filed in numerical sequence. This was the department's working copy. The vendor's acknowledgment and all other correspondence and documents pertaining to the order were accumulated in the folder. When the order was filled, the folder was transferred to a completed-order file. Thus, the numerical file constantly provided a record of all outstanding orders and automatically showed which ones had been longest outstanding. The second copy was filed alphabetically by vendor's name. It was used as a cross-reference when inquiries about an order were made by vendor's name or when a buyer had any other occasion to refer to the status of a given vendor's orders. This copy was destroyed when the numerical file copy was transferred from the open file. References according to the material involved were made through the purchase record card, where each purchase order was entered as issued. The third copy was used for follow-up purposes.

One copy was sent to the originator of the requisition as a notification that his request had been taken care of, and one copy to production control as an aid to scheduling. If the vendor's delivery promise did not coincide with the date requested on the purchase order, these departments were kept informed.

Four copies, in a collated set with carbon sheets retained, went to the receiving department, advising the latter of the expected shipment. When goods were received, this set was filled out as a receiving report. One copy was returned directly to the purchasing department, and one was retained as a receiving record. Two copies went with the goods to the inspection department. One of these was used as an inspection report to purchasing, certifying that quality was acceptable or serving as the basis for rejection. If goods were accepted, the fourth copy went with the goods to the stores or using department to identify the shipment. The receiving department was provided with supplementary sets, in blank, to use in reporting partial shipments; the purchase order form itself was returned to purchasing only when an order was completed.

The twelfth copy of the order went to the accounting department, apprising them of the commitment. This obviated the making of a daily summary of expenditures. Vendors were required to send invoices in duplicate. One went directly to accounts payable. The other was checked against the receiving report and the working copy of the purchase order to certify the correctness of quantities, prices, and terms; it was then sent with the receiving report to the accounting department as authorization for payment and for the distribution of material changes. Wherever the terms included a cash-discount privilege, a red sticker was attached to the margin of the invoice.

Follow-up procedure was delegated to the buyers who issued the respective purchase orders, on the principle that the buying responsibility ended only when a delivery was satisfactory. There were two further practical considerations: (1) that the buyer, through his contact with the vendor, was in a position to expedite most effectively, and (2) in the event that expediting was not successful in getting a needed delivery, the buyer must procure the goods from some other source. Follow-up copies of the orders were distributed to the appropriate commodity-buying sections, and were filed there separately, in numerical sequence. A 1-to-31 scale was printed along the top margin of this order copy, indicating the date of the month. When an order was placed in the file, a yellow tab was attached to flag the date five days after issue. If an acknowledgement had not been received by that date, the follow-up clerk sent a routine follow-up request. As soon as a delivery promise was received, a blue tab was affixed at the date two days before the promised delivery; at that time the clerk sent a postcard request for information on the status of the order and attached a red tab at the date of promised delivery. The follow-up clerk went through this file each day, removing all orders on which receiving slips had been received, and taking appropriate action on tabbed orders for that date. Only red-tabbed orders were brought to the attention of the buyer, who then took whatever steps were necessary by letter, wire, telephone, or in person, according to the urgency of the item.

A management consultant engaged by the company to evaluate organization and methods spent several days in the purchasing department. The purchasing director explained the reasons for each purchasing form and record, stressing the factors of control. Before making an appraisal of the procedures, the consultant analyzed all orders placed during the past 60 days. Among the things revealed by this analysis were the following:

Cost of issuing and processing a purchase order amounted to $9.42.

About 20 per cent of the orders issued were for $50 or less; 14 per cent were for $10 or less. All but a very few of the smallest orders were in the category of miscellaneous operating supplies, and 80 per cent of these were placed with three local supply firms.

More than 70 per cent of all requisitions originated in the stores department, and were repetitive as to item and quantity; most of the corresponding purchase orders were repetitive as to source or were divided among several sources according to an established ratio of distribution.

Dollarwise, 70 per cent of total expenditures were made on 12 per cent of total orders, representing a limited number of major commodity classifications.

About 55 per cent of the orders were acknowledged by vendors without any follow-up action. Follow-up secured acknowledgements from another 25 per cent, but in quite a number of cases only when the goods were ready for shipment. On the remaining 20 per cent, goods were shipped without formal acknowledgement of the order.

Less than 15 per cent of all orders required any intensive expediting. During the two-month period under study, not a single order in the supply category had been followed up.

With these facts in hand, he again discussed methods with the purchasing director and recommended that procedures be reviewed and revised on a more selective basis.

What advantages, if any, are there in handling the entire gamut of purchases with a single, uniform procedure? Can the purchasing director exercise the control he desires by any other means than through the detailed procedure on each transaction?

If alternative procedures are to be applied, what should be the basis of distinction, for example, nature of the item, repetitive versus special purchase, production versus nonproduction materials, or value of the order?

Can the number of requisitions, number of purchase orders, number of purchase-order copies, or number of processing operations be reduced without impairing the effectiveness of the system? Are there any instances of duplication or lost motion in the present procedure?

Suggest possible simplification of the requisitioning forms and procedure that would serve the same purposes at less expense. Suggest a solution for Charlton's small-order problem that would not sacrifice essential purchasing control over these expenditures.

Charlton's experience in getting acceptances from vendors is typical. Conceding the desirability of receiving such acknowledgements as assurance of delivery on schedule, is Charlton's follow-up for acknowledgements worth its cost and effort? This system is only 55 per cent effective on delinquent vendors; can you suggest any more effective or economical way of attacking this problem?

20. MENTON ELECTRIC CORP.

Purchasing Policies

Menton Electric Corp. is a large, diversified electrical manufacturing company that manufactures a wide line of appliances and equipment in regional plants throughout the country. Its major home application division, for example, is located in the Midwest but also serves the Northeastern section. Another plant, located in the Southeast, ships to areas in the Midwest and sends a large part of its production to Gulf ports for shipment abroad.

Purchasing, which is a strong, highly regarded department in most Menton divisions, includes the traffic function. A vice-president of purchases and traffic is on the corporate headquarters staff. Menton buyers and purchasing agents, most of whom have both business administration and engineering backgrounds, are well known inside and outside the company for their aggressive, competitive, but fair approach to procurement.

Their view of reciprocal buying reflects the traditional view of the company management, the attitude of the purchasing vice-president, and their own professional training. It could be summed up this way: Theoretically, reciprocity when "all other things are equal" is harmless, acceptable, and, in fact, preferable to an intelligent purchasing executive. But all other things are rarely equal—or, at least, should not be if a competent purchasing department is doing its job of stimulating competition among a number of suppliers. Therefore, reciprocity could inhibit good buying in many cases and should be avoided as much as possible. Decisions to pay premium prices for reasons of reciprocity should be made by top management. Reciprocal pressures from customers should be handled tactfully, and every attempt should be made to send the supplier away feeling that he has had a sympathetic reception—but without making any concrete commitments to him. Conversely, the Menton Company was justified in trying to use reciprocity to gain its own ends, but should do it realistically, diplomatically and legally.

One case where a reciprocal-buying situation existed almost as a matter of tradition and with no specific commitments on either side was in the purchase of transportation. The Midwest appliance division, along with several other divisions, was a good customer of certain railroads in terms of freight shipped. Many railroads, in turn, bought Menton diesel engines. In the appliance division's case, a valued corporate customer was also the lowest-priced supplier. The division shipped some of its production to nearby states in company-owned trucks, but all of its output for the Eastern states went by three different railroads to a central distributing point on the East Coast. One railroad had a siding at the division plant. The two others tracked Menton products to freight terminals near the plant at no extra cost. These three railroads alone spent close to a million dollars a year on Menton engines.

In the case of the generator division, no reciprocal considerations appeared to be involved. Company trucking moved most of the generators sold in the Middle West and the Northeast. The single rail line serving the plant was used for shipping Menton products to Southern ports.

One day the manager of purchases and traffic of the appliance division received a call from the division manager, who asked for a breakdown of the amount of merchandise shipped east on the three railroads, the rate paid, and the rates for shipping the products by truck. Following are the figures he supplied:

No. of units shipped annually	60,000
Average weight per unit	350 lb.
Rate per rail carload, 15,000 lb. minimum	$218
Rate per rail carload, 24,000 lb. minimum	$146
Rate per truckload, 16,000 lb. minimum	$217
Rate per truckload, 22,000 lb. minimum	$162

Meanwhile, the small generator plant's purchasing and traffic department had been preparing similar figures on shipments to Gulf ports. They were as follows:

No. of units shipped annually	8,400
Average weight per unit	1,350 lb.
Rate per rail carload, 24,000 lb. minimum	$165
Rate per rail carload, 30,000 lb. minimum	$145
Rate per truckload, 22,000 lb. minimum	$170

The information from both plants was forwarded to corporate headquarters, where the executive vice-president had been presented with a blunt demand for a part of both divisions' freight business from a Menton Company customer. The demand had come from his counterpart in Worldwide Industries, holding company that had recently purchased Trans-State Trucking Corp. Trans-State's system covers both the areas served by the two Menton divisions.

Worldwide's executive had put his case very frankly: several of the company's subsidiaries placed a substantial amount of business with the Menton Company.

Among them were a brass mill, two chemical processing plants, an air-conditioner maker, and a stage lighting equipment manufacturer. Their combined purchases of motors and other Menton products ran to over $3 million a year. On the basis of this purchase volume, he said, the Menton Company owed it to a good customer to use Trans-State's trucks for some of its shipments.

The Worldwide executive suggested that he and Menton's vice-president sit down and "negotiate" an arrangement immediately.

The Menton Company's vice-president stalled him for a while, but was finding it difficult to hold out against his insistence that they come to some agreement. He called in Menton's vice-president in charge of purchasing and traffic for consultation.

Evaluate the Menton Company's purchasing department's "realistic" attitude toward reciprocity. How should the vice-president in charge of purchasing and traffic apply it in this case?

Are reciprocal situations involving the purchase of transportation different from those involving other types of purchases? Discuss the implications of your answer in respect to the whole Menton purchasing program.

Discuss the advantages and disadvantages of establishing a separate organization to handle reciprocal problems in a large corporation like the Menton Company, including the question of whose jurisdiction such a section should come under.

21. BESTON FOOD PRODUCTS COMPANY

Ethics of Purchasing

Carl Hopkins was in his second year as director of purchasing for Beston Foods. He had come to the company after eight years as purchasing agent of a division of a major steel company to succeed a man retiring from the post after 30 years' service. In his first year with the company, he had concentrated on improving his understanding of those areas of food-industry purchasing for which his experience in heavy metals had not prepared him—primarily, the technical and commodity market phases. When he felt sufficiently grounded in the basics of these specialized areas, he began turning his attention to some of the broader phases of procurement common to all industries—including such aspects as administrative procedures, purchasing policies, vendor relations, and buyer training. He had had no other mandate from the food company management other than to see that the department was kept "up to date" and at a high level of efficiency.

In the process of reviewing procedures and policies in the Beston Company's purchasing manual, which had not been revised in several years, Hopkins came across a section that read:

> We believe that our vendors carry out their responsibilities to us when they provide us with good service and high quality at lowest possible cost. Any effort on their part to go further than this through the giving of gifts or gratuities is unnecessary and should be courteously but firmly discouraged.

The policy on gifts and gratuities in Hopkins' former company had been written at company headquarters and was much more precise and stronger. It had specifically forbidden any employee to accept gifts of any kind, other than advertising items, or to accept entertainment or lunches from suppliers. It pointed out that any employee accepting gifts was, at worst, involving himself in commercial bribery and, at best, violating company policy. Mr. Hopkins had personally endorsed the policy, and he and his buyers had scrupulously followed it.

Mr. Hopkins had no desire to try to force this stricter code on his new company, or even on the purchasing department. Yet he felt that there was an obvious contradiction between the Beston Company's policy and the practice of his department. During his first Christmas season with the company, he had seen a few gifts—a bottle of liquor, a box of cigars, and similar items—on his buyers' desks. He knew also that at least two buyers had attended Sunday World Series' games as guests of one of the Beston Company's best and most respected suppliers.

Mr. Hopkins decided to bring some consistency into the situation. He called his supervisory buyers together for a frank talk about this phase of vendor relations. To his surprise and gratification, they were not only glad to discuss the matter but indicated that they would welcome a more specific prohibition of gifts and entertainment. "They're more bother than they're worth" was the consensus; such gifts were accepted only to avoid embarrassing reputable vendors of long standing. Several pointed out that they were aware of the statement in the manual, but had never heard of anyone trying to implement it.

They agreed that a letter should go out over Mr. Hopkins' name to the Beston Company's entire vendor list, carefully explaining a new purchasing policy on gifts and gratuities and asking the recipients to refrain from offering them to members of the purchasing department. The following letter was prepared for mailing right after Thanksgiving:

In recent years employees in our department have received Christmas gifts from some of our suppliers. They generally have been modest tokens of the esteem and friendship we know exist between our organization and those with whom we do business. We feel, however, that it would be in the best interests of all if we kept our relationships on a strictly business basis.

We have therefore decided on a policy of not permitting any member of this department to accept personal gifts from any firm or individual doing business with our company. We sincerely hope you appreciate our position that quality, service, and price should be the only considerations in our buying.

Meanwhile, the Beston sales department was aggressively merchandising a new line of canned luxury foods—paté de foie gras, vichysoisse, smoked oysters, and similar delicacies. Pictures of the foods were displayed in the company's reception room and mentioned in a new "welcome booklet" for visiting salesmen. A small selection of several items had even been mailed as a gift to all Beston Company stockholders at the end of the last fiscal year with a note encouraging them to recommend the delicacies to their friends.

During the fall season, the sales manager had what he considered a brilliant idea. Among the many reports run off on the company computer that were available to his office was one listing every supplier with whom the Beston Company was doing business, together with their addresses. Here, he reasoned, was a captive audience on which he could try a first-rate merchandising idea. Without informing the purchasing department, he sent a letter addressed to the sales manager of every Beston supplier during the first week of December. It read in part:

> During the coming holiday season, what better way could you find to express your gratitude to customers for their business during the past year than with a gift of fine food? And what finer food is there than Beston's Gourmet Specialties. . . . Remember your special business friends with a boxed selection of Gourmet Specialties. . . . Available beautifully gift wrapped in $3, $5, $10, and $20 sizes. . . .

It did not take long for Mr. Hopkins to discover what had happened. Within a few days he had one mildly sarcastic letter from a supplier, containing copies of the letter on prohibiting Christmas gifts and the one promoting Beston products as gifts. Which one, he said in effect, am I supposed to believe? Mr. Hopkins, furious, went directly to the executive vice-president and complained of the embarrassing situation he and the company had been put in. The executive vice-president called in the sales manager, who seemed only slightly amused by the whole affair.

Was the director of purchasing justified in complaining? Had his approach to the problem of gifts been too arbitrary? Too naïve? What other methods might he have used in establishing a no-gift policy that would have avoided the situation described above?

What do you think of the sales manager's tactics—were they businesslike, ethical? Do you think he should have had free access to the purchasing department's vendor list? Why? Assuming you were the executive vice-president, what action would you take to solve the problem?

22. RUMFORD MACHINE COMPANY

Legal Aspects of Purchasing

After careful investigation of competing types of equipment, a committee that included representatives of purchasing, engineering, and production decided to buy a new multipurpose machine tool for the Rumford Machine Company. It was the latest model of a numerically controlled unit that could perform drilling, milling, and boring operations on a single piece in any sequence. The machine was manufactured by Bradley-Donald Machine Tool Company, a leader in the field and a supplier to Rumford on numerous occasions in the past.

During the negotiations for the equipment, in which all committee members participated, Rumford Company engineers had asked for several modifications on the machine to meet their particular problems. The supplier's technical representatives agreed that the changes could be made. The price finally agreed upon was

$93,000, and the Bradley-Donald representatives were told they would receive a purchase order by mail.

The Rumford Company's purchasing agent asked his engineers to send him a detailed listing of the changes they wanted made on Bradley-Donald's standard model of the machine. From this he had a set of specifications transcribed to the purchase order; then he issued the order carrying the price of $93,000 agreed on previously.

Within a few days, the Bradley-Donald Company acknowledged the order, but not on the copy of the Rumford Company purchase order designated for this purpose. Instead of his own acknowledgement form, the purchasing agent received Bradley-Donald Company's contract form. He examined the form closely and reviewed the clauses carefully with the company's legal department. They agreed that there was nothing inimical to Rumford's interests in the "fine print" on the contract order. The purchasing agent, however, was not satisfied with the simple statement that the contract called for "one Brad-O-Matic, Model 64, installed . . . $93,000." No mention of charges previously agreed to appeared on the form. He called Bradley-Donald's district sales manager in to discuss the matter.

The supplier's representative pointed out that it was customary for the company to acknowledge orders on that form—and, in fact, it had done so previously on orders from the Rumford Company.

When the purchasing agent objected to the fact that his original specifications were not included in the contract, the sales representative replied that he did not have authority to change the contract. But, he added, he would insert the words "Changes to come" beneath the model description and notify his home office that the order would be followed by a letter from the purchasing agent detailing the modifications to be made on the standard machine.

The purchasing agent agreed, and after the words had been inserted in the contract, both men initialed both copies. Before the day was out, the purchasing agent had sent a letter to the Bradley-Donald Company's home office specifying the changes to be made on the machine and mentioning the contract he had initialed.

In the final stages of the installation of the machine, the Rumford Company received an invoice for $101,500, covering "one Brad-O-Matic, Model 64" at $93,000 and additional charges of $8,500 for "modifications as per your letter." Just before he planned to call Bradley-Donald's sales office, the purchasing agent received an urgent call from the shop. The test runs on the machine were not up to expectations, and it was obvious that it could not meet the performance standards which the Rumford Company's engineers expected of it. They could get no satisfaction from the supplier's technical representatives, who said that there must have been some understanding as to the capabilities of the machine. They suggested that the matter be taken up with their district sales office and perhaps the company's home office.

The purchasing agent called the district office and protested to the manager. He asked for an immediate change in the invoice and adjustment of the machine to meet the Rumford Company's requirements. Following his call, he dictated a letter to the Bradley-Donald Company home office outlining the situation and making the same demands.

The Bradley-Donald Company answered that the extra charge was justified because it covered instructions given after the contract had been signed for a standard machine. It claimed that the words "Changes to come" merely indicated that such instructions would follow but were not a part of the contract and were not included in the contract price. As to the performance of the equipment, they would be glad to continue giving technical assistance and advice at no cost, but would not be held to any warranties in the contract. The machine to which the warranties applied, they claimed, had been altered at the customer's instructions and to the customer's specification.

The Rumford Company refused to accept the machine, and the Bradley-Donald Company sued for the full amount of the invoice.

Who comes into court with the strongest case? Why? Analyze the mistakes in the Rumford Company's conduct of negotiation and contract procedure, pointing out how the company could have protected itself by alternative approaches.

23. HICKMAN & HOGE

Settling a Contract Termination

Silsby Corporation received a large government order for instrumentation in military aircraft. The contract contained the standard clause providing for contract termination and required that the same clause be included in Silsby's contracts with its suppliers. Silsby contracted with Horan Engineering Company for one of the major assemblies required in the device. Horan ordered the instrument panel from Durland and Company. Durland ordered the wiring assembly to be mounted on the back of the panel from Hickman & Hoge.

The part to be made by Hickman & Hoge required the purchase from outside sources of a cast-aluminum alloy frame of intricate design and four small special relays for each unit. The wire was to be formed, the terminals and connectors fabricated, and the entire part assembled in Hickman & Hoge's own shop. The purchasing agent placed orders for 3,000 frames with Milltown Metal Process Company and for 12,000 relays with Watson Electric Company. He also ordered the necessary wire for the company's own production.

Some weeks later, before any of the frames or relays had been delivered, Hickman & Hoge received a telegram from Durland advising that the order had been canceled and instructing them to cancel immediately any commitments that had been made in connection with it. The manager called Durland for further information. It was Durland's understanding that the contract had been halted because of major design stages but had not been abandoned. They were hopeful that the order would be reinstated and that they would participate in the new program; there was no assurance of this, and there would be a considerable delay in any case. So far as the present order was concerned, the termination was absolute.

Hickman & Hoge had done no actual work on the Durland order pending receipt of the frames and relays. The materials for their part of the job were standard and could readily be applied to other orders. Their expenses up to this point were negligible. They had expected to make a profit of about $600 on the order, which was presently lost but might be recouped if the order were reinstated. Durland was an important source of subcontracting orders, and the company was anxious to maintain the best possible relationship with this customer. The partners considered waiving any claim for their own account, as a gesture of cooperation that might simplify the termination settlement for Durland, but deferred this decision until they found out the extent of their obligation to Milltown and Watson.

The purchasing agent immediately telephoned both of these companies to stop work on the order and made appointments with them to arrange a settlement. He confirmed this by registered mail.

The contract price for the frames was $1.10 each. Milltown had completed one-fourth of the order, or 750 units. The finished frames were useless for any other purpose and had only nominal value as scrap. Milltown felt, however, that they should be billed at the full contract price whether Hickman & Hoge took delivery of them or not. The purchasing agent saw these completed parts and verified the count. Beyond this, Milltown had spent $300 for special tooling, an expense which they had intended to spread over the cost of the total order. They had purchased 1,000 pounds of the specified alloy, at 40 cents per pound. They had no other orders calling for this particular material, and it was not returnable. It could, however, be used on other orders that would normally take a less expensive metal, at 30 to 35 cents per pound. The company had expected to make a profit of 15 cents each on the frames.

Watson Electric Company had nothing tangible whatever to show the purchasing agent. The quoted price of 90 cents each for the special relays had included an indeterminate amount for engineering. This development work was well under way, but the result up to this point was only an unfinished drawing. Watson's cost system did not provide for an exact allocation of the expense of engineering studies. There were usually several projects going on simultaneously, involving the time of various members of the engineering staff, in consultation as well as in actual designing. It was the practice in this company to average these costs over total production in the form of a 15 cent overhead charge for engineering services. Watson's best estimate was that the work on Hickman & Hoge's order had cost between $450 and $500 to date. No materials had been specially procured or allocated to the order. The expected profit was also an indeterminate figure. The company's balance sheets for the past year showed an average profit of 8 per cent on total sales.

Suggest a reasonable basis of settlement with each of these suppliers. To what extent can Watson's inconclusive development work be justified as a claim? Does the purchasing agent have a responsibility to keep suppliers' claims at a minimum? Should the purchasing agent negotiate these claims, or should the settlement be an auditing procedure?

Suggest a reasonable basis of settlement between Durland and Hickman & Hoge. In view of the fact that the cancellation came before the company had started work on the order, is there any valid basis for making a claim for loss of profits?

Is there any merit in the proposal to waive any claim to which it might be entitled? To what extent should business relationships and the possibility of future orders influence this decision?

24. GUNTHER STOVE COMPANY

Evaluating Purchasing Performance

The board of directors of Gunther Stove Company in 1956 employed Franklin Associates, a management consulting firm, to make a thorough study of the company's organization and procedures and to recommend any changes which might be made to improve efficiency. This was prompted, not by any serious dissatisfaction with present performance, but to get the benefit of an expert, objective evaluation. The study was made in great detail, covering every department, using check lists and standards which the Franklin organization had developed for the purpose. When the data had been assembled and analyzed, Mr. Franklin presented his report to the directors. It was generally favorable, with a number of suggestions regarding each department designed to simplify or expedite the work. His recommendations concerning purchasing were to bring traffic control under the jurisdiction of this department; to add one buyer, preferably with engineering training; to set up a special fund that would permit the handling of small local orders on a petty cash basis, eliminating considerable paper work on these dealings; and to transfer the checking of invoices to the accounting department, because he felt that no department should audit its own transactions.

"By the way," said Mr. Gunther, chairman of the board, "how is our purchasing department doing? I've been in the management of this company forty years and I've never had a satisfactory answer to that question."

Mr. Franklin said that, in his judgment, the department was doing very well.

"How well?" Mr. Gunther persisted. "Would you rate it as 95 per cent, 90 per cent, 85 per cent, or what?"

Mr. Franklin said that it was impossible to set objective standards of performance that would permit a rating of this sort. There were too many variables and intangibles involved. A rating depended, first, on what you expected, and second, on whether that expectation was reasonable.

"But you must have some basis for saying that our buyers are doing a good job, and that's what I'm trying to get at. After all, purchasing is a pretty tangible business. We spend X number of dollars, and we buy X tons or carloads of iron and nickel and bolts and coal and shipping cases. What I want to know is whether we're getting full value for our dollars, and whether it's costing us more than it should to buy those materials. I'm not interested in how many purchase orders we issue, or how much we deduct in cash discounts. I'm interested in the quality of our buying performance and in results. What I'd like to see is a simple report, maybe six or eight really significant figures, that would give me the picture."

"I think we can get the figures for you," said Mr. Franklin. "You'd have to make your own evaluation, as we do. At the start I doubt that you could rate them any closer than *excellent, good,* or *fair.* After the first few months, when you have a chance to make comparisons, you may be able to apply some sort of scale—if you still think it's worth while."

Mr. Franklin went back to the purchasing agent, and together they worked out a type of report to give Mr. Gunther the information he wanted. Their first step was to define the areas of purchasing activity to be considered in an evaluation; the second step was to select measurable factors in each of these areas that were known or available from existing records and that would indicate to a significant extent the quality of performance and results obtained. The areas they decided on were:

1. Effectiveness of procurement as a service of supply.
2. Price performance in buying.
3. Cost reductions; specific savings.
4. Inventory performance.
5. Administrative performance; efficiency; cost of purchasing.
6. Miscellaneous and intangibles.

Under each of these headings they jotted down everything that came to mind pertinent to that area of activity and responsibility. Despite Mr. Gunther's aversion to statistical information, they found that much of the information was basically of this nature. However, the figures acquired more than statistical significance when they were related to other figures in the form of a ratio or as a proportion of the total; one of the problems was to find the appropriate standards of comparison and methods of presentation. Some of the factors were of a negative nature, inverse to the quality of purchasing performance; nevertheless, they were important in any complete evaluation. "We'll have to differentiate," said Mr. Franklin, "between those that are rated on a low score, as in golf, and those that are rated on a high score, as in bowling. If we get to the point of making a numerical rating, there are simple mathematical means to take care of this, but we'll run into the even tougher problem of assigning weights to the various factors."

The list of suggested possible indicators grew much longer than the half-dozen criteria which Mr. Gunther had requested, but this was a necessary preliminary to the process of selection. When they had finished, the following factors were noted on their work sheet:

1. *Service of Supply*

Number of delinquent deliveries
Machine downtime due to lack of material
Schedule revisions necessary due to lack of material
Successful substitutions made by purchasing department to avoid downtime or schedule revisions
Number of rush orders handled (Proportion of total orders? Of dollar volume?)
Number of change orders issued
Follow-up action (Number of orders? Cost of follow-up?)
Number and amount of premium transportation charges paid to get deliveries on time

Number of deliveries rejected by inspection department
Cost of reworking substandard materials
Number of overdue orders in open-order file
Commodities for which alternate supply sources have been established and
   used

2. *Price Performance*

Number of price changes, up or down from previous prices paid
Number of orders placed on competitive bidding
Number of orders placed by negotiation
Commodities covered by term contracts (How long a term?)
Actual prices paid compared with published market (Market at time of
   purchase or at time of use? Should this be shown for individual key
   commodities, as currently kept in chart form in purchasing office, or
   could it be put in the form of comparative price indices?)
Inventory valuation, actual cost versus replacement cost
Variances from standard costs
Direct material cost per unit of product
Average cost of selected commodities, year to date and projected to annual
average on the basis of current price

3. *Cost Savings*

Specific instances; savings projected on basis of annual usage; cumulative
   totals
Savings through change of source
Savings through change in method of buying
Savings by substitution
Savings by change in specification
Savings by standardization
Savings in transportation costs
Savings in manner of packaging

4. *Inventory Performance*

Ratio of dollar inventory to sales volume
Inventory increase or decrease during month
Extent of forward coverage (Weeks)
Inventory turnover (By commodity classifications)
Number of items under maximum-minimum stock control
Number of stock-outs
Quantity discounts earned by revision of stock limits

5. *Efficiency of Operation*

Total cost of purchasing, related to dollar volume
Number of buyers
Number of nonbuying personnel (Breakdown by functions)
Number of requisitions unprocessed within 24 hours
Number of small orders ($10 and under)
Cash discounts earned and forfeited
Average waiting time for salesmen

6. *Miscellaneous*

Sales of scrap and waste
Hours spent in staff training courses
Number of vendors' plants visited
Business and professional meetings attended

"I have evaluated your department on a number of other, intangible factors," Mr. Franklin said, "such things as morale, public relations, organization, supervision, and the like, as well as adequacy of records and procedures. You'll hear about these when the general manager discusses my report with you and other department heads. There's no doubt that they have a distinct bearing on performance, and they are reflected in many of the items we have set down here. They are measurable, too, but not in the same sense as your specific activities. They are factors that you, as department head, should be evaluating for yourself, and on which top management will evaluate you. I have recommended a simple plan for doing this systematically and confidentially throughout all departments of the company."

Consider, first, the general areas selected for evaluation. Are they all pertinent? Are they all necessary for this purpose? What changes, if any, would you suggest in this approach? Should the various areas be weighted according to their relative importance? How? Should an effort be made to include the intangibles that Mr. Franklin has reserved for separate rating? Assuming that his proposal for a general evaluation system is adopted, would this obviate the need for, or reduce the usefulness of, the detailed evaluation of performance, which was not included in his original recommendation?

Consider the measurements suggested under each heading. Which of these are most significant? How should they be presented? Prepare an outline for a monthly performance report based on the selected factors.

It is suggested that price performance be measured by means of comparative price indices, actual versus market. How would you go about preparing price indices applicable to and representative of a specific purchasing operation?

Is Mr. Gunther unreasonable or impractical in asking for a mathematical rating of purchasing performance?

What advantages, if any, would accrue to the purchasing department from systematic evaluation?

Bibliography

General

Alford, L. P., and J. R. Bangs (editors), *Production Handbook*. New York: The Ronald Press Company, 1944.

Aljian, G. W. (editor), *Purchasing Handbook*. New York: McGraw-Hill Book Company, Inc., 1958.

Ammer, Dean S., *Materials Management*. Homewood, Ill.: Richard D. Irwin, Inc., 1962.

Berry, Harold A., *Purchasing Management*. Waterford, Conn.: National Foremen's Institute, 1964.

Cady, E. L., *Industrial Purchasing*. New York: John Wiley & Sons, Inc., 1945.

Colton, R. R., *Industrial Purchasing: Principles and Procedures*. Columbus, Ohio: Chas. E. Merrill Corp., 1962.

De Rose, L. J., *Negotiated Purchasing*. Boston: Materials Management Institute, 1962.

England, Wilbur B., *Procurement: Principles and Cases* (4th ed.). Homewood, Ill.: Richard D. Irwin, Inc., 1962.

Hodges, Henry G., *Procurement: The Modern Science of Purchasing*. New York: Harper & Row, Publishers, 1961.

Lusardi, F. R., *Purchasing for Industry*. New York: National Industrial Conference Board, 1948. (Studies in Business Policy, No. 33.)

McMillan, A. L., *The Art of Purchasing*. New York: Exposition Press, Inc., 1959.

Peck, M. J., Scherer, F. M., *The Weapons Acquisition Process*. Boston: Harvard University Press, 1962.

Pooler, Victor H., *The Purchasing Man and His Job*. New York: American Management Association, 1964.

Reck, Dickson, *Government Purchasing and Competition*. Berkeley, Calif.: University of California Press, 1954.

Ritterskamp, James J. Jr., Abbott, Forrest L., and Ahrens Bert C., *Purchas-*

ing for Educational Institutions. New York: Bureau of Publications, Columbia University, 1961.

Westing, J. H. and Fine, I. V., *Industrial Purchasing* (2nd ed.). New York: John Wiley & Sons, Inc., 1962.

Chapters 1–3

Alford, L. P., *Principles of Industrial Management.* New York: The Ronald Press Company, 1940.

Davis, R. C., *Industrial Organization and Management.* New York: Harper and Row, Publishers, 1940.

Haas, George H., *et al., Purchasing Department Organization and Authority.* New York: American Management Association (Research Study No. 45), 1960.

Lansburg, R. H., and W. R. Spriegel, *Industrial Management.* New York: John Wiley & Sons, Inc., 1947.

Lewis, H. T., and C. A. Livesey, *Materials Management: A Problem in the Airframe Industry.* Boston: Harvard University, Graduate School of Business Administration, 1944. (Research Studies, No. 31.)

Pfiffner, John M., and Sherwood, Frank P., *Administrative Organization.* Englewood Cliffs, N. J.: Prentice-Hall, Inc., 1960.

Rautenstrauch, Walter, *The Economics of Business Enterprise.* New York: John Wiley & Sons, Inc., 1939.

Spriegel, W. R., and E. C. Davies, *Principles of Business Organization and Operation* (2nd ed.). Englewood Cliffs, N. J.: Prentice-Hall, Inc., 1952.

Terry, G. R., *Principles of Management.* Homewood, Ill.: Richard D. Irwin, Inc., 1957.

Chapters 4–12

Abramovitz, Moses, *Inventories and Business Cycles.* New York: National Bureau of Economic Research, 1950.

Agnew, H. E., and Dale Houghton, *Market Policies.* New York: McGraw-Hill Book Company, Inc., 1941.

American Standards Association, *American Standards Year Book.* New York, published annually.

Backman, J., *Price Practices and Price Policies.* New York: The Ronald Press Company, 1955.

Baer, J. B., and O. G. Saxon, *Commodity Exchanges and Futures Trading.* New York: Harper and Row, Publishers, 1949.

Brady, G. S., *Materials Handbook*. New York: McGraw-Hill Book Company, Inc., 1957.

Bratt, E. C., *Business Cycles and Forecasting*. Homewood, Ill.: Richard D. Irwin, Inc., 1953.

Clark, John Maurice, *Competition As A Dynamic Process*. Washington: The Brookings Institution, 1961.

Davis, R. C., and M. J. Jucius, *Purchasing and Storing*. New York: Alexander Hamilton Institute, 1947.

Dewey, E. R., and E. F. Daken, *Cycles: The Science of Prediction*. New York: Holt, Rinehart & Winston, Inc., 1947

Fearon, Harold E., and Hoagland, John A., *Purchasing Research in American Industry*. New York: American Management Association, 1963.

Hamilton. W. H., *Price and Price Policies*. New York: McGraw-Hill Book Company, Inc., 1938.

Harriman, N. F., *Standards and Standardization*. New York: McGraw-Hill Book Company, Inc., 1938.

Jiler, Harry (editor), *Commodity Year Book*. New York: Commodity Research Bureau, published annually.

Juran, J. M., *Management of Inspection and Quality Control*. New York: Harper and Row, Publishers, 1945.

Knight, H. A., *Materials Buying Manual*. New York: Conover-Mast Publications, 1951.

Lyon, L. S., and Victor Abramson, *The Economics of Open Price Systems*. Washington, D. C.: The Brookings Institution, 1936.

MacNiece, E. H., *Industrial Specifications*. New York: John Wiley & Sons, Inc., 1953.

Melnitsky, Benjamin, *Management of Industrial Inventory*. New York: Conover-Mast Publications, 1951.

National Bureau of Standards, *Directory of Commercial and College Testing Laboratories*. Washington: Government Printing Office, 1945.

National Bureau of Standards, *National Directory of Commodity Specifications*. Washington: Government Printing Office, 1945.

Nelson, Saul, *Price Behavior and Business Policy*. Washington, D. C.: Government Printing Office, 1940.

Newbury, F. D., *Business Forecasting*. New York: McGraw-Hill Book Company, Inc., 1952.

Newschel, R. F., and H. T. Johnson, *How to Take Physical Inventory*. New York: McGraw-Hill Book Company, Inc., 1946.

Nourse, E. G., *Price Making in a Democracy*. Washington, D. C.: The Brookings Institution, 1944.

Oxenfeldt, H. R., *Industrial Pricing and Market Practices*. Englewood Cliffs, N. J.: Prentice-Hall, Inc., 1951.

Shewhart, W. A.. *Economic Control of Quality of a Manufactured Product.* Princeton, N. J.: D. Van Nostrand Company, Inc., 1931.

Skuce, W. C., *Control of Industrial Inventory.* New York: National Association of Purchasing Agents, 1945.

Welch, W. E., *Scientific Inventory Control.* Greenwich. Conn.: Management Publishing Corp., 1956.

Chapters 13–17

Culliton, J. W., *Make or Buy?* Boston: Harvard University, Graduate School of Business Administration, 1942. (Research Studies, No. 27.)

Cuneo, Gilbert A., *Government Contracts Handbook.* Washington: Machinery and Allied Products Institute, 1963.

McDonald, Paul R., *Government Prime Contracts and Subcontracts.* Glendora, California: Procurement Associates, 1961.

Miles, Lawrence D., *Techniques of Value Analysis and Engineering.* New York: McGraw-Hill Book Company, Inc., 1962.

Rowland, F. H., *Business Planning and Control.* New York: Harper and Row, Publishers, 1947.

Wright, W. E., *Forecasting for Profit.* New York: John Wiley & Sons, Inc., 1947.

Chapters 18–25

Brink, V., and B. Cadmus, *Internal Auditing in Industry.* New York: Institute of Internal Auditors, 1950.

Conyngton, T., and L. O. Bergh, *Business Law.* New York: The Ronald Press Company, 1949.

Gallagher, James D., *Management Information Systems and the Computer.* New York: American Management Association, 1961.

Garrett, Thomas M., *Ethics in Business.* New York: Sheed & Ward, 1963.

Gray, A. W., *Purchase Law Manual.* New York: Conover-Mast Publications, 1954.

Hayes, E. A., and Renard, G. A., *Evaluating Purchasing Performance.* New York: American Management Association, 1964.

Henrici, S. B., *Standard Costs for Manufacturing.* New York: McGraw-Hill Book Company, Inc., 1947.

Kellor, F. A., *American Arbitration: Its History, Functions, and Achievements.* New York: Harper and Row, Publishers, 1948.

MacDonald, J. H., *Practical Budget Procedure*. Englewood Cliffs, N. J.: Prentice-Hall, Inc., 1939.

Specthrie, S. W., *Industrial Accounting*. Englewood Cliffs, N. J.: Prentice-Hall, Inc., 1947.

Taeusch, C. F., *Policy and Ethics in Business*. New York: McGraw-Hill Book Company, Inc., 1931.

Williams, J. H., *The Flexible Budget*. New York: McGraw-Hill Book Company, Inc., 1934.

Winters, F. J., *Purchase Follow-up Systems*. New York: National Association of Purchasing Agents, 1947.

INDEX

INDEX